Best wishes

SMELL TEST

Stories *and* Advice *on* Lawyering

ABA Section of
BUSINESS LAW

illustrations by Joe Azar

ABA
Defending Liberty
Pursuing Justice

Printed in the United States of America.

12 11 10 09 08   5 4 3 2 1

Library of Congress Cataloging in Publication Data

Freund, James C., 1934-
 Smell test / James C. Freund.
  p. cm.
 Includes index.
 "My idea was, first, to entertain readers (lawyers and non-lawyers) with some fictional short stories about lawyers, and second, to pass along to my younger colleagues some septuagenarian pointers."—Introduction.
 ISBN 978-1-60442-089-0
 1. Practice of law—United States—Case studies. 2. Lawyers—United States—Fiction. I. Title.

KF300.F74 2008
340.092—dc22   2008026403

*To my wife and soulmate, Barbara Fox; to my mother, Marcy Freund,
honoring her recent triumphal conquest of the 100-year hurdle;
and to the innumerable skilled, ethical, and problem-solving business lawyers
I've worked alongside and encountered over the years.*

TABLE OF CONTENTS

ACKNOWLEDGMENTS

Let me start by paying tribute to my long-time collaborator Joe Azar for the skilled and insightful illustrations that enhance the cover and text of the book. Joe has a real knack for illuminating in pictorial terms just what I'm trying to get across in words.

My thanks to a number of friends and colleagues who have read drafts of the stories and given me helpful comments; to my wife, Barbara Fox, who read them all, put up with my time-in-seclusion, and was unfailingly supportive; to Susana Darwin and her publishing colleagues at the American Bar Association, plus Art Garwin; to my secretaries, Ann Leyden and Fay Hill, and the word processing unit at Skadden Arps; and special thanks to Raymond.

I also express my appreciation to Charlie McCallum and the other worthies at the Business Law Section of the American Bar Association for sharing my vision and having the gumption to publish a work of fiction.

Needless to say, these good people are exonerated from responsibility for all characters, situations, opinions, errors, omissions, or excesses in these pages, for which I take full responsibility.

—Jim Freund, July 2008

INTRODUCTION

I've tried to do something a little offbeat in this book, so you might want to read this introduction and see what I had in mind.

The Concept

My idea was, first, to entertain readers (lawyers and nonlawyers) with some short stories about lawyers, and second, to pass along to my younger colleagues some septuagenarian pointers.

In coaching lawyers and law students over the years, I frequently used examples to illustrate the points I wanted to emphasize. When the point involved lawyering, although I preached a ton of "how to" gospel, my favorite approach was to depict the *wrong* way to do something, followed by analysis and advice on how it might better be handled.

As I penned these fictional tales, I saw that while much of the lawyering involved was praiseworthy, a portion was questionable, and some of it stunk up the joint. So I decided to write a commentary to each story, aimed at getting readers to focus on the actions taken, decisions made, and rationalizations offered by the fictional attorneys. "How'd they do?"—that's the recurring question I pose to you, before offering my own views on both the specific instance and certain broader related issues.

Although you need to have read the story for its commentary to be worthwhile, it isn't necessary to read the commentaries to enjoy the fictional tales on their own terms. This is especially true for those of you who aren't lawyers—the commentaries are just an added feature that you can peruse or pass on by.

By the way, my hope is that you nonlawyers will find these stories readily accessible. The issues posed are well within your experience, at least those of you with a foot in the business world. I took special pains not to let a lot of "law" intrude on the action, and you'll search in vain for a Latin maxim or any phrase beginning with "hereinafter."

About the Stories

The ten short stories in this collection share a common thread—there's at least one lawyer at the core of every tale.

After a lifetime of writing nonfiction instructional books, I decided to test my fictional chops. I chose lawyers as my subject because, for almost thirty-five years, I was an active member of the profession and a close observer of the breed.

The backdrop for most of the fiction involving lawyers in print today—to say nothing of the innumerable lawyer-centric television shows and movies—is criminal law. Even when civil law comes into play, it's usually portrayed through the prism of the litigation process. America seems fascinated by judges and juries, and by lawyers who strut and posture in dramatic courtroom scenes or make life-or-death decisions the night before a trial. So let me come clean at the outset—with the exception of the trial excerpt depicted in the tale "You Gotta Get Me Off!," that's not what you'll find in these stories.

What I did for a living—except for some requisite lawsuits in the 1980s when I was defending companies against hostile takeovers—was to try to keep my business clients out of litigation. I helped fashion deals and negotiated agreements designed to move things forward on an amicable—though rarely warm and fuzzy—basis, so as to accomplish mutual aims, ward off potential disputes, or both.

As a result, I rarely saw the inside of a courtroom. Most of my hours were spent in offices, around conference tables, and on the telephone. (For an extended metaphor of what we business lawyers do for a living, check out the story entitled "Father's Day.") My activities were seldom as dramatic as the litigation you see portrayed nowadays—although in truth, large chunks of actual litigation are quite tedious, as anyone who has served on a jury is likely to attest. But one thing a business lawyer's practice does have is conflict—albeit in a mostly civilized form—and conflict is the stuff of fiction.

Many of the conflicts I faced or observed took place lawyer-to-lawyer, frequently at the negotiating table. There were also conflicts between a lawyer and his own client or prospective client. Conflicts existed within the law firm itself—between partners or between a partner and the associate working for him. Some of the most wrenching conflicts took place within the lawyer's mind, as his better and baser instincts wrestled over how to deal with a sticky problem. And all the while, family conflicts involving a spouse or child often intruded on what was happening at the office.

The topics explored in these stories emerge out of such conflict-prone relationships. In some cases, there's an ethical issue at the core—a law firm deciding whether or not to take on questionable business ("The Smell Test"), a lawyer who discovers he may be sponsoring false testimony ("You Gotta Get Me Off!"), a lawyer directed by his client to perform a distasteful action that raises ethical questions ("The Reluctant Eulogist"). Wrestling with the implications of telling the truth is a recurrent theme—most notably in "Partnergate" (vis-à-vis one's partners) and "Sex, Lies, and Private Eyes" (in dealing with a client).

The lawyer-client relationship also abounds with other issues, such as the client who doesn't level with his own lawyer ("On-the-Job Training"), and the lawyer who has the misfortune to see a client at his worst ("The Corollary Axiom"). In "Negotiating 101" this relationship is viewed from the vantage point of a client under pressure and concerned with the soundness of the advice he's receiving.

Partners in a law firm can sometimes find themselves at cross-purposes with their colleagues over issues like taking on new business ("The Smell Test" and "On-the-Job Training") and making new partners ("Partnergate"), while intergenerational tensions can undermine collegiality ("The Reluctant Eulogist" and "The Smell Test"). Partner-associate relations may also become strained, as detailed in "Awash in Associates," "Sex, Lies, and Private Eyes," and "Partnergate."

The subject of negotiating deals takes center stage in "Negotiating 101," "On-the-Job Training," and "Awash in Associates." Family connections that impinge on legal practice are explored in "The Smell Test" and "The Corollary Axiom" (spouses), and in "Father's Day" (parent-child).

In three of the stories—"Awash in Associates," "The Reluctant Eulogist," and "On-the-Job Training"—the lawyer is handling more than one assignment simultaneously. That's a way of life in a commercial practice—only rarely are we able to concentrate all our energies on a single matter.

When someone writes stories about his former profession, the question naturally arises whether the tales are fiction or just thinly veiled fact. There are two dimensions to this question—the incidents described and the people involved.

The happenings depicted here very well *could* have happened to me or other business lawyers. But, as far as I am aware, they *didn't* occur—at least not in the way they do in the stories. This is what fiction is all about—the author making up plausible tales to stoke the reader's interest. If I had wanted to relate what actually happened to me, I would have chosen the memoir format, à la certain lawyer-authors like Louis Nizer. But though there were times in my career when I was tempted to transcribe my personal experiences, I always shied away from doing so in the end—concluding that my clients and colleagues were entitled to their privacy.

As for the people who populate these stories, I'll begin with the usual disclaimer that no character is intended to resemble anyone living or dead. Sure, certain of them may exhibit a trait that's shared by someone I've known over the years, but one trait does not a character make, and I didn't set out to pattern any of these folks after a particular acquaintance.

In this case, however, I have to go one step beyond the usual disclaimer, and here's why. In my professional career, the great bulk of lawyers I interacted with, both at my firm and elsewhere, as well as most of the clients I served, were competent, decent individuals with good intentions and an absence of malice. The problem with depicting such people in a work of fiction is that the resulting characters are . . . well, let's just say, boring. I didn't want to write boring fiction. So in order to inject some juice into the stories—to create conflict and tension and also to enhance the educational aspect—I found myself honing in on less desirable traits exhibited by a small minority of people I've come in contact with over the years. These include:

- an excessive drive to bring in new clients, retain existing ones, win a case, make money, gain prestige or power—the excess causing the lawyer to turn a blind eye to questionable behavior and unsavory situations
- the temptation to lie on a minor matter, which then leads into a tangled morass that's tough to climb out of
- large doses of hubris that accompany modest success and ultimately undermine good judgment
- the urge to find scapegoats in the aftermath of failed enterprises
- the compulsion to manipulate people and things to accomplish goals that may otherwise be out of reach
- the glib rationalizing that strives to justify questionable personal conduct.

In addition, the stories display other shortcomings (less reprehensible but still worthy of scrutiny) that many of us fall prey to—the reluctance or inability to deal with sensitive personal issues and relationships, a paralysis of action in the face of a major problem, the loss of confidence experienced when finding oneself on unfamiliar ground. (This is why, in titling the book *Smell Test*, I dropped the definite article from the name of the first story,

"The Smell Test." There's plenty of stuff in these pages—going well beyond the finite limits of a corporate securities scheme—that could benefit from the scrutiny of a well-trained sniffer.)

The lawyers in these stories exhibit these and other undesirable traits. As a result, I frankly don't like some of the characters I've created—and, based on the reactions I received from my former secretary as she typed a few of these stories, you probably won't either. A number of these people would not be my choice as colleagues or clients. Half a dozen or so of the lawyers—Ralph Landry in "On-the Job Training," Paul Garson in "Partnergate," George Troy in "The Reluctant Eulogist," Jack Lawrence in "You Gotta Get Me Off!" and "Sex, Lies, and Private Eyes," Lenny Tatum in "The Smell Test," Alex Gibson in "The Smell Test" and "The Corollary Axiom"—may be smart, or at least shrewd, but I wouldn't want to pal around or do business with them. They give in too easily to human frailties and display negative traits I find abhorrent. But—heaven help me!— I do relish them as fictional characters.

As for myself, well, no one in this book is intended to be me. Even where there's a first-person narrator who occupies the kind of niche I may once have filled or who finds himself in a situation I used to face, he's not yours truly. A character may make a statement or take some action that's comparable to what I might have said or done under the circumstances—and in the commentaries, I point out a few places where those actions or views hit pretty close to home—but other characters react in ways that are completely alien to me.

In case you're interested in what attributes of a lawyer I find praiseworthy—and don't wish to wade through my book *Lawyering*, which is all about the subject—there's some indication of my views in the penultimate section of the last story ("The Reluctant Eulogist").

I want to mention two decisions I made in connection with the book. First, I decided to have all the stories relate to a single law firm—or in the case of "Negotiating 101," to a lawyer who was formerly at that firm. This made sense for several reasons: it enabled certain characters from one tale to reappear in a later episode so as to expand their personalities; the firm didn't need to be redescribed in each story; and I could show the breadth of functions that a lawyer in a commercial nonlitigation practice undertakes.

However, I don't want anyone to think that the fictional firm in these stories—Jenkins & Price—is the firm I was a partner of for so many years. (Nor, by the way, is Jenkins & Price intended to resemble any other particular firm.) Anyone who knows my actual firm will realize that at once. My firm was (and remains) a first-class collection of worthwhile, hard-working, smart, and sensible individuals. By contrast, I would not want to be a partner of the fictional firm of Jenkins & Price.

My second decision involved the time period when the stories take place. I've been retired from the active practice of law for eleven years now. As a result, I felt most comfortable with the idea of placing the action in a period when I was actively engaged in lawyering. The period I chose for the stories is the late 1970s—1977, 1978, and 1979, the Jimmy Carter years. That's a period I knew well—I was in the thick of my practice, while simultaneously writing the *Lawyering* book.

So that's the world I've tried to convey in these pages. There won't be any cell phones or emails or faxes. It was a time when there were relatively few women lawyers, and even fewer women partners of law firms, so most of my characters are male. (That accounts for the preponderance of "he" and "him" pronouns over "she" and "her," for which I apologize to the innumerable and estimable women who so enhance the profession today.) There are certain other differences in detail from today, including the contemporary references the characters make. But I believe that most of the essential situations facing business lawyers back then weren't dissimilar to what they face now. The issues that give rise to ethical problems or client concerns or negotiating impasses or internal firm squabbles still ring true today.

Concerning the Commentaries

I've included a commentary on each story, positioned right after it. Unless the book is being used for group discussion purposes (as noted in the next section), I recommend reading the commentary after finishing the story—while the particulars are still fresh in your mind—before going on to the next tale.

Each commentary contains a number of italicized questions directed to you, the reader. I typically set the stage by describing some action, decision, or statement of the fictional lawyer and then "stop the action" to ask whether or not you approve of the character's performance—and if not, how you would have handled it in his shoes.

You can, if you're so inclined, breeze right through these queries and read my own views on the subject, which follow immediately thereafter. But I think you'll be giving up something of value if you don't pause first and spend a few moments facing up to the problem posed. It's a good opportunity to formulate your own uninfluenced reaction—to test how sharp your instincts are.

Since most of these queries involve matters of judgment, reasonable opinions can differ and there may be several acceptable ways to approach the problem. I encourage you to disagree with my views on the subject if they fail to resonate. My aim is to provoke thought by having you reflect on these situations—not to drill some "correct" response into your head.

Many of the challenges facing the fictional lawyers are not just idiosyncratic episodes but fall into broader categories of professional behavior. Because you're unlikely to encounter in life the precise fact pattern occurring in the story, I've included in the commentaries my thoughts on certain elements of the larger issues illustrated by the tales. I hope you'll find such discussions helpful.

Using the Stories and Commentaries for Group Discussion

This section is primarily for those readers who may be interested in using the book as a resource for training or classroom purposes.

I envision these stories and commentaries being useful in law firm or law department training sessions as well as law school classrooms. (I'll refer to all these collectively as "group sessions," to the leaders or instructors as "leaders," and to the lawyers or law students attending as "participants.") For instance, several of the stories would be useful in seminars on negotiating; others could work for programs on ethics or professionalism, on lawyering generally, law firm dynamics, or lawyer-client relations.

I think the process will work best if the participants read the story or stories to be discussed in advance of the session. It takes a big chunk of time to read the material for the first time in the session. By preparing in advance, the participants will also have more opportunity to reflect on the issues raised. Still, if enough time has been scheduled for the session, there's nothing wrong with spending the first half hour or so in a silent read-through.

On the other hand, I think it would be preferable for the participants *not* to have read the applicable commentary before the session. If this can be arranged, then the session can be treated, in effect, as a multiparty commentary. The leader can refer to the particular circumstances from the story, pose the issues raised by the discussion questions, ask the group for their views, and then either paraphrase my views, give his or her own opinions, or both. Hopefully, some differing viewpoints will emerge, making for a livelier session.

If the participants have read the applicable commentary in advance of the session, the leader can still handle things the same way, although some of the spontaneity is bound to be lost—plus, it's hard to determine whether views expressed that are close to my own are original. So I suggest approaching this situation a little differently. Rather than take the group through each twist and turn of the plot, I'd run the session in a more free-wheeling manner. I might ask the group what significance they took away from the tale, what views in the commentary they disagreed with, whether they've encountered similar situations, what aspects may be different today, and so on. Skipping around like this is one way to elicit the group's real areas of interest. Toward the end of the session, the leader can discuss any particular points he or she feels are important that haven't been previously covered.

In any of these iterations, the leader needs to decide how much he or she wants to stick to the specifics of the story, versus taking off from these to the broader points raised in the commentary or to other generalized concerns that the leader considers significant. This is purely a matter of individual judgment, tempered by how much time has been allotted to each story and situation.

In case anyone is interested in further elucidation of the more general themes, I've included references to chapters or sections from some of my books, especially *Lawerying—A Realistic Approach to Legal Practice* (Law Journal Seminars-Press, 1979); *Smart Negotiating—How to Make Good Deals in the Real World* (Simon and Schuster, 1992); and *Advise and Invent—The Lawyer as Counselor–Strategist and Other Essays*. (Prentice-Hall Law and Business, 1992). There is also considerable material on negotiating in my first book, *Anatomy of a Merger—Strategies and Techniques for Negotiating Corporate Acquisitions* (Law Journal Seminars-Press, 1975).

For video examples of my penchant for depicting the *wrong* way to do something and recommending how it might better be handled, there are two instructional videos I made for the Practicing Law Institute that involve the mistakes lawyers make in dealing with clients and how associates cope with some hairy situations. Also, the final section of my *Smart Negotiating for Lawyers* PLI video course (entitled "The Lawyer's Report Card") allows viewers to test their evaluation of how effectively the actor-lawyers are negotiating or handling clients (mostly not-so-well) against my own analysis.

Well, that's enough introduction. I hope that readers will find these tales entertaining and that lawyers will consider the stories and commentaries useful in imparting some worthwhile tips on professional behavior.

THE SMELL TEST

T he door to Dwight Bentley's office swung open with such force that his suit jacket slipped half-way off the hanger on the inside panel. "Got a minute, Dwight?" said the younger man, barging into the room.

Bentley, seated behind his old-fashioned desk, peered at the intruder over his half-moon reading glasses. *They don't even bother to knock nowadays,* he thought—*so much for the niceties in the year of our Lord 1977.*

Dwight was sixty-four and looked every day of it—his posture stooped, his movements sluggish, the large pouches under his eyes and prominent neck cords framing a wearied face. His unkempt office—piles of papers strewn about on tables and windowsills, dozens of folders from bygone transactions littering the carpet—mirrored his personal appearance.

Dwight put down his pen and leaned back in his desk chair. "Hello, Alex."

Alex Gibson, without waiting for an invitation, dropped into a tattered pull-up chair near the desk. He was one of Dwight's nineteen partners in the sixty-lawyer Manhattan law firm of Jenkins & Price. Short and wiry, at thirty-seven he still reminded

1

Dwight of one of those 140-pound hard-bellies on college wres-tling teams. Gibson had made only a few sojourns to Bentley's office in recent years; none, in Dwight's mind, had left a pleasant aftertaste. Their relationship was, at best, edgy.

"Haven't seen you in a while," said Alex. "How've you been?"

He wants something, Dwight thought while mumbling a non-committal reply.

"You look great, Dwight. It must have something to do with being married to Helen. A remarkable woman—how is she?"

Dwight smiled inwardly, recalling how repugnant his wife found the brash Mr. Gibson. "Listen, Dwight," she had said to him more than once, "I don't care how successful he is—your partner Alex Gibson is nothing but a conniving, manipulative SOB." *Still,* he thought, *Alex is right about one thing—Helen is indeed remarkable. She speaks her mind, lets you know where she stands—but then has a real knack for resolving conflict.*

"She's fine," Dwight replied. "And you?"

"Can't complain. Very busy—but that's what it's all about, isn't it?"

No, Dwight mused, *that's not what it's all about—but I seem to be the only lawyer in the firm who harbors any such reservations.* Dwight conceded that Alex wasn't alone here, but rather in the vanguard of a thundering herd that seemed determined to sweep into the coffers of Jenkins & Price an outsized share of the lucrative legal business available in New York City. Dwight had no objection to picking up new business—he had just never pursued it with the avidity he now observed all around him.

And that, he reckoned, *is why I've become a virtual relic—isolated on a floor of the firm's offices used mainly for administrative functions, ignored by the Jenkins & Price power structure, and making less money than all but my youngest partners.*

Dwight decided to cut short the preliminary chatter. "So, Alex, to what do I owe the honor of this visit?"

Gibson, excused from the need for further pleasantries, seg-ued directly into his mission. "Well, I've got a new deal from the Breckenridge folks who have been giving us so much busi-ness over the past two years. Pretty straightforward commercial arrangement—I don't see any problem with it. Still, in an excess of caution, I decided to check with Bill Price. Bill reacted favorably but asked me to run it by you as our ethics guru—just to make sure it passes muster."

Well, at least someone remembers I exist. . . . A flood of suppressed feelings welled up suddenly in Dwight Bentley. It had been painful for him in recent years to be shunted off to the side of the firm as that thundering herd galloped by. He was well aware that he'd become a source of mirth among the younger partners for his old-fashioned ways.

And yet, when matters of ethics and propriety are involved, I'm still the partner to whom Bill Price turns for comfort and good judgment. Bill Price—the managing partner of the firm, whose name is sitting up there over the door. And Dwight took special pride in the fact that whenever he'd been negative on a troublesome situation—"Don't take this one on, Bill, it really stinks"—Price hadn't once overridden Dwight's recommendation, even though it meant the firm had to pass up some hefty legal fees.

"Okay," said Dwight, taking a fresh yellow pad out from under a pile of papers on his desk, "let's hear what it's all about."

Alex stood up and paced around the cluttered office as he spoke. "All right. Now by way of background, there have been four great financial developments in the '70s: the money market fund that Fidelity pioneered; selling stock mutual funds directly to ordinary investors like Magellan does; Schwab's discount brokerage; and this year, Merrill's cash management account. The Breckenridge guys have come up with an idea that, in effect, combines the best elements of all four! And, need I say, that with the Dow heading down to 800, the goddamn stagflation in the economy, and the largest trade deficit in our history, this could be a real lifesaver."

Gibson then proceeded to describe the complex proposal that was on the table, making extensive use of financial jargon and trendy buzzwords. Dwight knew he was in trouble the minute he heard those references to new-fangled financial constructs. Having assiduously avoided them in both his professional and personal lives, he had no desire to become better acquainted with their intricacies. *It's like those damned new computers I keep reading about—everyone I know has a horror story about them.*

Meanwhile, Gibson was forging ahead, gesticulating emphatically, never pausing to make sure Bentley understood what was being said. *Is it because Alex assumes I'm following right along, or is he just trying to dazzle me so I'll meekly acquiesce?* Still, Dwight was reluctant to interrupt the narrative for an explanation each time Gibson used an unfamiliar term or introduced an abstruse concept.

"Okay," said Alex, his hands resting for a moment on the back of the armchair, "that's pretty much the basic situation. I assume you're with me so far, right? Now, here's the interesting twist. . . ."

Dwight *wasn't* with him so far, but didn't speak up, hoping that further elaboration might clarify things. Instead, the complexities just increased. Dwight was now finding it difficult to look at Alex. His gaze began to wander, exploring various objects in the room. There were those little lucite cubes commemorating his legal specialty of bond financings, all of them long since closed. On a banquette was his favorite photo of Helen, under the maple tree at that cozy Adirondack retreat. *God, what I'd give to spend an uninterrupted month with her in that idyllic spot.*

Bentley's glance now lingered on the piles of papers that littered the office, resisting his dedicated secretary's sporadic clean-up forays. "Dwight," she would implore, "why can't I just scoop up the lot and send all this old stuff to central files?" To which his stock reply was, "Because someday, Joan, when I have the time, I'm determined to teach at law school, and these documents you so scorn will then become my primary course materials." What he was loath to admit, even to Joan, was that gazing out at the detritus of bygone deals made him feel less removed from the center of things than if he were forced to focus solely on his sparse current caseload.

When his mind returned to the problem at hand, Dwight realized he was utterly lost. So he interrupted the narrative to ask Alex some questions, trying to clarify in his mind what was being proposed. And gradually the broad outlines of the deal began to emerge.

In brief, the client Breckenridge, which was in the financial services business, would be setting up a new multifaceted program for its customers, in partnership with a publicly owned company named Excel, controlled by a man named Edwards. Those were the main players, except for a separate service provider which Excel had introduced into the deal—a privately owned company named Panoply, whose particular function remained unclear to Dwight.

The financial arrangements regarding all this were quite complex. Dwight tried to probe the trail of the funds involved in the deal but had trouble doing so, since he still couldn't quite comprehend what would be happening. He got the distinct impression, though, that this represented a quite favorable financial arrangement for Breckenridge, and also that Panoply would be making a lot of money.

"I don't understand the role of this Panoply company," Dwight said. "Why are they in the middle of this thing?"

"Well," replied Alex, "they're reputed to be an excellent supplier."

"All right, but couldn't Excel handle Panoply's role itself? Or, if it's not equipped to do so, why can't Breckenridge shop around and pick out its own supplier—perhaps on less expensive terms than the large amount of money that seems to be heading Panoply's way?"

Alex gave Dwight one of those "boys will be boys" looks. "Hey, no one has said anything, and there's nothing in the public record about this, but the Breckenridge people suspect that Panoply is indirectly owned by Edwards. So, what the hell, his minions at Excel know how to please the boss."

"Would that ownership be disclosed in the public information Breckenridge files about the deal?"

"No, it's not required, and we don't even know for sure whether that's the case."

Through the technical haze, Dwight began to sense what there was about the proposal that might cause a problem. Underneath the camouflage, the firm's client, Breckenridge, by means of a convoluted scheme involving multiple companies, would be compensating the individual, Edwards, through his ownership of Panoply. Edwards, in turn, would cause the public company (Excel) that he controlled to enter into a contractual arrangement on terms favorable to Breckenridge—and all without adequate public disclosure.

Alex Gibson was still talking, justifying the transaction, when Dwight Bentley decided he didn't need to listen to any more dazzle.

"Hold it," Dwight interrupted. "I think I've heard enough."

"So then it's okay?" said Alex, half-turning as if about to leave the room.

"No, it's *not* okay," replied Dwight.

"What the hell's wrong with it?" Alex asked—his curt tone and the sudden rigidity of his wrestler's body evincing a pugnacious quality that hadn't surfaced previously in the meeting.

Dwight leaned back in his chair. "I'm afraid it doesn't pass the smell test."

"You must be kidding," said Alex, shaking his head vigorously. "This is just straight financial services stuff, packaged a little differently to deal with the particular circumstances. And there's good precedent in the way that Merrill partnered with BancOne."

"I can't comment on how this compares to other financial services deals. All I can say is that Breckenridge appears to be participating in a scheme to line Mr. Edwards' personal pockets at the expense of the Excel stockholders—and not telling anyone about it."

"I don't believe what I'm hearing. A 'scheme'—oh my God, shades of Sherlock Holmes!"

As Alex spoke, Dwight noticed him looking at the old files that littered the room. Dwight detected an expression of scorn in his young partner's eyes. *I'll bet it's because Alex can tell these are all closed deals from days of yore.*

Alex continued in an exasperated tone. "Look, Dwight, if you examine the steps of the transaction, each one is completely justifiable."

"But that's just what you need a nose for." Dwight now adopted an avuncular manner. "Listen, I don't blame you—all of us can sometimes be led astray. Let me tell you a story that's quite apropos here, involving myself—something that happened many years ago when I was a young partner at the firm."

Gibson stopped pacing and leaned against the back of a chair, exuding impatience. Dwight paused briefly. *Have I told him this one before? Probably so, but what the hell—it's right on point now and deserves retelling.*

Dwight pursed his lips and twitched them twice before beginning his tale—a gesture he'd adopted in recent years that made him resemble, in Helen's simile, a fish about to take the hook. "A corporate client of mine was, in effect, being shaken down by a corrupt state official. The official made it clear that if the client didn't take a certain legitimate-looking action—the result of which would be to indirectly put some money in the official's pocket—then the client wouldn't get a government certificate that it badly needed and fully deserved on the merits. The official's scheme was ingenious and unlikely to raise any eyebrows. And the client really wanted the certificate.

"My nostrils started quivering—I wasn't at all happy about this. But then, as the client's tale of woe unfolded and the arguments of legitimacy were pressed, I found myself beginning to rationalize."

Dwight paused to marvel at how just the act of recalling the incident made him uneasy. It was a vivid reminder to him of how insidious this kind of thing was, even in a situation where he had been sensitive to the problem—unlike Alex in today's case.

Dwight continued. "So I decided to consult with old man Jenkins, who was still head of the firm at that time. It took him about three seconds to reply"—and here Dwight's voice erupted in a noisy caricature of his late partner's fabled decisiveness—"'FUHGEDDABOUTIT!!'"

"Jenkins was right, of course, and afterward I was chagrined for even bringing the issue to him. I knew damn well how it should have come out. But instead of following my gut instinct, I was trying to devise a way to accommodate a client who was being wronged." Dwight put down the pen he'd been waggling to signal the end of the tale.

"Yeah," said Alex, rising abruptly to his feet. "Well, thanks for the history lesson, but I'm not chagrined one bit. You're telling me a story about bribing a public official—that's a goddamn crime! There's no bribe here, or any other criminal act."

Dwight backpedaled. "I'm not saying it's a bribe in the classic sense—just that the two situations share a common—"

"And what old man Jenkins detected back then, something that *you*—no offense—failed to spot, sounds like it was goddamn obvious. But the situation here is much more complex than the simplistic way you're looking at it. This is *not* what you think, Dwight—it's different, and the difference hinges on the new ways we have of doing business in 1977."

"I fail to see the relevance of the distinction," Dwight replied, although wondering whether he just wasn't knowledgeable enough to recognize it.

"Besides," Gibson continued, as he resumed pacing around the room, "we're not as ultraconservative today as the firm was back then. We've got to think about what's good for our clients— *they're* the ones we're in business to serve."

"But that's the most interesting part of my story—the denouement." Dwight again reached for a pen to punctuate his words. "When I went back to the client to say that Jenkins and I strongly advised them not to have any part of this scheme, instead of bitching and moaning about their goody-two-shoes legal advisors, the senior executives seemed genuinely pleased that we had come out forcefully against it. They didn't like the scheme any more that we did, but they just needed to be told it was wrong by someone with moral authority in such matters." Dwight paused briefly to give his punch line the appropriate flourish. "And that someone was—and hopefully still is—the firm of Jenkins & Price."

Gibson wasted no time in dashing Bentley's hope that his morality tale had hit home. Taking quick strides around the office, he spoke through a clenched jaw, punctuating the words with a chopping motion of his right fist.

"Happy antiquity, Dwight. Now, let me introduce you to the real world of today. It seems that Breckenridge—probably concerned that we might turn out to be a little tight-assed—has already consulted another law firm about the transaction, and that other firm said they'd be pleased to do the deal if we shied away from it. I got this straight from the Breckenridge CEO—point blank. In other words, the effect of our being prissy here will not only cost us a very lucrative piece of business, but it won't prevent the deal from happening." Alex stopped pacing to deliver his clincher. "And, need I add, it will undoubtedly mean the permanent end of our relationship with this world-class client."

Dwight tried not to show it, but he was taken aback by the news that another firm had sanctioned the deal. *Someone else—someone who probably understands these financial services goings-on better than I do—has looked at this situation and found no problem.*

Then, almost as a reflex, the skeptic in him briefly materialized. *Could the Breckenridge CEO have been bluffing Alex? Might that other law firm lack the credentials to make its authentication meaningful?* But Dwight, who prided himself on being his own man, didn't raise these points with Alex—fearing they would give rise to the inference that his judgment was capable of being influenced by the reaction of another lawyer outside the firm.

Still, this particular item of information bothered him. *What will Bill Price say if I turn the deal down, and Gibson then tells him—as he undoubtedly will—that there's another firm itching to forge ahead? Hell, I bet Alex has told him already. Will Bill still follow my advice? And even if he does accept my judgment on* this *deal, will Bill want me as the partner who passes on new situations arising down the road?*

Dwight was debating whether to reply that Jenkins & Price would never sell its birthright to please an unprincipled client when he heard Alex start in again. But this time, the younger man—having relaxed his posture to lean against the back of a chair—spoke in a more modulated tone. It was a voice, Dwight sensed, that was usually reserved for Gibson's clients.

"But look, I don't need an answer right this minute—although I did tell the Breckenridge people, who seemed anxious to move ahead, that I'd get back to them by tomorrow. I've thrown a lot of facts at you in just a few minutes, involving a somewhat technical area that you might not be in touch with on a daily basis." Alex handed him a folder that Dwight hadn't previously noticed. "I brought along this file, which contains the relevant documents and shows the justification for each of the elements. Why don't you review the papers tonight, sleep on it, and we'll talk in the morning."

"That's a good idea," said Dwight, relieved that the immediate confrontation was about to end.

Alex turned to leave, then paused briefly at the door. "I didn't mean to get upset there, Dwight. I know you're just doing your job. This is a great firm, and one reason is the spirit of camaraderie that exists among partners—the sharing of burdens, the sense of 'I help you, you help me at another time,' and so on. There's no place like it." Alex exited the office, more deliberately than he had entered it, uttering a final "I'll come by tomorrow around 10:00 A.M." over his shoulder.

That evening, when Dwight arrived home, he found a note from Helen on the kitchen table. She had gone over to her mother's apartment, to bring her "some fresh vegetables and a little TLC" Dwight's dinner was in the microwave. He heated it up, mounted a stool, and ate at the kitchen counter.

After drinking a cup of coffee kept warm in a thermos, Dwight took the thermos and his briefcase down the narrow hall to the maid's room he'd converted into a home office some years back. Their apartment, located in an affluent East Side building and attractively furnished, was on the small side, though adequate for a childless couple like the Bentleys. The converted maid's room—the one spot Dwight could call his own—contained a desk, a well-worn armchair in the corner, and a low table covered with piles of vintage papers, folders, and yellow pads.

Dwight took out the documents he'd been given by Alex, spread them on the desk, and began reading. But it was tough sledding—the unfamiliar lingo and methodology hindering his efforts to get at the essence of the transaction. The little room, which Dwight found so cozy when he was operating in his comfort zone, began to feel almost claustrophobic.

His mind began to wander. *I'm living in a strange new world. A Georgia peanut farmer gets sworn in as president at the beginning of the year, shuns the traditional limousine, and walks with his family the mile and a half down Pennsylvania Avenue from the Capitol to the White House. Then Jimmy Carter gives a television speech to the nation wearing a sweater. Where are we headed?* Dwight recalled the uncomfortable words that Henry Kissinger had uttered last year on the occasion of America's bicentennial celebration. "The United

States has passed its historic high point, like so many earlier civilizations."

He heard footsteps outside, and Helen then appeared in the doorway. Although she was Dwight's contemporary, Helen was in better physical shape, looked much younger, and radiated energy. Starting out as a teacher, she had become aware over time of her ability to manage people and things, and now helped run one of the city's elite private schools. "Hi, honey," she said. "Hope I'm not disturbing you."

"Not a bit," replied Dwight, rising to kiss her cheek. "How's your mother?"

"She's fine—just needed a little company, that's all." Helen glanced at the papers on his desk. "Isn't it unusual for you to bring work home nowadays? I thought you had put that frantic phase of your life behind you."

"Caught in the act," said Dwight with a smile. "Well, since you're interested. . . ." He began to relate the day's events—omitting the name of the client and, given Helen's antipathy toward Alex, referring to him as "one of my younger partners."

But Helen wasn't about to let such imprecision pass. "*Which* partner?" she asked with more than a hint of suspicion.

Dwight knew he couldn't play games with her. "Oh, it was Alex Gibson," he replied—his casual tone designed to suggest that omitting the identity earlier had been a mere oversight.

"I knew it!" exclaimed Helen. "As soon as you started telling me the story, I could picture that little twerp pacing around your office, gesticulating wildly."

"Now, Helen," said Dwight, "please don't get started with all that again."

"All right," she said, but he realized she wasn't mollified. "I'll refrain—at least for the moment." She took a seat in the tattered armchair. "Tell me the rest of what went on."

Dwight related the balance of his conversation with Alex, although consciously softening the latter's harsh edge. He also omitted Alex's parting remark—"I help you, you help me another time." Since their meeting, Dwight had been trying hard—with limited success—to ignore its possible implications. *If Alex had said, "You help me now with this, and I'll help you another time with something else that's important to you," that would have been blatant—but Alex turned the concept around the other way.* Something was nagging at Dwight, but he couldn't—or wouldn't—come to grips with it.

"And so, my inquisitive spouse," Dwight concluded his narrative, "that's why I'm looking through these papers tonight—to try to better understand this financial services gobbledygook and see if perhaps the negative reaction I had earlier today wasn't warranted."

Helen said nothing for a few moments. Dwight waited, knowing there would be a response. The two of them had been together for almost forty years, and he could count on the fingers of one hand the number of times she had declined to express her opinion on a significant issue affecting them. He frequently disagreed with her point of view and didn't always heed her advice, but he valued her pragmatic intelligence—her shrewd, if somewhat cynical, view of the world.

Helen leaned forward in the armchair. Her expression was earnest, and when she spoke, the words tumbled out in a steady stream. "Dwight, there's something I need to discuss with you. Up to now, I've stayed away from raising the subject because I know how painful you find it, but the time has come."

Dwight hunkered down in his chair in uneasy anticipation. Still, the playful part of his mind couldn't help relating Helen's "the time has come" phrase to the current Paul Masson advertising slogan, repeated endlessly in the media, "We will sell no wine before its time."

Helen's expression was dead serious. "As we both know very well, this is the year you turn sixty-five—about four months from now. That's the date when Jenkins & Price makes its decision whether or not to allow you to stay on as a partner for the next five years. Am I right?"

She was correct, so he nodded in the affirmative.

Helen continued. "Now, my darling, you know I consider you the finest lawyer I've ever known. But your strengths don't lie in the areas that these people value nowadays—like bringing in new business."

Dwight had to admit she was right about this, too. A number of years had passed since he'd attracted any significant new clients to the firm.

"So, it follows that you're *not* a shoo-in to be retained on the basis of performance, using their yardstick of success. As for sentiment, I don't see any of that old-time 'good feeling' anymore. I hate to say it, but they could boot you out to make room for a few more young J&P hotshots without feeling a pang of remorse."

Dwight winced. *How could they do that to me?* As if anticipating his reaction, Helen moved to counter it. "And if you have any doubt on that score, just recall what happened to Mack when his time came up two years ago. You remember Mack, don't you—your ex-partner and friend, Michael McKinley?"

"Wait a minute," Dwight interrupted. "You're right that Mack wasn't allowed to continue with the firm, but you're leaving out the key fact that he had an acknowledged drinking problem."

"A problem," Helen countered, "that hadn't bothered anyone at J&P for over three decades—not until that cold, calculating firm committee that makes the stay-or-go decision noticed that Mack's billings were down for the last few years."

Dwight shook his head slowly from side to side—a gesture he'd adopted years back to indicate that he disagreed with Helen's viewpoint but didn't want to prolong the debate.

She forged ahead. "We discussed this subject the year they tossed Mack out. And my recollection is that Alex Gibson was—and presumably still is—on the committee that makes the decision. Am I right?"

Dwight nodded slowly. He could sense what was coming. Helen's face morphed into one of those "Aha!" looks as she leaned forward and launched into her peroration.

"In other words, to put it baldly, this monster who you accused today of proposing something unethical—this little monster holds your future at J&P in his hands. Do you think he's going to respect you because you have the guts to stand up to him? No way! In fact, he's going to punish you for it, in the most effective way he can—by booting you right out of the firm!"

"Now, hold it right there," said Dwight, shaking his head vigorously in denial of Helen's aspersion. "You're way off base here.

Alex wouldn't do such a nasty thing. A law firm isn't about ret-ribution. And besides, he's only one of *five* partners on that com-mittee. And the committee only makes a *recommendation* to the Executive Committee. A number of other partners are involved in the decision."

But Helen was undaunted by his defense of the firm bureauc-racy. "Sure they are, and each one will have taken home fewer dollars this year—and may be missing out on some big paydays in the future—based on your determination that Jenkins & Price shouldn't get involved in this deal that Alex is proposing. Not only that—it's a deal they'll find out was perfectly acceptable to another law firm. Do you really believe your other partners are going to appreciate you?"

"Come on, Helen," he protested weakly, "you're really going too far this time. . . ."

"I don't think so." But her tone now modulated, as if in tacit recognition that she may have overstepped the line. "Dwight, I'm just asking you to open your eyes—to think about the conse-quences. Our finances, for example."

It was a topic Dwight usually shied away from discussing with her. Early in their marriage, they had agreed that Helen would handle the family finances so that he could concentrate on his lawyering. Helen didn't raise the subject often, but tonight was different.

"Right now, we're pretty comfortable, but that's because of your monthly check from the firm. If that were to stop, how would we be able to pay the steep rental on this apartment? Cer-tainly not from that meager pension your beloved partners have never seen fit to improve. We wouldn't starve, but we'd have to move to more modest digs, as well as cut down on other things we've been enjoying—like our annual holiday in the Adiron-dacks. . . ."

Helen paused briefly—as if to consider whether or not to express the next thought—and then, apparently overcoming her reluctance, did so. "It would be different, honey, if this were hap-pening fifteen years ago, when any firm would have given their eyeteeth to land you as a partner. But let's face it, at your age, with your low energy level and—I hate to say this, but I have to—your questionable health, are you really likely to land a job practicing law with someone else? And if not, what else could you do that would provide comparable income? . . . Dwight, dear, we just can't afford for you to be forcibly retired right now."

It stung, but there was little Dwight could say in response. Allowing for the hyperbole, he knew she was closer to the truth than any defense he might muster. At his age, he couldn't imagine finding any work that would approach even the modest level of his present compensation. And, although reluctant to admit it, he was concerned about his health, especially after the questions raised during his last physical. *Younger men than I are dying every day.* His favorite jazz saxophonist, Paul Desmond of the Dave Brubeck Quartet, had passed away prematurely just a few months earlier.

Helen now leaned back in her chair, relaxing her posture and modulating her tone of voice. Dwight couldn't help noting a parallel to the shift in Alex's manner toward the close of their encounter that afternoon.

"Now, I know my virtuous husband would never go along with anything improper, and I wouldn't want you to. But isn't it possible that your instincts were a little off earlier today? Financial services isn't something you deal with on a regular basis—maybe you can't trust your intuition as much here as you can on more familiar ground like trust indentures."

A smile of conjugal esteem crossed Helen's face. "I also know how creative you are when you put your mind to it. I'm sure you'll be able to figure out an ethical way to let Alex do the business." She paused a beat. "That way, you won't have created an enemy. Even better, you'll have made a friend. And friends know how to reciprocate. . . . What better way for him to pay you back than for the firm to keep you on as a partner."

Helen stood up and walked to the door. "Okay, I've had my say—thanks for listening. I'm sure you know that I'll support whatever decision you make." She gave him a warm smile. "Coming out the right way here is *not* a condition of our marriage. Let me know when you're ready to come to bed." And with that, she left the room.

But it wasn't her final words that rung in Dwight's ears after she had departed. It was that phrase of Alex's—"I help you,

you help me at another time"—which now bore Helen's Good Housekeeping seal of approval.

Later, Dwight sat alone in the small room, leafing through pages and pages of Breckenridge documents. The unfamiliar words and phrases assaulted him, but it wasn't just the alien subject matter that clouded his judgment. Helen's reality check had gotten him thinking about how Alex Gibson—and Bill Price, and his other partners—might react if Dwight were responsible for the firm turning down the Breckenridge business.

Much as I hate to admit it, Helen has a point. Actually, several points. Alex Gibson, bless his cold heart, would not be above retribution. At the other extreme, if his parting remark meant anything, Alex might well feel the need to reciprocate if I came out his way. And Helen's concern that the Bentley family wouldn't be in good financial shape if I were shown the door at Jenkins & Price—that's hard to argue with.

Dwight stood up and shook himself vigorously. *Wait a minute! What kind of ethics guru would I be if I allowed considerations of that sort to sway my decision? After all, my real "client" here isn't Breckenridge— it's Jenkins & Price. Bill Price is reposing his trust in my judgment. A law firm can't afford to get itself involved in a shady deal. That's my job—to head off such things. I've got to call 'em as I see 'em.*

Some years back, Dwight had decided that the usual test to detect whether considerations of personal interest were influencing one's judgment—Would I come out the same way if the personal interest didn't exist?—wasn't strenuous enough. So he devised a tougher standard for himself, posing the issue this way: Assuming the consideration of personal interest ran *in the other direction*, would I still come out this way? In other words, in order for Dwight to pass the test, the advice he was proposing to give had to actually fly in the face of his self-interest. If it did, then he knew he was on sound ground.

Dwight now attempted to apply this test to his current predicament. He tried to visualize a situation where it would do him good—would be in his personal best interest—to turn Alex down flat. *Let's say Bill Price had whispered in my ear that he really doesn't want to take on this Breckenridge business, but he needs a negative opinion from me to use as a cover against an irate Alex. Given that premise, would I still feel the need to decide in favor of the firm taking on the matter?* But by this time, Dwight's thinking had become so befuddled that he wasn't sure how he would come out.

He perched on the armrest of the chair and visualized himself years earlier, lecturing to a group of eager young associates. *As a business lawyer, always trust your nose. My nose has kept me in business. There are lots of agile minds around, numerous ways to shape facts and justify actions—but when you cut through the smoke and mirrors, and what you find isn't kosher, then your nose should start to twitch. And when something doesn't pass the smell test, avoid it like the plague.* But he couldn't help wondering whether his nose still worked in evaluating this newly minted 1977 stuff.

He also pondered the related issue of whether to rely on one's gut instinct or be swayed by sober second thoughts. It was another sermon he'd often preached to younger colleagues. *Trust your gut. There may be great pressure to abandon your initial intuition, to allow yourself to be overwhelmed by those fearful—or fanciful or rationalized—second thoughts. But you should never lose sight of your first, uncluttered reaction, before the sugaring over begins. . . .* Still, he thought, it may be that when the subject matter is unfamiliar, those sober second thoughts are entitled to greater weight.

Dwight opened the thermos and poured himself some coffee. By now it was lukewarm, but the caffeine helped him to formulate alternatives. *What if I decided to pass on this one—just tell Bill Price I don't understand this financial services stuff well enough to reach a judgment?* He turned the concept over in his mind, but the more he considered the possibility, the less he liked it. *Copping out— letting the firm down—that would mean curtains for me around Jenkins & Price. What use do they have for an old warhorse who can't even handle the one duty they keep him around to perform?* He was struck by how apt the lyrics of one of his favorite Beatles' songs were—"Will you still need me? / Will you still feed me? / When I'm sixty-four."

He considered other possible ways out of his predicament. *I don't have to go that far. What if I just asked Bill Price to assign one of those savvy young associates to help me analyze this deal, with the ultimate judgment still mine to make?* Back in those memorable years Dwight spent in the army during World War II, especially after the Allied invasion of France, he'd put a lot of reliance in the younger

generation. But he feared that his judgment would then be influenced by others with their own agendas. That, together with his pride, made him reluctant to seek assistance.

Dwight now crossed the room and settled into the armchair, where he'd done some of his best thinking in years past. *Let's say I'm forced into early retirement. What would life be like after Jenkins & Price? Will I be able to land at another firm? Perhaps a corporate legal department could use my skills—or do they shun senior citizens? How about teaching at law school?* He formed a mental image of himself as Professor Bentley, foraging through those voluminous files on his office carpet, digging out nuggets to convey to eager young law students who hung on his every word. Still, he couldn't help wondering: *What school will want me? What subject can I teach? How much do they pay?*

His mind then turned to thoughts of Helen and how she'd adjust to a reduced scale of living. *She wouldn't be happy, but she does have great coping powers. Would there be a lot of second-guessing and recrimination? No, I don't think so. An occasional jab, perhaps, but grudges and resentment just aren't her thing. But would I feel I'd let her down? Can't say for sure. . . . On the other hand, we'd have a lot more time together, which would be delightful.* And he daydreamed once more about a month in that Adirondacks hideaway—assuming he could still afford it.

At intervals, he turned over in his mind different possible outcomes. *What if I nix our participation in the deal, the other firm does it, and then things go south—leaving the other firm in a lot of trouble, and my partners overjoyed that I've saved them from disaster? On the other hand, what if we pass on it, but the deal turns out to be a big hit—there's no trouble at all—and my partners wonder why we weren't the law firm doing it? Then again, what if I okay the deal, only now it turns sour and the firm gets into the soup?* He recalled the words of an esteemed colleague from years back: The false positive (the slick scheme) is much worse than the false negative (the missed opportunity)—it's never the deal you *don't* do that kills you.

It was after midnight when Dwight finally left the little room, trudged down the hall, performed a few ablutions, and went to bed. As he slipped beneath the covers next to Helen, he could feel the warmth radiating from her body—a warmth he equated with a sense of determination that he himself appeared to lack.

Early the next morning, after a short fitful slumber, Dwight woke, dressed, and left the apartment before Helen arose. He had his breakfast, consisting mostly of black coffee, at a diner near his midtown office.

Jenkins & Price was located in an undistinguished postwar high-rise building. There was a newsstand in the lobby where Dwight stopped this day for some mints. One of his partners, Lenny Tatum—who specialized in trademarks and copy-rights—was thumbing through a magazine. Dwight had never liked Tatum, whose annoying know-it-all personality grated on him.

After a brief exchange of greetings, Tatum said, "I happened to ride home with Alex Gibson yesterday, and he was telling me about the new Breckenridge deal he's doing—the one he ran past you yesterday afternoon. It sounds really interesting and, I might add, potentially lucrative for the firm."

"Deal that he's *doing*?" said Dwight, looking up sharply from the mints counter. "At this point, the firm hasn't even taken on the matter."

"Oh, sure," replied Tatum, handing a five dollar bill to the newsstand attendant to pay for his magazine. "I understand—it still has to be cleared. But, I must say, Alex sounded pretty con-fident that you would okay it."

"He did? I don't recall saying anything yesterday that might have given him that impression."

Tatum pocketed his change from the attendant and turned to leave. Smiling faintly, he said, "Well, maybe that's because he felt you'd be highly motivated to help out."

Dwight bristled. "Highly motivated? Just exactly what do you mean by that?"

Tatum backpedaled swiftly. "Nothing, nothing at all. I simply meant to say that Alex seemed to be quite satisfied with the pro-priety of the deal he was proposing. . . ."

The firm's offices covered all of three adjacent floors—21, 22, and 23—plus part of the 16th floor, which was used primarily for back office functions. The overall design on 21, 22, and 23 was an undistinguished blend of traditional and modern decor.

The space on 16, taken over a few years earlier from a small accounting firm, hadn't been renovated and bore no resemblance to the three main floors.

Dwight reached his office on the 16th floor shortly after 9:00 A.M. and settled in behind the old desk. A few minutes later, his secretary, Joan, came in to go over some housekeeping matters. The only item of consequence in the incoming mail was the bill for the annual premium on his life insurance—an amount that was becoming more significant with each passing year. It hadn't been factored into his monthly budget, and the balance in his checking account wasn't sufficient to cover it. Dwight was unsure whether he had enough other ready funds to handle the premium or would have to liquidate some securities.

But he didn't want to think about that right now. He had a big decision to make in the next hour. And, contrary to his normal practice of being fully prepared before taking action, he still hadn't decided how he was going to come out on the Breckenridge matter.

As Joan was leaving his room, she handed him a handwritten note from Bill Price that had come in late yesterday after Dwight left the office. It read: "Dwight, I'd meant to call you earlier today, but couldn't get out of meetings. By now, you've probably seen Alex on his new Breckenridge deal. He and I went over it briefly, and it seemed all right to me—and Breckenridge has been a good client, with great prospects for the future—but I did want you to vet it, just in case I'm missing something."

Dwight read the note a second time. *The way Bill puts the issue—basically, "We'd like to take on this business unless you tell us we can't"—makes it easier for me to say "go ahead." In effect, I'm not so much* approving *the deal as* not disapproving *it. Or is that a distinction without a real difference?*

He pushed his chair back from the desk. In the old days, he recalled, this was one of those moments when he'd routinely light up a cigarette. *What really bothers me is that Alex is already mouthing off about this to the other partners, like Lenny Tatum. Even worse, Alex—and presumably everyone else—has already forecast a favorable outcome to my deliberations. I'd like to know on what basis they think that's the case. . . .*

Strictly on the merits, and even assuming he could grasp the underlying technical considerations, Dwight considered this a close call. *But close calls were just what I always specialized in.* Yesterday, he acknowledged to himself, his "nose" had probably oversimplified what was a more complex issue. He still found it difficult to analyze the business deal apart from the technical aspects. And he worried that without a better understanding of the business side, he couldn't really evaluate what was proposed. *But at least I'm better prepared today.* He flipped through his yellow pad, finding the pages where he'd jotted down certain questions to ask Alex. He hoped the answers would help clarify his thinking.

At precisely 10:00 A.M., Alex Gibson strode briskly into Dwight's office without knocking and took a seat. "Good morning, Dwight. Did you get a chance to read those papers? Especially the one that described . . ."—at which point Alex proceeded to launch into a dazzling display of financial acumen. As Dwight listened, he became increasingly frustrated. Alex seemed to understand the complexity of what Breckenridge was proposing in a way Dwight couldn't grasp, even after having wrestled with the documents half the night.

When Alex finished, Dwight began raising the questions he had prepared. He was concerned that these might seem elementary to his young partner. But Alex answered each query cogently, without impatience or any trace of a putdown. Dwight was pleasantly surprised, but realized he shouldn't have been. Alex undoubtedly sensed he had made some progress from yesterday—when Dwight's mind seemed made up against the deal—but wasn't all the way home yet. *So, he's deliberately staying away from any "extraneous" factors that might get the Bentley dander up.* Still, at various points along the way, Alex did manage to subtly reinforce Dwight's lack of comfort with the subject matter.

The issue that most troubled Dwight was the lack of public disclosure regarding the probable affiliation between Excel and Panoply. But Alex defended Breckenridge's posture skillfully: We don't know that Edwards owns Panoply; we have no duty to inquire into that subject; if there is any disclosure problem, it belongs to Excel, not to us; the prices charged by Panoply are at their customary rates, so the Breckenridge stockholders aren't harmed; and so on.

Then, when Dwight completed asking his questions, Alex played what he undoubtedly considered his trump card. "By the way," he said, "I spoke last night to one of the financial guys at Breckenridge, who confirmed the information I mentioned yesterday about the other law firm being willing to take this on. Turns out it's the Peterson firm and the partner involved is Greg Rose."

Dwight took a deep breath. This was significant news, as Alex must have realized. The Peterson firm was widely regarded as one of the best in town, while Rose—a leading corporate lawyer, reputed to have a solid financial services background—was a gentleman whom Dwight had always respected.

Dwight felt his resistance weakening. He didn't like Alex—that was for sure—but he realized how smart the younger man was. He felt that Alex's strong conviction about the propriety of the deal couldn't be ignored—especially because the situation involved specialized financial matters he didn't fully understand. Bill Price's note and Lenny Tatum's attitude—undoubtedly representative of most of the partners—created in his mind a rebuttable presumption to do the deal. And the icing on the cake was the knowledge that a prominent lawyer, Greg Rose, had no problem with the transaction.

And now, clearly sensing it was time for the moment of truth, Alex moved forward in the chair, his body tense, and asked: "So, Dwight, how do you come out?"

Dwight didn't answer right away. Unconsciously, his lips pursed and twitched twice in that habitual fishlike gesture of his. As he spoke, the words seemed to him disembodied—almost as if he were just as interested in hearing his reply as his listener was.

"I've given this a lot of thought, Alex. Bottom line, and provided a few changes are made in the current proposal, I don't feel strongly negative enough to disapprove the firm's taking on this business."

"That's great," said Alex with a big smile. He seemed not at all concerned with the lukewarm, backhanded form of Dwight's blessing. "I knew you'd ultimately see it that way. Tell me the changes you want, and I'll see if we can convince the Brecken-ridge people to put them in place."

Dwight went through the changes with Alex, who had no problem with any of them. *There's no reason he should,* thought Dwight; *they're simply Band-Aids—cosmetic touches that don't get any-where near the heart of the matter.* His brain entertained a more vivid metaphor. *They're just a fig leaf to cover up the nakedness of my contrary gut reaction yesterday. And Alex is no dummy—he must have realized this right off the bat, which is why he didn't bother to withhold his favorable reaction until after having heard my changes.*

When Dwight finished, Alex said, "Those are good changes, Dwight. They help the appearance of the deal without detract-ing from the financial substance. I'm sure Breckenridge won't have any problem with them." He rose from his chair to leave. "Thanks so much, Dwight."

Dwight looked up. "Why thanks? I'm just doing my job."

Alex paused briefly at the door. "I know. And I'll do mine."

After Alex Gibson left, Dwight Bentley sat at his desk, ponder-ing what had just occurred. He went over again in his mind the rationale for his decision—retracing his thought process step by step.

He also reflected on how favorably this outcome would be viewed not only by Alex but also by Bill Price and his other partners—all of them anxious to keep the Breckenridge account where it belonged, right here at Jenkins & Price.

But as he silently mouthed the name of his firm—and particularly that of its founder, old man Jenkins—Dwight experienced a strong sense of déjà vu. He saw himself as a young man, standing in the senior partner's office—reliving the incident with the corrupt state official that he'd related to Gibson yesterday. All he could hear was Jenkins' stentorian "FUHGEDDABOUTIT!!" And Dwight realized that Jenkins was speaking to him *right now*—not about some corruption plot long ago but about the Breckenridge scheme that he had just sanctioned for the firm.

Dwight took a deep breath as he realized what he'd done. *I used the technical stuff as a crutch, a rationalization for my unwillingness to take a stand. And that notion of some kind of presumption in favor of doing the deal was strictly my own invention—Alex's urgings were just what you'd expect from a proponent of new business, while Bill's routine message carried no overtone or subtext.*

Worst of all was how I allowed myself to be influenced by the opinion of the Peterson firm. I should have been more skeptical—how deeply did Greg Rose delve into Breckenridge's plans? And the old Dwight would have been cynical about their motives—recognizing the situation as Peterson's golden opportunity to steal a prime client from us. But no, I swallowed it whole and let it tilt me toward nondisapproval of the deal. "Nondisapproval"—as if the difference between that and "approval" made the slightest difference in anyone's mind but my own. . . .

And now Dwight confronted the painful truth—previously blocked under layers of rationalization—as to why he came out the way he did. *It was concern about making enemies of my partners, fear of being forcibly retired by the firm, anxiety over displeasing Helen—all the wrong reasons.*

What's more, Dwight realized, he had flunked his own test for self-interest. If, contrary to fact, both the firm and his wife had wanted him to say "no" to the proposal, he would *never* have approved it—even in the backhanded fashion he did.

Now that Dwight was aware of why he had come out the way he did, he presumed his partners would also jump to that conclusion. He recalled with distaste Tatum's slimy innuendos, to say nothing of Alex's "I'll do mine" remark.

A wave of shame engulfed Dwight at the notion that his partners would think he'd approved the deal because he had something to gain personally from that result—*even though their assumption would be correct.* He felt an overpowering need to avoid that happening. He didn't want a single day to elapse without clearing the record on this point—eradicating any conceivable interpretation that he'd been bought off by his partners.

And, just like that, he knew what he had to do.

Five minutes later, Dwight knocked at the open door of Bill Price's office. Bill looked up from his desk and waved Dwight in, motioning him to one of the pull-up chairs.

Price's office was larger than the others and its artifacts befitted the longtime leader of the firm. The walls were chock full of framed awards, pictures of Bill with financial celebrities, and such. Price was well into his seventies, heavyset and jowly with thinning gray hair. He kept his vest and jacket on even in the privacy of his office.

"Good to see you, Dwight. I assume this visit relates to the Breckenridge matter, which I appreciate your having reviewed for us. Alex has just informed me that you blessed the deal."

Dwight twitched uncomfortably in his seat. "I'm not sure I'd use that terminology, although I guess the outcome is about the same. To be more precise, what I told Alex was that with a few small changes—which he had no problem with—I didn't feel strongly negative enough to disapprove our taking on the business."

Price gave him a quizzical look. "Does that represent a significant difference from 'blessing the deal'?"

"I think it does," Dwight replied, shrugging his shoulders, "although I'm not sure anyone else gives a damn. Look, Bill, I viewed my assignment from the firm as, 'Hey, Dwight, this Breckenridge company is a valued client, and we'd like to take on this piece of significant new business, which seems kosher enough, unless you tell us we can't.' A sort of rebuttable presumption to do the deal. And, bottom line, I couldn't overcome that presumption."

Price's eyes narrowed. "Does that mean you have some doubts about the deal?"

"Well, I have to admit that my first reaction was negative. Something about it smelled fishy. . . ." His voice tailed off.

"What happened then?"

"Well, Alex let me know in no uncertain terms how wrong I was—how I didn't understand the technical aspects and the way they impacted the deal. Fact is, I still don't fully understand it—I'm not sure how everything fits together. So I couldn't be certain something was wrong. Then, after hearing that Greg Rose and the Peterson firm had no problem with it, I realized that reasonable minds could differ. . . ."

Price was staring hard at him but said nothing. Bentley shifted in his chair, took a deep breath, pursed his lips and twitched them twice before continuing. "And that's the reason I'm sitting in your office right now, Bill. I'm here to tender my resignation from the firm, effective on my sixty-fifth birthday later this year."

Dwight paused briefly to clear the obstruction in his throat that he attributed to his momentous announcement. "It's time for some new blood. There's a state-of-the-art financial world out there today, but I'm still mired in the old one. To paraphrase Groucho Marx on club membership, I wouldn't want to be a member of a law firm whose ethics guru no longer trusts his nose."

Bill Price took his glasses off, rocked forward in his chair and erupted. "What kind of bullshit is this, Dwight? 'Rebuttable presumption'—come off it! And this technical stuff may be hard to follow, but it doesn't change the ethical equation. What the hell, you don't have to understand how a carburetor works to drive a car—or more to the point, to know when the car isn't functioning properly."

Dwight was taken aback by the vehemence of Price's outburst. He sat silently as it continued.

"No, I refuse to believe it was goddamn technical hogwash. There's something else that caused you to shift ground from your first negative reaction."

Dwight was impressed with how quickly Price saw through his rationalization. Still, he couldn't get himself to articulate the real reasons for his decision, so he replied lamely, "I guess I just didn't want to stand in the way of progress."

Price snorted. "Crap! Is this the Dwight Bentley I've known all these years? I don't recognize the person who's uttering such rot."

Dwight slumped lower in his chair, awaiting the balance of the tirade. But Price's voice now took on an earnest tone. "Hell, Dwight, I depend on you and your nose. Sure, I want to latch onto new business as much as the next guy—maybe even more—if it's good business. But I don't want to sign onto something that's questionable—something that runs the risk of harming the firm."

Everything Bill is saying seems so self-evident. What could I have been thinking?

"There's nothing wrong with your nose, Dwight. You spotted a problem right off the bat." There was real emotion now in Price's voice. "And then you wimped out—for reasons I won't even try to understand. I'm ashamed of you. You should be protecting the firm, not endangering it."

Price paused to take a sip of water from the glass on his desk. "Now, as for your retirement."

My retirement! Temporarily overlooked in the brambles of Breckenridge was the fact that he'd announced his retirement. *Why did I do that? And in such haste—not even pausing to sleep on it or discuss my intentions with Helen. . . .* But, though reluctant to put it into words, he already knew the answer.

Price put down his water glass. "You know, just a few weeks ago, I discussed your situation with our executive committee. We realized that your sixty-fifth birthday was coming up this year. I personally advised the group how stupid it would be to retire you. 'We need Dwight,' I told them—having in mind all these Young Turks around here, hustling their butts off but sometimes lacking in judgment—'we need him to protect us from plunging into something harmful.' And every member of the committee agreed 100 percent with me."

Price paused to let his words sink in. "But I guess I was wrong. If I can't depend on you to give me a forthright reaction to potential danger, we don't need you around. So, I accept your resignation. Only forget about turning sixty-five—let's make it effective immediately. Now get the hell out of here, so I can get back to work." And with that, Price put on his glasses, picked up a document from the desk, and started reading it.

For a long time after returning to his office, Dwight sat almost motionless at the desk. A welter of emotions washed over him, the most persistent being—*How could I have been so stupid? If I'd known what Price's reaction on Breckenridge was going to be before resigning, I never would have resigned. But I was in such a hurry to spit it out—I didn't even wait to hear what Bill had to say.*

One lesson he'd always hammered home to the younger lawyers, when they were negotiating a deal or challenging a regulator on behalf of a client, was: *Stop and listen to what the other guy is saying before leaping off the platform.* But he'd failed to follow his own advice, and now it was too late to take the action back. *Price wants nothing to do with me, and I don't blame him.*

Dwight found the irony overwhelming. He'd always had an eye for irony, relishing its intrusion into the lives of public figures—but the effect wasn't nearly as congenial when it hit home. He had done what his instinct told him not to do—bless the deal—because he didn't want to be forcibly retired by the firm. However, even if he'd declined to bless the deal, his partners wouldn't have made him retire, according to Price. But then he rushed ahead to make his retirement a certainty by voluntarily proposing it. Why? He knew why and now allowed himself to face the fact. It was so that no one would think the reason he blessed the deal was to keep from being involuntarily retired—*which, in fact, was exactly the reason. Awwww!*—a silent scream of agony filled his lungs.

He thought about Helen. *How will she react when she hears about my rush to resign without consulting her first?* He could visualize the nonplussed expression on her face, the incredulous tone of her voice: "Let me get this straight—you did *what?!*"

He looked at the venerable files littering the office—*what I refer to as my 'primary materials' for that law school course I've long been threatening to teach?* He picked one up. It was eight years old—and the applicable law had undergone some significant developments since then. At the moment, the prospect of revisiting the detritus of deals past, plucking out morsels of wisdom for inquisitive young minds, seemed unappetizing in the extreme.

He continued at this nadir for what seemed an eternity—but was actually less than ten minutes—when Bill Price appeared at the door of his office. "May I come in?" Price said.

Dwight nodded and Bill entered. After seating himself and removing his glasses, he looked Dwight in the eye and said: "As I grow older, I'm distressed to find I'm much quicker on the trigger to react negatively when something upsets me." He took a breath, then continued. "At the same time, it pleases me to discover that I'm faster to recognize those instances when my initial reaction wasn't warranted."

Price now cocked his head in mock self-reproof. "I acted too hastily with you earlier, Dwight. I don't want you to retire"—and here he paused for emphasis—"provided, that is, the 'you' I'm addressing is still the old Dwight Bentley, the one I could always rely on. A single slipup doesn't necessarily mean you've undergone a sea change, but the question remains: Can I still send you the hard ones? Can I trust your sound judgment?"

Can he? Dwight struggled to react to this turn of events. Bill was posing the key question, but Dwight wasn't sure he could give the answer sought. *How far have I slipped? How good is my nose? Am I willing to stand up to the Young Turks? Am I dead and gone—or is this my resurrection?*

In the cauldron of his conflicting reactions, one factor loomed larger to Dwight than all the others—a surge of rejuvenation to his deflated ego. *Bill Price still has confidence in me. I screwed up, and yet he's willing to place his trust in Dwight Bentley. This means everything.* After a few moments, Dwight replied, almost in a whisper, "I can try."

Price stared at him intently for a moment, then relaxed his gaze. "All right, that's good enough for me. And on that basis, I hereby refuse to accept your resignation. In fact, I've already forgotten that you ever submitted the damn thing—it never happened—so no one else will ever know."

Price rose from his chair. Dwight stood up and shook his hand with great warmth. Dwight thought he detected the trace of a smile on Bill's normally serious face.

"Oh, one more thing, Dwight. I wouldn't want to leave without giving you your first assignment. Remember what I said— I've got to be able to send you the tough ones.

"The assignment is—what do we do about this goddamn Breckenridge situation? I don't want the firm to take on the deal if it doesn't smell right to you. But you told Alex it was okay to go ahead, and I'll bet he's already got a team up and running on the project. So your first job is to come up with a way to get us out of it."

Price turned to leave Dwight's office, pausing at the door. "Understand, Dwight, I'll back you to the hilt on this—but I can't be the bad guy here. I don't want my fingerprints on the thing—I've got enough problems with these wunderkinds as it is. . . ."

Helen was, in Dwight's mental image, lying in wait for him when he arrived home that evening. Although she made some small talk, he could tell from her expectant air that she was itching to find out what had occurred at the office. He poured himself a drink, sat down on the living room couch, and began, "Okay, here's what happened. . . ."

The narrative he related bore a resemblance to one of those chopped-up World War II V-mail letters home from GIs overseas—letters that Captain Dwight Bentley had been in charge of censoring to blot out sensitive information. The principal omission in Dwight's tale was the fact of him tendering his resignation. He wasn't proud of having taken this step, especially without consulting Helen in advance; any mention of it would just lead to some unpleasant bickering; and, given Bill's ultimate rejection, its inclusion wasn't needed to make things understandable. *What the hell—Price himself said, 'It never happened.'* Nor did Dwight make mention of his epiphany as to what the true motives for his "nondisapproval" had been.

The rest of the story, however, was mostly there—including the Executive Committee's strong desire to keep him on the job past sixty-five and Price's renewed trust in the Bentley nose. Dwight resisted the temptation to call attention to how wrong-footed Helen's advice had proven. He knew she would grasp her lapse in judgment. *Not that she would acknowledge it or—heaven forbid!—apologize.* Dwight ended the narrative by relating the assignment Bill had given him—the first test to prove he was still worthy of the firm's confidence.

When he'd finished, Helen wasted no time rehashing what had occurred, but instead zeroed right in on the issue Price had thrown in Dwight's lap—how to get the firm off the hook on the Breckenridge deal. *That's so characteristic of her—cutting right to the chase. Her old man has brought her a new problem, so what's the Bentley team going to do about solving it?*

"Okay, Dwight, let's talk about how to deal with Alex. You can't just tell him you've changed your mind—that would be too bald. I think I've got a better way to go." *Amazing! Last night she was pressuring me to bring the Breckenridge business on board, and tonight—with the same zest—she's counseling me on to how to get rid of it. And telling me not to say I've changed my mind.*

Helen warmed to her subject. "You spoke of a few 'Band-Aid' changes you had proposed to the deal that Gibson had no problem with. How about if you were to come up with an additional change that you'd previously 'neglected to mention'—only instead of a Band-Aid, this one happens to be a bloody field dressing. . . ."

Early the next morning, Alex Gibson stopped by Bentley's office, as Dwight expected he would. There was no small talk this time.

"Hey, Dwight, I ran those changes you proposed yesterday past the Breckenridge people, and they had no problem with any of them. So we're up and running."

Dwight was seated in his desk chair. His posture was erect, and the pouches under his eyes seemed to have diminished. When he spoke, there was no trace of that habitual lip-pursing or twitch, and his voice was crisp.

"You know, Alex, I'm still troubled by the nondisclosure of Panoply's role and possible ownership. My first choice remains to pin that down, and if it turns out as you suspect, to disclose Edwards' ownership—"

Alex interrupted. "Wait a minute. I thought you and I put that issue to rest yesterday. We don't know for sure about his ownership, it's none of our business, we don't have a duty to inquire, our stockholders aren't hurt—and worst case, if there's a problem, it belongs to Excel, not Breckenridge."

Dwight didn't hesitate before replying. "I hear you, but what bothers me is the money trail—the fact that, by our client paying Panoply directly, Breckenridge could be deemed to be abetting an undisclosed plot to feather Edwards' nest."

"Oh, come on—"

"So anyway, here's my solution. If Breckenridge is unwilling to make appropriate inquiries and live with the disclosure consequences, then let's recommend to them a reconfiguration of the deal. Instead of Breckenridge dealing with Panoply directly, make Panoply a subcontractor of Excel. Then all the money we pay goes straight to Excel. How they then choose to whack it up with Panoply becomes their business, not ours. That way, we're not involved in any possible nondisclosure."

Alex stared at Dwight as if he were balmy. "What the hell are you talking about? That changes the whole transaction. Breckenridge doesn't want to start renegotiating the terms—it's a good deal for them just as it is. And even if Breckenridge were willing to do something like that, Excel would never go for it."

"If Excel were unwilling to make the change, that might be good evidence they have something to hide."

"Oh, come off it, Dwight! This is ridiculous. I'm not even going to raise this with Breckenridge. It's so presumptuous—the lawyer telling the client to change a favorable business deal."

Dwight rose from his chair, delivering his final words in a voice full of resolve. "If they won't inquire and disclose, or alternatively, make this change in structure, I'm not going to approve the firm's taking on the deal."

Alex's eyes blazed. "Why, you antique sonuvabitch—you *already* approved it! You can't pull this stunt now—I won't let you sandbag me like this." He started for the door. "We'll see about this bullshit—I'm going down to tell Bill Price the whole incredible story right now!"

"That," said Dwight calmly, as he bent down to pick up some old papers off the carpet for his secretary to send to central files, "is your prerogative. . . ."

Commentary on
THE SMELL TEST

T
he Smell Test" is a story about a skilled and highly ethical lawyer who for a few bad days (in Margaret Thatcher's memorable phrase) goes wobbly. As you read it, don't just tut-tut over Dwight Bentley's temporary weakness, while patting yourself on the back as an exemplar of professional morality. The fact is (and I know this, from painful experience), it can happen to *you*. Once you grant that premise, you'll find that the story contains some useful lessons.

The basic situation here—a superannuated underutilized partner of the law firm serving as its ethics guru—is a plausible one. It's prudent for the firm leadership (exemplified by Bill Price, the managing partner of Jenkins & Price) to have a wise individual review any questionable stuff the firm is asked to undertake. The arrangement works best when the reviewer isn't in the everyday line of fire and can be trusted not to let such pesky factors as making money get in the way of sound judgment.

Although this and the other stories in the book are set in the late 1970s, the broader issue for lawyers addressed by "The Smell Test"—stated simplistically, the recurrent conflict between the almighty dollar and professionalism—is still very much with us today. In this regard, I call your attention to an excellent piece on professionalism by Charles McCallum, present chairman of the ABA's Business Law Section, which appeared in *Business Law Today* (Jan/Feb 2007 pp. 43–46).

As for the specific clash here between a gentleman of the old school and a Young Turk, this was a common occurrence in the '70s. Although it's less prevalent today—with so many of the old-timers having passed from the scene—my hunch is that in many smaller and midsize firms that haven't yet fully subscribed to a "go-go" legal practice, the friction still exists.

There's also another, more timeless factor at work here. It's obvious from the start that a real edginess exists in the relationship between Dwight Bentley and Alex Gibson—a mutual distaste that extends well beyond their difference in age. Practicing law in a partnership format creates some singular kinds of relationships that I'll address more fully in the commentaries to the stories "Partnergate" and "On-the-Job Training." Suffice to say here, you need to learn to coexist with your partners and associates, but you're not required to be enamored of each one. Just make sure not to let any negative feelings you may harbor about a colleague get in the way of functioning together professionally.

The main point I'm trying to make in this story—a point that has implications not only for young or aspiring lawyers but also for seasoned veterans—is how, when faced with an insidious situation, any of us can temporarily lose our bearings.

Take Dwight Bentley at the beginning of the story. To be sure, he's aware that he's been shunted off to the side of the firm, exiled to an obscure floor, and even a source of mirth among the young partners. But he still knows that on matters of professional ethics, he's the guy that Bill Price (the managing partner) turns to for comfort and good judgment. And Dwight also knows from experience that when his judgment on a matter is negative, Bill Price doesn't override him—even if it means Jenkins & Price will be passing up some big fees. So in this respect Dwight is in a position of real power, and therefore, when he's called upon to act within his bailiwick, you'd expect him to call it as he sees it. Yet he doesn't do so—and *why* he doesn't is a central theme of the story. It's an important theme, because you don't want to let this kind of thing happen to *you*!

We view "The Smell Test" through the prism of a third-person narrator, but with much of Dwight Bentley's thinking rendered in his own words (in italics). The narrator does not go inside the head of any of the other characters, so we only get to know them from the narrator's surface observations and Dwight's personal reactions and insights.

Let's begin by taking a look at Alex Gibson. Here he comes, barging into Dwight's office to obtain the Bentley imprimatur on the firm handling the proposed Breckenridge deal. How does Alex proceed with his task?

At the risk of oversimplifying the issue, there are two basic ways we lawyers can go about imparting intelligence, persuading others and exerting influence. We can communicate or we can dazzle.

I always thought of myself a communicator. I attempted to persuade others by the logic of my presentation, which I strived to make the listener understand. On the other hand, a dazzler—of which breed Alex is a prime example—puts on a bravura display of subject matter grasp, intended to intimidate the listener (who doesn't fully understand what's going on) to fall into step. We may not get inside Gibson's head, but we can draw a reasonable inference that this is just what Alex is trying to do with Dwight. And, at least for a while, it works—a befuddled Dwight is swept along by the force of Gibson's presentation.

My first question is directed to those of you who have been (or may in the future be) subjected to someone like Alex:

What should you do when you feel yourself being dazzled?

My advice is to risk the embarrassment of confessing that you're not as much on top of the subject as the dazzler, tell him to slow down and explain things, and—if you're likely to be called upon to decide or act on the basis of the information being imparted—make a real effort to understand what's being said. Don't remain silent, feel yourself getting lost, and then have to act on your flawed intelligence.

As to which kind of communicator you should be, that's a personal decision for you to make. Some of us do a bit of each, depending on the circumstances. One basic distinction here relates to whom you're dealing with. If it's a business client (and certainly if it's a partner), communicating should prevail. The client is ultimately calling the shots, so she should understand what she's doing. Talking over the client's head, making no effort to explain—with a baffled client across the desk, who's reluctant to ask questions for fear of seeming ignorant—is just no way to handle the relationship.

Here's a litmus test you can use. Assume you decide on the best course of action and try to persuade your client to accept it. She ends up agreeing to do so. Would you be pleased at her acquiescence if you suspected she never really understood what you were talking about?

On the other hand, in haggling with an adversary, there's clearly more room for dazzle. (Your reply to the litmus test then can be—"Hell yes, I never meant for him to understand me anyhow!") As for dealings with regulators and judges, perhaps a little of each may be in order. I leave it to you to find the right groove.

Back to "The Smell Test." Dwight finally jostles himself into action, asks some questions, draws some inferences, and then his nose—behaving like the proboscis every good lawyer should employ as his or her personal smell test—goes to work. He hones in on the heart of the matter—the unnecessary company named Panoply, the flow of funds, the nondisclosure to the public. Through the obfuscation and haze, he sees this for what it is: a scheme to benefit Edwards personally, at the expense of the Excel stockholders, without telling them what's going on. Once he comes alive, Dwight performs precisely the way a savvy business lawyer should. And when Alex argues that each step of the proposed arrangement is "completely justifiable," Dwight's reply— "But that's just what you need a nose for"—is right on the money.

Dwight's anecdote about the shakedown by a corrupt state official derives, I'm embarrassed to say, from my own experience. I was the "young partner" who tried to come up with a way to accommodate a client who was being wronged. To my chagrin, one of my senior partners saw through the whole cabal in a minute and jolted me out of my phantasm. The experience was painful, but it seared a lesson into my brain that I never forgot.

By the way, the denouement of that incident occurred just about as Dwight relates it. The executives didn't like being shaken down, but needed to be told it was wrong by someone with moral authority in such matters— namely, their lawyers. The lesson is clear. No matter what those who are trying to get your ear might say or imply up front, don't be afraid to give your client (or your colleagues) your best and most objective advice—even if this means they have to pass up a seemingly golden opportunity to profit.

Well, Dwight's initial use of his sniffer concludes the good lawyering segment of "The Smell Test." The rest is frankly something of a mess.

I cast Alex as a modern-day Satan, tempting Dwight away from his original negative conclusion by sowing seeds of doubt in his mind, to wit:

Hey, Dwight, this is the "real world" of today, not your "happy antiquity."

The client has already contacted another law firm that would have no trouble taking on the transaction—so our firm's prissiness won't thwart the deal from happening.

That flashback of yours is distinguishable as a simplistic situation involving a bribe; the Breckenridge deal is complex with no bribe.

And, bottom line, passing this one up means our firm will permanently lose a world-class client.

A more virile Dwight might have had no problem shaking off this assortment of temptations to eat the apple. This Dwight has more trouble doing so—the primary reason being that, in the particular situation, he's out of his comfort zone. Every lawyer, at one time or another, has to face this plight—where, due to unfamiliarity with the subject matter, you can't be as confident that the judgment you're bringing to bear on a thorny issue is entirely sound.

And so, the doubts seep in to Dwight's brain. *Might the other firm understand the problem better? How will Bill Price react if I come out in the negative?* And so on. Try to picture yourself in the same predicament. I can envision myself there, and it's not a pretty sight. If and when this occurs, the important thing is to recognize what's happening and shake it off—but Dwight can't seem to do so.

Alex, no dummy, realizes he ought to give Dwight a little room to "sleep on it" in order to rescind that initial negative judgment. But far from taking the pressure off, Alex keeps it on with the following trifecta. He schedules the next session for ten o'clock the following morning—not much time at all. He leaves a voluminous and complex file to be absorbed overnight, adding to Dwight's uncertainty. And he exits with that enigmatic line, "I help you, you help me at another time."

The ensuing scene between Dwight and his wife Helen, which serves to heighten the pressure he feels, is purely out of my imagination. I can't recall either of my two estimable wives getting involved in the substance of some determination I was being called upon to make. And I was always careful not to reveal any confidential client information, even to my wife. You'll note that Dwight, in discussing the matter with Helen, does not disclose the name of the client involved, and I'm sure he doesn't go too deeply into the details of the client's business plan.

The reason for this scene is that I wanted to introduce a character who could bypass the merits of what Dwight is examining and focus on the practicalities of the situation. And for this sort of role, a spouse like Helen is hardly an unfamiliar presence. Her role is especially germane when those practical considerations are unlikely to occur to someone like Dwight, whom Helen sees as being in a state of denial.

And so in she charges—the love of Dwight's life—and promptly performs a complete circuit of all Dwight's hot buttons:

At sixty-five, will he be retained by the firm or canned like Mack (who, by the way, we meet in "Negotiating 101")?

That "little monster" Gibson is going to hold Dwight's fate in his hands.

Dwight won't be supported by his other partners, all of whom will make less money by his determination to turn down the Breckenridge business.

How will the Bentleys survive without that J&P paycheck?

What else can Dwight really do at his age to make money?

And finally, the unkindest cut of all—the insinuation that maybe Dwight's nose isn't as trustworthy on this new stuff as it used to be on devious schemes of the old school.

Then—shades of Alex Gibson!—Helen pulls back to let Dwight sleep on it. But her parting remark—"friends know how to reciprocate"—puts Alex's "I help you, you help me at another time" into bold relief.

In the next scene, Dwight is alone, late at night, wrestling with his problem. For me, this is the most true-to-life scenario in the entire story.

Many hours of a lawyer's professional time are spent in the company of others—with clients, with partners and associates, with adversaries, with regulators or judges. But there's a big chunk of time when the lawyer is alone in his or her office (or at home, in a car, or on a plane) thinking through a problem. That's the way it should be. To be sure, you can't neglect the fruits of your give-and-take with others and should not ignore any decent advice you've received. But you also have to reserve some time to ponder the problem on your own—because in the last analysis, this is going to be *your* determination, not theirs.

There's a section in my book *Lawyering* (called "The Modes and Moods of the Reflective Process") that deals with how best to go about analyzing a problem. On certain issues, I concluded, you're probably better off commandeering another smart, knowledgeable lawyer in your firm or company to bounce the problem off. The interplay of two minds can often improve your chances of arriving at an intelligent solution. Also I found that the act of articulating the problem to another lawyer helped me to analyze what was significant and what was not, to discover how much I knew about the problem and what I needed to find out, to ascertain what assumptions I was making, to see how differing alternatives could lead to different results, and so on.

For me, though, a lot of analytical time was best spent alone—where I could let my mind loose to dwell on an issue. As multiple matters compete for your attention, the luxury of uninterrupted reflective thought about a problem is greatly to be treasured. It's especially beneficial for (1) separating what is material from what isn't, (2) grasping the real significance of an already known but previously unobtrusive fact, (3) recognizing how the modification of a basic assumption can drastically alter your perception of the dynamics of a situation, and (4) formulating a new and different course of action.

Now let's return to Dwight Bentley, whose solo endeavor isn't going well at all. I think it's pretty obvious why this is so. Instead of focusing on the substantive problem he's been called upon to address, he's dwelling on the various permutations of Helen's reality check. Along the way, though, he touches on some important themes—in addition, of course, to the vital "trust your nose" advice—and these deserve a few words of elaboration.

First, there's the test Dwight propounds to determine whether considerations of personal interest are influencing one's judgment. Business lawyers need to be especially alert to the elements of self-interest that crop up all the time in their practice. We have to assess the motives and actions of those with whom we deal, because of the unescapable reality that the positions people take can be as dependent on factors personal to them as on the objective merits of their rationale. What makes this fertile ground for the bug of self-interest to flourish is that so few of the issues we consider in the course of counseling have objectively right answers; rather, most of them call for essentially subjective judgments on how to proceed.

So take some extra time to examine what might be going on at the subliminal level. Evaluate whether the reasons someone gives for pursuing a particular course of action appear to have intrinsic weight. Then ask yourself: What reason could he or she have for reaching this conclusion? A simple rule of thumb might be that the less persuasive the merits (from someone who's capable of worthier rationale), the more likely something else is at work.

What we may not always realize is how insinuating, how subtle the bug can be—to the point that it even affects our unaware self. And so we also have to examine our own motives for coming out the way we do. Are there considerations of personal benefit to us, financial or otherwise? Are we bending things too much to arrive at the result the client wants to achieve? Are we seeking revenge or retribution? And finally—perhaps the most insidious of all—are we looking to protect our own tails?

On this latter point, what you have to watch out for are situations where the principal virtue of your advice is its consistency with past advice you've given on the situation, even though it might not represent the optimum approach under the new circumstances. In my book *Advise and Invent*, I had this to say on the subject:

> Perhaps some of you are having trouble ascribing such dubious motives to yourself. If so, try this simple drill. Imagine that a client calls you to discuss an unpleasant situation that has arisen. The subject matter is ostensibly covered by an existing contract—a contract that you originally drafted and negotiated, but which you haven't reviewed in some time. The client is anxious to know whether he's protected by the agreement. He sets forth the facts; you promise to get back to him promptly with an answer. You hang up the phone and take out the contract, to check just how well you provided for the possibility of this particular contingency arising.
>
> Now, if you can't envision the way your heart begins to thump as you near the page containing the crucial language—if you can't feel the initial surge of relief upon discovering that the subject is indeed covered in the contract—if you can't experience the terrible sense of dismay when the provision appears to come out the

wrong way—if you can't visualize the exhilaration of discovering other language, in a different part of the contract (to which you've turned in panic), fully supporting your position—then I suggest an immediate visit to your family doctor: you may well be brain dead!

The real question is how to determine if self-interest has affected your judgment. Let me ask you:

Do you have a personal test for determining whether self-interest has entered into your determination. If so, what is it?

Do you recall the test Dwight seeks to apply to purge the bias? It's not just how you would come out on the issue by pretending the bias doesn't exist; it's going further and assuming the consideration of personal interest runs in the *other* direction—that is, that your determination flies in the face of your self-interest—in which case, you know you're on sound ground. That's a test I feel has a lot of merit—especially since it's hard to fool your subconscious by pretending the personal interest doesn't exist.

The other subject touched on here is the significance of gut reactions. The tough case occurs when there's a serious conflict between your initial reaction to something and the second thoughts that follow in its wake. How about you:

Do you typically go with your gut or heed those nagging subsequent doubts?

The framework here is decision-making. At the heart of decision-making is the appreciation of significance—the ability to sort out what is significant from what is unimportant or irrelevant. You can't make good decisions by simply lining up the factors and striking an arithmetic balance—the weighing process is critical to sound judgment. Most bad decisions are the product of giving too much weight to a factor that didn't deserve it, or failing to appreciate the significance of a factor at the heart of things.

It's clear to me that one of the most important factors in any situation is your first reaction to it. Unless your instincts are really flawed, that initial response has to deserve a lot of weight. So, whatever happens, don't lose sight of your first uncluttered reaction. A lot of what ensues is rationalizing, sugaring over, self-interest, and such.

Now, to be sure, if your track record of relying on that first instinct is bad, or you're in a learning process, or the issue isn't up your alley, then prudence may dictate that you rely on those sober second thoughts. But if you pride yourself on good instinctive judgment, and you're in your comfort zone, then go with your gut.

Dwight's problem, of course, stems from having convinced himself that he's out of his comfort zone. Now, try to put yourself in Dwight's shoes—but pretending you are Dwight Bentley and not yourself—and I ask you:

What might Dwight have decided to do here that would have helped him escape his quandary?

Well, I'll give you my reaction. It's understandable why Dwight didn't want to tell Bill Price he couldn't handle this—I would have felt the same way. But if I were Dwight, I would have cozied up to the notion of getting some help from a savvy young associate who understood the business aspects of the deal better than I. The narrator tells us it was Dwight's pride, plus the fear that his judgment would be influenced by someone with his own agenda, that kept Dwight from moving in that direction. To my mind, though, that's a foolish pride, given the circumstances, and Dwight should be sharp enough to see though any associate who isn't giving him the straight scoop.

The next scene, with Lenny Tatum at the lobby newsstand, is intended to raise the stakes for Dwight—both in terms of letting him know his partners are aware of the deal, want it to happen, and assume that it will, and then in insinuating a tie-in between his decision and his future at the firm. These factors, sad to say, influence Dwight's conduct over the next few hours of his life.

I upped the pressure a little more when the first thing Dwight encounters in his office is a life insurance premium he needs to pay—an expense that exceeds his monthly budget and reminds him of his shaky personal financial condition. And this comes at a time when he still hasn't decided how to come out on the Breckenridge matter.

Dwight now reveals his edgy mental state by giving an unduly emphatic reading to an otherwise neutral note from Bill Price. Dwight—his lawyer's mind working overtime—uses this as a pretext to convert the task he's been given from one of approving the deal to not disapproving it. In effect, he creates a sort of rebuttable presumption in favor of the deal, which he then construes as setting a higher standard for him to go against the flow. It reminds me of the rule invoked for challenges of calls on the field in National Football League games—if the evidence of the camera review isn't conclusive the other way, the referee has to go with the original call made by the official. That may be okay for the NFL, but it's nonsense here.

And now here comes Alex with some more dazzle that he saved up from yesterday, designed to clinch approval from a bewildered Dwight. At least this time Dwight does ask some questions, but Alex parries these neatly, making an effort not to get Dwight's dander up, and skillfully defending the nondisclosure aspect that most bothers Dwight. And then Alex plays his trump card by identifying the other law firm and lawyer who are willing to handle the deal—not some fly-by-nighters, but a highly respected firm and individual partner.

It's all too much for Dwight, who succumbs to the pressure. Given a few Band-Aid changes, he doesn't feel "strongly negative enough to disapprove the firm's taking on the business." It's lukewarm, it's back-handed, but Alex knows he's achieved his goal and treats it that way.

Alex Gibson may be brainy, but as is so often the case with people of his ilk, he lacks judgment. What he does next is just about the dumbest thing he could have said to someone of Dwight's proud character. Do you recall what it is? On his way out, Alex makes a definite link between Dwight's self-image of his decision ("I'm just doing my job") and Alex's role in the upcoming firm decision about whether to keep Dwight on ("and I'll do mine."). Well, all I can say is, thank God the Alex's of this world so often self-destruct—even if it takes a while for the demolition to occur.

The next scene finds Dwight alone, musing on what just happened, when suddenly everything about his conduct becomes clear to him. He used the technical stuff as a crutch not to take a stand, he invented the rebuttable presumption to do the deal, he created a false distinction between approval and nondisapproval, he was influenced by what another firm would do. He uncovers his real but misguided motives—the fear of being forcibly retired, his anxiety over displeasing Helen. And he realizes he has flunked his own self-interest test. Then, aghast at the notion that his partners may assume he's approved the deal because of his own self-interest (in which assumption, they would be correct), he decides he can't let that impression stand for even a moment, which leads directly into the disaster that follows.

I give Dwight a mixed report card here. I'm encouraged that he finally figured out what he was doing and why (although, lamentably, after the fact). But then for him to swing into immediate action to rectify it—that's very dangerous indeed. If and when that proverbial light bulb flashes over your head to signify a discovered personal error or omission, give yourself some time (perhaps with help from a trusted colleague or friend) to figure out what to do next. Your psyche may be too fragile at that moment to produce the kind of good practical judgment of which you're usually capable.

But Dwight is a man on a mission. He scurries over to Bill Price's office, confirms his nondisapproval of the deal, and tenders his resignation from the firm, confessing that he "no longer trusts his nose." Price reacts with some heat, telling Dwight he "wimped out." After recounting the vote of confidence Dwight has recently received from the Executive Committee, Price accepts Bentley's resignation on the spot (because "I can't depend on you to give me a forthright reaction to potential dangers"). A little hasty on Price's part, to be sure, but the force and clarity of his reaction does serve (as it may have been intended) to bring Dwight to his senses.

Now Dwight is back in his office, wondering, "How could I have been so stupid?" How could he indeed? He violated his own valid precept of hearing what the other guy has to say before acting—not waiting for Price's reaction on the Breckenridge deal before blurting out his resignation. And now Dwight wakes up as to why he resigned—so that his partners wouldn't think the reason he blessed the deal was to keep himself from being forcibly retired (which is precisely why he did do it!). Pardon any immodesty, but I must say, the irony is delicious.

Well, fortunately Bill Price has cooled down and arrives to offer a reprieve—providing he can still trust Dwight's sound judgment. The fact that Price still has confidence in him after his screw-up bolsters Dwight enough for him to reply, "I can try." And wisely, Bill doesn't press for a more definite response, but accepts this and treats the resignation as if it never happened. So Dwight is off the hook.

But not quite. Price now gives him the assignment to come up with a way to get the firm out of the Breckenridge deal that it's already working on—and without Bill's fingerprints appearing. (By the way, we'll run into that "no fingerprints" admonition in other stories, as you'll note later on.) So my final question to you is:

If you were Dwight, how would you handle this latest assignment from Price under all the circumstances?

In the story, Helen now rides to the rescue. Of course, she's not about to acknowledge how mistaken her prior judgment was, but she does turn on a dime and provides Dwight the clue as to what he should do. I suppose we should give thanks for the insights of the Helens of this world, even if they can't get it right the first time.

The Bentley we see the next day in his office is a different Dwight from the one we've witnessed earlier. He looks younger, more self-assured; the voice is crisp; the lip-pursing and twitch are gone; he's back in control. He even decides to send some of that junk on the carpet off to central files.

And now Dwight, confronting Alex, takes the position that if Breckenridge refuses to inquire and disclose (as he knows they won't), there needs to be a reconfiguration of the deal (which he knows the client won't accept). Alex goes ballistic, but Dwight is now serene, knowing that Bill Price (this, after all, doesn't bear *his* fingerprints) will back him up.

So that's "The Smell Test"—a morality tale that ultimately comes out the right way, but only after some troublesome miscalculations and missteps. I'll close by repeating the lesson I've tried to get across here. You don't need to be old-fashioned, bereft of business, and shunted to an auxiliary floor to have this kind of situation—complete with considerations of personal interest—come knocking on your door. Let's just hope that when it happens, you're better prepared than Dwight Bentley.

FATHER'S DAY

S o, here's the thing, Dad—I know you're a lawyer, but I've got no idea what you *do*."

Mark and I are in a rented car, driving from the airport in Denver to the ski resort at Steamboat Springs—just the two of us on vacation over the New Year's holiday. We've made the turn north off Route 70 and are heading up to the pass called Rabbit Ears. A light snow is falling. At three-thirty in the afternoon it's starting to get dark, although there's still adequate visibility.

"I mean, Josh's father is a surgeon—he cuts people up, takes out the bad stuff, and sews them back together. Kyle's dad is an architect—he makes up the design for a school or office building. I *know* what they do. But you—the big-shot lawyer Dan Barton, who likes to brag that in all his days at Jenkins & Price he's never seen the inside of a courtroom—what do *you* do?"

This, I'm thinking, is some precocious twelve-year-old. Dammit, I wish I could spend more time with him—like the many hours we'll have together on this vacation. It's the first trip the two of us have ever taken on our own. Ever since Alice and I split last summer, it's just been weekends for Mark and me. And I fill those Saturdays and Sundays with such nonstop activity—ball games, workouts, movies, and so on—that there's little quiet time to hold a serious conversation.

I miss those hours of prebedtime "guy talk" with Mark on weekday evenings in our Bronxville home—not that I always made it home on time. Nowadays, my weekday nonworking evenings are mostly spent chatting with the date du jour. And while there are some definite advantages to dealing with the other gender, the talking part doesn't always score high on my list.

"See what I mean, Dad? I can't *picture* your work, the way I can with those other guys' fathers."

As a kid, I always knew what *my* father did. He owned a company that made those little ball bearings they used in roller skates. But the business wasn't interesting, and I took no pride in it—I guess it seemed so inconsequential. I remember avoiding the subject when other kids discussed their fathers' professions.

Funny, I never thought Mark had any interest in what I do for a living. And the last thing I wanted was to bore him with war stories about my heroics on some current deal. So I just stayed away from the subject. But now, having posed a sensible question, he's entitled to a helpful reply.

"You know, I'm glad you asked the question. I'll try to answer it in a way that makes sense to you."

But how do I give him the flavor of what I do—make it seem interesting, in terms he can understand—without piling on all the baggage I have to deal with? Well, I'm not in a rush now, like I usually am. There's no client or other activity getting in the way. If I can't handle this inquiry, I'm not much of a lawyer—or a father, either.

Actually, I'm not sure how good a father I am to Mark, who's my only child. It's tough to excel at parenting when you're not around that much. But what the hell, I had to get out—our marriage just wasn't cutting it.

Hey, don't get me wrong—Alice is a nice enough lady, a good mother to Mark, and I bear her no ill will. I intend to be generous to her financially when we get around to filing for divorce. But the plain fact was that she made no effort to keep up with me. There I was—sprinting ahead in the law firm, mingling with all those slick investment bankers and corporate honchos with their worldly wives—while Alice was teaching kindergarten kids how to draw stick figures and cooking early dinners for our boy.

I feel bad for Mark, of course, as an only child in a—what's the clinical term?—in a broken home. But I'll say this for the kid—to all appearances, he seems to be handling the situation very well. When we get together each weekend at my apartment in the city, I always start out by asking him how things are going. He invariably answers, "Fine." I'm inclined to take that at face value and not probe too much—we never talk about the marriage or the separation. I'm sure if our split was causing him problems, he'd let me know.

"When you get right down to it, Mark, most of what I do is assist my clients—those people, mainly from big corporations, who come to me for help—in making difficult decisions."

"Decisions about what?"

"About different kinds of business matters—deals, contracts, disputes. And questions like what's the best path to take when there's a choice, what tactic should we adopt in a negotiation, how can we make the other side move closer to our position, and so on."

Mark doesn't respond right away. I infer from his silence that my answer to his question was too abstract. But unfortunately, it's not that easy to describe what I do to a nonlawyer.

Take Alice, for instance. She always seemed uninterested in my work, so I rarely brought it up. . . . You know, come to think of it, maybe she *was* interested, but didn't want to intrude after my long day at the office. If I'd volunteered some morsels, she might have gotten more involved. She's not unintelligent—it's just that she inhabited another world that I knew nothing about and wasn't interested in.

It's getting darker now, and my headlights sweep the narrow road as it ascends steadily toward Steamboat. There's still enough light to glimpse my son in profile across the front seat. We share a distinctive feature—a slightly crooked nose. Mine came from a football injury—the handiwork of a second-rate doctor who reset it off-center. The trauma of Mark's broken nose—the result of a fall from his crib—is something I'd just as soon forget. It happened on a night when Alice was at a PTA meeting, leaving me as the parent in charge. I was speaking on one of those endless conference calls in the next room when I heard the crash. . . .

"So, Dad, if these clients all come from big companies, they're probably smart guys—why do they need *your* help?" I can see, out of the corner of my eye, that when Mark talks, he turns in his seat to look directly at me. I've been trying, as much as possible, to keep my eyes glued to the road.

"Good question. Well, on some of the problems, there's a tough legal issue involved. They want to get an expert opinion from a lawyer who specializes in the area."

I don't like the way that came out. It's all right for others to call me an expert, but I shouldn't be making that boast to my son.

I never boasted to Susan Collins, but then again I didn't need to. We'd worked together on a couple of deals, so she had a golden opportunity to see me in action. Susan was a bright, good-looking Jenkins & Price junior partner who spoke my language, covered for me with clients, and worshipped the ground I walked on. And boy, did I have the hots for her.

Mark's next question catches me by surprise. "You said that 'some' of the problems are legal—does that mean that other ones *aren't* about legal stuff?"

"Oh, what a sharp kid—you picked right up on that, didn't you? As a matter of fact, a lot of what I advise on isn't legal at all."

I don't look over, but I can tell from his voice that Mark is pleased with himself. "Well, if the problem isn't legal, then why do they need help from a lawyer like you?"

This boy is setting me up to blow my own horn, but I may as well play it straight. "Because I have a reputation for giving good advice—I'm said to have good judgment."

That, in fact, is just what Susan Collins said to me—the night we spent in Akron on the Voyager deal, when I knocked on the door of her hotel room. She opened it a crack to be heard but kept the chain on. "Use your good judgment, Dan—I'm using mine. I think you're great, but I'm not into breaking up marriages. I won't sleep with you as long as you're still with Alice."

Susan's resolve remained firm. As far as I could tell, her stance was sincere. I'd never accuse her of withholding sex as a lever to get me to leave Alice. But I can't help but wonder—was that, in fact, what pushed me over the edge?

Mark persists. "The questions they ask you—are those so tough that they need to bring in an expert?"

Tough, I'll tell you what's tough—the first relationship you jump into after leaving your wife. Susan was pretty and bright, but there was a by-the-numbers quality to her lovemaking that make me feel like I'd stumbled into a sex therapy clinic. Bottom line, she's a better lawyer than a lover. And maybe so am I—which might account for the steady turnover of ladies who have succeeded Susan in my bed.

"Well, I wouldn't call it rocket science, but the solution isn't always obvious. Sometimes the underlying facts aren't clear, and the determinations that need to be made can be uncertain."

"Hey, whoa, you've lost me. Listen, why don't you give me an example of a tough decision you help people on—one that's not legal."

Oh, this kid is tenacious. But I don't want to disappoint him—like I'm sure I did on the subject of that London trip Alice proposed a few weeks ago. My sister and brother-in-law—and their son, Willy, who's Mark's favorite cousin—have been living in England the past few years. Alice wanted to take Mark to visit them in March during the upcoming spring break, provided I went along—since, as she said, "they're *your* relatives."

Now, I wouldn't mind seeing my sister, but traveling with Alice could prove to be dangerous. Did this strike me as an oblique overture on her part to get back together? If I had said "yes," might that have been misconstrued? You betcha! So I said "no"—but I could tell from Mark's reaction to the news he was unhappy we weren't making the trip.

"Okay, give me a minute to come up with a good example."

My mind strays to my own family. This has been happening often lately, doubtless influenced by the *Roots* series that's such a big TV hit now. I picture myself at Mark's age on a car trip with my parents and younger sister. Typically, I'd be curled up in the back seat, devouring a book or magazine, off in another world.

At twelve years old, did I ever initiate a serious conversation with my old man, like Mark's doing now? Maybe, but I don't recall one.

How about on my father's end? He seldom spoke to me on those rides, other than to call attention to some point of interest along the road. Was he respecting my privacy? Or had I rebuffed his prior attempts at dialogue once too often. Oh, God, I hope not.

My father and I always seemed to be on two different wavelengths. He was so wrapped up in his business that there wasn't much time left over for me—even to talk about the business. We never took a trip, just he and I together, like I'm doing now with Mark—although, to be fair, this is a first for us.

As for my mother, well, she was a sickly woman who lacked warmth. She spent most of her time relentlessly pruning the garden behind our Montclair home. My father would probably have been a lot happier with someone else, but back then, things weren't anything like they are in today's 1977 world. I just read that almost *half* the marriages now are destined to end in divorce. Not for my father, though—he stayed with my mother until she passed away. And now, he's gone too.

I return to the present. I'm hesitant to explain to Mark the elements of a real problem, which would be over his head. But maybe I can get across what I do as a lawyer by using a hypothetical.

The snow is heavier now, the visibility reduced. I alternate between my brights and the regular headlights, which sometimes outline the road more clearly. A car passes us in the other direction with its brights on, blinding me for a second. And then—prompted, I'm sure, by our present surroundings— something comes to me that I can use with Mark.

"Okay. Now, this isn't a real problem that clients ask me about, but it's got some correlative characteristics."

"Some *what?*"

"Sorry—it's difficult to keep lawyer-speak from creeping into my vocabulary, but I'll try harder. Anyway, let's say you're driving a rented car on a deserted road, and you look at the dashboard and notice that you have very little gas—the tank is practically empty."

"I'm not driving illegally, am I? After all, I'm only twelve years old."

"No, no, this takes place after you've gotten your driver's license."

"So it's six years from now—"

"Don't be a wise guy—your age has nothing to do with the situation I'm trying to explain."

I catch a glimpse of Mark waggling his finger at me. "Hey, don't get so bent out of shape. I just want to make sure I understand the example."

Why am I so testy? I should be thankful he's interested and responsive. "Right, right—I'm sorry. Those are fair questions to ask—I should have made things clearer. So now pretend you're eighteen and driving a big sedan by yourself on a lonely road in the California desert. And the car is a real gas-guzzler."

"Okay, I got it."

"Now, you don't know for sure, but you think there's a gas station about ten miles down the road—and it's the only one in the whole area."

"How much gas do I have?"

"You think—but again, you're not sure—that you have one gallon left in the tank."

"Will that get me there?"

"Well, you've been told—but, of course, it's not certain—that in this car, driving at thirty miles per hour on the open road, you get 12 miles to a gallon."

"Thirty miles an hour—why, that's almost like walking—"

"Yes, but that's the speed at which you get your best mileage. And if you're correct in thinking that the station is ten miles away, and that you've got at least a gallon of gas left, you would make it all the way at that speed."

"What if I want to go faster?"

"Ah, that's a problem. You've also been told that at a more normal sixty miles per hour, the car gets only eight miles to the gallon—so you might run out of gas two miles before reaching the station."

Mark is silent for a few moments, presumably thinking. The only sounds in the car are the slap-slap-slap of the windshield wipers and the crunch of snow beneath the tires. I steal a glance his way. It's curious, but when he's deep in thought, he strokes his chin with his index finger, brushing the bottom of his lip one way and then back the other—like one of those windshield wipers or the arm of a metronome. It's a gesture I had long considered my own private preserve.

He breaks the silence. "Am I in a hurry to get somewhere? Do I have a date with a pretty girl in the next town?"

I smile. "No, there's no rush."

"So the safe thing for me to do would be to drive at thirty—at turtle speed."

"Right—if that were all there were to the problem. But there's more."

His voice is cautious now. "What else?"

"Well, let's do a little simple math. At thirty miles per hour, how long does it take you to cover the ten miles?"

Mark thinks for a moment, then says, "Ten is one-third of thirty. . . . So it would take one-third of an hour—twenty minutes."

"Good. And how long would it take you at sixty miles per hour?"

Mark doesn't hesitate on this one. "Sixty is twice thirty, so half that time—ten minutes."

"Right again." Oh, I like the way this kid handles math problems in his head. It's just another indication of how well adjusted he is. I take his obvious brainpower as a positive sign of effective parenting by Alice and yours truly.

"Now, here's the other key fact. You think—but again you're not sure—that the gas station closes at 6:00 P.M. You're not wearing a watch, so you glance at the car clock—which may, but also may not, be on time—and it reads 5:45 P.M. Do you see the problem?"

Mark ponders this for a while and then gives a little laugh. "Sure. If I speed at sixty, I'll get there in ten minutes, and that's before closing time—*if* I get all the way there, which I may not. If I slow down to thirty, my chances of making it all the way there are better—but since it takes me twenty minutes, the station may be closed."

I'm ecstatic—he's analyzed the problem perfectly. And very lawyer-like, too. Hmmm. . . . I've always avoided bringing up with Mark the subject of him becoming a lawyer. I guess I've been following my own dad's lead here—he never put any pressure on me to go into his business, which I appreciated. It's clear, though, the boy would be a natural in the profession.

"You nailed it! And just to repeat the complicating factors: The clock's ticking, so there's time pressure, and you're really not sure about a whole number of items—is the station ten miles away, do you have a full gallon of gas, does the station close at six, is the car clock accurate, and are the mileage estimates at different speeds correct? So you've got a real problem."

I glimpse the furrows on Mark's brow. He's trying to figure a way out of the dilemma—just like I would be doing for a client.

"Do I have a map?"

"Not one that's helpful."

"Is there anything in the driver's manual about how many gallons are left when the needle gets to a certain point."

"Nothing that solves the problem."

Another pause. "Are there any phone booths along the road?"

"No."

"Damn! You know, Dad, someday some smart guy is gonna invent a phone you can use in a car."

"Yeah, like a Dick Tracy two-way wrist radio."

There's a brief silence before Mark speaks. "Okay, I see the problem. But how do *you* help the clients? You once told me they pay you two hundred bucks an hour for your time. But you're no expert on gas mileage. How do you know how far the car is from the station—or whether it closes at six?"

"Good question. I help them to analyze the pickle they're in and come to a reasonable decision about what to do. It gets into risk-reward analysis and a lot of other stuff that I'll save for our next chat on the subject."

"Yeah, I think we've just about used this one up. But if Josh asks me what my father does, I still don't know how to answer."

I chuckle. "Tell him I'm a kind of surgeon—I operate on people's psyches."

"What?"

"Just kidding."

We're quiet for the next few minutes. The snow is getting a lot heavier. Our car comes up behind a snowplow, and I slow down to follow in its wake. I'm really not that experienced in driving under these conditions. Should I have chains on the tires? Do people still use chains? Even if the car has a set of chains, which I doubt, would I know how to put them on?

My mind shifts ahead to a more agreeable topic—how marvelous the skiing will be after this snowstorm. I envision myself schussing down a moderate slope that's floating in new powder. In my vision, I'm skiing alone—because Mark, who has already far outstripped me in technique, is undoubtedly a hundred yards ahead, whooping it up.

There's a wonderful solitary aspect to skiing, even when you're accompanied by someone. The rest of life is strenuous, with all kinds of problems. The business issues are complex, and the personal relationships aren't easy either, with lots of subtleties filling your head. But when you're skiing, the entire focus is on getting your body down the hill in one piece. No distractions— maybe that's why I enjoy it so much.

I muse about Steamboat Springs, which Alice, Mark, and I visited once before a few years back. It's a place with two different characters. Near the mountain are some modern resort high-rises, which appealed to me at first. But after a while, I found them too antiseptic for my taste. I was taken with the old parts of the town, where the streets have a rugged western feel that's more . . . well, more in line with reality.

The silence lasts for a while. I sneak a look over at Mark and can see he's deep in thought. But I notice that his expression is different now than when he was trying to solve the car problem. It's more troubled, almost painful. When he does speak, his tone is more earnest than before.

"Dad, does every business decision your clients make—after you've given them advice—turn out okay?"

Now that's an intriguing question for a kid to ask. "I wish it were so, but I have to admit they don't all turn out as well as we hoped they would."

The follow-up comes quickly now, as if Mark had anticipated my answer. "And when that happens, do you sit down with your clients and try to figure out what went wrong?"

Another uncommon query—is he heading somewhere? "We do. That's very important—to be able to see where you erred, and then to learn from your mistakes."

The car seems to wobble in the thicker snow, which causes me some concern. I realize I've forgotten what my father used to drill into my head over the years—about the protocol to follow if the tires should start to skid on the snow. You turn the steering wheel—uh—in the direction of the skid—or is it in the *other* direction? And what does that mean—"in the direction of the skid"? Is it the way the front of the car goes, or the rear? God, I just hope we don't start to skid. . . .

Mark continues, more slowly now, a tentative note in his voice. "And you were saying before that there's a lot of stuff you're not sure of when you make the decision—the mileage, whether the store closes at six, if the clock's on time. You *think* you know, but you're not sure. Is that ever the problem—that it turns out you were wrong about what you thought you knew?"

Can you believe this—I'm being cross-examined by my son about my line of work. Go, kid, go. "Yes, that can happen. As I was saying, that's what makes the decisions so tricky."

"So, the decision seems right when you make it, but when you look back at it, the decision wasn't so hot."

"Yes."

He absorbs this, pauses—almost as if he's girding his loins to proceed—and then says, "Dad, do you ever go through the same thing when you're making your *own* decisions—on stuff that has nothing to do with business or with clients?"

"Absolutely. That's my style."

There's no hesitation now—the words come tumbling out in a rush. "Well then, did you go through it when you made the decision to split with Mom?"

Bam! I had no idea where this was heading. Our failed marriage is a topic Mark and I never talk about, so I'm stunned.

My mind goes back to all those brief father-son exchanges—"How are things going?" "Fine"—that I never followed up on. I have a sinking feeling that things haven't been fine for Mark—that his cheery replies masked deeper emotions—disappointment, distress, even anger.

I'd like more time to work out my response, but he deserves an answer right now. "Well, maybe not in a formal way, but I'm sure I analyzed the pros and cons."

He's ready for me, and I can sense some of that pain in the tartness of his tone. "In the gas problem, you said there were a lot of things you can't be sure of at the time you have to make the decision. So, with Mom, were there some things that turned out later to be different than you thought they'd be?"

You know how in cartoons a light bulb flashes on above a guy's head when something suddenly dawns on him? Well, my bulb just came on about 500 watts worth! The kid is right—there *are* such things.

My mind begins to sprint through some of the postsplit letdowns. . . . I thought Susan would be more fulfilling than she proved to be. . . . I thought I'd enjoy my freedom more than I do. . . . I didn't think I'd miss coming home to a dependable Alice each night, with dinner on the table no matter what the hour. . . . I never realized how much I treasured the weekday time I used to spend with Mark. . . . I didn't appreciate the marvelous job Alice has done in raising this terrific kid.

In short, the mileage estimates were understated, the tank had two gallons of gas, and the station—which was only five miles away—stayed open until midnight!

But I don't say these things. "What are you getting at, Mark?" This time I take my eye off the road to look over at him. Do I detect the glimmering of a tear in the corner of his eye?

"Nothing, Dad, nothing at all. Hey, you're a grown-up—you made your decision."

Just then, the snow plow I've been following slows down abruptly to get off the road at an unmarked exit. I brake—but much too forcefully, forgetting to pump the damn thing as my father taught me years ago. The car starts to skid. I'm paralyzed in terms of which direction to turn the wheel, so I leave it in the center.

The only action I take is an involuntary response, left over from my boyhood days in the passenger seat before seat belts were invented. I reach out my right arm to restrain Mark from hitting the windshield—just like my father used to do for me.

It's a scary moment—the swaying car seems to have a mind of its own. I catch a look of terror in Mark's eyes, although no sound comes from his mouth. Meanwhile I'm frozen into immobility, contemplating the abyss beneath the side of the mountain road, and aghast that we're relying on my minimal driving skills.

And then, much to my amazement, something happens underneath the chassis to restore the alignment of the tires—without me ever being forced to guess the proper direction to turn the wheel. In short—and no thanks to my driving ability—the car rights itself and we're okay.

I exhale in relief. "Whew! Sorry about that."

I look over at Mark, who mimes wiping his brow to indicate relief that the car crisis is over. My mind goes back to where things stood before the skid, and I'm wondering if we'll return to the subject matter. The answer isn't long in coming.

"Hey, Dad, do you think you earned your two hundred bucks an hour on making the decision to split with Mom?"

There's a wry smile on Mark's face. He knows he got off a good zinger that his old man can't help but appreciate—and I do. I reach over and give his arm an affectionate squeeze.

But I also realize that, from now on—Dummy! Are you finally awake?—I've got to find a way to get beneath Mark's cool exterior, down to where the pain lies, and try to be helpful. A new mantra pops into my head—*inaction is for skids, not kids.*

I've slowed the car down now, to avoid any further mishaps. I'm pondering where to go with this dialogue. And then it hits me. Instead of more talk, there's something positive I can do right now—something that will raise both my parental and spousal batting averages in a single stroke.

"Enough questions, Mark. But now, let me ask *you* something. Did you have your heart set on that London trip over spring break that Mom proposed?"

I can almost sense his excitement. "I sure would like to see my cuz Willy."

"Well, let me talk to your mother again, and maybe we can work things out. . . ."

Commentary on
FATHER'S DAY

L et me begin with an overall question for you, before getting into my own analysis of the subject:

What did you take away from this story?

You may be wondering about the relevance of "Father's Day" in a collection of stories about the practice of business law. To be sure, there's a lawyer involved—Dan Barton of the Jenkins & Price law firm. But he's not practicing law in the story. As a matter of fact, he's in a rented car with his twelve-year-old son, Mark, driving up a snowy road to Steamboat Springs, Colorado, on a father-son ski vacation.

If you are wondering why "Father's Day" is in here, then you may be one of those lawyers who can profit from both of the underlying messages I had hoped to convey in the story.

The first message is that for a practicing lawyer, there ought to be more to life than practicing law. And while hobbies, exercise, public interest work, and such are all

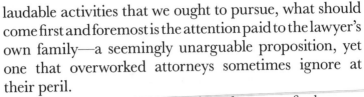

laudable activities that we ought to pursue, what should come first and foremost is the attention paid to the lawyer's own family—a seemingly unarguable proposition, yet one that overworked attorneys sometimes ignore at their peril.

The second message is that it makes sense for lawyers to step back on occasion and take stock of what they've been doing in their profession. A good exercise for this is to pretend you're trying to explain the complexities of what you do to a youngster—avoiding legalese and trade jargon, perhaps concocting a nontechnical example to place your work in some understandable perspective. This is especially worthwhile for a business lawyer, much of whose day may be taken up with activities that don't fit into the classic view of legal practice.

Let's begin with the family issue, as to which Dan Barton is a good (or, one might say, bad) example. We have to get at his problem by inference, since Dan is the first person narrator of the story and, at least at first, very much in denial. I think a strong inference can be drawn, though other factors may be at work here, that Dan's relentless pursuit of his profession has played a major role in the breakup of his marriage and has resulted in a less-than-ideal relationship with his only child.

We don't get to meet Dan's estranged wife, Alice, in person, but even viewed through Dan's distorted lens, she seems like a good person. He admits she's "not unintelligent" and has been a good mother to Mark. And we can appreciate the importance of both her mothering and her work as a kindergarten teacher, although Dan passes them off lightly.

Dan's main complaint seems to be that he outgrew her—that Alice hadn't made an effort to keep up with him as he moved ahead in the firm, spending his time with big-shot clients and their "worldly" wives. That's a tough conjugal attitude for Dan to take, especially since he seldom discussed with her what he was doing (because, he says, Alice "always seemed uninterested" in his work).

I'm not going to dwell further here on this relationship, but for those interested in the nuances of husband-wife issues, they're explored in more depth in the story "The Corollary Axiom" and its applicable commentary.

The focus of "Father's Day" is on Dan Barton's relations with his son Mark. The boy is twelve now, yet this is the first trip Dan has ever taken with him on their own. Well, I guess you can excuse this omission during the years that Dan and Alice were together and vacationed as a family, but how about in the period since they split up—why hasn't Dan been more proactive with his son?

I'll tell you why—because he has been up to his ears in lawyering. And then, when he wasn't lawyering, he was busy with extracurricular affairs, such as the one with his partner, Susan Collins. (I have a hunch—what do you think?—that his initial infatuation with Susan may have been a major contributor to his decision to split with Alice.) And then, after Susan didn't work out, there has been the "steady turnover of ladies who have succeeded Susan in my bed."

But even if Dan is too occupied to go on trips with Mark, that doesn't account for his obtuseness with the boy when they do get together on weekends. Dan has programmed these occasions with nonstop activities, ball games and such, leaving little quiet time to talk. He considers that he has done his duty by asking Mark each weekend how things are going, to which Mark answers "fine"—a response that Dan takes at face value and doesn't probe further. And (most oblivious of all) is Dan's comment, "I'm sure if our split was causing him problems, he'd let me know." WRONG! Young boys like Mark know how to suck it up and hold it in. (This is a painful lesson I had to learn myself as a father many years ago.) The true effect of the marital breakup on Mark can't be so easily passed off.

So that's the situation forming the backdrop for the father-son conversation at the heart of the story. Although Mark initiates the dialogue, he can't have contemplated where it would ultimately lead, since he couldn't have known how his father was going to respond. I take Mark at face value—that he's actually interested in Dan's work and would like to know what this parent does for a living. It's certainly a fair question, which every attorney parent ought to welcome. Unlike some other professions (such as medicine) that don't need much of a description, and in contrast to courtroom litigators whose antics are on display on the tube every night, a business lawyer's occupation isn't readily discernible by someone who's not at least peripherally involved in it.

Dan's initial reaction—he never thought Mark had any interest in what he did and wasn't keen on boring the boy with war story heroics, so he stayed away from the subject—cuts pretty close to my personal bone here. (This is one of those do-as-I-say moments, as contrasted with doing what I did.) My kids appeared uninterested in my work and I don't recall them asking about it. As a result, I rarely made more than cursory references to what was occupying my time. Both of them (now forty-ish) ended up following pursuits miles away from the legal profession. I've habitually attributed that to their observing me, week after week, working long hours under high pressure. I'm sure it just didn't seem attractive to them at all. Hmmm . . . maybe I should have tried harder to get them interested. . . .

Now let's leave for the moment the father-son relationship and go to the other significant aspect of this story—how Dan, through conjuring up an everyday situation, tries to give Mark a sense of what his legal practice is all about. Actually, writing the story gave me a good excuse to step back, after all those years in the office, and try to capture the nature of what I had been dealing with. By the way:

How would you attempt to describe to an unknowledgeable layman just what it is that you do?

Until my retirement, I was a business lawyer with an emphasis on mergers and acquisitions. As my career progressed, I found myself getting away from performing narrowly legal functions and instead acting more as a counselor-strategist. I was providing the client with advice on issues that weren't primarily legal—helping the client understand the problem, analyze alternatives, reach a sound decision, and come up with a workable course of action.

In "Father's Day," the import of the gas-guzzling extended metaphor can be summarized in these terms:

We lawyers often deal with decision-making, usually in terms of helping clients make their own determinations.

Those decisions generally involve a variety of pertinent factors.

These factors tend to point in several different (and frequently conflicting) directions.

At the moment the decision has to be made, we don't possess all the information we'd like to have.

In the hypothetical posed in "Father's Day," the relevant factors are time, speed, distance, amount of gas, and usage at different speeds, and they're in clear conflict with each other. While pretty good information is available on each factor, you can't be sure about any of it, and if one of the premises turns out to be incorrect, that can change the overall result. Yet the decision—in this case, the speed at which to drive—has to be made right now. If the factors weren't in conflict but each pointed toward the same conclusion—or if you didn't have to decide now but could wait until all the information was rock solid—you wouldn't have much of a problem. But in the world we business lawyers inhabit, this almost never seems to be the case. By the way, we should be delighted that this *isn't* the case, because then the clients would have little need for our services!

Back in the go-go '80s, we M&A lawyers were subjected to a particular variant of this counseling quandary. The Delaware law (consisting mainly of judicial decisions) applicable to takeover matters was changing so rapidly that we were never sure what was coming next, and yet, we had to counsel clients on the actions they were taking—knowing that each step would be challenged by a vigorous adversary and scrutinized by a knowledgeable court. Since the considerations were highly fact-sensitive and few bright lines existed for appropriate conduct, we faced the ever-present fear of either not going far enough to accomplish our purpose (as, for instance, with a lock-up option on shares) or going so far that we would later regret it in the courthouse.

Getting back to the story, the discussion of the gas hypothetical ends before any attempt is made to solve it. Mark says, "Okay, I see the problem. But how do *you* help the clients?" And Dan replies—rightly, I think, under the circumstances—that he'll save the answer to that for another day. So while Mark understands the nature of the problem, he still has no idea what his father actually does. Hopefully, they'll resume the dialogue later on during their time in Steamboat.

Now let me ask you this:

When you're counseling a client on a problem that's not strictly legal, what are some of the ways you go about being helpful?

In my writings on that subject, I distinguished between "go/no go" situations (whether a client should proceed with a voluntary course of action, such as making an acquisition) and "way to go" decisions (where the client has decided to take the step, and the issue is how best to go about it). Go/no go often involves a business decision on which I felt that the lawyer could be helpful (analyzing considerations and such) but should avoid taking a strong stand. By contrast, once the client has decided to act, the way-to-go is right up a lawyer's alley, and his or her advice—including advice that transcends purely legal matters—can be crucial. Although it wasn't so clear-cut to others in the earlier years of my practice (the 1960s and 1970s), I've always believed that we business lawyers have a useful role to play outside our area of certified expertise.

Now, to be sure, there are times when your client is one of those birds who believes lawyers ought to know their place and let the business people handle these kinds of matters on their own. You have to be sensitive to any clues that this may be the case, and when you sense it is, you should tread very gingerly. What I found, however, was that in the great bulk of complex situations, the client was very much looking to his lawyer for advice— advice that often transcended the purely legal issues involved. The client was saying, in effect, I've made the decision to proceed; now *you* tell me the best way to go about it.

Business people discuss these matters (such as when they're comparing two possible courses of action) in terms of the so-called risk/reward ratio. When the risks of both course A and course B are the same but the rewards favor A, or when the rewards are the same but there's more risk with B—or in the infrequent case where both the greater reward and lesser risk point to A—it's easy to opt for A. The difficult questions arise when A holds the greater reward but also entails the greater risk, while B couples the lesser reward with the lesser risk—and what has to be decided is whether A's incremental reward justifies the added risk.

I first wrote about this subject in section 8.5 of *Lawyering*, entitled "The Way To Go," which applies this principle to a specific hypothetical situation. In chapter 9 of *Lawyering*, which contains extended analyses of seven demanding situations an attorney could be called upon to face, the segment entitled "The Corporate Opportunist" is also relevant. A number of years later,

I revisited the subject in my book *Advise and Invent* (which focuses on the lawyer's counseling function), pointing out a few additional distinctions. Let me quote several paragraphs I wrote back then on the subject:

> The strategic issues I deal with arise mainly in the way-to-go area. The lawyer-counselor has to be able to handle two basic kinds of way-to-go situations, which while often overlapping, possess distinct characteristics and call for different skills.
>
> In the first situation (*"advise"*), which can involve either a problem or an opportunity, the issue typically is what path to take; although the choice itself may be murky, the alternative routes are clearly marked. Here, the lawyer's primary role is to help the client in sorting out the various considerations, assigning priorities, measuring risks against gains, and so forth. All the elements are on the table—it's the arrangement that's lacking; and the solution occurs when things finally fall into place, so that the path for the client to take becomes obvious.
>
> In the second situation (*"invent"*), which usually involves a problem facing the client, the issue is how best to solve it, but here, *no* workable solution is readily apparent, although one may lie hidden in the underbrush. Now, the lawyer's role—to help the client arrive at a satisfactory outcome—calls for some creativity on the lawyer's part, in sifting through the details and discovering a way to proceed that hasn't occurred to anyone yet (or, if it has, remains blocked by some impediment which the lawyer must sidestep in order to make the resolution feasible). In *invent*, the trick is to find the crucial missing ingredient—the novel idea or fresh way of looking at things—that breaks through and solves the problem.
>
> One or both of these two aspects are present in most counseling situations I find myself in. At times, they overlap; for instance, when the client has to choose between two clearly marked courses of action, but where one of them—the one that would otherwise seem the best—contains an obstacle that, unless overcome,

makes this alternative nonviable, and to overcome it requires considerable inventiveness.

At other times, appearances can be deceiving. The client may describe his dilemma to you as a prototypically *advise* situation—"There's path A and path B, and I can't seem to decide which one to take." Then, when you get involved, you realize that neither path is particularly desirable—which is precisely why the client is having so much trouble figuring out which way to go! So, although you haven't explicitly been asked to do so, you *invent* a path C that constitutes a better way to deal with the situation.

Now, having isolated the two functions, let me say that they have more in common than not. Their principal common ground is that when the client walks into your office, he is uncertain over what to do; and when he walks out—with no further events occurring or new facts presenting themselves, nothing beyond an exchange of information and views, plus some rigorous *thinking*—the client has a plan of action. And *that* is what we're selling.

That book also contained an extended analysis of a realistic complex problem a lawyer might face, entitled "The Lawyer-Strategist." I'll just summarize here the half dozen steps that I suggest you address when faced with one of these problems.

- *Specifying the question:* The client isn't always sure what he wants or needs, and whether it's a legal issue or a practical business issue. Make sure you know what's really being asked.
- *Getting the facts:* You need all the material facts relevant to the situation (or as many as you can pin down—as the gas hypothetical indicates, you almost never can get them all). Good judgment often hinges on assigning varying weights to conflicting factors; if you don't know all the factors, it's tough to assign the appropriate weights. And you can't rely on the client to provide you with all the information required,

or assume that what he does provide you with is accurately stated.

- *Understanding the context:* You have to broaden your focus to the context in which the question arises, making sure you're in sync with the client's ultimate direction. You don't want to devise a solution for the narrow issue posed that's unfavorable in the larger picture.

- *Knowing the personalities involved:* Their characteristics and idiosyncrasies generally play a significant role in working out a plan to deal with strategic-type issues. You ought to fit your strategy to the person at whom it's aimed.

- *Ascertaining the client's objective:* What is the result he or she wants to achieve? Unlike legal questions, where you have to let the chips fall where they may, on issues of strategy your prime goal is to achieve what your client desires (assuming it's legal and ethical and that he knows his own mind). Your solution not only has to possess intrinsic merit, but it must also appeal to the people who will be making the ultimate decision.

- *Assessing the timing:* Every situation operates within a time frame, which often influences the result. Sometimes, if you dig a little, you realize that the apparently rigid time constraints you've been operating under aren't so ironclad. The resulting flexibility may well lead to a quite different course of action.

Getting back to "Father's Day," the two parts of the story come together at the end. Mark neatly converts the dialogue on the decisional process into questioning the basis of his father's split with his mother. Dan wakes up to a triple realization: that the marital breakup may not have been so wise, that Mark isn't as unaffected by it as he may seem, and that there's still time for Dan to do something positive on both fronts (i.e., sponsor the London trip).

Along the way, there's a moment of suspense when the car starts to skid and Dan is paralyzed into inaction (other than the involuntary pre–seat belt instinct of his arm restraining the passenger). I'll leave it to the reader—after all, there has to be some mystery left in fiction!—as to whether my intent here was just to inject some drama into the story, or to give myself an excuse to quote Dan's newly discovered mantra ("Inaction is for skids, not kids"), or to take aim at some deeper undisclosed objective.

What's important, though, is Mark's insight in terms of analogizing the gas hypothetical to the marital situation. Remember? He takes Dan's you-never-can-be-sure-about-things premise and reworks it to pose the key question: "So, with Mom, were there some things that turned out later to be different than you thought they'd be?" And, of course, Dan realizes that there were such things and that they called into question the wisdom of his decision to split.

There's a broader lesson here for us lawyers (over and above the domestic issue) in cases where our information isn't definitive. No matter how logically we think we've proceeded in helping a client work through a difficult decision, it's entirely possible we'll discover in hindsight that we blew it. Just stop and think about this, whenever you begin to develop a case of terminal hubris.

As a matter of fact, it's a good idea for you to revisit these kinds of decisions at some point after they're made, to see if any new information has subsequently surfaced that calls into question any of the basic premises used in reaching the original result. Would the conclusion have been different if you knew then what you know now? If so, it might still be possible to alter the course of action previously decided upon, in order to take your new knowledge into account.

PARTNERGATE

ood news, Paul. For the most part—with one minor exception I'll get to in a moment—things went smoothly while you were away."

"That's what I like to hear," replied Paul Garson, a partner in the corporate department of the New York law firm, Jenkins & Price. Paul, forty-five, was just back from a New Year's vacation in the Caribbean, and the ruddy tan that overlay his usual pallor made him look almost handsome. He was seated behind the desk in his office, being briefed on the prior week's events by Ted Ashburn, a senior associate who had been covering for him. Ted was thirty-two, but his blue eyes, fair skin, and sandy cowlick made him look ten years younger.

"I finished the papers on the Riverview deal and got them out to everyone well before the closing date."

Paul nodded, impressed once more with Ashburn's efficiency—such a desirable attribute, he noted, for a partner-to-be. Paul's own focus on productivity was reflected in the spare trappings of his office—a functional sofa, a few lithographs of city scenes on the wall, some photos of his wife and children, an uncluttered desk.

"And the closing was basically a nonevent—no problems."

As he listened to Ted's report, Paul was keenly aware that Jenkins & Price would be selecting new partners later in the month. After all, he was chairman of the committee that evaluated the candidates and made recommendations to the full firm.

"I fielded a few phone calls from the Amalgamated CFO about that recent SEC regulation."

Paul was prepared to push hard for Ashburn's candidacy in the deliberations coming up in early 1978. Ted was smart, mature, and earnest, and had all the professional attributes that qualified him for advancement. He would have been a shoo-in any other year, but the problem now was that the corporate department also had another top-rated candidate, Curt Bell. And the executive committee of the firm—for financial reasons and to avoid setting a troublesome precedent in years to come—had decreed that only one of them could become a partner this year. So a choice would have to be made.

"But the regulation doesn't really apply to their situation—for which news the CFO was quite grateful."

For Paul, who had worked much more with Ashburn, the choice was clear. Although he acknowledged Bell's competence, something about the young man had always bothered Paul. But other corporate partners—most notably, George Troy—were very enthusiastic about him.

What complicated the situation was that Paul Garson and George Troy were viewed in the firm as rivals for preeminence in the mid-forties age group. As a result, the partnership prospects of the associates whom each of them mentored became an additional arena for their rivalry to play out.

After a contentious meeting on the subject, the committee that Paul chaired had decided to recommend both Ted Ashburn and Curt Bell, in order to allow the full partnership to make the final decision. Paul expected some real fireworks to erupt at the upcoming firm meeting.

"I made sure the firm's name got mentioned favorably in the article about summer associates that appeared last week in the *Tribune*."

This was another thing that Paul really liked about Ashburn—his sense of loyalty to Jenkins & Price. For Ted, it wasn't just a job or avenue to advancement. Paul realized the full depth of Ashburn's feelings for the firm a month ago, when they were discussing the impending partnership vote. At one point, Ted looked Paul in the eye and said—Paul could still recall the exact words Ted used—"If I'm not selected for partner, I'll stay on at Jenkins & Price as long as you'll have me and I can continue to contribute."

That was quite a pledge, thought Paul, especially in view of the hot job market out there for lawyers of Ted's age and experience. By contrast, other associates in past years had used the threat to leave as leverage on the firm to make them a partner. Ted's refusal to do so was, in Paul's view, vivid proof of his basic decency.

"There is one other matter that I need to tell you about," said Ted. "It's a little less pleasant." His usual affable expression darkened.

"What's that?"

"I got a call from Earl Caldwell a few days ago. I could quickly tell that he was beside himself—in fact, furious—I've never heard him so irate."

A look of concern crossed Paul's face at this troublesome reference to Caldwell, his most important client. "What was Earl's problem?"

"He had just gone back in the files to read the section regarding employees in the agreement terminating Caldwell's joint venture with Vortex. Specifically, it was the provision that says neither Caldwell nor Vortex can hire any employees of the other company for two years after the breakup. Evidently, he's had his eye on a key Vortex executive. But under the contract, he can't go after the guy for another year and a half."

"That's too bad, but that was the deal," said Paul. "So why was Earl furious?"

"He said he never focused on the provision at the time the contract was signed, and...and...."

"Yes?"

"...and he implied—well, hell, it was stronger than that—he *accused* you of, in his words, 'shooting him in the foot' by agreeing to the provision."

"He did what?!"

"Caldwell had really worked up a head of steam by the time he called, and he said some horrible things—"

"I can't believe this—"

"—so I decided to calm him down. I told him that the provision was inserted in the contract by the Vortex people while you were out of the country on that French deal. I said that none of the rest of us appreciated its significance, and no one brought it to your attention when you returned. That seemed to work—it brought Earl's temperature down below boiling." Ted sat back, his self-congratulatory expression akin to that of the indispensable lieutenant, returning from the successful skirmish, awaiting a hero's plaudits from his captain.

"But Ted, that's not true. *I* was the one responsible for putting that provision in the contract."

"I know," replied Ted.

Paul went on. "I felt it was in Caldwell's best interests to be protected against Vortex going after the Caldwell guys, since they had worked closely together on the joint venture. But in order to get that protection, I needed to make it reciprocal. I never thought it would adversely impact Caldwell—I had no idea Earl was interested in one of *their* guys."

"I realize that, but I can assure you that Caldwell was in no mood to hear any logical explanation. He was ready to eat you alive. I felt I had to do something to get you off the hot seat."

Throughout his professional life, Paul Garson had encountered situations like this one—where the truth could hurt, and a little shading of the truth eased the pain. At these and other moments of internal conflict, Paul habitually tuned in to an inner voice that he'd dubbed—mindful of the alliteration—his *Pal*. The inner voice could usually be counted on to offer wise counsel, albeit a tad opinionated for Paul's taste. Paul tended to take *Pal*'s advice, except when other factors *Pal* hadn't considered came into play.

Paul now issued a silent summons. "Hey, *Pal*, wake up—I've got one for you."

Pal's response was swift. *This one's not hard, Paulie. Ted's motives might have been admirable, but he shouldn't have done what he did. And you can't sanction it—after all, you're supposed to be his mentor.*

Paul could tell his *Pal* was on a roll, so he stayed out of the way. *Look, what the kid did wasn't so egregious, but you gotta deal with it. Use the opportunity to teach Ted an ethical lesson he won't forget.*

Paul approved of *Pal*'s advice here, though he needed to conduct the final downside analysis himself. The worst consequence of telling the truth was Earl Caldwell's wrath. A quick appraisal of the situation satisfied Paul that it was manageable—that his relations with the client were strong enough to survive this disclosure. And he reckoned he might even get credit from Earl for his candor.

The afternoon sun glinted through the window shades of Paul's west-facing office. As he shifted into avuncular gear—the voice low but forceful—he seemed older than his forty-five years.

"I understand your motive, Ted, but in order to accomplish it, you told a lie. And for a lawyer to lie—especially to a client—is never justifiable. I have to say that I'm very disappointed in you." He paused to let his words sink in.

Ted sat there, glumly examining the yellow briefing pad in his lap. All traces of heroism had vanished, and his body language acknowledged he'd done wrong.

"Facts are facts, Ted—and the fact here is that I knew all about the no-hire provision. Based on what I understood at the time, I thought it was in our client's best interests. My mistake was in not running it by Caldwell back then, so he wouldn't be able to second-guess me now. But since he's raised the subject, Earl is entitled to full disclosure, and I'm going to see that he gets it."

The room was quiet. Ted, thoroughly chastened, offered no defense.

"As a matter of fact," said Paul, punctuating his words with a flourish as he proceeded to dial Caldwell's number on the speaker phone, "there's no time like the present."

After a brief back-from-vacation exchange with Caldwell, Paul came right to the point. "I understand you're upset about the provision in the Vortex termination agreement that restricts either party from hiring employees of the other for two years."

"You're goddamn right I'm upset," said Caldwell. "How we ever agreed to that idiotic restriction I'll never understand."

"Well, I was personally responsible for it. I realize Ted Ashburn told you otherwise, but he was misinformed. I approved the provision, based on my understanding that we were more interested in protecting our employees from a Vortex raid than we were in picking off some of their guys. My mistake was in not running that supposition by you at the time, and for that I sincerely apologize."

No sound came from the other end of the line for a few moments. Then Caldwell said, "Well, I must say you're a stand-up guy, even if you're sometimes kinda stupid about business matters. I've decided to forgive you this time."

When the call ended, Paul turned to a remorseful Ashburn. "That's the way we do things at Jenkins & Price, Ted. There's no substitute for the truth."

A few days later, Paul was having lunch in the firm cafeteria with Stephanie Carroll, a partner in the litigation department and a member of his committee to recommend new partners. They were discussing the upcoming firm meeting. The room was noisy and lacking in charm—the food, merely passable.

Stephanie, a few years Paul's junior, was one of only three women partners at Jenkins & Price. Intelligent and conscientious, she got along well with her male colleagues at the firm. Paul valued her friendship and admired her professionalism, although at times he found himself wishing she possessed more "street smarts."

"I know you're a big fan of Ted Ashburn," Stephanie said.

"That's right," Paul replied. By now, any doubts he may have harbored about Ted over the Caldwell brouhaha had been banished, and he was once again a staunch Ashburn supporter. He didn't mention the incident to any of his partners and hadn't yet decided whether to say anything about it at the partnership meeting.

"I am, too. But Curt Bell has a lot of supporters, and the vote is likely to be close."

"I realize that."

"It's too bad we can't make both of them partners," Stephanie mused. "We'll probably lose the one we don't select—that's most unfortunate."

Paul, caught off-guard by her remark, briefly considered summoning his *Pal*, but instead opted to mumble something unintelligible as he bit into his pizza.

"Hold my calls for the next half hour, " Paul instructed his secretary over the intercom later that afternoon. He settled himself comfortably in the desk chair and summoned his *Pal*.

"We've got some work to do. The partnership meeting to decide on new partners is coming up in a few days, and I have to decide whether to say anything about Ted Ashburn's brush with Earl Caldwell."

Apparently drowsy, *Pal* replied in a rare low-key manner, *What's your inclination?*

"I can't help thinking that if the incident was serious enough for me to get my dander up, to make that mea culpa call to Caldwell, and to give Ted a stern lecture about not lying—then I ought to report it to the meeting."

Pal woke up in a hurry. *But that doesn't necessarily follow. You used the incident to teach Ted a lesson, and for that purpose it was right for you to respond strongly and act decisively—it probably scared the pants off him.*

"It did—you should have seen his face when I made that call."

Right—but in retrospect, is what Ashburn did so heinous? After all, he had the admirable motive of protecting you, and his actions didn't affect anything currently on the table—just the question of who should bear responsibility for a past event.

"That's so."

And let's face it, full disclosure here poses a sizable risk to Ashburn's chances. Keep in mind all those partners sitting on the fence between Ted and Curt Bell, looking for a reason to jump one way or the other. Can't you just hear them, Paulie—'Oh, oh, this shows that Ted lacks good judgment'— and we both know how that can become the death knell for a potential partner. Besides, for Ashburn to lose out to Bell because of this one incident wouldn't be fair to Ted, after all his years of splendid toil.

Paul leaned further back in his desk chair. "There's a lot to what you say."

And think of how a Curt Bell victory here—orchestrated by George Troy, the man everyone views as Bell's mentor—might affect your relative status

*in the firm vis-à-vis Troy. Right now, you're the standout—esteemed by all
your colleagues. And their respect for you will be further boosted by Ted's
becoming a partner. But that special aura you're presently exuding could
evaporate real fast if you can't pull it off.*

"I hear you."

*And there's one final thing, Paulie. To put it bluntly, Ted covered your ass
with Caldwell—now it's time for you to return the favor.*

The meeting to decide on new partners of Jenkins & Price was
in full swing. The twenty current partners were seated around
a large oval table in the firm's most spacious conference room.
There was a yellow pad and pencil at each place, with pitchers
of water and plastic cups in the middle of the table.

Chairing the meeting was Bill Price, seventy-four, head of
the firm. The room being slightly overheated, Price and most of
the male partners had removed their jackets, but he still wore
the vest of his three-piece suit. He used eyeglasses, but habitually
held them aloft by the earpiece when speaking to a group.

Paul Garson took the floor first in support of Ashburn's
candidacy, citing the splendid reviews Ted had received
throughout his career at the firm. Then George Troy—articulate,
knowledgeable, bristling with self-confidence—made an equally
forceful presentation on behalf of Curt Bell. Other partners
chimed in, and a lively discussion ensued.

Finally, Bill Price, waggling his glasses, addressed the
assemblage. "All right, we've heard from the various advocates
for each of these fine young men, and we have before us all
the glowing reports on both from over the years. Each has an
unblemished record. Just to bring things up to date before we
vote, let me ask you, George—since you've worked most recently
with Bell—did anything in the current assignment detract from
his prior record?"

"No," replied Troy, "If anything, Curt has improved."

"Thank you," said Price. "And now Paul—you've had the most
recent experience with Ashburn, so I pose the same question to
you."

Although Paul had decided not to bring up the Caldwell
incident voluntarily, the pointed manner in which Bill Price put

the question troubled him. Of course, the incident did "detract" from Ted's prior record. Could he ignore that in replying?

Steady, Paulie—remember the big picture. Pal's voice was right there on his shoulder.

Well, thought Paul, I've made my bed.... "Ashburn performed quite well, and the client, Earl Caldwell, likes him a lot."

Price nodded. "I want to thank both of you, George and Paul, for your forceful and instructive presentations here today."

George Troy spoke up. "There's just one more thing—and it's especially significant today in 1978, the first year of baseball's free agents. Curt Bell has told me that if he's not made partner on this go-round, he's outta here. That would be a damn shame, because Curt has developed solid relationships with several clients. Besides, we need guys like Bell to put in the late night hours."

Another partner, litigator Jack Lawrence, chimed in. "I agree with you that it would be tough to lose Bell, though it would be equally negative to lose Ashburn if we don't make him a partner. Of course, the best of all worlds would be if we could hang on to both of them—one as a partner and the other staying on as an associate with some hope of making partner down the road. But with the hot job market out there, and those other firms undoubtedly anxious to lay their hands on him, I have to assume that Ashburn would also leave if we pass him over. Paul, you've had the most recent experience with Ted. Do you have any insight on that score?"

Paul, taken aback by the direct question—even after Stephanie's remark in the cafeteria—was unprepared to respond. "I couldn't hear you, Jack—would you please repeat that?" he said, stalling for time to consult his *Pal.*

Listen, Paulie, the way Jack Lawrence stressed the great advantage to holding onto both of them, coming right after Troy quoted Bell as being 'outta here,' makes a truthful answer devastating to Ashburn's chances.

"I know, I know."

Now, I'd never advocate lying to your partners, but isn't there some sidestep you can do around this one? And you've got a ready-made rationalization— that whether or not an associate decides to hang around if he's passed over shouldn't impact his qualifications to become a partner.

By the time Lawrence repeated his inquiry, Paul knew how to handle it. "I never posed the question directly to him, Jack. I have to assume, though, that if Ashburn knew that saying anything other than 'I'm outta here' would hurt his chances in the partnership sweepstakes, he'd follow Bell's lead."

Very good, whispered his *Pal—that wasn't so hard, was it? A little sidestep, a half-truth, a neat refocusing of the issue on the not-so-subtle attempt by Troy and Bell to use the threat to leave as leverage—and presto!—I'll bet the issue is promptly dropped.*

"Well, that's about it, ladies and gentlemen," said Bill Price, doffing his glasses. "Let's put this to a headcount." The tally was promptly taken, with Ted Ashburn winning 11 to 9.

As head of the partnership recommendation committee, Paul was the individual who notified new partners of their election. So, shortly after the partners' meeting, he summoned Ashburn to his office.

"Ted, I'm delighted to inform you that the firm has elected you as a partner." Paul rose to clasp Ted's hand—his delight at Ted's good fortune mixing with satisfaction over his own personal achievement.

"That's great news," exclaimed Ashburn with a big grin. "I was really worried. I knew it was a close call between Curt Bell and myself."

"Well, close only counts in horseshoes."

"And, of course, I was concerned whether the partners would still choose me after they heard how I screwed up on that Vortex thing with Caldwell."

Paul summoned his *Pal*—obviously, there was still work to be done.

Ted continued. "All I can say is you must have been awfully persuasive to convince them that the Caldwell incident shouldn't be held against me."

Well, Paulie, said *Pal, you might as well tell Ted the truth, or at least a half-truth—that his mentor hadn't considered the Caldwell incident a big enough deal to require disclosure.*

Paul pondered this advice before replying to *Pal*. "That would be simple enough, but then Ted might consider the nondisclosure

of his screw-up as a blemish on his election—and is that what I want this fine young man to feel at such a joyous moment? Does he really need to know what *wasn't* said?"

I hear you. And you've already ducked the issue of how close the vote actually was. Besides, Ted didn't pose it as a question requiring a direct response, so it's easier to dodge.

Paul found his response. "Oh, come on, Ted—that incident is ancient history. Think of it as part of your professional learning process. Your new partners are delighted to have you aboard. And *now*"—Paul drew out the emphasis on the word to set up the little one-liner he liked to incorporate into such occasions—"let me acquaint you with the first obligation of partnership—you're personally liable on the office lease!"

As Stephanie Carroll left her office to go home late that afternoon, she saw Ted Ashburn heading her way in the hall.

"Well, if it isn't my newest partner," she said when he drew near. "Congratulations, Ted—I'm so pleased."

Ted clasped her proffered hand. "Thanks, Stephanie—I'm riding high. Especially after having convinced myself that I could say goodbye to my chances."

Stephanie seemed puzzled. "Why would you have thought that?"

"Because of the way I screwed up in that Caldwell-Vortex incident. I figured it just about killed my hopes of a partnership."

Stephanie put her attaché case down on the floor. "I don't know what you're talking about—what's the Caldwell-Vortex incident?"

Now it was Ted's turn to appear confused. "Why, that was when I lied to the client last month to try to protect Paul Garson. I guess Paul didn't mention the names of the companies when he told the partners about it."

Stephanie shook her head. "I don't recall Paul reporting any such incident to the partners." She found a nearby secretarial desk to perch on. "How about taking a few minutes and tell me just what happened...."

After his encounter with Stephanie, Ted Ashburn decided to walk home from the office. He was going out to celebrate with friends later that evening, but right now he needed some solo time to reflect.

He pondered the question of why Paul hadn't told the partners about his screw-up. Considering the fuss Paul made at the time, it was hard to believe that Paul didn't deem the matter serious enough to report. So it must have been that Paul badly wanted him to make partner and felt that revealing the incident would damage his chances.

But that, Ted mused, was a clear case of the end justifying the means. It was just like what he had done with Caldwell, only to get chewed out for it by Paul.

There was another nagging thought: Why hadn't Paul admitted not having told the partners about it, when Ted raised the subject with him in their meeting today? Was Paul embarrassed? Or, less charitably, could Paul have wanted Ted to think he *had* disclosed the incident—and then performed a Herculean feat to persuade the partners to select Ted notwithstanding....

Early the next day, Stephanie Carroll came to Paul Garson's office, looking troubled.

"I'm really upset."

"Why so?"

"As I was leaving the office yesterday, I saw Ted Ashburn in the hall. I congratulated him, and we had a brief conversation. At one point, he said something like, 'I really appreciate the firm selecting me, notwithstanding my screw-up.' I was puzzled, and asked him what he meant. He referred to the Caldwell-Vortex incident, which he assumed you had disclosed to the partners. He told me the whole story—including a vivid description of how angry you were with him at the time. Paul, why in God's name didn't you tell us about this?"

Garson, having quickly summoned his *Pal*, groped for the right words to respond.

Don't panic, Paulie—play it like the whole thing was a nonevent molehill that the kid blew up into a mountain.

"I'm sorry you're upset. Look, it wasn't such a big deal—I made a lot more of it at the time than was warranted, in order to teach Ted a lesson. So I can understand why he's sensitive on the subject. But all he was trying to do was protect me—and, after all, no one was harmed."

Stephanie shook her head slowly, her eyes still reflecting concern. "I don't know—I voted for Ted, but I'm not sure how I would have come out if I knew about this. And the same might be true of other partners who were on the fence. It goes to the issue of the candidate's good judgment. Even if the particular incident could be excused, the question is whether Ted, as a partner, might do something similar under other circumstances—something that could get the firm in a lot of trouble."

"Oh, I don't think so—Ted has learned his lesson, and he's basically an honest individual."

Stephanie, twisting in her seat, wasn't assuaged. "When Bill Price asked both you and George Troy if there was anything recent about the candidate to report, why didn't you at least mention it? You could have put the incident in context and assured us it shouldn't be a cause for concern."

Paul didn't wait for more advice from *Pal*. Stephanie was too good a friend for him to dissemble any further. "I'll level with you. Deep down, the reason I didn't mention it was because I sensed it might kill Ashburn's partnership chances—no matter what explanation or justification I could offer. And I just felt that Ted was too good a young man to be turned down for one mistake."

Pal interjected himself. *If you're going to take this tack, Paulie, be sure to cover your ass.*

"I'd really appreciate it, Steph, if you don't say anything about this to anyone."

She looked at him intently. Her expression, Paul noted, had at least become noncommittal. "I don't know. I want to sleep on it."

After Stephanie left, Paul held a damage control session with his *Pal*. The immediate issue on the table was what to say now to Ted Ashburn.

I told you so, said *Pal* in that know-it-all tone of perfect hindsight. *I told you to tell the kid the truth—that you had chosen not to air the Caldwell-Vortex dirty linen.*

"Okay, okay, I concede you did. But that was yesterday—what do we do *today?*"

Look, now that Ted knows you didn't bring it up with the partners, I'm sure he's wondering why. He's probably further confused that you ducked when he mentioned the subject yesterday. So, it's obvious what you have to do without delay.

"I guess I've got to go see him."

Of course. And while you're at it, find out if anyone else knows about the Caldwell incident....

Later that day, Paul appeared at the door of Ted Ashburn's small office. Ted was alone, working at a desk piled high with papers. Paul declined Ted's offer to sit and started right in.

"I have a confession to make. When we spoke the other day after the partnership vote, and you raised the subject of how the partners reacted to disclosure of the Caldwell-Vortex matter, I may have misled you by my silence. In fact, I never mentioned the incident to them. I'd made a judgment that you learned your lesson, and the incident wasn't significant enough to be brought up at that juncture."

Ted was glad that Paul had come around to set things straight between them. He nodded and said, "After your strong reaction when the issue first arose, I assumed you would report the incident to the partners. But when I mentioned my screw-up to Stephanie Carroll yesterday, she seemed puzzled—and then I knew."

"Stephanie told me about your conversation, which made me realize I may have unwittingly misled you. But Stephanie is my good friend, and I don't think she's going to say anything on that score to anyone else. Have you mentioned it to any of the other partners?"

This last inquiry caused a wave of uneasiness to wash over Ted. Why, he wondered, is Paul raising this? Memories of the 1970s Watergate scandal were still fresh in Ted's mind, and Paul's question seemed to smack of a cover-up. "No, I haven't."

"That's just as well—no need to enlarge the circle."

With the issue on the table, Ted now felt the need to go further in his answer than Paul's question had contemplated. "But I have to tell you—back at the time the incident occurred, I did tell one of my *associate* buddies, Jill Marsh, about it. And Jill happens to be a close friend of Curt Bell. . . ."

Paul didn't have to wait long. Later that day, Curt Bell came to his office. Curt was a sturdily built six-footer with a thick shock of dark brown hair, piercing eyes and a deep baritone voice.

"Come in, Curt. Have a seat." Paul summoned his *Pal* to stand by.

Bell balanced on the edge of a chair. "Let me come right to the point. I'm obviously upset about not making partner. I'd be less upset if I lost out to Ted Ashburn in a fair contest. But I learned something yesterday that causes me to believe the process wasn't equitable."

"What are you talking about?"

"Jill Marsh was consoling me over a drink last evening. She said she couldn't believe the partners chose Ashburn over me after Ted's screw-up in the Caldwell-Vortex matter. I knew nothing about the incident, so I asked her what it was. She told me the whole thing—the version she'd heard directly from Ted himself."

Bell cleared his throat. *Pal* took the opportunity to offer a few words of advice. *Say as little as possible, Paulie—let's find out what he's got on his mind, and then we can confer afterward on what to do.*

Bell resumed speaking, his tone angry and judgmental. "From Jill's description, this was definitely a screw-up. Let's face it, Ted lied. Lawyers aren't supposed to do that—especially to their clients. Now, obviously I wasn't there at the partnership election meeting, but I have to assume that none of the other partners were told about it—because I'm convinced that if they knew, they never would have chosen Ashburn over me. I'm right, aren't I?"

Paul, adhering to *Pal*'s directive, didn't respond. Bell went on, his voice rising.

"I'll take your silence for assent. So what I'm saying is that I feel you deliberately withheld vital information from the partners, in order to ensure that your candidate was selected instead of me."

Paul realized he could no longer remain silent. "Now, just a minute, Curt, I think you're going too far here—"

"Don't try to justify what you did. Just let me speak my piece." Bell lowered his voice, and the words emerged more slowly. "You know I could cause you and the firm a lot of trouble if I wanted to—such as starting a lawsuit to challenge the firm's procedure for making partners. There would probably be a lot of negative publicity about the firm, and especially about you as the partner involved.... But I'd rather not do that. Despite what happened to me, I care about the firm. And other than this incident, I have nothing against you personally."

Paul started to say something, but Bell wouldn't allow him to interrupt.

"Let me finish, please. I also want to make it clear that I'm not looking to have Ashburn 'unmade' as a partner. He's a good enough guy, and one screw-up shouldn't ruin his career. But *I* want to be a partner of the firm, too, and I think I deserve to be."

He paused to take a breath. Paul decided to hear the rest of what Bell had to say without commenting.

"So here's what I propose. Why can't the firm make *two* partners from the corporate department—especially when you have two such good candidates? I should think that you—as head of the partnership recommendation committee—could convince them to change their thinking and do just that." Bell stood up. "And if you help me become a partner, I promise I won't take any legal action or say anything negative."

Bell headed for the door, turning back briefly to say, "Think it over. I'll give you a week to get it done."

Paul spent a long night in deep discussion with his *Pal*.

"This is goddamn *blackmail*," said Paul mouthing the word with distaste.

That may be, but you've got to take Bell's threat seriously. He's angry, frustrated, and self-righteous—a volatile combination if ever I saw one.

"Volatile enough to bring a lawsuit? To speak to the media?"

I think so—and wouldn't that be a horror show! The legal publications—maybe even the Tribune—would eat it up. Imagine all that lousy publicity for the firm—to say nothing about how it would affect you personally.

"I don't know—his bark might be worse than his bite."

But look, Paulie, even if he doesn't sue or talk to the press, you have to figure that Bell will at least complain to George Troy, who in turn will tell Bill Price—and the shit will hit the fan inside the firm.

Paul could envisage a score of indignant partners turning on him—his prominent stature sinking fast, his burgeoning career irreparably sidetracked.

Besides, it's difficult to quarrel with Bell's solution—making a second partner. That one-partner thing isn't written on some stone tablet—it's the kind of administrative decision the firm is allowed to revisit. And you can justify it on the grounds that Jenkins & Price will end up with the best of both worlds.

Paul's resolve was weakening. "Okay, let's say I start the ball rolling toward making Bell a partner. Do I tell everyone *why* I'm doing that? Do I say, 'Hey, fellas, I'm succumbing to blackmail'?"

No, you can't do that. It would doom the proposal, and then you'd run the risk of the lawsuit, the newspapers, and so on.

"How about saying that the idea originated with Bell—after all, it's a very logical request for him to make—but just leave out the blackmail part?"

Pal thought that one over for a moment. *The problem there is that it'll just seem like sour grapes on Bell's part. If the idea originates with you—his adversary at the partnership meeting, so to speak—it carries a lot more weight. And that way, as a bonus, you can get credit from your partners for a big-hearted gesture toward George Troy's losing candidate.*

Paul wasn't convinced. "There's one thing we seem to be forgetting here—should the firm make someone a partner who stoops to blackmail to get his way?"

For the moment, *Pal* was reduced to splitting hairs. *Well, Bell didn't actually say he would sue—in fact, he said he'd rather not. So you could argue that technically it's not blackmail, and there are some special circumstances involved here.* Then *Pal* found his rhythm again. *You might say that Curt is just acting like a savvy commercial lawyer—using the leverage at his disposal to negotiate for a favorable outcome....*

The next day, Paul Garson settled himself on the small sofa in Stephanie Carroll's office.

"I've been doing some thinking," he said, "and I want to try something out on you before proposing it more widely."

"Go ahead—I'm listening."

"I don't feel good about the Curt Bell situation. He's a first-class lawyer, and I hate to see him leave the firm. So why the hell don't we just go ahead and make him a partner, too? Let's face it, a growing firm like Jenkins & Price can afford two new corporate partners. Limiting ourselves to one simply represents an excess of caution—a concern that the good times might not continue. But I believe that's a risk the firm can afford to take, where this kind of irreplaceable talent is involved. I'd like to reopen the issue— assuming you and the rest of the committee are in accord—and urge the firm to make a second partner right now."

Stephanie had been listening to him attentively. "That's a very good idea. Isn't it interesting how we sometimes lock ourselves into a fixed position and lose sight of what's important? From time to time, we need to reexamine the limits we've imposed on ourselves—to see if they still make sense. I believe this is one of those times."

"I'm glad you agree."

"Now that you've raised the idea, it seems so obvious. Did the notion just come to you out of the blue?"

Paul winced inwardly but decided to go all the way down *Pal*'s recommended path. "Yeah, it just seemed the appropriate thing to do."

The next day, Paul convened the partnership recommendation committee, which quickly endorsed his idea of making a second partner. A meeting of the full partnership to consider the matter was scheduled for the following afternoon.

That morning, there was a knock on the door of Ted Ashburn's office. He looked up to see Stephanie Carroll standing in the doorway.

"Come in," said Ted.

"No need," said Stephanie. "I just wanted to tell you that I've given some further thought to our conversation the other day.

What you said to Earl Caldwell was wrong, and Paul should have related the incident to his partners. But I've concluded that even if I knew about it, I would have voted for you anyway. So, I've put the whole thing to bed in my mind and don't feel any need to discuss it with the other partners."

"I appreciate your telling me."

She turned to leave, then looked back at him. "By the way, how do you stand on the issue of Curt Bell becoming a second corporate partner?"

"I'm fine with that."

"The firm should probably be aware of your feelings on the subject."

After Stephanie left, Ted knew he should feel reassured. After all, not only would she remain mum, but hers was a respected independent judgment that the Caldwell incident wasn't serious enough to bar him from partnership.

Still, he was bothered. It went back to Paul asking him if anyone else knew about the Caldwell incident—shades of a cover-up. And since Jill Marsh does know, she could well have mentioned it to her friend, Curt Bell, who would be apt to pass it along to George Troy. And now that Bell was being reconsidered, Troy might be tempted to use the incident to persuade the partners they hadn't selected the best man last week—banking on their collective contrition to promote Bell's current prospects.

That could really be bad, Ted thought—the incident being brought to light by Troy and made to appear as if Paul and Ted had tried to keep it under wraps. This, he knew, constituted the real lesson of Watergate—the cover-up was a hundred times more damaging to the Nixon administration than the original burglary.

As Ted continued to mull over the situation, it became clear to him that making Curt Bell a partner would go a long way toward easing his concerns. And a plan began to form in his mind—a plan that had the double virtue of helping that to occur and allaying his uneasiness over being viewed as part of a cover-up. The only problem he hadn't solved was how to keep Paul from becoming a wayside casualty.

Bill Price called the partners' meeting to order in the big conference room. "We've reconvened here today to consider the unanimous recommendation of the new partner evaluation committee that we reverse our prior position and elect a second corporate partner this year—namely, Curt Bell. In a moment, I'll turn matters over to Paul as head of the committee, but first I'd like to take note of the fact that our newest partner—Ted Ashburn—is with us today, attending his first partnership meeting. Welcome aboard, Ted." A round of applause greeted the newcomer.

Paul then went through the rationale for calling the meeting—namely, they all hated to lose Bell, they should reconsider making a second partner, business was good, the pros outweighed the cons. Much of the ensuing discussion was geared to firm economics. The notion appeared to be gaining headway, although approval was by no means certain. Some important partners still had reservations—financial soundness, setting a potentially troublesome precedent, and so on.

As Stephanie Carroll was completing her remarks in favor of making the second partner, George Troy tried to gain the floor. His eyes were directed at Ted Ashburn as he spoke. "I have something of importance to add to what's been discussed—"

"Excuse me, George, but I haven't finished yet," said Stephanie. "We'll get to you in a minute."

"Sorry," Troy mumbled. Stephanie turned toward Ted Ashburn, who hadn't participated in the discussion up to this point.

"Ted, inasmuch as making you a partner precluded us from making Curt Bell a partner—under the restriction we'd imposed upon ourselves at the last meeting—I wonder if you have any views on the subject before us today."

The query caught Ted at a time when he was pondering what was on George Troy's mind. That look Troy directed his way as George prepared to speak a moment ago—had Jill Marsh talked to Bell, and Bell to Troy? Was George about to reveal the Caldwell incident?

Maybe, thought Ted—but then again, maybe not. So often in the practice of law—and, he knew, in life generally—you're forced to act on the basis of incomplete information. He realized that if he was going to implement his plan, this might be the last moment he'd be able to do so. It was chancy, he acknowledged, but he considered the personal risk as acceptable.

What he hadn't been able to quantify was the potential harm to Paul Garson. This was a troublesome loose end for Ted. But Paul, after all, was the one who said to him that it's "never justifiable" for a lawyer to lie, and further that "there's no substitute for the truth." And so, with some trepidation, Ted addressed the meeting.

"I'd like to see Curt Bell become a partner—he's definitely qualified—although I don't know enough about firm economics to comment on the overall issue of making a second corporate partner. But since it's clear you would have made Bell a partner if you hadn't elected me, then there's something else you ought to take into consideration."

"What's that?" asked Bill Price.

"I believe in full disclosure. As a matter of fact," and here Ted turned in Paul's direction, "I've been tutored in that subject by a master. So here's what you ought to know—something that Paul Garson, for well-meaning reasons, I'm sure, chose not to share with you." Ted then proceeded to tell the hushed room about the Caldwell-Vortex incident in detail, not sparing his improper conduct, and concluding with these words: "So I say this to my new partners—especially those of you who are concerned about making two corporate partners. If today, knowing all the facts, any of you who previously voted for me now believe that Curt Bell is the better man and would like to change your vote, I think you should have the right to do so. And if the result of such a recount is that you wouldn't have elected me as a partner, then I will step down without any fuss and be content to stay with the firm—which I love very much—as an associate."

"But Ted," Stephanie blurted, "I thought that if you didn't make partner, you would leave the firm."

"To the contrary," replied Ted. "As I told Paul—"

That bit of byplay, however, was lost in the general commotion that resulted from Ted's disclosure of the Caldwell incident, which culminated in Bill Price turning to Garson. "Paul, let me voice the question we're all wondering about—how come you never mentioned the Caldwell matter to us?'"

Paul had not anticipated this turn of events. But the moment Ted began his confession, Paul knew he would have to speak to the issue, and so he held a hurried conference with his *Pal.*

Mea culpa, Paulie. Downplay the significance. But don't insult their intelligence by pretending you didn't realize it could have affected how they viewed the candidates.

Facing Price now, Paul said, "That was a mistake on my part. While the incident agitated me at the time, I didn't consider it sufficiently serious to disqualify Ted from making partner. And, quite frankly, I didn't want to hurt Ted's chances by bringing up something that might be overemphasized in the heat of the selection process."

Bill Price frowned. "Is this the reason—your sense of guilt, if you will—that you're now pushing us to make Bell a second partner?"

Despite Stephanie's initial inquiry, and even with his *Pal's* input, Paul had been unable to devise a satisfactory reply to this self-evident question. So he'd never resolved how to respond if it came up, trusting to the instinct of the moment.

Now the moment had come, and there was no time to consult his *Pal.* It was only when he began speaking, in fact, that he discovered what he was going to say.

"No, it's not my sense of guilt. I believe Ted may have been referring to me earlier as the 'master' who taught him, but today I've learned my lesson from the pupil."

Paul paused, aware now of where he was headed and recognizing it would be a rough trip.

His *Pal,* although unsummoned, rushed to intervene. *Watch out where you're going here. Just tell 'em a half-truth. Say you had a conversation with Bell and the idea grew out of that. You don't have to get into the blackmail.*

But Paul, sick of the deceit and having heard enough from this source, silently muttered, "Get lost, *Pal.*"

He spoke to his partners in a calm voice. "The fact is, I'm raising the second partner issue because Curt Bell is blackmailing me to do so—using the threat that if I don't, he'll take some actions that will hurt both me and the firm." Paul then proceeded to relate the details of Bell's visit. His voice was determined and forceful as he concluded his remarks.

"Ted Ashburn deserves to be a partner of this firm. His courage and forthrightness today are vivid proofs of that. Curt Bell, if he ever was deserving of a partnership, has forfeited that because of his attempted extortion. And for my misdeeds—withholding pertinent information from my partners, succumbing to a threat to save my own tail, misleading you as to my motives—I deserve to be severely censured."

At partnership meetings, Bill Price rarely acted in peremptory fashion, preferring to let decisions bubble up from the partnership as a whole. Now, however, as Paul concluded his confession, Price removed his glasses and took charge.

"This firm is not making Curt Bell a partner—yesterday, today, or tomorrow. In fact, let's tell him exactly how we feel about people who try to blackmail us—and then push him out the door immediately, no matter what the consequences are." Price turned to look at Ashburn. "Ted will remain a valued partner of the firm, having learned his lesson well."

Price now pivoted to face Garson. "As for you, Paul, you're absolutely right—you do deserve to be punished. In addition to other consequences that I'll be mulling over in the days ahead— to say nothing of the fact that your partners may never think of you the same way again—there's one thing I'm going to do right here on the spot. Effective today, you are no longer chairman— or even a member—of the committee to recommend new partners."

Bill Price put his glasses back on. "And now, ladies and gentlemen, I suggest we terminate these deliberations and get back to productive work."

In the hall that led away from the conference room toward their offices, Paul overtook Stephanie Carroll. No one else was in their immediate vicinity.

"I just wanted to apologize personally to you for—"

"It's a little late for that," said Stephanie as she continued walking. "You lied to me in order to get my support for your two-partner concept. But it wasn't *your* concept—it was Bell's. If I'd known Bell was behind it, I'd never have gone along and attempted to persuade others."

"That's why I'm so chagrined—"

"How could you have succumbed to blackmail? Where's your good judgment—your ethical center? What's happened to you?"

Paul had no words in reply.

"Our relationship was based on mutual respect. That's now gone, and I don't think our friendship can survive without it." Stephanie arrived at her office, entered the room, and slammed the door in Paul's face.

An hour later, Ashburn came to Paul's office. Ted knew that his confession had opened the door to serious consequences for Paul, and he felt the need to justify what he'd done. It wasn't just a matter of friendship, although that was part of it. Ted also reckoned that Paul—even in his weakened state—was still an important partner at the firm, whose support Ted would continue to need.

"I have to assume you're pissed at me for telling the firm about the Caldwell-Vortex episode," he said. "I'd like to explain my thinking—"

Paul waved Ted to a chair. "No, no, I'm not pissed and there's no need to explain. You did the right thing—in fact, I'm proud of you. Your disclosure persuaded me to be truthful. I realize there will be severe repercussions—professional tarnish, loss of friendships, who knows what else—but even so, my confession has made me feel clean for the first time this week."

This makes twice, Ted mused, that he had expected one reaction from Paul and gotten another. With Caldwell, he anticipated being treated like a hero, but got thoroughly chewed out. Today, he expected Paul to be mad as hell, but instead was receiving a hero's welcome.

Paul went on. "I was so damn self-righteous about your lie to Caldwell. I really believed I was an honest guy. Then I turned around and deceived my partners—the same thing I scolded you for! No, I deserved exactly what I got."

"I appreciate your attitude."

"The only good thing to come out of this whole mess is that we both learned a valuable lesson—namely, not to lie or cover up, even when it's done for a respectable motive, such as helping out a friend. Full and truthful disclosure is the only way to go."

"Amen," replied Ted.

Bill Price was seated behind his desk when, later that day, Ted Ashburn entered the managing partner's office—a room abounding in testaments to a distinguished legal career. Ted had crossed this baronial threshold only a few times in his tenure at the firm. Price told him to sit.

"A messy business," said Price. "But the reason I asked you here is to clarify one thing that's still bothering me."

"What's that?"

"Paul's failure to disclose the Caldwell incident and his neglecting to reveal Bell's blackmail—those were bad enough, and I've punished him for those indiscretions by stripping him of his committee. But at today's meeting, there was also a little byplay on another subject that got lost in the shuffle."

Ted sat there quietly, unsure of where things were headed but concerned nonetheless.

"I got the impression today that Paul may have lied to his partners at the first meeting, when he answered a question posed to him about what you were likely to do if passed over. At the time, I think we all came away with the impression that you would leave the firm. But that's *not* what I think I heard from you at today's meeting."

The phone rang on Price's desk. He excused himself and picked up the receiver.

Ted's body stiffened as he grasped where this was heading. He did recall having told Paul he would stay on if passed over. Had that been solely a hallmark of his loyalty to the firm? No, he realized—he also had thought he'd get credit for *not* using the threat of leaving as leverage on the firm to make him a partner. Now he sensed the opposite—that the firm might have been *less* inclined to select him if they knew he would have stayed on anyway.

But why, he pondered, had he repeated the pledge at today's meeting? Was it simply to give the partners maximum leeway to act in demoting him? No, once again he saw that his motives were mixed. He was betting that the partners would consider him such a stand-up guy for making both the offer to resign and the pledge to stay on that there was no way they'd revoke his partnership.

Price hung up the telephone and redirected his attention to Ted. "If Paul lied to us back then, the situation is a lot more serious than I thought, and I'd be forced to take much more drastic action against him." He paused, as if reflecting on what he was about to say. "It even calls into question whether he should remain a partner of the firm....So, tell me, Ted, what if anything did you say to Paul on the subject of your intentions should you be passed over?"

Ted realized that here was his second moment of truth as a new partner. He made a quick skim through some pertinent considerations, as well as the lessons he'd absorbed in recent days:

Staying or leaving is such a peripheral issue to the merits of making partner—why should it matter?

But, as Paul had just proclaimed, truth—the whole truth and nothing but the truth—is what it's all about.

No one wants to lie to the managing partner—but maybe a sidestep is possible.

Wait a minute, is this any way for me to start my career as a partner?

What it comes down to is, Paul covered for me—shouldn't I do the same for him?

But then, wouldn't I be doing the identical thing Paul criticized in the Caldwell incident?

Time was up. People can change, Ted mused—but do they really change that much? He looked Bill Price in the eye.

"Hey, I'm not a fool? Do you think that with the partnership decision coming up, I'd have told Paul I'm going to stay at the firm no matter what—and lose all my leverage? If I were that dumb, I wouldn't deserve to be a partner. Come on, Bill, give me more credit than that. . . ."

Commentary on
PARTNERGATE

Partnergate" provides a glimpse into the inner workings of an imaginary law firm. (We meet one client briefly at the outset, but otherwise the story is all internal.) Its main theme (and that of "Sex, Lies, and Private Eyes" later on) is the uneasy relationship some lawyers have with telling the truth.

What I've attempted to portray here is how two lawyers wrestle in their minds with a variety of situations that spawn powerful temptations to dissemble—an ongoing struggle between their better and lesser natures. It also touches on such themes as hypocrisy, loyalty, competition, trust, and blackmail, plus the use of bad means to accomplish good ends, and how we lawyers rationalize our questionable decisions.

All of this occurs in a story that deals with the process by which law firms go about making the crucial decision to promote an associate to partner. A word of caution, though. While the dramatics depicted in "Partnergate" could conceivably happen, let me assure you that I know of no instance where something like this really did occur—it's pure fiction. The actual process is generally much less animated and rarely evokes these various themes.

In today's law firm, great care goes into the selection of new partners, with painstaking evaluation of the skills, performance, and potential of likely candidates. To be sure, partners whose views are sought out may have their personal favorites, so it's not unlikely that some "grade inflation" occurs along the way. Nevertheless, to a great extent the evaluations are trustworthy, meritocracy rules, and in most cases a consensus evolves that makes the ultimate decisions appear in hindsight to have been inevitable. But not in "Partnergate."

The story begins with a briefing by the associate (Ted Ashburn) of the partner (Paul Garson) as to what occurred during the partner's recent vacation. Before getting into the heart of the story, let me offer a few comments on this more general subject matter.

A status report is one of the basic elements in the partner-associate relationship. It raises such issues for the associate as how often to approach the partner with general updates, what kinds of questions or problems ought to be run past the partner (or just resolved by the associate), and how to handle the actual briefing. Section 5.1.2 of *Lawyering* discusses these issues and provides some useful examples to illustrate the associate's choices. Here are two points worth emphasizing:

- First, associates should avoid the trap of only initiating contact with the partner when a problem or adverse development occurs. You don't want the partner to view you as solely the bearer of bad tidings, causing her to cringe involuntarily when she sees you coming. At least now and then, intersperse a "good news" (or at least neutral) partner contact, so that you're not in danger of being viewed as the local Cassandra.
- Second, if you come to the partner with a question or problem, be sure to proffer your own proposed answer or solution for the partner's ultimate determination.

It's much easier for a partner to react to a proposed solution than to devise one herself from scratch. View the encounter as a golden opportunity for you to display some real initiative.

The other pertinent aspect of this subject is just how to deliver to anyone (partner, client, etc.) an oral report as to what you've found out or heard. (This is discussed in section 3.3.1 of *Lawyering*, entitled "The Oral Report.") You have to learn how to distill the essence, to present refined conclusions rather than rough facts, to avoid encumbering the report with a lot of minutiae. This can be stickier when you're providing an assessment of a legal issue; in that case, the amount of detail to include is often geared to your listener's predisposition. As you gain experience, you'll want to function not solely as a reporter but also as an interpreter—putting your own imprimatur on what you're passing along and assessing its significance.

Getting back to "Partnergate," most of what transpired during Paul's absence was positive, but Ted has one piece of disturbing news to report. It's worth noting that Ted delivers the good news first, which seems wise to me—otherwise it might get lost in all the fuss that arises over the negative item.

The Caldwell-Vortex difficulty that Ted relates to Paul falls within a category of events that can occur from time to time—where a client, who is mad at the partner, vents his spleen to the associate. (This is discussed in section 5.1.2 of *Lawyering*.) The overriding question here is, should the associate be the bearer of bad tidings (risking the well-known fate of the guiltless messenger) or just ignore what's been said, hoping it will either blow over or that the client will let the partner know directly?

In many cases, when you cut through the client's rhetoric, his unhappiness boils down to a feeling that the partner isn't paying enough attention to him. Here's a case where the associate—in diplomatic fashion, to be sure—ought to let the partner know what's going on, because it can probably be rectified by a partner visit or phone call.

In the story, however, Earl Caldwell's complaint about Paul Garson is a substantive one—the discovery of a troublesome provision (at least in Earl's eyes) in an existing contract that was entered into on Paul's watch. When the client's complaint was voiced—with Paul away on vacation—Ted handled it in a way designed to protect the absent partner from the client's wrath. He told what he considered a "white lie" (but note its definition in the dictionary as a "trivial, diplomatic, or well-intentioned untruth," often "told to spare someone's feelings") that absolved Paul of the error, while taking the heat on himself for not appreciating the significance of the provision. Ted's intentions, if not his conduct, were decent. What's more (as we learn later), he fully expected kudos from Paul for his performance under fire.

We're now introduced to Paul's *Pal*, his inner voice that has been providing generally wise counsel over the years. We all have one of these, even if we're unaware of it. To graphically illustrate the nature of such existence, I decided to give that inner voice its own character in the story. Throughout "Partnergate," Paul and his *Pal* engage in lively silent dialogue.

The immediate issue raised by Ted's false statement is what, if anything, Paul should do about it in terms of communicating with Earl Caldwell, the client. So, before I discuss what Paul in fact did, let me ask you:

If you were Paul and had just received this report from Ted, what (if anything) would you have done about it vis-à-vis Earl Caldwell?

Pal's sound advice (which is hard to argue with) is that Paul has to rectify the current state of affairs and, in the process, teach Ted a valuable lesson about lawyer-client integrity. Paul agrees, but note what he does here. Before acting on the advice, he makes a practical check as to the downside of telling the truth—concluding that his relations with the client are strong enough to survive this disclosure. One is entitled to wonder what Paul would have done if he had determined that telling the truth might have permanently damaged the Caldwell relationship. . . .

Once Paul has decided to act, he handles the situation very well with the associate—broadening the message (clients are entitled to full disclosure) and creating maximum impact by acting on it *right now*, with Ted in attendance. Paul picks up the phone, calls Caldwell, and delivers an appropriate mea culpa to the client (it was my fault—I should have run the provision by you at the time). Like many clients, Caldwell values forthrightness and reacts positively (you're a stand-up guy). Paul concludes the tutorial with the mantra that will later prove prophetic (or counterprophetic): "That's the way we do it at J&P—there's no substitute for the truth." Paul makes it a memorable moment that Ted Ashburn will never forget—or will he?

Did you notice, though, that in the course of Paul's truth-telling conversation with Earl, I inserted one small instance where Paul was *not* telling the whole truth? Read those paragraphs again and see if you can pick out the fib.

Here it is. In explaining why Ted had said what he did to Earl, Paul characterized Ted as having been "misinformed"—but, of course, that wasn't the case. Ted knew very well who had been responsible for the contract provision. The spurious use of "misinformed" tripped readily off Paul's tongue, smack in the middle of his paean to veracity. Paul's motive here was to protect the associate (and, by extension, the firm) from having the client conclude that Ted had consciously lied to him. The intent may have been admirable, but the exculpatory word he used was nonetheless misleading. If you didn't catch it, this just goes to show how insidious the temptations to shade the truth can be. (We'll see more of this later in "Partnergate," as well as in "Sex,

Lies, and Private Eyes.") Oh, by the way, let me ask you:

If you were Paul, how would you have characterized to Caldwell what Ted's state of mind was when he lied to Caldwell?

For some reason, this bit of dissemblance doesn't bother me that much. I guess it's because Ted's prior state of mind isn't integral to the purpose of Paul's call to Caldwell. I can actually see myself uttering the word "misinformed" or something similar under these circumstances.

There are two points to note in the next scene, in which Paul and his partner Stephanie Carroll are discussing the upcoming partnership sweepstakes. One is that Paul says nothing about the Caldwell-Vortex incident. I don't find that too disturbing, since he still hasn't decided how to handle this (if at all) at the partnership meeting. On the other hand, given that Stephanie is a fellow supporter of Ted's candidacy, he might well have used the opportunity to explain the dilemma he was facing and perhaps get a useful reaction.

The more troubling point is Paul's nonresponse to Stephanie's comment about the firm probably losing the associate who isn't made a partner. We can infer that Paul recalls Ted's previous remark to him about staying with the firm no matter what the partnership result is, but Paul chooses to make no comment here. It's not exactly a lie—since he's not being asked to respond to a direct question—but his mumbling response is certainly construable by Stephanie as assenting to her observation. I don't like this, but tell me what you think:

Should Paul have spoken up at this point and revealed to his friend Stephanie the remark Ted made about staying with the firm?

The next scene depicts a full-fledged dialogue between Paul and his *Pal* on the issue of whether Paul should mention the Caldwell-Vortex incident at the upcoming partnership meeting. Paul's initial instinct is to say something about it—reasoning that if the incident was serious enough for him to handle as he did, then he should report at least a summary. How about you:

As Paul, would you have decided to disclose Ted's role in the Caldwell-Vortex incident to the partnership meeting?

In this dialogue, *Pal* is the voice of rationalization—a voice that each of us is familiar with. Here's how the dictionary defines "rationalize" (in the sense I use it here): "to devise superficially rational, or plausible, explanations or excuses for (one's acts, beliefs, desires, etc.), usually without being aware that these are not the real motives." Well, *Pal* is working overtime to make a persuasive case for Paul to justify saying nothing about the incident to his partners—and if you ask me, *Pal* is plenty aware that these are not the real motives. Recall the basic thrust of his case:

You (Paul) used the incident to teach Ted a lesson, but was his cover story to protect you really so heinous?

The subject matter of Ted's misstep is who should bear the responsibility for something that happened in the past—nothing of current interest.

Full disclosure here will put Ted's chances for partnership at risk.

For Ted to lose out to Curt Bell will damage your kingmaker status in the firm vis-à-vis George Troy.

Ted, after all, covered your ass—you owe him one.

It's a line of reasoning that may appear persuasive, but bottom line (in my view), it's wrong. Given its obvious relevance to the determination his partners are being called upon to make, Paul should have resolved to disclose what happened. He can, of course, put the incident in the best light for Ted, but his partners are entitled to know about this.

Now the meeting is taking place, and we learn that Paul has decided not to disclose the incident voluntarily.

But then he's asked a specific question by Bill Price, the J&P managing partner, about how well Paul has handled his current assignment and whether anything has occurred that would "detract" from his excellent record. Put yourself in Paul's place and assume you had previously decided not to volunteer anything about the Caldwell-Vortex incident.

Would this direct question from your boss in front of your partners have caused you to change your decision and mention the incident?

My answer to this one is "yes." Up to now, Paul may have been able to fool himself that this one blip didn't sufficiently mar Ted's splendid eight-year run to require bringing it up at such a crucial meeting. But once Bill Price asks Paul and George Troy a very specific question about whether anything current has tarnished their candidates' fine records, it's a mistake for Paul to remain silent. He can introduce his reply, if he wishes, along the line that he didn't think it sufficiently serious to Ted's overall performance to mention previously, but now that we're focused on the associate's *current* assignment, there was this one "minor incident."

The second issue that arises at the partnership meeting is of a somewhat different nature. There was no need in the first instance for Paul to mention Ted's remark about staying at the firm if he were passed over. Unlike the lying incident, it doesn't go to the merits of the decision the partners are being called upon to make. (Some folks with a more pragmatic bent of mind might argue that it does.) Nevertheless, when a direct question on the subject is posed to Paul, the issue has to be squarely faced. What do you think:

Under those circumstances, should Paul have responded by disclosing Ted's remark?

Paul had never decided how to handle this issue if it were to come up, even after Stephanie's remark on the subject in the cafeteria. That ought to have alerted Paul to the fact that this pragmatic consideration was very much on his partners' minds, and he should have worked out in advance how to handle any probe he got in that area. Advance preparation is always preferable to trying to think clearly under extreme situational and time pressure. In any event, without much thought, Paul listens to *Pal*'s advice—sidestep the question, because a truthful answer will hurt Ted's chances vis-à-vis Curt Bell, and also because whether or not a losing candidate will leave the firm shouldn't be a criterion for selecting a partner.

So that's what Paul does—he executes a wily sidestep. It's accurate for Paul to say he "never posed the question directly" to Ted, and Paul can be justified in speculating that Ted never thought saying it would hurt his chances. So Paul's cagey response is literally true, but let's face facts—it's misleading under the circumstances. This kind of issue—whether it's all right to mislead if your words are literally true—comes up with some regularity in the negotiating arena, and we'll return to the subject in the commentary to "Negotiating 101."

Let me just say, I would *not* have handled this the way Paul did. Rather, I might have replied along the following lines. Ted is very loyal to the firm (and I would point out other specific evidence of his loyalty, getting in some extra licks in Ted's favor). Because of this, he might very well choose to stay—although we can't be sure how he would actually react to the shock and disappointment of being passed over. However, I don't think we should hold this kind of loyalty against Ted. And, as a matter of fact, it sounds to me like Curt Bell is trying to use that unsolicited warning of his departure as leverage to put added pressure on us, which I don't like one bit (getting in a little jab at the competition). In other words, I would attempt to turn a potential negative into a positive, but without being misleading about Ted's intentions. Still, it's tough to come up with something like this off the cuff, so—as the Boy Scouts would say—be prepared.

The plot thickens in the next scene between Paul and his newly anointed partner. Ted expresses genuine surprise that he was selected notwithstanding the Caldwell-Vortex incident, which he presumes Paul has related to the partnership. I ask you:

If you were Paul, would you have informed Ted at this point that you didn't mention the incident to your partners?

I would have done so, and that's *Pal*'s advice also. But Paul—perhaps carried away by the giddiness over his victory and not wanting to spoil the joyous moment for Ted—ducks the issue (rationalizing that he wasn't asked a direct question) and segues briskly to the mock-serious ceremony of the new partner becoming liable on the firm's office lease.

By not, 'fessing up, however, Paul certainly implies to Ted that he did disclose the problem. Not only is that deceptive—it's also a dumb practical mistake, since (as Paul should well have known) once you start something like this on its trajectory, you can't control the actions and reactions of the rest of the world.

And that's exactly what transpires in the next scene with Ted and Stephanie, when Ted's reference to the incident is sparked by the prior inference he drew that Paul had disclosed it to the partnership. Stephanie, shocked to learn that such an incident occurred, tells Ted the partners didn't know about it. And we're off to the races.

At this point in the story, I decided that we needed to go inside Ted's head. (In most of these tales we're only privy to the inner workings of a single mind— "Partnergate" and "Sex, Lies, and Private Eyes" being the exceptions.) I made this decision because Ted has to go through some thought processes and take some actions that are integral to the story, but might not be readily understandable if the reader were privy only to the observations of an uninformed narrator.

When we do get inside Ted's head, we find him wondering about two things. First, why didn't Paul tell his partners about the Caldwell-Vortex incident? There he makes the correct assumption—that Paul didn't want to jeopardize Ted's chances for partnership. But Ted—thinking, as he apparently does, that it should have been disclosed—realizes it's a case of the end being used to justify the means. And that's a subject on which he earlier received such a dramatic lesson from Paul.

Ted's second question is why didn't Paul admit to Ted that he hadn't told his partners, when Ted specifically raised the point with him. This is an example of what I warned about earlier. When you don't level with people (as Paul didn't with Ted here), not only will they eventually find out about it, but when they do—and then attempt to figure out why this happened—they're likely to ascribe less charitable motives to your dissembling than were actually intended. Here, Ted surmises that Paul might have wanted to paint himself as a hero to Ted—the powerful partner who overcame the negative reaction to the disclosure and still presided over Ted's coronation. You may as well face it—in the absence of actual knowledge, the underlying rationale that others will attribute to your actions is likely to be something you wouldn't want to be caught dead actually contemplating.

Next we observe an upset Stephanie, seeking an answer from Paul as to why he didn't tell his partners about the Caldwell-Vortex incident—especially when Bill Price posed the direct question to him as to whether anything in Ted's current assignment detracted from his prior performance. What do you think:

Do you approve of how Paul handled this encounter with Stephanie? If you were Paul at this point, how would you have replied to her?

With somewhat more honor than he has exhibited up to this juncture, Paul does reveal the real reason for his silence—not wanting to harm Ted's partnership chances. However, by coupling this with a "don't say anything" plea to her, he undercuts the propriety of his stance. It would have been preferable for Paul to ask Stephanie whether, under all the circumstances, she thinks he needs to do something about this with the partnership right now—and then let the chips fall where they may.

Paul's next session with the know-it-all *Pal* (who is annoyingly chanting, "I told you so") results in their agreeing that Paul should say something about this to Ted, which is certainly the right course of action now. I cannot agree, however, with *Pal's* advice to find out who else knows about it. When Paul, following that advice, pops the question in the next scene with Ted, you can almost predict Ted's reaction—shades of the Watergate cover-up. At any rate, it does come out that Ted told Jill Marsh, who is Curt Bell's friend.

Sure enough, in the next scene Curt confronts Paul in the latter's office. Curt makes his accusations (to which Paul doesn't really respond) and then threatens dire consequences if he's not made a partner (to which Paul still doesn't reply). Let me ask you:

Do you agree with Paul's silence here, and if not, how would you have handled Bell's accusations and threats?

When someone threatens you overtly, my advice is to reply to the threat—don't just let it hang there. A lack of response can be misinterpreted by the maker of the threat as fear on your part, suggesting to him that his threat has struck a nerve and achieved the intimidation he sought. Paul should have risen up in righteous indignation here at Bell's crude tactic.

In negotiating situations, I usually make the further suggestion that after countering the threat, it may be worthwhile to then move to a more constructive level of discourse—focusing on whether there's some way for the two sides to resolve their differences. But I don't advise that with Curt Bell—he has already forfeited any consideration by Paul of a possible compromise.

In the next scene, a dialogue between Paul and his *Pal*, Paul has finally worked himself up into a state of righteous outrage over Curt's blackmail. But now *Pal* focuses on the practical considerations—warning Paul that he has to take the threat seriously, that even if Curt doesn't talk to the press, he'll probably complain to George Troy, and Paul knows damn well where that will lead. It may be blackmail, says *Pal*, but think of it this way: Curt's underlying notion—for the firm to make *two* partners—is really the best of both worlds. Well, how about it:

Do you agree that making Curt Bell a partner under the circumstances is the best of both worlds?

I don't. What Curt Bell does here—threatening dire consequences if he's not made a partner—is just plain wrong. He isn't the kind of person you would want as your partner, and Paul should not become a willing participant in Curt's blackmail scheme.

If Curt had come to Paul, expressed his sense of unfairness at Paul not disclosing the Caldwell-Vortex incident to the partnership, and requested reconsideration of his case—but without the threats and the time pressure—that might be something Paul could support. Of course, Paul would then have to disclose to the partnership what he omitted about Ted the first time around, together with a plea to his partners not to take their vengeance out on Ted, since it wasn't Ted's fault that Paul chose not to disclose the incident.

In the story, Paul isn't initially convinced by *Pal*, but as his resolve weakens, he decides to try out some aspects of the notion. A discussion ensues as to just how Paul would go about persuading the firm to make Bell a partner. They realize that for Paul to tell the truth about Curt's blackmail would doom the proposal. When Paul toys with the notion of saying the idea originated with Bell but leaving out the blackmail, *Pal* shoots it down—but (and this shows how far down the slippery slope Paul and his *Pal* have gone) not because leaving out the blackmail constitutes a material omission (which it clearly does). Rather, *Pal* feels the idea will have more weight—and actually redound to Paul's benefit—if it's made to appear to have originated with Paul.

Then, when Paul at last tries to face up to the real question of whether J&P should take on a blackmailing partner, that rationalizing inner voice of *Pal* starts to split hairs—Bell didn't say he would sue, but that he'd rather not; Curt's just using negotiating leverage as any commercial lawyer would; and so on. And Paul—his judgment weakened by the whole mess—falls for it.

The next scene finds Paul trying out the concept on Stephanie. He's purporting to take her into his confidence, but when it turns out she likes the idea, he promptly tells another lie—that it was *his* idea, with no mention of the threat from Curt. Can you believe it? Where is Paul's ethical sense? This is his good friend and partner Stephanie, who has already expressed her concern over Paul's past behavior in withholding the Caldwell-Vortex incident from his partners. The fact of his lying to get her on his side in persuading the firm to reopen the partnership consideration is bad enough, but it also reflects exceptionally bad judgment on Paul's part. The lie may work temporarily, but it sinks Paul in the long run. And in case you had any doubt on this score, it's the long run that we lawyers ought to be thinking about.

The following scene between Stephanie and Ted serves two purposes. One is for her to urge him to speak up on the issue of Curt Bell at the partnership meeting. As for the other, which concerns the Caldwell-Vortex incident, Stephanie says that she considers what Ted did to be wrong, and that Paul should have related the incident to his partners. But she acknowledges that even if she had known about the incident, she would have voted for Ted. As a result, she has decided not to discuss the incident with her partners. Although we don't get inside Stephanie's head, we can sense it was a close call on her part. So, let me ask you:

Based on the foregoing, do you agree with Stephanie's decision here?

I'm inclined to give Stephanie the benefit of the doubt. The anticipated subject matter of the upcoming meeting is Curt Bell and the question of the firm awarding a second partnership. I think she would come out differently if the meeting had been called to revisit the firm's prior action in making Ted a partner. But that's behind them now, and to bring the incident up at this time would only further muddy some already murky waters.

For the next scene, we're back inside Ted's head. He now knows that Stephanie won't say anything about the incident. He still has concerns, however, and they run in two seemingly contrary directions. On the one hand, he doesn't want to be seen as participating in a cover-up. On the other, he's bothered that Jill Marsh probably told Curt Bell, who undoubtedly told George Troy, who might well reveal all to the partners. Both these concerns could be eased by Curt being made a partner, so he devises a plan (that we're not told the details of) to help accomplish this.

Next we attend the reconvened partnership meeting, called to deal with the question of making Curt a partner. While the outcome is still undecided, there comes a moment when George Troy begins to talk ("I have something of importance to add to what's been discussed—"), but Stephanie cuts him off and asks Ted to offer his views on Bell. Ted, however, is pondering what's on George's mind—is he about to reveal the Caldwell-Vortex incident? If so, Ted would very much like to preempt the revelation, and it's right now (but presumably not later) that he has the opportunity.

Here's a situation that replicates what Dan Barton was telling his son Mark about in "Father's Day"— remember the gas station hypothetical? So often in our legal practice we're forced to act—make a decision, take an action—at a time when our information is incomplete. Ted's plan seems to be that if it appears the Caldwell-Vortex incident will be raised at the meeting, he wants to be the one to raise it. (What isn't so clear— an uncertainty that I intended—is whether he plans to say anything about the incident if it appears *unlikely* to come up.) Now, with George tooling up to discuss something that could very well be the incident, Ted decides to act.

There's one other aspect of interest here. Ted recognizes that what he's about to say will do harm to his mentor at the firm, Paul Garson. The way Ted gets past this potential obstacle is by reverting to that old standby of rationalization, but here with a special twist. Paul himself had previously said that it's "never justifiable" for a lawyer to lie, and that "there's no substitute for the truth." Well, that's all Ted will be doing—speaking truthfully on the basis of those words right out of Paul's own mouth—in effect, hoisting Paul on his own petard. (This is a subject we return to in a bargaining context in "Negotiating 101.")

So, deciding it's now or never, Ted reveals all about the Caldwell-Vortex incident, offers to step down as a partner, and adds that if this happens, he will nevertheless stay at the firm. (At the meeting, Stephanie tries to quiz Ted on the latter pledge, but her question is lost in the general commotion.) We learn, in the story's final scene, why Ted put that pledge on the table. It wasn't just to give the partners maximum leeway to act in demoting him; he was also betting that, by this offer to step down and stay at J&P, his partners will consider him such a stand-up guy that they won't revoke his partnership.

So now put yourself in Ted's position:

Do you agree with Ted's decision to reveal the Caldwell-Vortex incident? Should Ted have discussed what he intended to do with Paul before the meeting—either for guidance or at least to give him a heads-up? Do you agree with Ted's offering to step down as a partner? Do you agree with his saying he'll then stay with the firm as an associate?

I think Ted's plan is a good one—even including the offer to step down and the pledge to stay. The J&P partners will never take him up on revoking his partnership, now that he's come forward himself to reveal all—preemption being crucial here. Besides, he wouldn't want the nondisclosure of the incident to be hanging over his head in years to come.

I think Ted erred, though, in not telling Paul beforehand what he was intending to do at the meeting. If Ted was determined to press ahead with this in any event, then their get-together wouldn't have been to seek Ted's guidance, but just as a courtesy to alert him in advance—giving Paul some time to reflect on what his response should be. As for the additional trouble created for Paul by Ted's pledge to stay on, Ted has no idea that Paul previously dissembled to the partners on that issue.

The focus now shifts to Paul, who starts out with a mea culpa. He could have stopped his explanation at the level of "I didn't consider it sufficiently serious to disqualify Ted," but instead chose to go further and candidly admit that another reason for the omission was not wanting to hurt Ted's chances. How about it:

Do you agree with Paul's choice to go on and give the real reason?

I think Paul was wise to admit what was probably obvious to everyone. But immediately thereafter he's faced with the predictable question of why he's pushing the firm to make Curt Bell a partner, to which (surprisingly) he hasn't prepared an answer in advance. Boldly shunning *Pal*'s half-truth advice, Paul now comes clean on the blackmail. I don't have to ask you about this one—finally, Paul did the right thing.

At this juncture, Bill Price takes charge of the meeting, boots Curt Bell out of the firm, and strips Paul of his committee chairmanship.

Do you agree with the approach Bill Price takes? Should his punishment of Paul have been more or less severe?

I think Bill Price acted wisely and well. The meeting would have quickly gotten out of hand if he hadn't intervened. His decisiveness on Bell was right on the money—just the way old man Jenkins (see "The Smell Test") would have handled it. As for Paul, the immediate punishment was apt and related to the offense—and Price does say he'll mull over other possible consequences. He also alludes to the strongest repercussion of all—the loss of esteem in which Paul will now be held by his partners.

The ensuing scene between Paul and Stephanie confirms Bill Price's judgment as to how Paul's partners will react. It's too late now for Paul to apologize to Stephanie, who views him as ethically lost. The lie he told in order to get her support for the two-partner concept was the last straw. It's doubtful if their relationship will ever be revived. That's what happens when you lie to a friend—so don't do it!

Ted now comes to Paul's office. We learn (because we're inside Ted's head) that the visit is not just because Ted feels guilty about exposing Paul; he also wants Paul's continuing support at the firm. (This concept of having more than one motivation for our actions is echoed in the final scene, when Ted reflects on the dual reasons behind his pledge to stay at the firm.) Well, all I can say is that most of us have mixed motives for a lot of what we do, and some aren't as noble as others.

Ted muses about being surprised at the reactions he has gotten in recent days—expecting praise from Paul on how he handled the Caldwell complaint and instead getting chewed out; expecting an irate Paul after Ted's revelation to the partnership and instead hearing words of gratitude. (It reminds me of the plaque my former partner kept on his office wall, containing the maxim, attributed to a well-known jurist: "Never assume a damn thing!") Paul, thoroughly cleansed by his confession, behaves well at this meeting. He concludes it with his paean to full and truthful disclosure, to which Ted says "amen." And to which I say, "*ahem* . . . read on."

Now I urge you to review the final scene between Ted and Bill Price. The big question for you (or for any of us in Ted's position) is this:

If you were Ted, what would you do when Bill Price puts you in this damn box?

All the pertinent considerations that enter into Ted's decision are spelled out in the story, so I won't repeat them here. Ted's decision to sidestep the question might well appear cynical to the reader—a reminder that the admonition to tell "the truth, the whole truth, and nothing but the truth" is sometimes honored more in the breach.

Still, Ted realizes that to answer Price truthfully will cause severe damage to Paul. So here, truth comes up against loyalty to a mentor who has been responsible for Ted's rise at the firm. It can also be inferred that if Ted had known his pledge to stay was going to cause damage to Paul, he never would have made it at the partnership meeting; i.e. it was Ted's own inadvertence that triggered the issue.

I'm inclined to cut Ted some slack here. I wouldn't have handled it the way he did, but I would also not have conceded a prior settled intent to stay if passed over. Ted can admit that he mused about the possibility of staying at the firm he loved so well—especially if the prospect of becoming a partner a year from now seemed in the cards—but he by no means signed a pledge on the subject. Since Ted can honestly say that he doesn't know how he would have reacted to the shock of losing out, he can focus on that. And this would probably be enough to get Paul off the hook.

So that's the saga of "Partnergate." For me, it's a dramatic reminder of the multiple temptations faced by lawyers (to say nothing of nonlawyers) to shade the truth. This can be caused by undue pressure from clients who are dead set on achieving certain goals and hardly puritanical about what's involved in the journey. Or it may stem from the agony of having to cope with some ridiculous administrative regulations. Sometimes, it's triggered by the outrageous words and deeds of an overreaching adversary, where perhaps just a little dose of prevarication is needed to put the scoundrel in his place.

But unfortunately, we can't blame everything on our clients, regulators and adversaries. We manufacture much of the problem ourselves, and it's this homegrown variety that is on display in "Partnergate." Like the characters in the story, we often consider our intentions to be pure—it's almost like we're committing some victimless crime to achieve an unassailable end. And then, very shortly, we find ourselves on the proverbial slippery slope.

Part of the problem is that a handy lie often presents itself as the most facile way to proceed to your goal. Don't let yourself be beguiled by an untruthful shortcut to the place you're trying to go. Spend a little extra time on the problem, and figure out how, without resorting to a lie, you can still achieve a constructive favorable result.

You Gotta Get Me Off!

Judge Redmond, returning from the lunch recess, takes her seat on the bench, looks over at me, and says, "Call your next witness, Mr. Lawrence."

I rise from my chair. "The defense calls William Wilson."

Wilson, a tall man in his late twenties, strides briskly to the witness stand. His expression is serious, his hair slicked back, his manner confident. I notice that the blue suit he's wearing is frayed at the collar and cuffs.

The bailiff administers the oath. "Raise your right hand. Do you swear that the testimony you will give is the truth, the whole truth and nothing but the truth?"

"I do," replies Wilson. He sits down, then shifts several times in the hard wooden chair, as if trying to find a comfortable position.

I move a few steps toward the witness stand. "Please state your name."

"William Wilson."

"Where do you reside?"

"In New York City."

"Tell us about your education, Mr. Wilson."

"I graduated from high school and then attended college for two years but never got a degree."

"And what is your occupation?"

Wilson flashes a self-deprecating smile. "Well, I like to think of myself as an actor, but the roles haven't been coming with any regularity. So, for the last year or so, I've mostly been driving for Ring-Up Limo Service."

I pause to consult my notes. I'm definitely feeling the pressure of this case. Here I am, in my late forties—graying at the temples, bulging around the midriff—a litigator of business and financial disputes who hasn't actually tried that many lawsuits. This isn't unusual among partners at firms like Jenkins & Price—most of the commercial cases we're involved in get settled before they go to trial. Not this one, though—neither side has been willing to budge an inch.

So I'm handling this lawsuit, and although the dollar amount involved isn't that large, the case has become a high profile one in New York financial circles. The two business honchos involved are well known on Wall Street, and the clash between them has captured the Street's interest.

That's why I'm feeling the pressure. All the people I've been cultivating for business over the years are aware of the suit and of my role in it. A victory here would be a major boost to my career. Conversely, a well-publicized loss could really hurt my standing.

Well, at least there's no jury to deal with—it's the judge who will make the ultimate decision. Judge Redmond is a middle-aged woman who looks a little like Angela Lansbury wearing horn-rimmed glasses. So far, she seems reasonably competent.

But I'll tell you, I could have done without that early morning phone call today from Jill Marsh, the associate who's been helping me on the case. "Jack," she said in a muffled voice, "I feel terrible, must be the flu, can't get out of bed." So I'm going it alone in court, which adds to the stress I'm feeling.

I shake off the momentary black cloud and offer myself some silent encouragement. *Hey, Jack, take your time with this witness. He's the key to our case. If Judge Redmond buys Wilson's testimony, we're home free.*

"Now, Mr. Wilson, were you driving for Ring-Up Limo ten months ago, during January of this year, 1977?"

"I was. My car was then, and still is, number 365—easy to remember, the number of days in the year."

"And, in particular, were you driving car number 365 during the daytime hours on January 13, which I believe was a Thursday?"

"I consulted the company records to prepare for my testimony, and yes, I was driving January 13—on the day shift from 8:00 A.M. until 4:00 P.M."

I steal a glance at my client, Alan Carter, who is seated at the defense table, following Wilson's testimony intently. Carter has an aging boy-wonder look, full of nervous energy—fidgeting in his seat, drumming his fingers on the table. Twice during the trial I've had to nudge him to stop—I don't want Judge Redmond drawing any negative inferences.

The fact is, I don't know my client well at all. This was one of those out-of-the-blue referrals from a law school classmate with whom I spent some time at our last reunion. I have no direct experience with Carter, no past observations to rely on. So I've been giving him the benefit of the doubt— attributing his nerves to the significance of the case rather than the rumblings of a guilty conscience. Carter's anxiety about winning has been evident from the outset. My hunch is he's probably under some financial pressure—an adverse verdict here might have dire consequences.

Well, at least we got paid the bulk of the firm's fee in advance. When the subject came up in one of our early meetings, Carter surprised me. "I've just got to win this case," he said. "I want to pay you up front, Jack, so you'll be motivated to do your best work. Here's my check. Just get this guy Mickey Trent off my back."

I can't really blame Carter for being upset. It's bad enough to be sued on any grounds. It's especially tough when you're accused of fraud—as the plaintiff Mickey Trent has charged here—and the alleged fraud consists of *not* saying something you should have said. In that kind of case, a defendant like Carter carries a heavy burden—the burden of negating the negative by proving you really did say it!

I have a mental picture of the written complaint, containing Mickey Trent's allegations about how Carter defrauded him. The fraud occurred, according to Trent, eight months ago when Carter sold Trent a big block of shares in a record company called Slipped Disc Corp. There's a lot of stuff in Trent's complaint, but the only charge that amounts to a hill of beans is the Burnside contract cancellation. The fact is, this whole case—all $12 million of it—comes down to one point, and it's about to be served up.

"Now, Mr. Wilson, at the time in question, was the investment firm of Carter Resources a regular customer of Ring-Up Limo?"

"Yes, it was."

"And did Carter Resources order a car to pick up its president, Alan Carter, at 11:00 A.M. on January 13?"

"Yes. I know that because Ring-Up Limo assigned me to the job. According to the company's records, I picked up Mr. Carter at about 11:00 A.M. that day outside the Carter Resources office at 307 East Forty-second Street."

"If you see Mr. Carter in the courtroom, please point him out."

"That's him"—Wilson points a finger at Carter— "sitting at the table where you were sitting before. I also knew who he was back then on January 13, because I had driven him several times before."

January 13, January 13—the date is inexorable. It came two weeks after the prior December 30, when—as another witness has already testified—Slipped Disc received the dreaded letter from Burnside. The letter was a formal notice, advising that effective March 31—the requisite three-month notice period— Burnside was canceling its contract with Slipped Disc. And this wasn't just any contract, but the one that had been responsible for roughly 25 percent of Slipped Disc's profits over the past five years.

January 13 was also one week after January 6, the date the Slipped Disc board of directors held a special meeting to discuss the cancellation. Another witness has testified that Alan Carter— a director of Slipped Disc since its start-up days—attended the meeting.

Then, going in the other direction, January 13 was four days *prior* to January 17, when Carter sold his large block of Slipped Disc shares to Mickey Trent. And January 13 was a week prior to January 20, when Slipped Disc—after trying unsuccessfully to persuade Burnside to reconsider—finally put out a press release announcing the cancelled contract. On that day, the stock took a 35 percent nosedive in a massive sell-off.

In February, Mickey Trent commenced his fraud suit against Alan Carter. The gist of his complaint is that Carter, as a director of Slipped Disc with knowledge of the Burnside contract cancellation, had a duty to tell Trent about it before selling him the block of Slipped Disc shares, but failed to do so.

Carter's response has been that Trent is lying—that, in fact, Carter did tell Trent about the problem on January 13. This was the reason the deal wasn't made until four days later, according to Carter—because over the weekend, Trent tried unsuccessfully to renegotiate the price downward.

Trent, in turn, vigorously denies all this. Earlier in the trial, Trent testified that at no time during their talks about Slipped Disc did Carter ever mention a contract cancellation. The first time he learned of it, says Trent, was when the company announced the news on January 20. So, what we've got here is one man's word against the other—the financial world's equivalent of "he-said, she-said."

When I started out on the case, I figured that the truth probably lay somewhere in the middle. I admit to having my doubts whether Carter gave Trent the full scoop on the Burnside contract cancellation. Chances are, though, that he did say something with a negative slant, from which Trent could have inferred there was a problem. In my experience, people in the securities business frequently converse in oblique terms. It's often tough to determine whether what's been said is enough to put a person on notice.

Still, in my talks with him, Carter was quite certain about having imparted the bad news to Trent. And who am I to doubt my client's word? Besides, once the Burnside story broke, Trent must have been kicking himself for having gone through with the deal—and Carter was clearly the handiest scapegoat.

"Mr. Wilson, when you picked up Mr. Carter that day at his office, did anyone else get in the car with him?"

"Yes, another man."

"If you recognize this other man in the courtroom, would you please so indicate."

"Yes, I do. He's the man sitting there at the other table, in the gray suit and red tie." He pointed with conviction at Mickey Trent.

"Let the record show that the witness has identified Mickey Trent."

I remember the day at Carter's office, discussing the case, when Alan recalled that his first conversation with Trent about the Burnside contract cancellation took place in a limo. I encouraged Alan to track down the limo driver, on the off chance that he'd overheard something buttressing Carter's story and could still remember it today.

And then, lo and behold, there appeared in my office the key to Carter's case—Will Wilson. When the two of us first spoke, I recall having an uneasy sense of déjà vu . . . But this quickly vanished when I heard what Wilson had to relate.

"Now, Mr. Wilson, please tell us about the conversation you heard in your limo that day."

"Objection! Your Honor, counsel is leading the witness." Trent's lawyer, Carol Unger, an attractive woman in her early forties, is on her feet.

Judge Redmond, who has sometimes seemed distracted behind her horn-rimmed glasses, now perks up and rules on the objection. "Sustained."

I rephrase my inquiry. "Mr. Wilson, did you overhear any conversation between Mr. Carter and Mr. Trent on that day?"

"I did."

"And what was the subject of the conversation?"

"They were talking business, but mostly about one company."

"And do you remember the name of that company?"

"Yes, I do."

"What was it?"

"It was Slipped Disc."

I realize, of course, what the first question in Judge Redmond's mind has to be at this point—why does this driver remember the specifics of a conversation that he overheard between two passengers in his limo eight months ago? This was the question I specifically posed to Will Wilson in our first interview. Since Wilson's explanation makes a lot of sense, I've decided to let him testify about his reason for recalling this dialogue *before* the judge learns exactly what Will overheard. This way, when Wilson relates the actual exchange, it will have more credibility.

"Now, Mr. Wilson, this conversation occurred eight months ago. How is it that you remember today what was said back then?"

"Well, first of all, I'm a guy who's interested in business, especially the stock market. I play the market with the few bucks I'm able to save. I get to drive around plenty of corporate executives and investment bankers who are always talking business. So, when a conversation begins, my ears prick up.

"Next, I had driven Mr. Carter a few times before this. I knew he had the reputation of being one of the smartest financial guys on Wall Street, so I was especially interested in what he might say.

"But the main reason I paid special attention to the conversation, and remember it today, is because back in January, Slipped Disc was a company I was thinking of investing in."

Well done, Will Wilson—logical, understandable, not overstated. I just hope you do equally well on what you remember hearing.

"Now, if you please, Mr. Wilson, tell the court what you overheard on January 13 in your car."

"Well, I remember that the gentleman who's sitting over there—I'm sorry, what did you say his name is?"

Hey, that's a nice touch—establishing Wilson as a cautious witness. This guy's a natural.

"That's Mr. Trent," I reply, "the plaintiff, whom you previously identified as the man in the car with Mr. Carter."

"Yes. Well, as I was saying, Mr. Trent asked Mr. Carter, 'Why do you want to get out of Slipped Disc?'—or something along those lines. That's when my antennae shot way up. Here I was, thinking of buying into the stock, just as this savvy Wall Streeter was thinking of getting out."

"And what was Mr. Carter's reply?"

"Well, I think he gave a couple of personal reasons I don't remember. But there was one reason I do recall, because it involved the company itself. Mr. Carter said Slipped Disc was in a risky business that depended on a few key contracts—and that one of those was in real trouble."

"Why do you recall that?"

"Because I remember thinking to myself at the time, hey, if this other guy is a potential buyer, that's no way for Mr. Carter to go about selling stock. He's being real candid with this guy, but after what he just said, this deal probably won't happen."

"And, by the way, Mr. Wilson, did you go out the very next day and buy Slipped Disc stock?"

"Are you crazy? After what I heard Mr. Carter say in the car, I wouldn't have touched it with a ten-foot pole!"

"Thank you, Mr. Wilson. I have no further questions."

One thing I've learned over the years is when to stop. Here's a dramatic moment, and the direct impact on his own pocketbook of the information Wilson overheard adds credibility to his recollection.

I'm feeling ebullient. I glance up at the judge. Sometimes, after questionable testimony, I can tell from the cynical, disapproving look on a judge's face that he or she doesn't believe the witness. But I don't see that sort of expression in Judge Redmond's features, nor do I detect any negative body language. My sense is that she has bought into Wilson's testimony. I'm on a roll.

Carol Unger, Trent's lawyer, now rises and approaches the witness. "Just a few questions, Mr. Wilson."

I'm not that concerned about the substance of Wilson's testimony. We've gone over it several times, and Will is rock solid. And so far, he's proved to be an excellent witness. But there's one line of inquiry Unger might take that seriously worries me.

"I assume, Mr. Wilson, that these gentlemen were both seated in the backseat of the Ring-Up Limo?"

"That's right."

"In your limo, Mr. Wilson—number 365, I think you testified—is there any kind of partition between the front seat and the backseat?"

"No, it's completely open, just as in any passenger sedan."

"This was January, was it not?"

"That's right."

"In the middle of winter?"

"Yes."

"Am I correct to assume that in winter you use the limo heater for the comfort of your passengers?"

"Usually, if it's cold out."

"The heater has a blower, is that correct?"

"Yes."

"Which makes a whirring noise when in use?"

"A low hum."

This stuff isn't a problem. Let her probe Wilson's ability to hear their voices in the car on January 13 all she wants. What worries me are the relations between Wilson and Carter *after* January 13. . . .

The subject first came up when I was interviewing Wilson and routinely asked whether he had seen Carter since that key date. To my surprise, Wilson replied that he had. It seems that Wilson, who sometimes moonlights with his limo, acted as a chauffeur to Carter's wife and kids for several Saturday shopping excursions and sports events.

I asked Wilson how this came about. He said he received a call one day from Carter's secretary, who asked if he was available. Wilson assumed she had gotten his name from Ring-Up Limo, which knew he moonlighted and had no objections. I then asked Wilson if he had spoken directly to Carter in the course of these assignments. He said that he had—but when I asked whether they had discussed the case, his answer was no.

I was frankly troubled that Alan Carter hadn't mentioned anything to me about those subsequent contacts with Wilson. When I confronted him on the subject, Carter confirmed Wilson's private chauffeuring assignments. Why, I asked—why didn't you tell me? Because, Carter replied, I only saw Wilson for a few brief moments when he picked up my family, and we didn't discuss the case, so I didn't think it mattered. Besides, he said, you never questioned me about anything subsequent to the month of January—which, I had to admit, was true.

Still, this disclosure made me uneasy. Once, again, I had the feeling that there was a relevant trace of memory—some incident in my past, perhaps—but I couldn't put my finger on it.

If I were sure Carol Unger knew about the subsequent contacts between Carter and Wilson, or even suspected something, I would have gotten into this as part of Wilson's direct testimony. Clearly, the linkage would be less damaging if brought out voluntarily rather than through cross-examination. But I have no reason to believe Unger knows or has suspicions.

Then, when I originally raised the subject with my client, he showed some concern about the disclosure. "Look, Jack," Carter said to me, "it's your call. But my strong preference is to take a chance and not introduce the subject of chauffeuring. We have nothing to hide if it comes out, but I have a hunch she'll miss it completely." Somewhat reluctantly, I decided to go along.

Carol Unger continues with her cross-examination. "So the blower was humming while you overheard this conversation."

"The hum doesn't affect my ability to hear people in the backseat if they're talking in normal tones."

"But might not Mr. Carter and Mr. Trent have been whispering that day—since they were discussing such a private business matter?"

"No, they weren't. The made no attempt to keep from being overheard."

"But they weren't talking to you or with you, is that correct?"

"That's right."

"So you were eavesdropping, weren't you?"

"Well—"

"In fact, you made a conscious decision to take note of what they were saying."

"I guess so."

"Does Ring-Up Limo tell you to respect the privacy of your customers?"

"Sure, but I couldn't help—"

"Thank you, you've answered my question."

Well, that's snappy, but it doesn't really hurt us. After all, just about everyone—probably even Judge Redmond—has involuntarily eavesdropped on a conversation at some time in the past. It appears that Carol has no idea about the chauffeuring. And it sounds like she's coming to the end of her cross examination.

Carol Unger consults her notes briefly, then looks up at the witness. "Other than what you've previously testified to, did you overhear anything else that Messrs. Carter and Trent discussed that day?"

Wilson pauses for a moment before replying. "Yes, there was something else."

I can feel my body stiffen. I have no idea what might be coming now.

"What was that?" asks Unger.

"Well, after Mr. Carter mentioned the problem Slipped Disc had with the contract, Mr. Trent said that this should reduce the price he would be paying for the shares. Mr. Carter said, 'No way. A deal is a deal,' or something like that. But Mr. Trent wouldn't let up—he was trying like hell to negotiate the price down because of that troubled contract. They were still arguing about it when they got out of the car."

I'm stunned. Sure, this new testimony fits perfectly into my client's case, fully supporting the theory that I want the judge to accept. But Wilson hasn't mentioned anything to me about overhearing this aspect of the Carter-Trent conversation. Wilson is a smart guy, so he certainly must realize this testimony is significant—but he never once referred to it. There's something very fishy here.

And suddenly, the shard of memory that wouldn't surface earlier now pops into focus—the whole incident flashing through my mind in an instant.

I'm back in the Navy, right out of college and before attending law school—an ensign on a destroyer. In those days, when a seaman went AWOL or committed some other offense, he was tried at a special court-martial aboard ship. The newest officer had the duty of representing the unfortunate defendant—you didn't have to be a lawyer, as long as the prosecutor wasn't one.

I use the word "unfortunate" because the judges were crusty old salts with a dim view of defendants' alibis. Half listening to the testimony while doodling hangman's nooses on their yellow pads, they invariably convicted the hapless offenders.

One day I was assigned to defend Kinney, an arrogant young seaman who was disliked by officers and enlisted men alike. He had been accused of taking a swing at Petty Officer Porter. Kinney's story was that he threw the punch in self-defense after being attacked by Porter. No witnesses to the incident had been located.

As we discussed the case in my stateroom, Kinney suddenly turned to me, speaking with deep emotion: "Mr. Lawrence, you gotta get me off! I hate the goddamn Navy. I've only got three months left to serve before I get my discharge. But if I'm convicted, they can stick me in the brig for up to six months and then they add another six months to the time I have to serve. I swear, Mr. Lawrence, I won't make it through another year."

"Well, Kinney," I replied, "I'll do what I can, but it's a tough case for you—your word against that of Porter, a respected petty officer, who claims you assaulted him without provocation."

"He's lying," said Kinney. "He hates me from something that happened between us way back when, and this is just his way of evening up the score." He looked pleadingly at me. "Look, Mr. Lawrence, I've got to beat this rap. I've saved up some real money from my gambling winnings, and it's all yours if you can get me off."

I smiled. "Listen, Kinney, that's one of the benefits of being in the Navy—you don't have to pay your defense counsel! Don't worry, I'll try my best. Save your money for when you get out of the service—which I hope will be earlier rather than later." But I had little confidence Kinney would be acquitted.

Back in the courtroom, Carol Unger seems shaken by Wilson's latest recollection. Apparently deciding things can only get worse from Trent's standpoint, she says, "No further questions."

Three days after my meeting with Kinney, there was a knock on the door of my stateroom. A seaman named Seward entered. "They told me you're defending Kinney, Mr. Lawrence."

"That's right."

"I just wanted to tell you that I saw the whole thing between Kinney and Porter from up on the 40-mm turret where I was oiling the guns."

"You saw it? I didn't realize there were any witnesses. Well, tell me what happened."

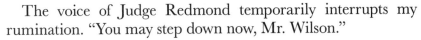
"They started yelling at each other, and then all of a sudden Porter took a swing at Kinney, missed him, then threw another punch that Kinney blocked, and then Kinney belted him on the chin."

I remember the excitement I felt. Seward's eyewitness account of the incident, describing Kinney's blow as having been struck in self-defense, represented total exoneration for my client. I tried the case, highlighting Seward's testimony. In what might have been the first acquittal ever obtained on the destroyer, the court dismissed the charges against Kinney. I was jubilant, and Kinney even more so.

The voice of Judge Redmond temporarily interrupts my rumination. "You may step down now, Mr. Wilson."

A week after Kinney's acquittal, I woke up one morning with a start. Suddenly it all came into focus—Kinney's desperation to beat the rap, his mention of having saved up some cash, Seward materializing after a previously unsuccessful search for witnesses— my God, I realized, Kinney used those funds to pay Seward to lie on the witness stand! It was all so obvious—and yet I was so wet behind the ears and so delighted with Seward's testimony that the thought never occurred to me while the trial was in progress.

I remember wrestling at the time with the issue of whether to do anything about my revelation. If I'd realized during the trial that I was sponsoring false testimony, I was sure I would have taken immediate steps to rectify it. But now, as I sat on my bunk, the trial was all over. Could I overturn what had already happened? And besides, I rationalized, there was no proof of what Kinney and Seward had cooked up—only my own strong suspicion.

So inertia ruled the day. I didn't nose around to see what I could find out, or have any further contacts with either Kinney or Seward, or approach the president of the court or the ship's executive officer to relate my suspicions. I had to live with the knowledge of my inaction through the law school years that followed. But I found it so troubling that, once I began practice,

I blocked the incident out of my mind—that is, until Wilson's too-glib testimony brought it back with a rush.

Will Wilson stands up, buttons his suit jacket, and starts to leave the witness stand.

And now I realize that the same thing—dressed up in more sophisticated guise—is happening here in a New York courthouse. Instead of two seamen, there's a different cast: Carter, a wealthy individual, desperate to win his case; Wilson, short on funds, appearing out of nowhere with crucial testimony; Carter and Wilson, involuntarily admitting to a "chauffeuring" relationship that could be the conduit for the payoffs. And then Will Wilson, an aspiring actor, pulls it off perfectly, blinding me to what's really going on—until he decides to gild the lily with that "negotiating" stuff. My God, I've been unwittingly sponsoring false testimony!

Back in law school, one thought always comforted me—that I would never let that Kinney thing happen again, especially if I got wind of it while the trial was still in progress. Up to today, the situation hasn't arisen. Now it's here in spades. But I've never worked out in my mind just what I'd do if it happened again. And the matter isn't so simple, in view of the ethical compulsion to zealously represent your client.

Still, I must act. . . . Suddenly, I find myself on my feet. "Excuse me, your Honor, but I'd like to take the witness on redirect."

Judge Redmond seems surprised at this turn of events, but nods and says to the witness, "Stay up here for a bit more, Mr. Wilson." Will turns around and resumes his seat.

Since I don't know for certain that Wilson's testimony was false, I realize there's little I can do at this point about what he has already said. But perhaps I can implant some doubt in the judge's mind about Wilson's testimony by bringing out those subsequent relations.

"Mr. Wilson, have you had any dealings with Mr. Carter since the January 13 date of the conversation you overheard in limo 365?"

Out of the corner of my eye, I can see the expression on Alan Carter's face—puzzlement mixed with impending terror. As for Wilson, whatever reaction he may be experiencing is well-masked by his actor's skill.

"As a matter of fact, yes, I have."

"What were those dealings?" I see Carter's mouth opening and closing, his eyes blazing. Serves him right—buying testimony like this—shades of seaman Kinney!

"I've moonlighted as a chauffeur for Mr. Carter's family on a couple of Saturdays."

"For which services Mr. Carter has paid you well?"

"I don't know about 'well,' but he paid me the going rate of $150 a day."

"And in the course of your chauffeuring duties, you've had occasion to spend some time with Mr. Carter?"

"Yes, a few times, for brief periods, while waiting for his wife."

"And you've had an opportunity to talk with him?"

"Yes, we've talked."

"And you've discussed this case and your testimony?"

"No, we haven't discussed the case. We both treated that subject as off-limits."

The blaze of my indignation has now eased. Given Wilson's carefully modulated answers, I decide it might be best for me to stop here and leave the rest up to my adversary.

"No further questions."

Carol Unger, who evidently didn't know about this and appears chagrined that she hadn't thought to ask, now starts in on the witness with a vengeance. I listen with one ear while trying to work out what else I'm going to do about the situation. Unanswered questions rumble through my mind: Do I dig deeper into this? Do I confront Wilson? Carter? Do I say anything to the judge? What are my ethical obligations to my client—to our system of justice? There are no easy answers, and it's difficult for me to think while Carol Unger is working Wilson over.

Wilson continues to prove unflappable under Carol's questioning, and although she insinuates much, she obtains no damaging admissions from him. When it's over, Judge Redmond looks at her watch—it's 3:00 P.M. and Wilson is the final witness.

The judge calls a fifteen-minute recess, following which the lawyers will present their closing arguments.

I realize that during the recess I'll have to deal with my client. Alan Carter, after all, is seated at the table right next to me. I haven't once looked over at him since I sat down, but the memory of his blazing eyes when I launched into the chauffeuring stuff is still very fresh. Anticipating Alan's fury, I'm wondering how to react. Should I tell him directly why I did it? Do I say I suspect him of bribing the witness?

I don't have long to wait. As soon as the recess begins, Carter turns to me. "Jack," he says, "that was brilliant. I'll admit I was against bringing up the chauffeuring voluntarily, and I was worried sick when you first got into it. But it worked out beautifully—it showed the judge we had absolutely nothing to hide. That's just the kind of smart judgment call I hired you to make for me."

Carter's praise catches me off guard, and I don't know how to respond. Can I now say what I'm really thinking: *No, Alan, that wasn't why I did it. I was trying to impeach Wilson, because I had a sudden realization—based on a similar incident from my Navy days—that you had bribed him to testify falsely.*

My mouth twitches, but the words won't come. I'm a cautious man by nature, and I feel the need for more time to think this through before taking irreparable action. So I bite my tongue and say nothing to Carter about my suspicions. I would have liked to grill Wilson on his unexpected testimony, but he left the courthouse quickly without a word to either of us, so I've missed my chance.

I go off by myself to think, finding an small unoccupied room down the hall. I'd like to consult with one of my partners, but nobody's around. Even if I could locate an unused pay telephone, the short recess isn't enough time to explain the situation sufficiently so as to get a useful reaction. I'm going to have to handle this on my own.

I focus on the immediate problem—what to say in my closing remarks. I can't tell the judge to disbelieve Wilson's testimony— that would be so adverse to my client's interests as to constitute malpractice. In my own mind—inflamed by the Kinney episode of several decades earlier—I'm convinced there's some funny business going on here, but I have no proof of Carter and Wilson conniving.

I ponder the question—what if I knew for sure that Wilson's testimony was false? I certainly couldn't sponsor it—that would be equivalent to lying to the court. I'd have to step up and take my lumps, even if it meant losing the case. . . . Or would I? I recall the nagging doubt I used to have about myself as a teenager—how I'd behave in wartime, prone in a foxhole, being fired at by unseen enemy forces. I realized then that you can't know for sure whether you'd be courageous or a coward until you're actually on the front lines.

And then, all too soon, the time is up, and I have to go back inside the courtroom and make my summation. Almost by default, I end up giving the speech I originally prepared. The only difference is that I dwell less on Wilson's testimony—never even referring to his "negotiating" recollection—and more on other evidence supporting Carter's position.

Judge Redmond then retires to deliberate on her verdict, telling the parties to stay around the courthouse. Carter goes off to make some phone calls, while I resume grappling with my dilemma.

I think about getting some help in deciding what, if anything, to do. I have the time now to place a call to one of my partners—like managing partner Bill Price, or our ethics guru, Dwight Bentley, although I've heard he's been under the weather lately. But I don't make the call. Why not? I must be afraid of what they'll tell me needs to be done. . . .

In the next hour, I manage to come full circle from the outrage I felt in the courtroom. In part, it's the power of inertia—doing nothing is much easier than facing up to angry confrontations with Carter and Wilson, or to the ethical uncertainty of approaching Judge Redmond. And in part—although I'm reluctant to admit this to myself—it's how important the outcome of this case is to my legal career. How sweet a victory would be—how devastating a defeat.

The final part is my lawyer's rationalizing machine, as it swings into high gear. *After all, it's only a suspicion. . . . Maybe*

Wilson did mention the negotiating to me and I forgot. . . . I shouldn't be influenced by something that happened twenty years ago in a completely different world. . . . There's other evidence supporting Carter's version of the events. . . . I gave my adversary every chance to destroy Wilson as a witness, and the man withstood it all. . . . I have ethical responsibilities to my client. . . .

So, to shorten a long and painful story, I don't do a thing. After an hour recess, the judge orders us to reassemble in her courtroom. My heart is beating so rapidly that I'm sure others around me can hear it thump. Carter tries to look confident but is clearly agitated—those drumming fingers give him away.

Judge Redmond starts out with a brief review of the evidence she's heard. As she gets to the conversation in the backseat of the limo, I find myself visualizing one of those weddings in the movies, when the minister says, "If anyone here objects to this union, speak now or forever hold your peace." In the movies, someone in the back row—or, better still, the groom himself—suddenly begins to babble, thereby sidetracking the otherwise inexorable course of the ceremony. But in Judge Redmond's courtroom, this groom's lips remain sealed—while the judge describes how credible she finds Will Wilson's testimony and why it completely undercuts Mickey Trent's case. . . .

The suspense doesn't last long. Judge Redmond announces her verdict in favor of Carter, dismissing Trent's case without awarding him a single dollar of damages.

Alan Carter is thrilled and effusive in his praise for my efforts. I accept his compliments, but frankly I'm in a state of shock. I don't know whether to be happy or saddened. Carter and I shake hands and leave the courtroom separately.

I arrive outside the court building a few minutes later, just in time to see Carter getting into a sedan at the curb. As the car pulls away, I can't help but notice, just above the rear license plate, a decal bearing the number 365.

Commentary on
YOU GOTTA GET ME OFF!

I'm writing a little out of my comfort zone in this story, not being a litigator and never having tried a case in court. But in terms of the flashback Navy incident that's at the heart of the tale—something like that actually happened to me, providing a useful frame of reference.

I always wondered what I'd do if a similar situation arose once I became a real lawyer—although by opting not to litigate, I minimized the chances of its happening. Not entirely, though, because analogous situations can arise for nonlitigating business lawyers.

At any rate, this is *not* a story about how to try a case in court. It's a story about a lawyer who is forced to face up to an ethical dilemma, which happens to arise in the middle of a trial. And keep in mind as we go through this that the tale is being told, in the present tense, by the very lawyer who's in the pickle.

Before getting to the central question posed by the story, I want to comment on some factors I've introduced into the narrative—factors that bear on the ultimate issue but also contain some worthwhile learning on their own.

Jack Lawrence is a litigator who hasn't tried that many cases, doesn't know his client well, is painfully aware of how important the outcome in the *Trent v. Carter* lawsuit is to him personally, and is operating under real time pressure. Let me touch briefly on each of these points.

In large business law firms, most of the litigators don't get to try that many cases. There's a lot of motion practice and the taking of depositions and such, but the great bulk of the lawsuits get settled before trial. So some of the anxiety that Jack Lawrence is feeling, even before being surprised by Will Wilson's "extra" testimony, and his flustered reaction when that occurs, are states of mind that many litigators might experience under similar circumstances. I think those of you in this line of work can appreciate the strain.

Jack doesn't know his client very well—the case came to him via a referral out of left field. If Jack had dealt previously with Alan Carter, he probably would have formed an opinion about his client's basic honesty or dishonesty, and that would have served him well in assessing the veracity of Will Wilson. But *Trent v. Carter* was the first time out for this lawyer-client relationship. So, while Jack's reaction to Carter's evident case of nerves—"giving him the benefit of the doubt"—may be understandable, it forms a doubtful premise on which to base weighty decisions. This doesn't mean that you should stay away from first-time clients—try that and your practice will definitely stagnate. It just means you should be more aware of the limitations that unfamiliarity imposes.

Part of the pressure on Jack here is the significance to him of the trial's outcome. Although the dollars aren't large, the case—involving two well-known figures—has a high profile in the financial community. Jack is convinced that his standing with prospective clients will be boosted by a victory and diminished by a loss. When a lawyer has a lot at stake in the outcome, he or she has to be especially careful not to let that factor unduly influence how important matters are handled, such as the ethical issue in the story. You can draw your own conclusion about the extent to which this affected Jack's response, but it was definitely a factor.

The subject of self-interest is treated in more detail in "The Smell Test" and its commentary. As indicated there—where the issue involves a law firm taking on some questionable new business—this isn't something that's limited to the outcome of litigation. Business lawyers have to face this often, with what's at issue sometimes impacting whether or not a deal gets done, or the price.

Usually when an issue arises like the one in this story, the lawyer has more time to reflect and reach a wise decision on how to proceed. But not always—and remember, this is a *short* story. In order to create dramatic tension, I had to put real time pressure on Jack. From everything I hear, though, business lawyers face extreme time pressures in today's world of technological wonders, with clients demanding instant Blackberry answers and such. So it's not unrealistic for Jack to be in a situation requiring a quick reaction. But generally speaking, unless the answer to the issue posed is quite clear, or the time pressure is real (not the artificial kind), taking time to reflect before giving your views or swinging into action is preferable to a knee-jerk response.

I want to say a few words about the role that inference plays in our legal practice. On many difficult issues that come to our attention, not only isn't the situation clear cut, but we lawyers are rarely in possession of all the facts. Yet we have to act, or refrain from acting, fully realizing that we don't have all the information we'd like to have. ("Father's Day" contains an extended hypothetical dealing with just this fact of life.) To fill in the cracks of our knowledge, we lawyers often turn to drawing inferences.

So, for instance, when Wilson's unexpected additional testimony switches on the light bulb over Jack's head, Jack doesn't know for sure that Wilson is lying. Rather, Jack is drawing a strong inference to that effect, based on the fact that Wilson had never previously mentioned anything about Trent negotiating the price for the shares, and on the further fact that the fresh recollection was so exculpatory of Andy Carter.

Now, to be sure, the ability to draw reasoned inferences is an important skill for a lawyer to possess. We do it all the time, and if we didn't, we wouldn't be as good lawyers as we are. But we have to be careful not to put too much weight on them. Note the dictionary definition of *inference*: "The process of arriving at some conclusion which, though it is not logically derivable from the assumed premises, possesses some degree of probability relative to the premises." I direct your attention to the words "some degree of probability"; that's all an inference is entitled to, and when we award it more, we do so at our peril.

In the story, there's an added factor at work. Jack is drawing an analogy between what happened to him in the Navy way back when and what seems to be happening in the courthouse today. In his mind, this lends weight to the inference he's drawn of shenanigans afoot. Again, this is something we often do but need to be careful about. An analogy can be useful, but the facts always differ to some degree, and you can't place undue reliance on the analogy. If you have any doubts on this score, just read any typical legal brief and observe how the author skewers the precedents relied upon by the opposition—distinguishing the facts, issues, motivations, and so on.

In the story, the trial is the financial world's equivalent of he-said, she-said. Jack went into it not fully convinced that Carter had been telling him the entire truth about his conversations with Trent. Jack admits to having his doubts as to whether Carter gave Trent the "full scoop" on the Burnside contract cancellation. More likely, he thinks, Carter provided just enough of a negative from which Trent could have inferred there was a problem.

But that skepticism didn't deter Jack from proceeding, comforted by several useful rationalizations, to wit: Securities people often converse in oblique terms; it's tough to determine whether what's been said is enough to put someone on notice; Carter was quite certain about having passed along the bad news (and why should a lawyer doubt his client's word?); Trent was angry about having bought the shares, Carter was a handy scapegoat—and presto! Jack has no problem representing Carter's side of the issue.

So, let me put the issue to you:

If you were Jack, would you have been willing to proceed with the defense of Carter, assuming you harbored serious doubts as to whether he had transmitted enough information about the Burnside contract cancellation to put Trent on notice that there was a real problem?

For me, the key here is whether there's honest room for doubt. If I were convinced my client was lying, I wouldn't proceed. (This must be why criminal defense lawyers never pose the question of guilt or innocence to their clients.) But if, after subjecting him to a thorough inquiry and reviewing other evidence, the matter remained unclear, I think I'd go ahead. This, after all, is exactly why we have judges and juries—to sift through conflicting evidence and render judgment. And I have a hunch that if you were able to get litigators to talk candidly about the true feelings they have regarding the stories their clients tell them, Jack's reaction wouldn't be an unfamiliar one.

Later in the story, we're given another crucial fact that Jack didn't allude to in his earlier rationalization. He's worried about the relations between Wilson and Carter *after* the key date of January 13—specifically, Wilson's weekend chauffeuring stints for the Carter family. Jack is especially troubled that he learned about this from Wilson; his client Carter never saw fit to mention it. And Carter's excuse for this seems a little lame.

Jack decides not to disclose the chauffeuring voluntarily in court, on both a litigation strategy basis and as a matter of client relations. Jack would reveal it if his adversary, Carol Unger, were aware of the subsequent contact, because it will be less damaging if brought out voluntarily. But he has no reason to think she knows or has suspicions about it—so, he contends, why undercut his own case? I leave it up to you whether this was a wise litigation judgment or just a handy crutch to support Jack's acquiescence in the "strong preference" Carter expressed to take a chance and not introduce it. So, let me ask this:

Do you agree with Jack's initial judgment not to voluntarily raise the issue of the Carter/Wilson subsequent contacts?

I consider this a close call that could go either way. To proceed against his client's wishes and introduce the subject would expose Jack to some fierce second-guessing from Carter if the judge decided for Trent and cited the chauffeuring as a factor in her decision. On the other hand, the very fact that Carter obviously didn't want it disclosed must have caused Jack to infer that the contacts weren't totally innocent. On balance, I'd probably not raise it unless I began to sense that it was likely to emerge in any event.

At any rate, Carol Unger seems unaware of the chauffeuring as she nears the end of her cross-examination. Then she asks one question too many: *Did you overhear anything else that Messrs. Carter and Trent discussed that day?* The problem here is that this is a question to which she doesn't know the answer. I'm sure litigators could wax eloquent on the lack of wisdom in that move.

Wilson replies with that fishy addenda about Trent trying to negotiate the price down. The good news is that it fits perfectly into the theory of the case Jack is trying to sell to the judge. The bad news is that this is something Wilson had never mentioned to Jack before—something that Wilson must realize makes Carter's case.

Jack's shock at this bombshell revelation causes the Navy incident to pop full-blown into his mind, and the analogy makes him think, "My God, I've been unwittingly sponsoring false testimony!" Jack has always told himself he'd never let that happen again, but he hasn't planned what to do if the situation were to arise. Now that it has erupted, he's forced to think and act quickly, because Wilson is coming down off the witness stand. So, here's' the question:

Do you agree with what Jack decides to do? What would you do in Jack's place at this juncture?

Jack decides to take Wilson on redirect. Since he doesn't know for certain that Wilson's testimony is false, he stays away from what has already been testified to, but opts to bring out the subsequent chauffeuring relationship—"to implant some doubt about Wilson's testimony in the judge's mind."

Well, that's not exactly a noble motive client-wise for Jack to subscribe to, but given the quandary of his situation and the time pressure involved, I think Jack's approach makes sense. He can't go back and try to get his witness to recant what Wilson just testified to under cross-examination. To do nothing would be hugely unsatisfying to Jack, given his state of mind at the moment. So, to introduce the post-incident chauffeuring—with all the possibilities that this opens up in terms of cross-examination and judicial inference-drawing—seems a reasonable alternative that's within Jack's power to accomplish.

As a result of Jack's ire, his redirect questions to Wilson have the negative tone of a cross-examination. But Wilson's answers are calm, and Jack (wisely, I think) sits down once his indignation has eased, leaving the rest up to his adversary.

Jack is left with some big questions. Should he contact Wilson or Carter over this? Should he approach the judge? What are his ethical obligations? Big questions with no easy answers. And it's difficult for him to deal with them while necessarily having to listen to Carol's ongoing cross-examination of Wilson.

When the recess is called, Carter catches Jack off guard—terming his judgment in voluntarily bringing up the chauffeuring to be "brilliant." Jack can't get himself to say that he did it to impeach Wilson, because he suspected—based on something that happened twenty years ago in the Navy, when he wasn't even a lawyer—that Carter had bribed Wilson to testify falsely. Jack decides he needs more time to think things through "before taking irreparable action." Here's a question for you:

What misstep/omission did Jack make/neglect at this point in the proceedings?

My clear answer to this is that Jack badly needed to talk to Wilson about his testimony. But he misses his chance when Wilson leaves the courthouse right away. At the very least, when Will came off the stand, Jack should have told him to stick around during the upcoming recess.

Now Jack goes off by himself to think. Considering the extreme time pressure, he wisely focuses on what to say in his closing remarks fifteen minutes away. Note that he would have liked to consult one of his partners, but bemoans that he probably wouldn't have been able to find an unused pay telephone. Here's where a modern-day cell phone might have come in handy, but remember, we're back in the late 1970s. Besides, he might not have been able to describe the situation sufficiently in such a short time to get a useful reaction. So he decides to handle things on his own.

Jack realizes he can't tell the judge to disbelieve Wilson's testimony, since he has no direct proof of Carter and Wilson conniving. So with the pressure of time, he decides to give much the same speech as he originally prepared—just dwelling more on other evidence in his client's favor and less on Wilson's testimony, and never even referring to Will's "negotiating" recollection. I can't argue with this decision, but you tell me:

Is that what you would have done under these circumstances?

After the closing arguments, when the judge retires to deliberate on her verdict, Jack has more time to reflect on what to do. Now he could call a colleague—perhaps J&P's managing partner, Bill Price, or Dwight Bentley, the firm's ethics guru, both of whom we met in "The Smell Test." This would have been the smart thing to do. It's not just their wisdom and experience that would have proved useful, but also their cool heads—not being caught up, as Jack is, in the middle of the turmoil. Moreover, Jack is a member of a law firm, and since what happens here could obviously reflect on the firm, someone (other than Jack) representing the interests of the firm should be consulted on whatever decision is made.

But Jack doesn't parley with any of his colleagues. And he suspects that the reason he doesn't is his fear of what a partner would tell him needs to be done. This is almost never a worthwhile rationale for declining to do something important—and it's certainly unworthy here. It's time to grow up, Jack. Life can throw you some curve balls, and you have to face up to them squarely— even if the proper response calls for you to do something uncomfortable.

To broaden the situation portrayed here, I should note that for nonlitigators, there are a variety of potentially similar circumstances. Take a securities lawyer handling a prospectus or other disclosure document—what if he doesn't believe some of the "facts" or forecasts his client is feeding him? How about an M&A type whose seller client wants him to dissemble by suggesting to the prospective buyer the existence of other strong bidders—does he indulge in such fictions? Or try a tax expert who has doubts about the validity of his client's claimed deductions—what to do? And for something really painful, read what client Dave Keating makes lawyer George Troy undertake in "The Reluctant Eulogist."

So now we come to the final reckoning in this tale—Jack's decision to do nothing. Take a look at the way Jack got there:

- The power of inertia—doing nothing is easier than facing up to angry confrontations with his client and the witness, to say nothing of the ethical uncertainty of approaching the judge;
- A reluctance to act because of the importance to his career of a victory in this case;
- And then, all that rationalizing—it's only a suspicion, maybe Wilson did mention the negotiating; the old incident shouldn't influence me; other evidence supports Carter's version; Carol Unger couldn't break Wilson down; I have ethical responsibilities to my client.

And I ask you:

What, if anything, would you have done in Jack's situation?

The one thing I know I would have done (in addition to trying to reach Wilson and have him come back to court) is confront the client with my suspicions. Where did that "negotiating" testimony come from? Did you ever discuss this case with Wilson? Does Wilson know that this fits right in with our defense theory? Have any payments (or other things of value) been made or promised to Wilson for his testimony? And so on. I might not gain anything useful, but then again it could help me decide if I had been sponsoring false testimony. Any further steps I'd take would depend on the outcome of such a grilling. But if I couldn't establish that a miscarriage of justice has occurred, I guess I'd reluctantly have to do what Jack did—which is nothing.

Well, anyway, Judge Redmond buys Carter's case and finds for him. Carter is thrilled; Jack's in a state of shock. And then there's the final image—the 365 decal on the sedan that Carter steps into leaving the courthouse. Now, I'm not telling you what to think, but if you're in the mood for inferences, here's a pretty powerful one to draw.

We'll meet Jack Lawrence again, as the central figure in "Sex, Lies, and Private Eyes." In that story, Jack gets involved in some active malfeasance, in contrast with what might be termed his passive nonfeasance in "You Gotta Get Me Off!"—after all, he didn't knowingly sponsor false testimony. This does raise the question of whether one is just an inevitable step up the ladder from the other. . . .

On-the-Job Training

When the dust settled, I came back to my office, sat alone at my desk, and pondered the significance of what I'd witnessed. As I rehashed the events, one unrelated image kept crowding out the others—the image of Muhammad Ali, having lost his heavyweight title to Leon Spinks this past February, winning it back in September.

"Ted, this is Ralph Landry. Can you stop by my office for a few minutes—I've got two new matters I'd like to get you involved in."

That's how it started, one morning less than a month ago—a call from one of the senior Jenkins & Price corporate partners to me, Ted Ashburn, J&P's newest partner.

The whole mess that erupted over my elevation to partnership—with Curt Bell as the villain and Paul Garson as the man caught in the middle—taught me a lot, mostly about telling (and, on special occasions, shading) the truth. But there's so much more I need to learn—like how to handle tough clients or bring in new ones.

So the call from Ralph Landry was welcome. He's a big hitter at the firm, but I had never worked for him before. I knew I'd learn a lot by observing him in action—how to do it and, from what I'd heard, sometimes how *not* to do it.

When I entered his room, Ralph was seated behind his desk, which overflowed with folders, books, papers—the man looked to be operating at 110 percent of capacity. He's in his late fifties, portly, with a ruddy face beginning to wrinkle and thinning black hair combed sideways to cover a big bald spot. In some ways, his appearance and self-important demeanor reminded me of Douglas MacArthur, the general so vividly described by William Manchester in his recent book *American Caesar.*

Ralph looked up, smiled, and put aside the document he'd been reading. "Ted, we haven't spoken recently, but I'm delighted that you've become a partner. We've never had a chance to work together, but I hope I'll now be able to see you in action. Are you involved in anything major that would prevent you from taking on some assignments for me?"

"No, I'm not," I said. "I'd very much enjoy the opportunity to help you out."

"Good. Actually I have in mind two unrelated matters—one large and one small. The small one is negotiating a simple purchase of real estate, but it's for Ken Hellman, one of my good long-term clients. I want to get you involved in several of Ken's projects, and this is a good opportunity for you to get started with him."

"Fine."

"Now let me tell you about the big matter, which is more urgent. Here's the situation. There's a large public company out in Dayton I'm sure you've heard off—Prime Industrials. They've been using a local Ohio law firm all these years. I've known one of their key directors, a man named Pat Duckworth, for half a dozen years—since the Allied deal in 1972. I bailed him out of a bad situation back then, so he owes me big time. I've been working hard on him to use his influence to get us in the door at Prime. But he always says, 'It's not the right time, Ralph—I'll let you know when.'"

Somehow, I doubted that Ralph had called me in to relate his unsuccessful efforts at landing new business. I didn't have to wait long to be proved right.

"Well, just yesterday I got a call from Duckworth, who said, 'Okay Ralph, *now* is the time!' Prime evidently has a big deal coming up, so they've finally decided to go first class and bring in some big-time lawyers. And, of course, Pat recommended me—uh, he recommended Jenkins & Price to do the job." The expression on Ralph's face was half ego gratification, half pedagogue. "Which, I might say, shows the value of persistence in going after business. Given all the times I pestered him, Pat couldn't have passed us by even if he wanted to."

I'd heard that when you worked for Ralph, you had to endure quite a few of these self-congratulatory moments. But hell, if we were getting the Prime Industrials business—a real coup for the firm—he was entitled to gloat. And it did illustrate the need to keep yourself poised to pursue good business when the time became ripe.

But now a look of annoyance furrowed Ralph's brow. "Of course, nothing is ever that simple. It seems that Prime's general counsel, a woman named Cathy Weaver, felt they had to go through a beauty contest before deciding which firm to retain. And the CEO, a guy named Rick Kane who I've met once or twice but can't say I know well, went along with Cathy. So we're in a goddamn competition. . . ."

Then, in an instant, Ralph's annoyed look was replaced by one of resolve and confidence. "Of course, it's ultimately Rick Kane's decision, not Ms. Weaver's. And my guy Duckworth has Kane's ear—you know why?" He didn't wait for an answer. "Because Pat was head of the search committee of Prime's board of directors that hired Kane for his job! So, even though we have to go through the motions here, we're in good shape to end up the winner."

Watching Ralph in action, I found myself wondering if I'd ever achieve this guy's degree of self-confidence—although if so, I'd prefer to go a little easier on the arrogance quotient. . . .

Ralph went on. "Duckworth also leaked to me the names of the two other firms in the beauty contest, but told me not to let on to Cathy Weaver that I know who they are. One is the Jackson firm here, and the other is the Anderson firm in Chicago. Hell, we can take those guys with one hand tied behind our back.

I happen to know things about both firms that would keep any sensible company from ever retaining them. . . ."

That last remark intrigued me, but I could tell Ralph was in no mood to go off on a sideline. So I just nodded my head and gave him a knowing look, feigning my awareness of whatever dirt he had on the two firms.

Ralph continued. "Now, Ted, here's why I asked you to stop by today. First of all, assuming we land Prime as a client, I'd like you to work with me on the deal—to be my number one deputy. Second, I want you to help me pull together the presentation we have to make for the beauty contest. And the third reason is that I have to return a call to Cathy Weaver, who phoned earlier when I was out. I've never spoken to her. She probably wants to give us formal notice that we're in the contest and describe the procedure. I'd like to introduce you as a key member of our team, since you'll probably be dealing with her over the next few weeks. So let's make the call."

When the connection was made, Ralph turned on his speaker phone, which I gathered was his usual mode of communicating long distance.

After some initial pleasantries and Ralph's introduction of me, Cathy Weaver said, "Ralph, as you know from Pat Duckworth, we've decided to hire new counsel for a major event coming up. We're considering several firms, including Jenkins & Price. We hear good things about your firm from Pat, who has recommended you highly."

Cathy had the businesslike tone of someone who knows exactly what she's doing. She'd obviously become aware of Pat's extracurricular communication to Ralph, and she let Ralph know it.

"Thank you, Cathy," said Ralph. "We appreciate being invited to take a crack at persuading you that we're the best firm for the assignment. Jenkins & Price would like very much to represent Prime, and, of course, Ted and I think we could do an excellent job for you."

"I'm sure you could," said Cathy. "I'd like you to come out to Dayton to meet with me and my senior colleagues in the general counsel's office. I also hope that our top executives—the CEO, the COO, perhaps the CFO—could drop by while you're here, at least to say hello. Would next week—say, Tuesday, November 7—be a good date for you?"

Ralph consulted the calendar on his desk. He didn't consult me. "That's good."

"I'll call you or Ted later with the details—what time, where to come, etc. Right now, unfortunately, I'm late for a meeting."

"We look forward to hearing from you."

"By the way," said Cathy, "your partner, Susan Collins, and I are old friends—we roomed next to each other during our last year in college. The two of us stayed up late many a night discussing whether or not to become lawyers. We see each other at reunions, but I haven't spoken to her for a while. How is she?"

"Just fine," replied Ralph. "She's in good health and doing very well at the firm. . . . Now, I think we should plan to take the early morning flight on the seventh, so that we have the better part of the day and can still get the last flight out later that afternoon."

"My secretary has all the information on that—I'll have her get in touch with you. Please give Susan my warmest regards. Bye now."

Hey, I thought, this is a terrific break for us, in terms of landing the Prime business. Susan Collins is a first-rate lawyer—one of the up-and-coming stars in our department and the only female corporate partner—and Cathy obviously has genuine affection for her. Clearly, we had a secret weapon that our competitors were unlikely to be able to match.

I remarked on this to Ralph, but he didn't reply, busying himself jotting some notes on a pad. When he finished writing, we spoke briefly about preparing for the beauty contest, but I could see he was impatient to get on to other matters. He said we'd be going to Ken Hellman's office that afternoon to discuss the real estate deal, and he would brief me in the cab on the way over.

We were seated in Ken Hellman's modest, rumpled office. Hellman, who I'd never met, is a large man whose short-sleeved shirt revealed muscular forearms. I had heard him described as a self-made wheeler-dealer with rough edges. Ralph introduced me as a new partner he wanted to get involved in Ken's legal work.

After a minute's discussion of general matters, Hellman leaned forward across his desk and said, "All right, that's enough foreplay. I've got two expensive lawyers sitting here, and I can hear your meters ticking away."

Ralph acknowledged the meter reference with a tight smile. I pulled a yellow pad from my briefcase.

Hellman spoke in a gruff voice, "Let's review the situation. As you know, I want to buy this property out on the Island that the locals call 'Old Mill Run.' It's owned by a guy named Charles Deane. When I contacted Deane last week, he said he hadn't contemplated selling it, but if I were interested, I should have my lawyer call his." Hellman leaned back in his chair. "Ralph, you take it from there."

"All right. So I telephoned Deane's lawyer, Peter Winters, who I don't know. Winters told me that because the property wasn't for sale, there was no asking price. If we're interested in it, he said, we ought to make a bid. But he warned that unless we're prepared to start the bidding with a number 'in eight figures,' as he put it, we shouldn't even bother coming around."

"I assume the reference to 'eight figures' was his code for an initial bid of at least $10 million?" Ken asked.

"That's right." Now Ralph's voice changed from that of a narrator to a negotiator. "But here's how I see it. While we can't ignore the warning entirely, to me it's simply part of the negotiating dance. You don't have to comply. If we come in with a reasonable first bid—even if it's not as robust as what they've signaled—coupled with a good argument as to why that's all the property is worth, but indicating a willingness to bargain, my experience has been that most sellers will counter. And then the negotiation will be under way."

"Thanks for your expertise, counselor," said Ken, although I didn't detect gratitude in his voice. "My gut comes out in the same place—especially since $10 million happens to be the price at which I'd like to buy Old Mill Run. So I certainly don't want to start the bidding there."

"Amen." Ralph seemed pleased at Ken's reaction to his advice. "But before we decide where to start out, let me ask you the key question. If you can't get the property at the price you want to pay, how far are you willing to stretch beyond that?"

Hellman didn't hesitate. "Oh, not very far at all. In fact, the $10 million is just about my upper limit."

Ralph's voice turned more serious. "Let me make sure I understand. What you're saying is that the price you'd like to pay and your outside limit are the same number?"

"That's right."

Ralph paused to take a sip from his coffee cup. A thought suddenly occurred to me and I used the lull to say, "I just want to make sure—"

"Okay," said Ralph, cutting me off in midsentence, his voice now all business. "I suggest we make an opening offer of $9 million. It's a respectable number, even though it ignores their 'eight figure' message. I'd like to have some financial backup— comparables and such—to provide a plausible rationale for the offer. Can your people get me that, Ken?"

"We'll work something up."

"Good. Apparently, Charles Deane prefers the negotiations to take place between lawyers. Is that all right with you?"

"It is."

"Then I'll convey our $9 million offer to Deane's lawyer, Peter Winters. And, without demeaning it, I'll suggest with some subtlety that you're not at your limit."

"Although I'm pretty close to it—"

"Of course, of course. . . ."

In the cab returning to our office, Ralph Landry suddenly chuckled.

"What's funny?" I asked.

"Ted, you've just witnessed the classic case of a client who won't level with his own lawyer."

"How so?"

"That $10 million figure—it may be the price that Ken would *like* to get Old Mill Run for, but in no way is it his top dollar. He's got more in his pocket—I'd bet anything on it."

I could tell that Landry was itching to educate me on a fine point of negotiating, so I helped him along. "Then why'd he say that $10 million was his top?"

Ralph smiled benignly. "It's just a little game that clients like to play with their lawyers—in fact, that all business people play with their advisors or representatives. When you serve as an agent—which is what we lawyers are—you get used to it. I don't think of it as lying or consider it venal—it's merely a case of the client not taking the lawyer into his confidence."

I continued as Ralph's straight man. "But what makes clients do that?"

"What indeed?" From Landry's expression, I could see him thinking, Puck-like, *Lord, what fools these clients be* . . . "I guess it's because they're concerned that once we know what the truth is—for a buyer client, his real top number; for a seller client, his actual bottom line—then, in our zeal to make the deal, we'll immediately zoom to the limit without even attempting to negotiate a better price." He snorted at the absurdity of it all. "They must unconsciously equate lawyers with investment bankers, brokers, and others who work on a contingent fee basis—who have a direct monetary interest in seeing a deal get done regardless of the price."

I nodded my head and made a little murmur to acknowledge this facet of client simple-mindedness.

"So, what you find is that your client likes to keep something in reserve—a little extra gas in the tank, so to speak. He figures that what you don't know won't hurt you, and that on the basis of what you've been told, you'll bargain harder to make the deal at a good price."

I decided to take a tentative step toward turning this tutorial into a dialogue. "Well, I can see why that line of reasoning has some appeal for them. I mean, it's always seemed to me—"

"It has some appeal—which is why they do it," said Landry, effectively relegating me once more to interlocutor status. "But what they don't realize is that it can produce bad results in the negotiations—bad results that would be avoidable if the client were more candid."

Ralph paused, as if to admire his own handiwork. "Look, in order to negotiate effectively for a client, I need to know his ultimate tolerance for pain. It helps me decide the right level to kick off the bargaining, how to characterize the other side's response, what moves we should make after that, and so on. Conversely, *not* knowing it impedes my ability to predict how things are going to turn out—a very important function for an advisor."

Well, I figured, I might as well feed Landry the ultimate straight line. "So, Ralph, if it's so vital, what can you do about it?"

"Well, with Ken, I didn't want to push the issue just yet. It's a very delicate subject, and good timing is essential. But I do intend to take my shot if, as I suspect, the other side comes back at a much higher level. . . . Just watch, Ted, and you'll learn something valuable."

At the end of the day, I stopped by the office of Susan Collins. She's one of my favorites at the firm—a clear-eyed brunette in her late thirties with a friendly open disposition. I'd heard word around the office that she had had an affair with our partner Dan Barton after his marriage broke up, but it evidently didn't last.

When I relayed Cathy Weaver's greetings, Susan replied, "Thanks, Ted, but Ralph already called to let me know."

"So I assume he'll want to pick your brain on how best to make our pitch."

"Well, he didn't say anything about that. I offered to be of help, of course. Ralph said he'd get in touch if he needs anything."

"Surely, though, a call from you to Cathy would be in order under the circumstances."

"I would think so, and I volunteered to do that, but he told me not to."

This all seemed very strange to me. I felt I knew Susan well enough to ask her, "Hey, what's going on here? Don't you and Ralph get along?"

Susan shrugged. "We get along reasonably well. He's not an easy guy to get close to, but we've never had any problems."

"Well, then, I'm sure Ralph will come around and make use of your contact. I'll speak to him"—and then added, as I saw the first inkling of a frown come over her face—"without making it seem like it's coming from you." Her expression relaxed. I was learning.

As I thought about this later that day—wondering why Ralph didn't take the logical step of getting Susan "on the team" for the Prime project—it occurred to me that maybe *I* was the problem. Ralph might have thought that if Susan came aboard, we'd be too top-heavy with three partners—and he didn't want to bump me off, now that he'd asked me in. But hell, I didn't really care if I was on this deal or not—there were plenty of other assignments around. So I decided to make Ralph aware of that and take him off the hook.

"I've been thinking about this," I said to him the next morning in his office. "We'd be in a much stronger position to get the Prime business with Susan on the team, in view of her past relationship with Cathy Weaver. But if you think that would make us too top-heavy with three partners, I'm willing to drop off, since I don't bring anything special to the table."

"No," said Ralph quickly. "I want you as my number two in handling that big deal they've got in the works."

"Well, I appreciate the vote of confidence. But even if she's not on the team, Susan could still be helpful to us in the beauty contest. For example, with the opening that Cathy gave us, it would be perfectly natural for Susan to make a phone call to her—"

"No, no, I don't like the idea of Susan phoning her now. It might look like we're trying to do an end run around the process Cathy has set up."

I didn't get that at all. End run? What was he talking about? Cathy practically invited a call from Susan by invoking those warm memories of college days and then noting, almost wistfully, that they hadn't spoken of late. But I realized it wouldn't be wise to press the point with Ralph right now.

"Well," I said, "at least Susan can give us some insights into how to deal with Cathy—what are her likes, her dislikes, her hot buttons, and so forth."

Ralph gave me one of those looks that said, hey, junior, don't presume to tell *me* how to land new business. "Look, the reality is that Cathy Weaver is *not* the key figure here. She's just coordinating things, but Rick Kane—the CEO—is the one who will make the ultimate decision. And he's going to be influenced in our direction by Pat Duckworth. That's who Kane will listen to—his boss on the board, not his employee in the general counsel's office."

It was clear that, for Ralph, this ended the discussion. But I was left with an uneasy feeling. Far be it for me to question a proven rainmaker like Ralph Landry on how best to hustle new business, but I must say that his views seemed out of date. They harked back to the days when the post of inside general counsel was more ornamental than substantial, and totally ignored the power GC's were now starting to wield with respect to the choice of outside lawyers.

Later that day, I placed a call to Ed Sinclair, the junior lawyer who is my counterpart in the Deane camp. He didn't know who I was, so I went a little overboard with my opening line.

"I'm calling on behalf of Ralph Landry, who represents Ken Hellman, to set up a meeting with Peter Winters, with regard to negotiating the purchase of the Old Mill Run property owned by Charles Deane."

"Wow, that's a mouthful," Sinclair replied. "Actually, I've been expecting your call. Peter is available at our office at 3:00 P.M. tomorrow, if that's convenient for Landry."

"Yes, that'll be fine."

"If you guys want everything to be fine," said Sinclair, "tell Landry to bring along a bushel-basket of money. Deane has a sentimental attachment to Old Mill Run, and he doesn't need to dispose of it—in fact, he had no intention of selling before Hellman raised the subject. So, it's going to take a very healthy price to get him to part with his baby. . . . So long."

After he hung up, I thought of a dozen clever replies I might have made to Sinclair's posturing—but at the time, I wasn't quick enough to come up with anything more than my tepid version of a snort. What, for instance, is less than a bushel—a peck? My riposte could have been, "He'll have a peck-basket with him." I've got to learn to think faster on my feet. . . .

Later on that day, I decided to have another talk with Susan Collins. But she cut me off before I got very far.

"Look, Ted, I know you're trying to be helpful, but you're treading on dangerous ground here. This is Ralph's call. We're only in the beauty contest because of his buddy on the Prime board. I certainly didn't have any success getting business from Cathy, although from time to time—in my more subtle fashion—I let her know we were interested. I've offered to help Ralph, but if he doesn't want any assistance, so be it."

"I hear you, but hey, a little call from you to Cathy on the sly wouldn't hurt."

"No, I can't do that, now that Ralph has told me not to. If I called, and then we *didn't* get the business, he'd blame it on my meddling in the process."

Susan took an incoming call from a client. While she was talking, my mind went to work in an unfamiliar area. I'm such a neophyte on the subject of internal firm politics and firm finances. Oh, I'd heard some stories, of course, but I lacked direct experience—a little like a kid who's been told the rudiments of sex but hasn't yet tried out the real thing.

At that moment, though, it became clear what this was all about—money, and to some degree, status. And I realized that this is the place to look when partners do or say something that, at first glance, appears weird.

The key in this case was the way Jenkins & Price determines each partner's share of the profits. The system is complicated and judgmental, but here's the gist. The credit for revenue received from a particular client is allocated among the partner who is responsible for bringing in the business (the "originating" partner), the partner who supervises the client's overall activity and sends out the bills (the "billing" partner), and the partner who's in charge of performing the legal services for the client (the "services" partner).

What had become obvious was that, in terms of Prime, Ralph wanted to be *all three* of those partners. He didn't want the powers-that-be to think that landing the Prime business represented a joint effort by Ralph and Susan. That's why he wouldn't let her call Cathy and even declined to consult Susan on how to deal with the general counsel. If Ralph was the sole originating partner, then he'd undoubtedly be the sole billing partner. And he didn't want Susan on the working team, because her presence—as contrasted with mine, too junior to matter—would dilute his credit as the services partner.

So, having figured it all out, I smiled knowingly when Susan got off the phone and said to her, "Okay, I know what's going on. But if Ralph won't deign to pick your brain, then how about just advising me—your old buddy—on how to deal with Cathy Weaver."

She hesitated for a moment and then said. "I will, but only if you promise not to tell Ralph that you got any information from me."

I could see that Susan had her guard up. She undoubtedly realized that Ralph would not be a good enemy to have at the firm. So I made the promise to her, and she then proceeded to give me some good dope about Cathy—what kind of person she was, her likes and dislikes, and such. One comment, in particular, hit home.

"At a college reunion a few years ago, Cathy and I stayed up late having a real heart-to-heart, mostly about the practice of law. As Prime's general counsel, Cathy has to deal with a lot of outside law firms who are trying to hustle her for business. The lawyers who turn her off, she said, are the ones who boast about how good they are, about what big deals they've done, and so on. For Cathy, modesty is a real virtue. And another thing she touched on that night—she hates to hear one firm run down another firm. That kind of badmouthing is anathema to her."

I let out a big breath. "This could be a problem for us," I said. "Let's face it, bragging is Ralph's stock in trade. And he's already outlined for me how he intends to dump on those other beauty contest entrants, now that he's found out from his buddy Duckworth who they are."

"That would not be wise," said Susan. "But remember, you can't tell Ralph you got that insight from me."

I could see this wasn't going to be easy. . . .

It was the morning after Landry's meeting with Charles Deane's lawyer. Ralph had called me into his office.

"Well," he said, "the good news is that Winters didn't boot me off the premises for not coming in with an eight figure number."

Ever the dutiful straight man, I asked, "What's the bad news?"

"The bad news is that, after chiding me for not meeting their precondition—which I'd anticipated—Winters countered with a strong $13 million."

"What do you mean by 'strong'?"

"Oh, you know"—and here Ralph's voice changed, apparently mimicking the other lawyer's tone—"'Deane's real price is $15 million, but he'd be willing to sell it for $13 million if Hellman is prepared to pay all cash, sign a contract with no contingencies . . .' and so on."

I decided to risk a substantive comment. "Well, that's bad, but not as bad as—"

"Wait, there's worse to come. After Ken approached him about selling Old Mill Run, Deane decided to get some competitive bids. They began shopping it and, according to Winters, have already been able to generate a good deal of serious interest. So, if that $10 million figure is Ken's real limit, we've got a problem."

"I can see that. It does strike me, though, that—"

Ralph cut me off. "Ted, this is one of the most difficult tasks a lawyer is called upon to do—telling a client that if he really wants the deal, he'll have to stretch beyond what he'd like to pay for it. Fortunately—or unfortunately, depending on how you look at it—this is something that, over the course of my career, I've been forced to become expert at. . . . So give Ken a call, and make a date for us to go over to his place. And then just watch old Ralph do his thing."

Back in my office, I phoned Hellman to set up the appointment. He was available that afternoon. Then, to my surprise—I thought I was invisible to him—he schmoozed a little and even tried to get a preview. "Well, do you have good news for me?"

I was leery about stealing Landry's thunder. "Since I wasn't at the meeting with Deane's lawyer, I'd prefer to let Ralph characterize it for you."

An hour later, Ralph and I went over the presentation we'd be making in Dayton. Actually, it was more about what *he* was going to say. Ralph had carved out one minor role for me— just so they'd know I wasn't mute—but this was going to be his show.

"So, after your segment, Ted, comes the part when I really get to blow our horn—talk about our experience, our depth, all the big deals we've done in recent years. And then I'll contrast our skills with those other bogus firms we're competing against—without, of course, letting on that I know who our competition is."

Here goes, I thought—it's now or never. "Ralph, if I may make a suggestion—"

"By all means."

"I've been talking with Cathy Weaver on the phone, making arrangements for our trip and such. I'm starting to get a feel for her style. I just have a hunch she's the kind of person who might not appreciate having us blow our own horn."

"Did she say that?"

"No, not in so many words."

"Well, then, my basic operating premise is not to hide your light under a bushel. When you've got something good to sell, hawk it loud and clear."

I played my last card. "I also got a sense that Cathy might react unfavorably to our badmouthing the other guys."

"Nonsense," said Ralph, with a dismissive wave of his hand. "Listen, everyone says they don't like to indulge in negatives—politicians are the most blatant example—but then they go right ahead and wade in. Those other firms would be doing it to us if they knew we were in the running. The fact is, a well-handled badmouthing can influence people mightily, even if they pretend it doesn't. The negatives you provide get through to their brains, if only subliminally, and then stick. Just look at what the Republicans are saying about Jimmy Carter. . . ."

I was itching to reveal that I'd gotten this advice from the horse's mouth, but I had given Susan my word. . . . So, I tried a different tack.

"You may well be right. But I've got an idea—why don't we run my notion past Susan Collins, who may have some insight on the subject?"

Ralph reacted sharply. "I've made my decision. Now let's move on."

At that point, I realized I'd better back off.

That afternoon, in Hellman's office, Ralph was completing his report on the meeting with Peter Winters.

"And so, Ken, that's the substance of what happened. We now have a choice as to what to do next. I must say, however, that with $10 million as your top number, none of the alternatives are particularly appetizing."

Ken frowned and replied with some impatience. "I told you, $10 million is what I want to pay for the property."

Ignoring Ken's tone, Ralph came on as smooth as silk. "I heard you. But just bear with me a few minutes while I run down the various negotiating possibilities. First, we could stick at our $9 million level for the moment, tell Deane his $13 million figure is ridiculous, and try to get him to bid against himself. That's a real hardball approach, though, and given the fact that he's out there talking to other possible buyers, it raises a real risk of our blowing any chance of a deal."

Ken gave a little nod, which I took as his way of acknowledging the riskiness of that alternative.

"On the other hand, we could go up to $9.5 million, which provides us with at least one more move to the $10 million level. This is less risky than sticking, but. . . ."

"But what?" asked Ken.

"Well, it deliberately defies Deane's eight figure minimum, which they've now made a lot more explicit. So, it may put them in a spot where they feel they have to break off the bargaining to save face."

Ken didn't nod this time, which suggested to me that he wasn't convinced on this score.

"The third possibility is to go all the way to $10 million on this round, clearly labeling it as our final bid. We'd have to muster up some special sincerity for Deane and Winters to believe us. Otherwise, they'll assume that no matter what words we use, you still have more dollars in your pocket. This requires real discipline in order to maintain the credibility of our position.

So, for instance, if they were to counter at, say, $12 million, we'd have to reject that without raising our $10 million bid even a penny."

I took Ken's slight wince as signaling a negative reaction to this course of action.

Landry, now gaining steam, continued his exegesis. "Understand, I would never advise you to take this last path if your actual top number is higher than $10 million. In that case, it would be a bluff. I don't like bluffs—and although there's always some chance one might work, in this case, I doubt it."

Ralph leaned forward, apparently to emphasize the significance—or, to his mind, the brilliance—of what he was about to say. "Actually, although it seems somewhat counterintuitive, the *worst* possible outcome for us in this last scenario is that they do, in fact, believe $10 million to be our limit—but they're just unwilling to sell at that price. Then, without ever getting back to us, they turn around and sell the property to one of those other guys they're talking to—at a number a little north of $10 million, a number that you would have been willing to pay!"

Ken sat there, doodling on his desk pad. I was impressed with Laundry's analysis—this guy is no dummy. Then, after a pause to let his insight sink in, Ralph moved into high gear. "And that's why it's so important for me to know what your real limit is. Look, if $10 million is all you're willing to pay, then we'll proceed along the lines of one of those three approaches I just outlined. But frankly, I don't think it's realistic for us to expect to succeed at the $10 million level. I don't see Deane as a seller at that price. And now that he's drummed up some competition for the property, the leverage has definitely swung in his direction."

Ralph paused again—hoping, I guess, for a reaction—but Ken remained expressionless. So Ralph continued.

"By contrast, if you were willing to go up to, say, $11 million, there would be a much higher likelihood of making the deal. We could put in a $10 million bid—which satisfies their eight figure condition—without having to characterize it as a final offer. Oh, sure, we could dress it up so as to suggest that moving to that level has been sheer agony—but at least the other side will realize that the negotiation is still alive."

With Ken still giving no responsive sign, Ralph went on. "Our hope would be that Deane then comes down between $11 and $12 million. For instance, he might drop to $11.5 million, characterizing it as 'splitting the difference' between his $13 and our $10 million, It's a little premature to offer a split, though, and since we would still be at $10 million while he's shown his willingness to go to $11.5 million, we'd have a good shot at getting the property for under $11 million."

I had the sense from Ken's lack of response that he might have gotten a little lost in Ralph's analysis, so I decided to express the same idea in a simpler fashion. "You know, another helpful way to look at it is that—"

But Landry was in no mood for interruptions. "Listen, Ken, I hope you don't feel that if you tell me your real number, I'll zoom right to it in the negotiations. On the contrary, I'll make every effort to buy Old Mill Run for you at a lesser price, if that's possible. But this way, by knowing what I have to work with, I won't lose the deal by sticking prematurely at a level that's less than what you're willing to pay for the property."

Finally, Ken spoke up in response, shaking his head from side to side in apparent resignation. "Well, it goes against my grain, but if the best you can do is $11 million, I'd still make the deal at that level . . . But not a penny more."

"That's a good decision," said Ralph, whose facial expression could only be described as beaming. "Don't worry, I'll bring home the bacon. I intend to meet with Deane's lawyer right after I get back from that Dayton trip I was telling you about."

As we left Ken's office, I was thinking how shrewdly Ralph Landry had handled the situation. I may have had reservations about him on a personal level, but give the guy his due—he went to the meeting with a purpose, had a well-thought-out game plan, encountered a tough nut to crack, and yet pulled the whole thing off in under fifteen minutes.

I would have come to those conclusions myself, but Ralph didn't give me much time to get there. In the cab heading back to the office after the meeting with Ken, he was figuratively prancing. "Did you see how I—" and "When Ken grunted, I realized I had to—" and "At which point, I came in for the kill—" and so on. He made sure I didn't miss a single nuance of his performance.

After our meeting with Ken, I called Ed Sinclair to set up Landry's next meeting with Winters for the day after our Dayton trip.

"Let me give you a heads up," Sinclair said, in almost a conspiratorial tone. "When we talk about a number in eight figures, that means $10 million *for openers*. There's now a lot of interest in this property. Your guy implied that $10 million was going to be his top number, but he better be prepared to move up from there in the bargaining, or he's not gonna end up with Old Mill Run."

A sudden fear came over me. If Charles Deane believed we wouldn't go higher than $10 million, and if one of those other bidders was already over that number, Deane might sell to the other bidder without even bothering to come back to us to test our resolve.

"Don't worry," I replied, "we have a certain amount of flexibility."

Later, I pondered whether I'd done the right thing. Was I being properly cautious in trying to preempt a real risk, or did I just panic and blurt out something that could undercut our negotiating position? It concerned me enough that I decided not to mention the byplay to Ralph.

The next day, Ralph and I went out to Dayton to spend several hours in a spacious conference room. Cathy Weaver brought along two of her assistants, and at various times during the meeting, the top Prime executives popped in for a few moments to say hello. When Rick Kane, the CEO, completed his short visit and was about to leave, Ralph said—very pointedly, for all to hear—"Please give my best regards to Pat Duckworth." I winced at the transparency of the message, but that's Ralph for you.

How can I describe Ralph's presentation? It was, shall we say, over the top. He's very brainy and articulate, I'll grant him that, but his style is so forceful that I worried how it was playing with Cathy and her aides. I watched them sitting there stony-faced as Ralph thundered on.

"So now, let me tell you about the various deals over $100 million that Jenkins & Price has done in the last three years. . . ."

Later on, Ralph went into attack mode, along these lines. "In this age of high morality, you want to associate with a firm like ours that has never been tainted in the slightest fashion. It's not something you can take for granted anymore. There are other firms in our fair city that can't make the same claim—and as a result, the value they bring to clients is severely compromised."

Now I realized what Ralph was up to. It was common knowledge that the Jackson firm, one of our competitors for the assignment, had recently defended a suit brought by an aggrieved client on conflict of interest charges—and the word was that the ultimate settlement figure reached well into the millions.

Ralph went on. "I don't know what other firms you're considering, but if any are from Chicago, there's something you should be aware of. Even the best of the Chicago firms, such as"—and here Ralph named three firms other than Anderson— "don't have the level of sophistication or extensive contacts of a leading New York firm like ours. As for the lesser Chicago firms, such as"—and here Ralph did name Anderson, sandwiched in between two decidedly inferior firms—"well, to be frank, it's not much of a step up above your present representation in Dayton."

Ralph, completely ignoring Cathy's negative reaction here— she was looking down at her fingernails, eyes half closed, lips pursed tight—kept on with a point-by-point indictment of just about every major law firm in the land, but always including something that indirectly tarnished the two other contenders.

I shuddered during this monologue, closing my eyes and trying to look on the bright side. Ralph's presentation about our firm was admirable in many ways—the kind of stuff a lot of clients eat up. And I have to admit that much of what I find off-putting about Ralph's style probably appeals to tough executives, who are looking for a lawyer strong enough to stand up vigorously for their interests. But what I could see with real clarity was that you had to tailor your pitch to the specific prospective client—what might work in some circles could well be anathema in others.

Our presentation, which seemed to go on forever, finally ended. We answered a few innocuous questions on our billing practices and the like. Cathy then thanked us for coming out and said she'd let us know the outcome in a few days.

While Ralph made a detour to the men's room, Cathy took me aside and said, "Ralph Landry is a very smart guy, I can see that, but he's so relentlessly negative about other law firms. Is that a shared trait of Jenkins & Price partners—are you all cut from the same cloth?"

I smiled, and rolled my eyes a little, signaling that I was on her wavelength and she didn't need to be concerned about the firm. "No, that's just Ralph's style. We're all competitive, but most of us are less out front about it. For instance, I've never heard your friend, Susan Collins, utter a negative word about anyone."

In the cab heading to the airport, Ralph seemed quite pleased with himself. "Well," he said, turning to me, "I guess we really showed them what a world-class beauty contest presentation is all about, didn't we?" At that moment, I got the feeling that the purpose behind my presence in Dayton was more as an observer of Ralph's technique than as a participant—so that, assuming we got the assignment, I could report back to the other partners how effective Ralph had been.

I managed to nod my head in the affirmative, although I had real trepidation as to our chances of winning.—especially after my sidebar chat with Cathy, which I decided not to mention to Ralph.

Two days later, which was yesterday, Ralph held his negotiation on the Old Mill Run deal. Early today, Landry's secretary called to tell me Ralph had arrived at the office and wanted to see me. He was seated at his desk when I entered the room.

"How did it go?" I asked.

"Just great," said Ralph, rising from his desk. "Here's a twenty-second recap." He circled the room as he spoke.

"I came in at $10 million, making a lot of noise about how hard it had been to get Hellman up into eight figures, and hoping we could make the deal at that level. But Winters wouldn't even consider it. He seemed convinced that, having crossed the $10 million bar, Hellman had a lot more in his pocket, and he bargained accordingly. . . . I wonder where he might have gotten that notion?"

Fortunately, Ralph was standing behind me as he spoke, so I didn't have to meet his gaze. Unfortunately, I knew where the notion had come from.

"Anyway," Ralph continued, "Winters countered at $12 million. I expressed my 'abject disappointment.' After some fencing, he said, 'We can get this done in the 11s.' I replied, 'No way. If it's going to get done, it'll be in the 10s.' Then there was a lot of back and forth, and we finally struck a deal at $10.8 million."

This was good news indeed. "Congratulations, Ralph—you pulled it off, just like you told Ken you would."

Ralph was really strutting now—his expression seeming to reflect how deserving he considered my praise. "I've advised Ken, and, of course, he's thrilled. It was the $200,000 savings below his top price that gave him a real kick, as I knew it would. It also proved my point that he shouldn't be worried about me zooming to the limit right away. . . . Anyway, give Ken a call to find out what his plans are about the financing arrangements. Then call Deane's counsel to discuss the schedule and the paperwork. We'll need a real estate partner to do the documents, so let's get Lou Struthers working on it."

When I reached Ken Hellman on the phone, I said, "I'm delighted you were able to end up with the Old Mill Run, even though you had to spend a little more than you would have liked."

"That's no problem," Ken replied. "Hell, I would have gone to $12 million if I needed to."

This took me aback. But then, a few minutes later, I got a double whammy when I called Ed Sinclair, my counterpart on the seller's legal team.

I started out by saying, " I'm glad the deal got done with our guy and not with one of those other bidders."

"Just between us," said Sinclair, "your guy was the *only* guy."

I was stunned. Unsure of how to reply to this candid disclosure, I said, "Well, at least the price was right."

Sinclair didn't hesitate. "It was right for Deane. I probably shouldn't tell you this, but—notwithstanding the stuff I said to you on the phone that day—Deane would have taken $10 million. We never could figure out why your guy felt the need to overpay."

So now I had a problem—namely, should I be the bearer of bad tidings to Ralph Landry? Could I risk him shooting the messenger?

I couldn't deny that there would be something delicious about spilling the beans—just to knock this pompous strutter off his high horse. Sure, he was a wily negotiator, and I learned a lot from watching him in action—particularly in terms of a lawyer dealing with his own client. But the deeper lesson was to be leery of making assumptions about others—particularly assumptions that exalt your own sense of self-importance— when you can't know for certain what's going on in someone else's mind.

But shattering pomposity wasn't enough of a reason to speak up. Hey, if reporting these two bombshells back to the man served some useful purpose, I wouldn't have hesitated to open my mouth. But here, the deal was already done— the negotiation was over. It wasn't as if Landry needed the information I got from Sinclair to help plan the next step in the bargaining. As for Hellman, while the news that he plays his cards close to the vest might be valuable for future client dealings, Ralph was perfectly capable of discovering that on his own.

And there was also the issue of my having unwittingly conveyed information to the other side that undercut any credibility we might have mustered up in trying to stick at $10 million. For me to repeat Sinclair's remark now would only serve to refocus Ralph on his puzzlement—why did Winters seem to know we had more in our pocket?—at which time, the finger might point more directly at me.

So I decided not to say anything about these revelations to Landry. It would just remain my own juicy knowledge—at best, the subject of a good yarn to be told to a couple of colleagues some late night over a beer.

An hour ago, I was summoned to a meeting in Landry's office to discuss the Old Mill matter with Ralph and Lou Struthers, the real estate partner who would be handling the details of the transaction.

I arrived outside Ralph's office a little early for the meeting. Lou wasn't there yet. A temp I knew was sitting in for Ralph's regular secretary, and we chatted at her desk in the hallway outside the office. At one point, the phone rang. She answered it and buzzed Ralph, saying. "Pat Duckworth is on the line." I couldn't see Ralph from where I was standing—and although I wasn't sure, I didn't think he could see me out there—but I could hear Duckworth's voice coming clearly over the speaker phone.

"Ralph, I've got some good news for you—Cathy Weaver is prepared to select your firm as Prime's counsel."

There was real satisfaction in Ralph's voice as he replied. "That's great news, Pat. Thanks so much for letting me know and for everything you've done to make this possible."

"There's just one thing."

"What's that?"

"Cathy wants to work with your partner, Susan Collins. That is, assuming Susan is available—Cathy hasn't even spoken to her in the last six months. Nothing against you, I'm sure, but Susan is an old friend of Cathy's from college days, and Cathy thinks they'll have a special chemistry together."

There was a pause before Ralph replied. "Well, uh . . . sure, Pat, if that's what Cathy wants, I can add Susan to my team—"

Pat broke in. "No, Ralph, maybe I didn't state it clearly enough. Cathy wants Susan to head up your firm's team."

I could hear a sense of urgency in Ralph's voice. "But Pat, what about the CEO? Haven't you talked to Rick Kane about me—about what a great job I can do for Prime, about the seasoned judgment I can bring to bear in advising him and the company?"

"I've talked to Rick, but bottom line, he thinks the world of Cathy Weaver, and he'll go along with whatever she decides—no matter what I might say."

"But hell, I want to work personally on Prime matters—"

"Sorry, Ralph, if you can't give us Susan Collins, then the business is going to go to the Anderson firm in Chicago—their lead partner is another law school buddy of Cathy's. Call me back when you've decided what to do."

The conversation ended. I was stunned by what I'd overheard. And I couldn't help but recall my brief exchange with Cathy after our presentation in Dayton. I certainly hadn't defended Ralph, and in fact, had contrasted him unfavorably with Susan. Was I wrong to have done so? Could this have played a role in Cathy's decision?

I waited a decent interval before entering Landry's office. Struthers had still not yet arrived. Ralph appeared to be deep in thought, ignoring my presence for several seconds. Then he shook his head vigorously—in a manner that suggested he had come to a decision—and looked up at me.

"So, did you get a chance to speak to Ken? Did he tell you how pleased he was with the outcome of the negotiations?"

"Uh . . ." I'd been thinking about the Prime situation and wasn't prepared for Ralph's direct approach on Hellman.

Ralph was beaming now. "Did Ken appreciate how constructive it was for me to get him to stretch beyond his top number, in order to clinch the deal?"

I didn't want to lie, so I said, "Well, not exactly. . . ."

"Hah! That's the thanks you get. But surely he wasn't bitching about having to go up to $10.8 million."

At this point, with Ralph pressing me, I became uncomfortable about dissembling further, and all my good intentions went out the window. "No, as a matter of fact, he indicated he would have been willing to go to $12 million if it were needed."

"Bullshit!"

"That's what he said."

Landry muttered something about "ungrateful clients," but the glow that had covered his face was now replaced by an expression that suggested glimmerings of self-doubt.

I suddenly realized that this overweening guy was a mere mortal—he was vulnerable, capable of being wounded. First, the startling news from Duckworth, then, my embarrassing revelation. The moment of pleasure I experienced seeing him flounder passed quickly.

And now an idea flashed into my head—a way that I might help Ralph recover his composure and, at the same time, appreciate me more. Before I knew it, the words were out of my mouth.

"But hell, Ralph, I understand perfectly why you didn't push Ken to the 12 level."

"You do?"

"Sure. He might have gone there, but then he would have resented you muscling him up that high—never a desirable situation with a good long-term client."

"No, never." I realized that Ralph was actually listening to me, for the first time.

"What's more, your instinct was that you'd be able to do the deal for less than 11. And you also knew that if it didn't work out at that level, you could always go back to take another shot at Ken—using the unfavorable course the bargaining had taken as ammo for why he needed to pay the higher price."

"Yes, yes," said Landry, "that's precisely what I thought. I could always have gone back later for another round with Ken."

My strategy seemed to be working. I marveled at how the ability to rationalize events rejuvenated a faltering self-image. The uncertainty had left Ralph's face and the old timbre came back into his voice as he retook center stage.

"But anyway, that extra authority I got from Ken was crucial here."

I bit my tongue, reminding myself that this was a subject I really didn't want to get into.

Ralph began to strut. "I needed every penny of that to make the deal with Peter Winters."

Once more, my good intentions went out the window—influenced, I think, by the realization that this would provide another opportunity to promote myself with Landry. "Actually, Ralph, that wasn't quite what his associate, Ed Sinclair, told me. He said that Deane would have sold at $10 million."

Landry started to sputter again. "Why . . . I don't believe that for a minute . . . it's not possible . . . not with those other interested bidders chafing at the bit. . . ."

I drove the final nail into the coffin. "Sinclair said they were never a factor."

Landry, his expression troubled, sank into a chair. It was time for me to ride to the rescue once more.

"But I could see, Ralph, that even though you probably suspected there was no real competition, you needed to keep the specter of it alive—in order to raise *Ken's* sights."

"Hey, that's right."

"And although it undoubtedly occurred to you that Deane might have taken less, you also realized that, at the lower price, he may have felt the need to do some more shopping around. And you, very properly, didn't want to take the chance that he might stumble upon a new higher bid. . . ." I was on a roll, so what the hell—I decided to go all the way. "It was, if I may say so, very good thinking on your part."

"Yes, yes . . . that's exactly the way I analyzed it." Once again, Landry was beaming. He'd been down and now he was back up—just like Muhammad Ali earlier in the year. And I was happy too, because now Ralph knew for certain that I wasn't just some spear-carrier but a savvy negotiator in my own right.

At that point, Lou Struthers entered the office. "I understand you need my help with some documents on a new property deal for Hellman out on the Island."

"That's right," said Ralph, smiling broadly. "Lou, I know you enjoy the give and take of a good negotiation. Let me tell you the tale of Old Mill Run. It's got some terrific twists—just the thing for our next associate-training session."

The ensuing monologue by a rejuvenated Landry contained nary a nod in my direction. My facile contributions had been forgotten, and once more I was invisible.

When our meeting ended an hour ago, I hung around outside Ralph's office for a few minutes to speak to the temp. Again, I couldn't help but overhear Ralph place a call to Duckworth on his speaker phone.

"Okay, Pat, if that's the way things are, I'll go along. But I want you to do me a favor. Here's the way I'd like this news to be played. . . ." At that point, Ralph apparently picked up the handset and talked to Duckworth in a low voice. I was unable to hear the balance of their conversation, so I returned to my office.

Twenty minutes ago, I got a call to come by Ralph's office. This, I thought, is going to be interesting.

When I sat down, Ralph smiled at me across the desk. "Well, Ted, I have to hand it to you—you were right and I was wrong."

"About what?"

"About the value Susan Collins could bring to our cause in landing the Prime business. I got a heads-up call from Pat Duckworth earlier today. He told me that no official decision had yet been reached in the beauty contest, but he'd heard through the grapevine that it would increase our chances of winning if Susan—who, as you know, is Cathy's old college friend—were on our team."

I didn't hesitate. "Well, then, by all means, bring her aboard. And as I told you, I'm perfectly willing to drop out if that will make the team too top-heavy."

"I appreciate your gesture, but I've been doing some thinking. You know, I've got so much else on my plate. . . . Maybe I'll step aside from taking an active role on Prime—assuming, of course, that Cathy would be willing to forego my participation—and let Susan and you handle the deal."

At that moment, the door opened and Susan entered. "You wanted to see me, Ralph?"

"Yes, please have a seat." Ralph smiled in her direction and made a friendly gesture. "I'll come right to the point. As you know, we're in a beauty contest for Prime Industrial's business. We're in it because of my prior relationship with Pat Duckworth, one of the key directors of the company."

Susan nodded in acquiescence, her face expressionless.

"Well, today Pat gave me an interesting heads-up. He said he'd heard through the grapevine that because of your longtime friendship with Prime's general counsel, Cathy Weaver, having you on the team would increase our chances of getting the business." He paused, making certain to emphasize the point. "And that, after all, is what's really important for our firm—to get the business."

Susan's eyes widened. I could tell this news came as a surprise to her. Knowing Susan, I was sure no backdoor conversation with Cathy had occurred—although if the roles had been reversed, I wouldn't have put it past Ralph to call *his* old college buddy. . . .

Susan replied, "Whatever you say, Ralph. I'd be delighted to work for you on Prime if it will do the trick."

He smiled back at her. "That won't be necessary. With both of us on the team, it would be a little top-heavy, and I've got a lot of other things on my plate. So, if you're able to take this on, and assuming that Cathy is willing to forego my active participation, I'll step aside from the operational end—staying available, of course, for any crises that might arise—and just remain as the originating and billing partner. Ted here will serve as your number two."

Susan looked puzzled but seemed to be pleased. "If that's the way you want it. . . ."

"Yes, I believe that would be best."

At that moment, I appreciated for the first time the wisdom of the old "half a loaf" adage—or rather, in this case, two-thirds. . . .

That brings us up to the present moment. I stayed in Ralph's office for a while after Susan left, discussing Old Mill Run with Lou. When I returned to my office a few minutes ago, my secretary told me that Susan Collins had just come by and left a note in an envelope. I didn't read it right away. I wanted to ponder—while events were still fresh in my mind—what I'd learned from my double immersion in the Ralph Landry Follies.

Watching the man in action, there was one thing I could see with absolute clarity—that none of us is perfect. Like so much in life, it's basically a package. The same individual who is capable of superb performance can also commit serious blunders. And that's true in spades when money and status are involved—those twin sirens capable of luring us in such misguided directions.

I'd observed two distinct sides of Ralph Landry. In the Hellman property deal, it was Landry the consummate negotiator, performing on behalf of an existing client he knew well. In the Prime beauty contest, it was Landry the overweening hustler of new business, dealing with a potential client he didn't know well and utterly failed to read, and letting his urge to hog all the credit get in the way of landing the assignment for the firm.

In the Hellman deal, Ralph did some admirable lawyering and achieved a good result. The only thing that marred his triumph was a bad case of hubris—self-acclaim for outmaneuvering everyone else in the deal—but that was soon undermined by the revelations I conveyed from client and adversary.

By the way, hubris isn't something that's limited to Landry and his ilk. I just witnessed it also in . . . myself. After weeks of being kept under wraps, not allowed to contribute anything of substance, I spotted my opening, delivered the bad news, and then came up with a clever rationalization to make it palatable to Ralph. I thought I'd be greeted as a big hero. *That* was hubris—I learned soon enough that Ralph doesn't have any heroes other than himself.

In Prime, by contrast, after starting out well positioned via Duckworth for a shot at the new business, Ralph proceeded to make a number of mistakes in judgment. I could see this happening along the way, but I was powerless to steer him in a more constructive direction—the man just doesn't take guidance. As a result, Jenkins & Price could easily have lost out on the Prime representation. If Cathy Weaver had concluded that Ralph was a fixture in the J&P lead chair, but she was unwilling to deal with him, she might well have just gone ahead and selected her buddy at the Chicago firm. Fortunately for us, Cathy took a different tack, using Duckworth as an intermediary to have Ralph replaced by Susan.

And then Ralph absorbed the blow, took a deep breath, and rolled into action. I don't like what he did—manipulating the facts to keep the lion's share of the new business credit. But it was a real wake-up call for me. My gut tells me I'm going to see a lot more of that stuff in the years ahead—and not just from Ralph.

Another lesson I learned from these cases is that an effective lawyer has to be resilient and pragmatic. Shocks to the system are bound to occur—what counts is how you respond to adversity. For all his foibles, Ralph Landry is the epitome of resilience— he's mastered the knack of extracting whatever's obtainable from a situation and moving on. You won't find him paralyzed by his own rhetoric—he'll never get carried out on his shield.

Now I took out Susan's note and read it: "Ted, I'm confused. What's going on here? That was so uncharacteristic of Ralph to 'step down' like that. Do you know something about this? Please give me a call."

I can see I'm in a spot here. Unless I do something about it, Susan won't get the share of the credit she deserves for J&P landing the Prime business. But what can I do?

I can't just walk into the office of Bill Price, the J&P managing partner, and announce that a wrong has been committed relative to partnership compensation. That's no way to start out my career as a partner. I also don't want to confront Ralph directly and tell him I overheard his conversation with Duckworth. I can just hear him now—"You snooped on me?!" My life at the firm would never be the same thereafter. And I certainly don't intend to ask Cathy Weaver to write a letter to the firm, making it clear why J&P got the business.

So, the only way for me to do something about this is to tell Susan what I overheard. But then she's likely to say, "Thanks, Ted, but forget it." Or she might be suspicious and ask if I played a role in this—in which case I might feel forced to tell her about that little exchange I had with Cathy Weaver after our Dayton presentation. And Susan might be critical of what I did—might consider it as interfering.

But look at it the other way. Let's say that my report of the Duckworth call gets Susan's dander up and she decides to make an issue of it with Ralph. She might then have to say she heard it from me—a disclosure I wouldn't like at all. Even if she invented some other source, Ralph might put two and two together—recalling a glimpse of me outside his office the day of the call, aware of my friendship with Susan—and then school's out.

So here I am—torn between doing the right thing for a woman I respect and watching out for my own ass vis-à-vis one of the firm's tough guys—it's a modern-day take on the lady or the tiger!

I pick up the phone and get Susan on the line. "Susan, it's Ted. I have your note about Ralph. Hey, I'm just as surprised as you are. . . ."

Commentary on
On-the-Job Training

T he first thing to note here is that this story is told entirely in the first person from the point of view of Ted Ashburn. We met Ted a few tales ago in "Partnergate," where he was in the process of being anointed as the newest partner of Jenkins & Price. I don't want to poison your mind, but based on what we learned about Ted from that story, there may be cause to speculate whether he's an entirely trustworthy narrator in the present tale.

My purpose behind "On-the-Job Training" is to portray some components in the education of a young partner. As an associate, Ted mastered the practice of law sufficiently to receive the honor of being made a partner in a substantial law firm. But as an associate, he was always working for someone else at the firm (namely, the partner) on each deal or other assignment. Now, although on some matters there may still be a more senior partner over him (as in this story), Ted has to prepare himself to take full responsibility for a client's affairs. Then too, as an associate Ted didn't get very involved in such partner duties as trying to land new clients. As a partner, he has to start paying more attention to that aspect of practice.

So I paired Ted up with an experienced J&P business lawyer, Ralph Landry. And I picked Ralph in particular because he's the kind of senior partner who likes to instruct juniors on the fine points of what he's accomplishing as the assignment progresses. Although he performs this function in part for educational purposes, it's also designed to show off Ralph's skills, which he obviously relishes doing.

Many senior lawyers, less prone to showing off than Ralph, undertake the educational function with their juniors, and this can be very beneficial to the junior's learning process. (This subject is discussed in section 10.2.1 of *Lawyering.*) Allowing the junior lawyer to observe the senior in action with the client or adversary or regulator can be beneficial in and of itself, but the senior can't be assured that the junior appreciates the full significance of what he or she has observed. This often calls for a brief postmortem after the session, during which the senior points out what really went on. It's especially useful if the senior can generalize some advice from the specific item under discussion, so that the junior can appreciate the broader applicability.

By the way, not all seniors believe in doing this. Some favor a technique that's the equivalent of teaching swimming by throwing a kid in the water—learning by immersion, you might call it. A senior partner of my law firm hailed from that school, and if you ever get me over a late night beer, I'll tell you a delicious anecdote about what happened on my first day at the firm.

In "On-the-Job Training" (which begins and ends in the present, with the bulk of the story taking place in the recent past), Ted is working on two assignments simultaneously, and the story swivels back and forth between them. I set it up like this to illustrate two different aspects of Ted's education—one, how to negotiate a deal, and the other, how to bag a new client. But this kind of oscillation is often the order of the day for a business lawyer at the partner level. Except when you're in the middle of a really big deal, it's rare that you can blot everything else out and concentrate on just one matter.

Ralph Landry is the central character here. Like most people of any significance, Ralph is what might be termed a package deal. There's some good stuff in him, and then there's some that's not so good. On the positive front, he has brains, self-confidence, lots of drive, and a ton of resilience. Ralph understands the skill of negotiating, including the often overlooked but vital interaction between lawyer and client. Apparently, he has also been successful over the years in attracting new business to the firm.

On the negative side, he suffers from hubris, a penchant for manipulation, an unwillingness to listen to others, and a disdain for trying to read his audience. He's certainly not what you would call a team player, and some of his maneuvering is quite unattractive.

But that's enough characterization up front. Now let's follow the tale, examining Ralph's conduct (as well as that of Ted and some others) along the way. We'll take up the negotiating segment first, going all the way through that before turning to the pursuit of new business.

One of the first things a good negotiator should do at the outset of a possible deal is to size up the people—lawyer and client—on the other side of the table. In this case, at the initial meeting Ted attends, Ralph Landry and his client Ken Hellman begin by reporting what has taken place prior to the meeting in conversations with Charles Deane (the owner of Old Mill Run) and his lawyer, Peter Winters. Let me ask you this right off the bat:

Based on those first reports, do you derive any information that indicates whether or not Ken and Ralph are up against a savvy team of negotiators in Deane and Winters?

I'll give you my view, but first I need to step back and make some general observations about an important aspect of negotiating—the opening rounds. (This is discussed in greater detail in chapter 8 of *Smart Negotiating.*)

If an owner of property (such as real estate) decides to sell it, he or she sets an asking price, which in effect kicks off the bidding. Here, however, Deane says he hasn't contemplated selling Old Mill Run; but if Hellman is interested, he should have his lawyer contact Deane's.

To oversimplify a bit, there are two obvious ways a seller can create bargaining leverage in his favor. One is through generating competition among several buyers, in the hope that the auction aspect causes them to raise their offers to outbid competitors. The other way (which isn't usable if the property has already been put up for sale) is to take the position that it's not for sale, and thus only a hefty price will persuade the owner to part with it—especially if the buyer wants to close the deal before the seller has a chance to check out what other prospective purchasers might be willing to pay. This second tactic is the one that the Deane/Winters team chooses to use in this case; and because having an asking price might be considered inconsistent with their position that the property isn't for sale, they invite Hellman to make a bid.

This raises the related question of whether it's preferable to go first on the issue of price or to let the other guy go first—a question whose answer can shape the resultant course of the bargaining. The conventional wisdom is to let the other side make the first proposal, to see where your counterpart is coming from before committing yourself. The premise is logical enough. If you're the seller, the buyer might propose a higher price than you would have sought. If you're the buyer, the seller may value his property below what you would have offered. And if you go first, you'll never know. Besides, even if you don't get lucky, you'll pick up valuable information before having to bid.

At times I go along with the conventional wisdom. A buyer who lacks enough data to make an intelligent bid, for example, should hold his fire. A seller who wants to preserve the posture (whether true or fictional) that he hasn't made up his mind whether or not to sell (as is the case with Deane here) may do better letting the buyer go first, underscoring the message that it will take a blockbuster offer to move the seller off the fence.

Nevertheless, when there's a choice in the matter, I frequently counsel my clients to put their number on the table *first*. I advise sellers to let the buyer know what price they're looking to receive; I advise buyers to tell the seller what they consider an appropriate price to pay.

Why do I often go against the conventional wisdom? Because I think it makes good sense for a negotiator to take control of the price issue. For instance, put yourself in the shoes of the knowledgeable buyer. You want the seller negotiating off your opening number, not his own. Your bid sends a message to your counterpart: If he wants to play ball, here's the ballpark where the action will occur. Or to change (and mix) metaphors, think of this as a first-strike deterrent against the seller shooting for the moon.

In my experience the chances of the seller asking for less than the buyer would dare offer are slim. In the real world, negotiators worry about just the opposite— a seller who trots out an exorbitant figure and goes to great pains to support it, thereby digging a hole that's tough to climb out of. This makes for rough sledding in the resulting negotiations.

Just one note of caution, however. Don't go first unless your side knows value (or is well advised on that score) and has formulated a realistic expectation to guide its negotiating strategy.

How about when you're a seller? The last thing you need is a lowball offer, requiring lots of energy to elevate the buyer into the realm of reason. True, you can't eliminate this risk, even if your asking price is reasonable. But you increase the chance of it occurring when you invite the buyer to put the first number on the table without any guidance.

And (finally!) that's just the point here. Peter Winters didn't want to have to dig out of a hole after receiving a lowball Ken Hellman offer. So, when he told Ralph to have Hellman make a bid, he added this warning—that unless Hellman was prepared to start the bidding with a number "in eight figures," he shouldn't bother coming around.

I like what Winters did here, and I certainly have taken that approach myself on more than one occasion. Without putting the first number on the table (which is tough for the seller to do when he's trying to give the impression that the property isn't for sale), Winters nevertheless provided some guidance to the buyer, designed to dissuade him from making an offer at a much lower price. I call that savvy bargaining, and this is what the Hellman/Landry team is up against here.

So now Ralph puts on his negotiator's hat. He tells his client that although the $10 million signal can't be ignored, it's just part of the negotiating dance—Ken doesn't have to comply with it, and Ralph explains why. My question to you is this:

Do you agree with Ralph's advice here? Is he overstepping the lawyer-client boundary?

This is a fair question to ask, and it deserves a considered response. By encouraging his client not to comply with the explicit direction given by the seller's lawyer, Ralph is taking a definite risk. If the client follows his advice and the resulting offer of less than $10 million is rejected (as not having complied with Winters' instructions), and if Deane thereupon refuses to engage in further bargaining with Hellman (reverting to his original posture that Old Mill Run isn't for sale), then

Ralph Landry is likely to bear the brunt of the adverse result. And besides, one might ask, what's the lawyer doing advising on something that is basically a business question?

Here's my reply to this. I do caution lawyers not to give ultimate advice or take a strong stance on what I call "go/no go" decisions (e.g., should Hellman be buying Old Mill Run at all) or on the price a client/buyer should pay for something (or a client/seller should accept). These are clear business judgments, to be made by the client, utilizing advice from others skilled in those areas. The principal role of the lawyer should be to clarify, summarize, and help analyze the various considerations that enter into the determination, in order to assist the client's decisional process. For the lawyer to go further and offer his or her personal view on the matter can lead to serious second-guessing if things don't work out well.

On the other hand, I feel differently about what I call "way-to-go" judgments. (These are covered in section 8.5 of *Lawyering*.) Here, I think the lawyer should take a larger role—at least if it's within her area of expertise and the client hasn't indicated (as some do) that he doesn't want the lawyer messing with such things. Strategizing about the bargaining necessary in order to reach the client's goal is an area where I've usually been willing to go out on a limb and advise clients—even if, as here, I can be second-guessed should the advice prove faulty. So, I approve of Ralph stepping up to the plate on the issue of how to deal with the "eight-figure" message from the seller's attorney.

As for the substance of Ralph's advice here, I also agree with that. I have frequently given similar counsel—especially when representing business people who would otherwise have been afraid to open the bidding below $10 million, for fear the seller would (figuratively) get up and walk out of the room. Those kinds of buyers usually end up overpaying for properties. Ralph's analysis is just about right here—if you come in with a reasonable first bid, although lower than what has been signaled, plus a good argument (not necessarily a conclusive one, just plausible) as to why that's all the property is worth, and you indicate a willingness to bargain further, most sellers will counter. That has certainly been my experience.

Next comes the byplay between lawyer and client about what price Ken Hellman would be willing to pay. This is another important negotiating topic on which I need to provide some background. (The subject is discussed at length in chapter 7 of *Smart Negotiating*.) It's crucial for the lawyer who's advising the client on bargaining strategy to know where the client is looking to end up—and to know that, if possible, before the bargaining starts. Without what I call a "realistic expectation" on price and other important issues, you don't know where to start the bidding, you'll have trouble figuring out what steps to take along the way, and you won't know where to stop. It serves as a prominent—although not inflexible—compass point as you go through the process.

I view someone's realistic expectation as a good outcome of the negotiations—a price (or other term) that you (which, for lawyers, means your client) would be agreeable to pay or receive, and that your counterpart could well accept. Your efforts to achieve that outcome should reflect a hard-headed determination. It's neither the best price (or terms) that you might get if your counterpart caves in, nor the worst that you may be forced to pay or take if she hangs tough and you're dying to do the deal.

The ideal outcome, of course, would be to cut a better deal than your realistic expectation. But under my approach, you don't get there by revising your expectation. Rather, you take your shot by giving yourself some room in terms of your initial position. And you neither count on getting a bargain nor let that possibility dictate your overall strategy.

Your realistic expectation is *not* a bottom line. At the outset of a negotiation, before all the information is available and prior to the necessary investment of time and effort, your client often doesn't know how far he'll be willing to reach. My experience is that lurking beneath the surface of most realistic expectations is some less favorable outcome that he may find himself willing to accept, if necessary.

I call this the "stretch." It's not a first-class outcome of the negotiation, but it's still satisfactory, in the sense that your client decides it's better to do the deal on these terms than not to do it. Phrased another way, as you near the end of a negotiation, you often have to pose this key question to your client: If you stick on your terms and thereby lose the deal, will you then regret not having paid (or accepted) your counterpart's higher (or lower) price?

Frequently this is the key to deal-making—not how far you've had to travel in the negotiations, or whether you're irritated by your counterpart's bargaining, but how much you're willing to stretch. Most of the time there aren't any magical solutions just waiting around for contracting parties to discover. Rather, there are satisfactory outcomes, which have to be ground out inch by inch. If, ultimately, your client is willing to stretch, it's usually because either necessity, competition, time pressure or strong desire is motivating him (more than his counterpart) to make the deal.

Naturally, however, you'll try to get the other side to believe that your client's realistic expectation—and perhaps even some positions you take before retreating to that point—represents a real stretch. But since your credibility is important, it shouldn't be squandered on unrealistic postures. You're also out to persuade your counterpart that her own expectation won't swing the deal—that she should start thinking seriously about her own stretch. And, of course, the real or apparent leverage you can bring to bear will carry considerable weight.

The rest of this meeting (and the ensuing dialogue in the cab between Ralph and Ted) deals with the cat-and-mouse byplay that often occurs between client and lawyer. It's a negotiation in which the client doesn't want his own lawyer to know how much he's really willing to pay—perhaps out of fear that once the lawyer knows the number, he'll zoom right to it in his zeal to make the deal. Ralph's explanation of this in the cab, and his assessment of the trouble it presents for the negotiator, are right on the money.

Although Ralph recognizes that he has this problem with Ken Hellman, he chooses not to push the issue at this time.

Do you agree with Ralph's restraint here?

I do. It would be premature to confront the issue now. Ralph knows what Ken's goal is here—to buy the property for $10 million. Whether it's an expectation that will prove to be realistic (which Ralph has obvious doubts about) is something that will become clearer as the negotiations proceed. It's often difficult to assess the feasibility of achieving a desired result at the outset.

Besides, the $9 million offer they decide upon appears to be a prudent first bid, no matter what ultimate price Ken has in mind. In view of the seller's eight-figure warning, they can't go much lower than this, and they wouldn't want to start out higher, inasmuch as Ken may ultimately decide not to pay above $10 million.

A side issue raised during these two scenes is the byplay between Ralph and Ted. Both at the meeting with Ken Hellman and in the cab where it's just the two of them, Ralph rudely cuts off any attempt by Ted to get a substantive word into the conversation. Putting aside Ralph's obvious rudeness, let me ask you:

Do you agree with Ralph's muzzling of Ted?

In answering this, I must make a distinction here between the two venues. In the scene with the client,

I'm inclined to excuse Ralph, on the grounds that since he hasn't worked with Ted before, he doesn't know what his new partner might say. Ralph is performing a delicate operation with a client he considers to be unrealistic, and he doesn't want some irrelevancy (or worse) emanating from Ted to interfere with what he's attempting to accomplish.

This point, by the way, is magnified tenfold when the senior and junior are together in a room negotiating with their adversary. I confess to having always had a strong desire to control my side in any negotiation. I worried about what an associate or a tax accountant or some other unskilled negotiator on my team might utter spontaneously that would undercut the position I was trying to take.

But if Ralph is going to play it this way, he should alert Ted in advance. ("Ted, I'd appreciate you not getting involved in the byplay with the client until after you've had some more experience with Ken, who can be a very prickly fellow. . . .") At the very least, if Ralph hasn't prewarned Ted, he should explain matters in the cab. ("Ted, I'm sorry to have cut you off in the meeting, but I wasn't sure you knew where I was headed, and I thought it best that we discuss this outside the client's office.")

On the other hand, when the two of them are alone in the cab, there's no excuse for Ralph refusing to listen to what Ted wants to offer. Ralph may not agree with Ted or choose to follow his advice, but Ralph should be open to it and grateful that his new partner has some thoughts on the subject.

In the ensuing brief conversation between Ted and Ed Sinclair, the junior lawyer in the Deane camp, Ed sends a message intended to intimidate the Hellman team: tell Landry to bring along a bushel basket of money—it'll take a big price to get Deane to part with his baby. I have no problem with what Ed is doing here—he's just trying to reinforce the eight-figure message previously delivered.

But now let's focus on Ted in that same phone call. In a negotiation, when someone on the other side pulls a stunt like Ed's, I don't like the idea of just leaving it out there as the last word on the subject. I'm concerned that the speaker might thereby infer he has been successful in establishing the intimidation. So I think a reply is in order. It can be of the joking variety, such as the "peck basket" rejoinder that Ted came up with—but unfortunately, only after the call had ended. That's too late for such a riposte—it's either done at the moment or not at all. Or the response could be of a more serious type, along these lines. "Don't get too cocky here, Ed. Hellman is interested in the property, but he's not enamored of it. Ken's not going to pay more than a reasonable price to buy it." This serves the purpose of getting things back in the middle.

The next encounter between Ralph and Ted occurs after Ralph's first meeting with Deane's lawyer. Again, Ralph is uninterested in anything that Ted has to offer and cuts him off twice—bad show. But Ralph does analyze the bargaining situation with some acuity, and realizes he will now have to work on getting his client to stretch beyond his initial expectations.

In the call to set up the meeting, Ted is correct not to preview for Ken what occurred at Ralph's session with Deane's lawyer, and his reply to Ken's probe is about right. Ralph will want to put his own spin on this, and Ted is well advised not to get in the way.

The dialogue at the ensuing meeting that Ralph and Ted have with Ken is at the heart of the negotiating segment of "On-the-Job Training." Tell me:

What do you think of Ralph's performance here, in terms of raising his client's sights with regard to the likely purchase price that will be required?

I like it very much. After relating what happened at the meeting, Ralph explains why, with $10 million as Ken's top number, none of the alternative next steps are appealing. If, nevertheless, Ken's real limit is $10 million, Ralph indicates he's prepared to move ahead on that basis. But he warns that it's not realistic for Ken to expect to succeed at that level—particularly with the leverage factor of competition now working in the seller's favor.

Note that Ralph is careful not to say or even imply that $10 million is less than the real value of Old Mill Run—nothing emerges that would cast doubt on the client's financial assessment of the property. That's the way to do it—to get the point across without implying any criticism of the client.

Along the way, Ralph tells Ken why he doesn't like the idea of bluffing that $10 million is his top number, if in fact it isn't. It's a speech I've made to clients, lawyers and law students about a thousand times by now.

Ralph then runs through the much preferable negotiating possibilities that open up if Ken "were willing to go up to, say, $11 million." I like that wording—Ralph slips in the number he obviously thinks Ken should aim for, but only as an example. Still, Ralph has managed to get it on the table, and he then goes on to utilize it for his discussion of possibilities. The crucial aspect of an $11 million realistic expectation is that it will allow Ralph to raise his next offer to the $10 million level— thus satisfying the seller's eight figure condition, which might be riskier to ignore the second time around.

Notice what Ralph does next. In addition to showing Ken how this might lead to a deal under $11 million, he couples it with a statement to rebut the inference Ken might otherwise draw that Ralph will use the extra authority to immediately zoom to $11 million. If you're trying to pry his real number out of the client, this is the best method to do it. Otherwise, he doesn't know what might be on your mind.

By the way, another means of handling this with a long-term client is to say, in effect, that you understand the little game your client is playing with you, and you don't want to deprive him of his fun, but if he'd just throw you a wink or a nod to show there's a little more room, you'll know how to conduct the negotiations. It's what might be termed implicit leeway, which is often all you need.

Sure enough, as Ralph foresaw, Ken has more dollars in his pocket. Ralph then proceeds to prance all the way home in the taxi. It's certainly appropriate for Ralph to point out to Ted what his strategy was and how well it worked, but we could do without the prancing.

The next scene is the telephone conversation in which Ed Sinclair signals to Ted that the $10 million figure was for openers, and that Hellman had better be prepared to move up from there or he won't end up with the property. It's a forceful tactic on Ed's part, but let me ask you:

How do you evaluate the wisdom of Ted's rejoinder, "Don't worry, we have a certain amount of flexibility"?

Ted says this because of his fear that Deane might believe Hellman really won't go over $10 million—at which point Deane might sell the property to one of the other bidders for a price slightly in excess of $10 million, without ever coming back to give Hellman another chance. But that doesn't stand up. Ted knows that Ralph isn't going to characterize the $10 million as Hellman's top number—especially after having worked so hard to raise Ken's sights. Now, however, with Ted having made it clear to Ed that the $10 million is just a starting point, there's little hope of acquiring the property at $10 million or even very close to it. I would call Ted's response a real blunder.

Then Ted compounds the mistake by not reporting his byplay with Ed to his senior partner. Even if Ted realizes he did the wrong thing, at least he had a plausible reason for doing so, and this is pertinent information that Ralph, who is responsible for conducting the negotiations, is entitled to know about.

Well, Ralph makes the deal at $10.8 million and is really strutting. He gives Ted an ebullient recap of the negotiations and receives the congratulations due him. Note, by the way, Ralph's puzzlement over why Winters wouldn't consider a deal at the $10 million level—the other lawyer seemingly convinced that Hellman had a lot more in his pocket and bargaining accordingly. This, of course, is the effect of Ted's ill-considered rejoinder to Ed Sinclair, and I think Ted now realizes he blundered.

Then come Ted's two calls, first to Ken and then to Ed. I must confess, what Ted learns on those calls is something that doesn't happen too often in real life. Adversaries and even clients tend not to admit this sort of thing. It would be particularly unusual for this to come from an adversary, since the deal is still just at the agreement in principle stage and could easily be aborted. And the Hellman side may be particularly miffed that Ed dissembled earlier about the other bidders, as well as stating that $10 million wouldn't take it. So you'll have to forgive me a bit here—but it does make for a more interesting story.

Now Ted has to decide what to do. Should he relay the contents of these two calls to Ralph? He determines not to.

At this point, do you think Ted should have decided to pass along this information to Ralph?

I agree with Ted's decision to say nothing, for all the reasons stated in the story (not least, because of his own error). Ted's understandable desire to burst Ralph's pompous bubble just isn't strong enough to overcome all that. And, by the way, Ted can't be sure that Ken and Ed are leveling with him—perhaps they too just want to get in a poke at the insufferable Ralph. I might come out differently on the question, however, if at this point the basic deal hadn't already been struck.

In the final meeting between Ralph and Ted, Ralph struts again—but when the conversation gets specific,

Ted's resolve suddenly weakens, and he spills the beans on what he's learned in the two calls. What do you think:

Now that Ralph has specifically put the issue on the table in the form of a question to Ted, do you agree with Ted telling Ralph all?

At this point, I can understand why Ted's resolve weakens. But what really tips the balance is Ted sensing an opportunity to get Ralph to notice him for the first time, especially after the demeaning way Ralph has treated him up to now. It's payback time!

Ted's rationalizations are clever and do the trick. But if he expected to receive plaudits from Ralph, forget it—by the end of the scene, Ted is once more invisible. That's the way life is with the Ralphs of this world. And Ted is insightful enough to recognize his own hubris in thinking he'd get some recognition.

Turning now to the client-getting activities, we first encounter Ralph Landry telling Ted Ashburn about the call he just received from Pat Duckworth, a director of Prime Industrials—a heads-up that Jenkins & Price is being considered as the firm to represent Prime in connection with its upcoming big deal. Ralph, reviewing his past efforts with Duckworth, cites the news as evidence of the value of persistence in going after business, and I agree with him. There's very little instant gratification in attempting to bring in new business. Part of what's needed is perseverance, keeping yourself on tap in a potential client's consciousness.

On the other hand, we're subjected to Ralph's cynical view that the selection of a law firm will ultimately be the decision of the Prime CEO, Rick Kane, and that Kane will listen to Duckworth who chaired the Prime search committee that hired Kane. This kind of thinking—the seemingly shrewd observation that may prove to be right, but can also be dead wrong—is too simplistic for my taste.

The first sign of trouble comes when Cathy Weaver, the Prime general counsel, makes it clear that she is fully aware of the relationship between Pat Duckworth and Ralph, and knows they communicate out of normal channels. This woman is on to Ralph's game. He should have taken note of that, but he's too full of himself.

Then there's the good news—or is it?—that Cathy is a friend of one of Jenkins & Price's corporate partners, Susan Collins. Ted is puzzled by Ralph's seeming disinterest in that piece of good fortune. He's later surprised to learn that Ralph has told Susan not to call Cathy and isn't looking for any insights from her about the Prime general counsel.

Ralph's explanation for this—that Rick Kane will be making the ultimate decision—doesn't assuage Ted. He thinks Ralph's view fails to take into account the power that inside general counsel started to exercise in the 1970s, especially in terms of such matters as selecting outside counsel. This power was greatly expanded in the '80s, '90s, and beyond, so I don't think Ralph would make that same mistake today—but he also shouldn't have made it in 1978.

In his subsequent meeting with Susan, Ted finally figures out what's going on here. Of course, we'll never know for sure (since we don't get inside Ralph's head), but I think we can draw a pretty strong inference that Ted's assessment—it's all about money and status—is right on the button.

Firms go at these matters differently, but in any firm where partner compensation is measured by client generation and client billings, the potential for Ralph's kind of aggrandizement is there. But, to be fair, let's look at this from Ralph's viewpoint. He's been sweating to get the Prime business for years, finally sees it in sight, and doesn't want this young woman partner to rain on his parade. So let me ask you:

Now that you know what Ralph is trying to do, what do you think of it?

I tell you what I think—it's lousy. In a law firm, teamwork among partners should be the order of the day—not only to service clients but also to attract them to the firm in the first instance. Ralph ought to be making positive use of Susan's connection to help get the firm selected, instead of trying to hog all the glory for himself—with possibly disastrous consequences.

Ted then receives Susan's insight (which he's told not to repeat to Ralph) that Cathy values modesty and no bashing of the competition. It's 180 degrees away from Ralph's methodology, and this knowledge puts Ted in a tough spot.

At his next meeting with Ralph, Ted tries to get the message across without citing Susan as the source. Ralph puts him down, and Ted backs off. What do you think:

Was Ted right in not revealing to Ralph what Susan told him?

My answer here is yes. Ted promised Susan he wouldn't reveal it, and he shouldn't welsh on that promise.

Now Ralph and Ted travel out to Dayton to make the J&P presentation in the beauty contest. Ralph is forceful but, in Ted's phrase, "over the top." He brags without ceasing about the firm's abilities and experience, and he relentlessly badmouths the other firms that Prime has under consideration.

Even assuming, for purposes of argument, that this sort of approach might be well received in some potential client circles, it's nonetheless critical to tailor your new business pitch to the likes and dislikes of the people you're pitching. If you don't know what to expect, watch for body language clues. Here, Ralph ignores his "stony-faced" audience and Cathy's obviously negative reaction—avoiding eye contact, lips pursed tight. We can't give Ralph high marks here.

Then, when the session ends, Cathy privately asks Ted if all Jenkins & Price partners are as relentlessly negative as Ralph.

If you were Ted, how would you handle Cathy's question? Do you believe that what Ted actually says is wise?

Well, I think Ted should do something to rebut Cathy's obviously negative reaction—at least as it applies to the firm in general, if not Ralph himself. Ted's reply is all right until he mentions Susan Collins by name. I don't consider that wise—it points up the distinction between Ralph and Susan too sharply. This sidebar dialogue between Cathy and Ted also raises another question:

How do you feel about Ted's decision not to mention it to Ralph?

I agree with him. Cathy would not have liked her remark to get back to Ralph; Ted would be shot by Ralph as the messenger; and nothing would be gained now, since the J&P presentation is complete. It might be different if the comment was made before the presentation, and Ted could cite it as proof of his "hunch" that Cathy doesn't like this kind of stuff.

Now they're back in the office some days later, and Ted overhears Ralph's phone call with Pat. For Ralph, it's both good news (Jenkins & Price will get the assignment) and bad news (provided that Susan replaces Ralph as lead counsel).

"Half a Loaf" was one of the possibilities I considered for the title of this story. That (or actually two-thirds) is what Ralph now swings into action to accomplish through manipulating Pat Duckworth, Ted, and Susan. I won't even ask you about this brazen display. Pretending that it's still his deal, the servicing of which he's generously passing along to Susan out of the goodness of his heart—when, in fact, the firm would have lost the deal if he were unwilling to substitute Susan for himself as the lead partner—is shameless, and not what you're entitled to expect from your partner.

In this story, because it involves Ted Ashburn's education as a young partner, I let him ponder at the end what he'd learned from his dealings with Ralph Landry. These musings, to which I generally subscribe, might ordinarily be found in the commentary to the story and are worth absorbing.

As the story concludes, Ted is reflecting on whether he should say anything to Susan about what happened, in response to her query. I have two questions for you:

First, knowing Ted from "Partnergate," what would you have predicted he'd do here? Second, if you were Ted, how would you come out on this?

In my view, Ted's decision to play dumb is quite consistent with his actions as the new partner who feigned "no pledge" to Bill Price in the last scene of "Partnergate." As for what Ted should have done, it's not an easy call.

After due consideration, here's what I think I'd have done in Ted's place. First, I would make Susan promise not to tell anyone what I was about to tell her and not to take any action based on it without first checking with me. Then I'd tell her about overhearing the Duckworth call and what Ralph said to me after receiving that call. I'd suggest to Susan that if she wants to know more about what happened—how she ended up heading the J&P team—she should talk to Cathy Weaver, but without mentioning what I had overheard. I think Cathy will set her straight. And that way, whatever Susan chooses to do about it (if anything), will flow from her conversation with Cathy and not be attributable to me.

Well, that's my analysis. So now I ask you:

Do you think Ted Ashburn is any wiser at the end of the story than before his dual encounters with Ralph Landry?

I have no doubt that he is. A lawyer can learn from seeing something done the right way; and he or she can also learn from applying a critical eye to the conduct of another attorney, taking note of errors and omissions. With Ralph as the role model, all of the foregoing comes into play!

So Ted picks up some valuable negotiating tips, with a special emphasis on a lawyer's dealings with his own client. But he also sees how hubris can take the sheen off a positive result. And he realizes it's not just the pompous Ralphs among us who can be infected with delusions of grandeur. Finally, he comes to understand—from his own painful experience—how an ill-conceived remark can affect the course of the bargaining.

With respect to landing new clients, on the positive side, Ted learns the value of persistence and keeping up useful contacts. By negative example, he realizes the importance of tailoring your pitch to the particular audience. And he's now alert to the possibility of manipulation among partners, while having a fresh appreciation of the importance of teamwork in putting the firm's best foot forward.

Not a bad couple of weeks for the new partner, I'd say.

THE COROLLARY AXIOM

"P lease raise your glasses, ladies," said Joe Miller, hoisting his own by the stem, "and join me in a toast to the brilliant young man who pulled my irons out of the fire—Alex Gibson!"

"Hey, it wasn't so special," said Alex, in a tone that his wife, Lynn, recognized as a halfhearted attempt at false modesty. *And now*, she correctly predicted, *here comes his dab of self-deprecating humor.* "I just did what any workaholic, overcompensated, sleep-deprived lawyer would have done under the circumstances." *Hmm . . . he forgot to add wife-neglecting.*

Joe Miller let out a loud snort. "Listen to this guy, Vicky," he said, putting down his wine glass and turning toward his wife. "He's making nothing of it—'any lawyer could have' . . . blah, blah." Then, shifting around to face Alex's wife, Joe waggled his finger for emphasis. "But let me tell *you*, Lynn, something you ought to know."

Joe paused, sneezed, muttered "this damn flu," and then, looking directly across the restaurant table at Alex, lowered his voice and spoke in measured cadence. "This man here is one of the great young deal lawyers in New York."

Alex Gibson lifted his hand as if to deflect an undeserved compliment, but Lynn could tell he was savoring every word. She knew full well that in his circles, the ultimate compliment was to be thought of as a "great deal lawyer." (She reckoned that, although in his late thirties, Alex had already excised from Joe's blurb the adjective "young" as being unnecessarily restrictive.) Lynn was also aware of how much it meant to him for those words to be uttered by Joe Miller, who Alex considered the hottest investment banker on the Street. *He's already thinking of how to convey that glowing endorsement to his senior partners at Jenkins & Price.*

The two couples were dining in one of Manhattan's trendy and pricey restaurants, at a time in the late seventies when dining out had become the "in" thing around town. Every table was occupied by avid New Yorkers, many of whom had clipped the three-star review that appeared the prior month in the *Times* and were ordering the signature dishes of the highly regarded chef. The noise level, while not lacking in decibels, was still reasonable by New York auditory standards—the result of opulent carpeting underfoot and some expensive dampening equipment in the ceiling.

Joe Miller took another quaff from their second bottle of wine and continued his paean. "I'm not sure anyone but Alex Gibson could have bailed me out of that mess—created, I might add, by another well-known law firm whose name we won't mention." Joe was a tall handsome man in his early forties, well-tailored, hair brushed back, suspenders—in Lynn's eyes, the whole nine yards of successful investment banker look.

"What firm was that, Joe?" asked his wife, Vicky, in her husky voice and soothing inflections carried over from girlhood in the mid-South. The woman's sultry features and sleek proportions brought to Lynn's mind Faye Dunaway's classic Vicky in *The Thomas Crown Affair.* Lynn couldn't help but observe the goofy expression on Alex's face whenever Vicky spoke—*my brilliant husband is smitten by the wench.*

"Oh, that white shoe play-it-by-the-book bunch of robots at Struthers & Pierce," Joe replied. "I can't believe I've put up with them representing me all these years. But I'll tell you something"—and here he turned to face Alex—"that's going to change in the future. From here on in, Alex, when I run up against a tough one, you're the guy I want in my corner."

Lynn missed nothing—the expression on Alex's face signifying I'm-eternally-grateful-in-advance, the slight movement of his lips that told her Alex was memorizing Joe's last words for verbatim transmission to his partners. And she knew what he was thinking—that if Joe Miller started to use him as Joe's regular lawyer, this would catapult Alex ahead of all his peers at the firm.

Lynn's feelings about all this were decidedly ambivalent. She recognized, of course, the importance to Alex's career of gaining Joe Miller's approval and obtaining his future business. *How could I not be aware of that,* she thought, *after the patronizing lecture Alex gave me during the cab ride to the restaurant. I can't believe he had the nerve to tell me, 'And be careful what you say, Lynn—sometimes you don't think before you speak—just don't screw things up'* . . . *as if I were some unruly child. Okay, so I once happened to mention to the CEO of his best client that Alex used to admire George McGovern* . . . Still, she was taking no chances tonight and had remained buttoned up since they had arrived at the restaurant.

At first, Lynn had been skeptical of the praise being heaped on Alex. *Is this just the wine, so liberally poured, that's doing the talking?* By now, though, she was disposed to treat it as—in a new phrase she'd coined for the occasion—*sincere hyperbole.*

Lynn realized she should be proud of Alex. They had met in college, dated nonstop senior year, and were wed shortly after graduation. Since then, she had been a constant companion to what others saw as his meteoric rise. But Lynn couldn't help thinking that, by some standards of comparison, what Alex did for a living wasn't really so heroic. *Now Anwar Sadat—there was a man who made a bold stroke this year, actually visiting Jerusalem. Even Israeli prime minister Begin talked about Sadat's courage, and how much the Jews appreciated that.* . . .

Also tempering her enjoyment of the moment was the recognition that a lot of additional business from Joe Miller would mean more long hours for Alex—more nights that she would be eating takeout dinners alone in front of the television set, while Alex was busy elsewhere performing self-styled legal miracles. *Is it worth it?* She was painfully aware of how immersed Alex had become in his career—wrapped up in his work, his clients, his position in the law firm. The two of them rarely had time to enjoy themselves the way they used to.

"Lynn, honey," said Vicky, setting down her wineglass with a small flourish, "you should be extremely proud of your handsome Lex Gibson. It's not every day that Joe Miller delivers such a ringing endorsement of a young attorney. In fact"—and here she fluttered her eyes and tilted her head toward Joe—"what I usually hear Joe telling some young lawyer on the phone is"—and now she attempted a rough parody of Joe at his imperious best—"'You idiot! How could you have screwed this up so badly?!'"

Lynn murmured in acknowledgment, but her eyes were on Alex. *My husband is gazing at Vicky as if he's on the verge of having an orgasm right at the table! I can't believe what a flirt that Vicky is, with all that 'handsome' stuff.* Lynn considered Alex to be manly looking and possessed of strong features, but she'd never thought of him as movie star handsome in the sense of cinema heartthrobs. *And where does this* *woman get off referring to him as "Lex," a name that only a few of his high school friends and family members still used—where the hell did she dig that one up from? The jerk must have mentioned it in a weak moment.*

Before this evening, Lynn had never met Vicky—or for that matter, Joe—although she knew that Alex had spent time at the Millers' beach home the past summer, while trying to work out Joe's legal problem. *So how come Alex never mentioned how seductive this woman is—was he trying to conceal something?*

Vicky motioned for the waiter to pour some more of the wine before she continued. "I just know how much Joe Miller thinks of your man, Lynn, because even though Joe seems to have picked up that damn flu bug that's going around, and really should be in bed, he insisted on keeping this dinner date with the two of you."

Lynn could guess what was probably going through Alex's mind right about now—a side-by-side comparison of Vicky and his wife—*in which I don't come off well at all. And it isn't just that she's physically attractive—albeit in an obvious way—while I'm not exactly showgirl-glamorous. I'm sure Alex is also marveling to himself about how Vicky bolsters Joe's efforts, elaborates on his motifs, and so on.*

That's certainly not my strong suit. Alex always tells me I don't understand anything about client relations—that I'm completely insensitive on that score. He says he always holds his breath when I chime in during social occasions with clients or senior colleagues at his firm. Lynn recalled how angry Alex had gotten the evening she quoted verbatim his offhand remark that "all investment bankers are whores"—repeating it to a small audience that included a Goldman Sachs partner whom Alex had been hustling for business.

Her husband's seeming infatuation with Vicky made Lynn ponder once again just how faithful he had been through the years. *I'm sure he's had stirrings from time to time—after all, sex is all over the place in this late '70s scene.* She'd read recently in the paper about the opening of a West Side club named Plato's Retreat, dedicated to casual heterosexual sex—the article noting the delicious irony that it occupied the same location where Continental Baths used to service the gay community.

One thing that works in my favor—Alex is so busy with his work that he has very little time to fool around. My guess is that he doesn't seek out sex—but on the other hand, he might not be strong enough to withstand a come-on from an alluring woman. How about this Vicky? Hey, even assuming she were available, Alex would have to think twice before getting involved. After all, she's married to his meal ticket for the millennium—that's too much baggage for him.

Alex lifted his wine glass and said, "I want you both to know I really appreciate this dinner, and what Joe said before, especially with him not feeling so great."

"Hey, Alex," said Joe, "I meant every word of it. As a matter of fact, I intend to call you in the next few days about a new deal I've got cooking. If you can spare some time this Saturday—I hope Lynn won't mind me borrowing you again—maybe we can brainstorm the whole thing out in Easthampton, where Vicky insists we spend our late fall weekends."

Lynn listened with one ear, while continuing to ponder Alex's fidelity. *I've always trusted him, but is my trust misplaced? How faithful is the guy when he's a little tipsy? What if he starts working a lot with Joe*

Miller, like next weekend, and then this vixen—uh, this Vicky—starts to come on strong with all that 'Lex' crap . . . ?

Lynn's mind segued to the subject that she now found herself dwelling on more and more often—children. She didn't want to pressure Alex, but she did manage to work it into their conversation, one way or another, almost every month. *God knows*, she thought, *Alex never brings it up himself.*

When Alex did deign to reply to her on the subject, it was always the same thing—"It's not that I don't *ever* want to be a father, Lynn—this is just the wrong time. My career is barreling ahead full steam, and a baby would be too much of a distraction."

Lynn, who worked as an administrator at a prominent art gallery, was much less wrapped up in her career than Alex. The idea of giving it up entirely at age thirty-seven to raise a family didn't bother her in the least. *So that's a big contrast between us—plus which, it's not* his *biological clock that's starting to tick so loudly.*

The celebratory meal now resumed with the arrival of the main course, served by skilled waiters with a great deal of flourish—albeit a trifle pretentiously, to Lynn's mind. The food was rich and the wines full bodied. The clientele was well-heeled, spiffily attired, and generally attractive.

At the Miller table, the conversation was dominated by Joe who, between large mouthfuls of food and drink, was relating anecdotes of recent deals with great panache—more like bombast, to Lynn's mind. Alex was listening attentively, reacting when a response was called for, and interspersing supportive commentary from time to time. Lynn, making little pretense of interest in Joe's stories, continued to dwell on the possibility of Vicky seducing—or of having already seduced—her husband. Vicky gave every appearance of listening, although Lynn was sure that she had mastered the art of looking interested while focusing her mind on other subjects.

"So, net net, I bailed the Barstow guys out, found a buyer for the shares"—Joe Miller paused for emphasis, coughed twice, took another quick swig of wine, and delivered the punch line a little shakily—"and what do you think—not only did those bastards never thank me, they actually used it *against* me in the other deal! It's a perfect example of the old axiom that goes, 'good deeds' . . . no, that's not it . . . that 'no bad deed' . . . uh . . . oh yeah, that 'no good deed goes unpunished.'"

Lynn, whose attention refocused on Joe when she heard him utter the uncharacteristic word "axiom," wondered if he was getting sloshed. She sneaked a glance at her watch, hoping the evening would soon come to an end.

But Alex, whose tongue had evidently been loosened by the wine, seemed to be caught up in the camaraderie of a couple of world-class dealmakers swapping tales. "That's a great story, Joe—really unbelievable. Now let me tell you one that stands for a corollary of that axiom. You'll understand, I'm sure, if I omit the names of the individual and company involved."

Alex began with a rhetorical question. "Do you know what your proudest moment is as a lawyer?" He didn't wait for an answer. "It's the legal profession's equivalent to a surgeon performing brain surgery. It happens when the client is up against the wall—in *extremis*—and there you are, by his side, providing wise counsel, guiding him through the crisis."

Joe Miller nodded in agreement. Vicky looked interested. Lynn was apprehensive about what was in store, and her face showed it. If Alex saw her troubled expression, he ignored it and resumed the narrative. "But there's one caveat I've learned all too painfully over the years, and it's this: While you're performing this intricate maneuver, you must avoid getting into a position where you see your client at his worst—because he will *never* forget it or forgive you for being there."

Lynn had now identified what story Alex was going to relate— she had heard him tell it on other occasions in the past. She wondered how appropriate it was for this audience. Although usually trustful of Alex's judgment in such matters, she realized he'd had a lot to drink tonight.

"I'm not sure I know what y'all mean, Lex," said Vicky in her come-hither voice, "but I'm all ears." Lynn winced.

"Well," said Alex, "a few years ago I was representing a big corporation in negotiating a major acquisition of another company. My client's CEO, who was really hot to do the deal, had taken personal charge of shepherding the difficult negotiations. But as the days wore on and things didn't get resolved, he became increasingly frustrated. Everything peaked on December twenty-third—remember that date, it's significant."

Alex paused, reached for his wine glass, seemed to think better of it, and instead took a sip of water before continuing. "We were having one of those late night bargaining sessions with the other side in the conference room of our client's office. Our CEO was there—I had asked him to be available for any decisions that needed to be made, because I could tell this was a crucial moment in the negotiations. The other side was being ornery on several issues, but the deal was definitely there to be done. If we stuck it out, I was sure we'd be able to reach agreement. But if we didn't shake hands that night, I was worried that the whole thing might crater—since it had to be signed up by year-end or the numbers wouldn't work."

Lynn noticed that Joe appeared to be drifting off—he was facing in Alex's direction, but his eyes were unfocused and glazing over. *Hey, Alex*, she wanted to stage-whisper, *you're losing your audience . . .* But after observing the scene more closely, she surmised that Alex was aiming his narration more at Vicky than at Joe. *Has Alex noticed Joe's glaze, or is he just trying to impress that . . . that . . .* Lynn looked again at Vicky, who was sitting in rapt attention, drinking in every word Alex spoke, resonating on his wavelength with every fiber of her being, urging him irresistibly onward . . . *that slut!*

Now that she'd found an apt noun for her rival, Lynn realized that Alex might be no match for Vicky's wiles—*especially since it looks like he's going to be spending lots of time at the Miller home on business.* Lynn wondered whether, if Alex were to succumb to a sexy lady like Vicky flouncing around in short-shorts, it would just be a fling—*or could Alex ever seriously consider leaving his 'partner-for-life?' That's what he once called me, in his idea of a tender moment . . .* Lynn's conjectures now began to take on an antic tone. *Could Alex's lusting after this slut be the real reason he keeps putting off having a kid?*

Alex now warmed to the heart of his narrative. "Well, the negotiations in the big conference room were going hot and heavy. The CEO became more and more restless and finally retreated to the confines of his private office. I went in there several times to brief him on what was happening. He was unhappy, impatient and irritable.

"So it's about 11:00 P.M., and I'm sitting in the conference room with the other side's lawyer—Russ Simmons. You know him, don't you, Joe—he's a real pro. And now Russ introduces a new point into the bargaining. It wasn't anything crucial, but it did run counter to something both sides had agreed on earlier.

"'You don't want to raise that point, Russ,' I said to him, in my most menacing tone of voice. Russ knew exactly what I was getting at, but he just shrugged and replied, 'Yeah, Alex, I hear you, but my guy brought it up. You've got to ask your guy for it'—which, of course, was his way of telling me, in the shorthand code we sometimes use, 'Don't worry, Alex, we'll be able to work this one out.'"

"So I went into the CEO's office, where he was all alone, pacing the floor. I began to report on this new issue that Russ had raised—but before I could even tell him about Russ's coded signal to me, the CEO started bouncing off the wall. 'That's it,' he screamed, 'the deal's off! I'm going home.' And he threw a yellow pad and two pencils halfway across the room!"

"I couldn't believe it. 'Wait a minute,' I said, 'we can work this out'—but he wasn't listening. 'It's the night before Christmas Eve,' he wailed. 'My kids are in from college, and I'm not home with them. I feel lousy, and these fuckers'—sorry about the language, ladies—'are jerking my chain. If I give in on this, they'll want ten more things. The hell with them—I'm history.'"

"And with that, the CEO put on his overcoat and started to leave the premises. Can you imagine that?! The head of a big public company, and he's ready to throw away this major deal, where we've worked out very favorable terms, just to sing some carols with his kids."

Alex took another sip of water. He had come to the part of the story that, as he once told Lynn, made him feel a little uncomfortable. He didn't like to toot his own horn unduly, but he considered it necessary here in order to set up the punch line.

"I honestly think that what followed was one of my finest performances ever as a lawyer. I was calm and tactful; I was patient; I was painfully rational. I brought the CEO down off the wall, reminded him of how significant he considered the deal to be, put the minor point at issue in context, predicted the shape of the ultimate compromise, convinced him to stay around just a little while longer—and then I marched into the next room and beat Russ Simmons around the head and shoulders until he gave us the terms we needed to sign the agreement. Hooray! My client's wonderful deal was saved."

Alex paused to let this sink in before delivering the punch line. Joe seemed a little more interested, probably sensing the story was coming to an end. Vicky was all ears. If Alex had bothered to glance over at Lynn, he would have seen the troubled look in her eyes—the kind of warning signal he usually heeded. But he wasn't looking in that direction.

Alex now served up the finale with great emphasis, speaking the words very deliberately. "That ... client ... never ... used ... me ... again ... as ... his ... lawyer ... after ... that ... night!"

For a few moments, there was no reaction at the table. Then Vicky broke the silence. "Why not, Lex?" she asked, in a soft purr. "Why didn't he use you, after all you did to save his precious deal?"

Alex turned in his seat to face Vicky. To Lynn's mind, the beatific expression on his face fairly screamed out, "Oh you wonderful woman—that's just the question I wanted you to ask." He held his palms aloft in apparent bemusement at the ways of the world. "In light of the results I had achieved, Vicky, I can think of no other reason than that I had seen him at his absolute worst—impetuous, irrational, self-pitying—and he would never feel comfortable with me again. He just didn't want me around as a reminder."

Vicky nodded in acknowledgment, and then asked him, "Did you know right then—that very night—that this was going to happen?"

"No way," replied Alex. "Just the opposite—I was so proud of my performance, I thought I'd be his lawyer for life."

Alex stopped talking, leaned back in his chair, and took a deliberate sip from his wineglass as if to signal the others that his narrative was concluded.

"That's really something, Lex," said Vicky.

"Yeah . . ." muttered Joe, seemingly from a great distance.

Alex beamed, apparently pleased with his delivery and confident that the tale had gone over well.

"Well, personally, I've never liked that particular war story," said Lynn from out of nowhere. All eyes turned to her. *Oops,* she thought, *what am I saying—why am I criticizing my husband in front of his new meal ticket? It must be that damn Vicky, with her rapt attention and adoring eyes—shades of Pat Nixon! And her breathless 'That's really something, Lex' just touched me off. But I'd better soften the blow now with some typical wifely inanity . . .* "I could never understand what Christmas had to do with the whole thing."

Although Alex replied in a patient tone, Lynn could see he was upset that she had broken the spell he'd worked so hard to create. "The holiday season just heightened the CEO's emotions—his kids had come home, they were trimming the tree and singing carols—the whole ball of wax. He was basically a rational guy who in that moment became irrational, and Christmas might have just been what put him over the top."

"Of course," gushed Vicky, adding with a twinkle, "Oh, you're so observant, Lex. I might say in passing that's *not* a quality one usually associates with corporate lawyers."

Lynn's gaze now moved over to Joe Miller, but what she saw didn't present a pretty picture. Joe's head was bobbing back and forth. His color could aptly be described as "green around the gills." Vicky noticed Joe's shaky appearance at about the same time. "Honey," she said, "are you all right? Is that flu bothering you?" Joe didn't answer. Lynn then chimed in, saying, "I don't like the way Joe looks—"

Alex responded immediately. He stood up, walked around to the back of Joe's chair, and said, "C'mon, Joe, let's you and me take a walk outside. It's getting stuffy in here."

Joe said nothing, but readily acquiesced. With Alex's help, he pushed back his chair, rose, and began to walk unsteadily toward the restaurant entrance. They passed by tables of New York's beautiful people, all absorbed in their food, wine and conversation. Alex steered Joe out of the dining room and into the foyer heading for the street.

Suddenly a look of desperation appeared on Joe's face. Alex again reacted quickly, reversing course and aiming Joe toward the men's room. When they got there, Alex pushed open the lavatory door, and Joe rumbled in behind him, heading desperately for the nearest toilet.

But he didn't make it. Halfway there, Joe made a detour to the sink, gave a big heave, and retched his roast duckling, candied sweets, and the better part of two bottles of wine all over the sink, the counter, and a large section of the floor. It was an ungodly mess. He shook a few times and then heaved again—here came lunch and probably some leftovers from breakfast. Alex had his arms firmly on Joe's shoulders, which trembled as he prepared for another round.

The vomiting finally ended. Alex guided Joe over to one of the toilet stalls where, without removing his pants, Joe sat down to compose himself. Then Alex swung into action. He turned the faucets on full blast to wash the bulk of the mess down the sink. Grabbing big handfuls of paper towels from the dispenser, he blotted up what had landed on the counter.

Alex had just knelt down to wipe the floor when there was a noise outside the room. Rising quickly, he hurried over to the door and bolted it from the inside, just as the handle began to turn. After a moment, there was a loud knock. "Who's in here?" demanded a voice. "Just give us two minutes," Alex replied. "We'll be right out."

Now Alex finished sopping up what was on the floor, flushing the most soiled paper towels down the other toilet. He moistened a tissue, which he used to wipe some drippings off Joe's suit and tie. He even produced a few breath mints that he always carried in his coat pocket.

"Are you feeling better?" Alex asked. Joe nodded affirmatively. "Then let's go out to the street and get a few minutes of air." Alex helped Joe to his feet, unlatched the door, and the two of them exited. The man who had knocked was still outside, giving them a dirty look—as if he suspected they had been having a homosexual encounter in the restroom.

Alex escorted Joe out to the street. Joe inhaled a few gulps of air, walked about twenty feet, circled back, and said,

"Okay, Alex, I'm ready to go back in. Thanks a lot for helping me out."

When they returned to the table, Vicky looked concerned. "How are you, baby?" she said.

"I'm okay," Joe replied.

Alex spoke up. "We just took a little walk outside," he said. "It had gotten too stuffy in here. Sorry we were gone so long, but we had a few deals to talk over . . . you know how it is."

Vicky seemed mollified. Lynn said nothing. The waiter came over, suggesting dessert and coffee, but there were no takers. Joe Miller asked the waiter for the check. While they were waiting, Vicky held the floor, commenting on the quality of the food they'd eaten, comparing this place to several other trendy restaurants where she and Joe had recently dined. Joe paid the bill with a credit card.

They all arose from the table. Alex and Lynn thanked Joe and Vicky for a delightful dinner. The four of them exited the restaurant. Since they were heading in opposite directions, each couple hailed a separate taxi to go home.

In the back seat of their cab, Lynn turned to Alex. "Well," she asked, "what really happened?"

"Oh, you wouldn't have believed it—what a mess!" And Alex proceeded to offer up all the gory details of their men's room odyssey. "Lynn, you know me—I have trouble even clearing the plates from the dining room table and putting them in the dishwasher. Can you picture me down on my hands and knees, sopping up the barf with paper towels? I really came through in the clutch."

Alex shuddered at the recollection. "And how did you like the cool way I handled it when we got back to the table? . . . Joe didn't say much, but I could tell he was very grateful . . . First, I got him out of that legal mess a month ago, and tonight I pull him out of another kind of mess . . . I wonder what the new deal is—the one he mentioned he wants to talk about later this week?"

Lynn sat there quietly, taking in Alex's graphic report. After a minute or so, for the first time that night, the corners of her mouth turned up in a smile. Soon after, when they arrived at their apartment building and were exiting the cab, Lynn's face broke into a big grin, as she realized that the flirtatious Vicky—who had been such a concern to her only a half hour ago—was no threat at all to their marriage.

For in that instant—which Lynn punctuated by giving her hero husband a playful slap on the rump—Lynn knew for a certainty there would be no more seductive Saturday evenings in Easthampton for Alex. *After all*, she thought, silently mimicking her sometimes insightful husband, *it's the 'corollary axiom'—there's not a shadow of a doubt. After tonight, and for as long as he practices law, Alex Gibson will never see another piece of business come his way from Joe Miller.* . . .

Commentary on
The Corollary Axiom

In certain of these stories, I've scattered points throughout the narrative for lawyers to ponder. By contrast, my intention in "The Corollary Axiom" was to make a single point, but in the kind of graphic detail that will hopefully bring it to mind if the reader ever encounters a comparable situation.

The point in question has particular meaning for me because it's something I've encountered personally several times—in fact, I like to treat it as my private discovery. (I'm sure others have come to a similar conclusion; I just haven't heard their versions.) It's in the same ironic vein as its well-known corollary that "no good deed goes unpunished." The point, as expressed in the story by Alex Gibson, is "Avoid getting into a position where you see your client at his worst—because he will *never* forget it or forgive you for being there."

But although it was designed to make that one point memorable, the story does touch on several other matters of interest along the way. So I'm going to save the axiom for later and start by discussing these other items.

At the heart of the story is a young Jenkins & Price partner, Alex Gibson. Remember Alex? He was Dwight Bentley's nemesis in "The Smell Test"—using all his wiles to get J&P to take on a questionable assignment. Alex wasn't a very appealing personage back then. "The Corollary Axiom" presents another side of him, and the question is, do you like the guy any better now?

The other characters are Alex's wife, Lynn, an investment banker named Joe Miller, and the latter's wife, Vicky. I'll have more to say about each of them after a few words on the setup for the story.

As contrasted with "On-the-Job Training," which features a first-person narrator (Ted Ashburn), the narration in this story is in the third person (as in "Partnergate" and "The Smell Test"). And, like "The Smell Test," we only get to peer inside one person's head.

In my original draft of this story, the head we were inside was Alex's. On further reflection, I saw it would be more interesting to have Lynn observe and comment on the proceedings from her vantage point. So, although Alex is the central character, any insights into him have to be based on the detached observations of a third-party narrator and the more personal musings of his wife.

In contrast to other stories that take place over a period of days or weeks in differing locales, this story (akin to the car setting of "Father's Day") is related in a single continuous scene, with all but the final taxi segment taking place in a trendy Manhattan restaurant.

"The Corollary Axiom" touches on two separate relationships—lawyer/client and husband/wife. Let's examine the lawyer/client interaction first.

In "On-the-Job Training," we observed two aspects of this: servicing an existing client (Ken Hellman) and going after a new client (Prime Industrials). In "The Corollary Axiom," the focus is on a third chore dear to the heart of business lawyers—attempting to pry more business out of an existing client. And here, it's not just any client, but rather Joe Miller, whom Alex considers "the hottest investment banker on the Street."

Well, Alex is heading down the right track. What makes investment bankers special for business lawyers is that if they esteem your abilities, they'll introduce you into deals you wouldn't get near otherwise—often representing one of the parties, whence most large fees emanate. And although historically the investment banking firms had ties to a single law firm each, things had changed by the time of this story in the late 1970s, and deal-oriented investment bankers were reaching out to utilize other lawyers possessing special skills. Today, of course, this has become very much the norm.

As the story begins, it looks like Alex has already made a lot of progress in courting Joe Miller's business. For openers, note that Joe is taking Alex and his wife out to dinner—not the other way around. At the dinner, Joe toasts Alex as "a brilliant young man" and "one of the great young deal lawyers in New York." Alex has bailed Joe out of a mess (created by another law firm), for which Joe is very grateful. From now on, Joe tells Alex, "You're the guy I want in my corner." And Joe makes the kudos more tangible by alluding to a new deal he's got cooking that he wants to discuss with Alex over the weekend.

It sounds to me like Joe Miller is a real Alex Gibson fan. The praise may be a little overblown—Lynn dubs it "sincere hyperbole"—which can be attributable to the wine. But Joe's wife, Vicky, reinforces its genuine nature by noting how seldom this happens—what she mostly hears is Joe bawling lawyers out.

How about Alex? On the surface, we observe a display of false modesty as he tries (not too hard) to deflect the compliments. But we know better, via Lynn's sharp eye. Underneath, he's eating it up, savoring every word (except "young," which she's sure he has already excised from Joe's "great deal lawyer" accolade). Lynn speculates that Alex is memorizing the plaudits verbatim for later transmission to his partners, where word that Joe Miller will be directing business Alex's way is likely to propel him ahead of his peers at the firm.

But this isn't just a meal between lawyer and client. What makes it more engaging is that they have their wives along. And while the two men are pretty much in synch—seemingly cut from the same cloth—the two women to all appearances couldn't be more different.

Let's start with Vicky, Joe Miller's wife, as she's observed through Lynn Gibson's eyes. A sultry and sleek Faye Dunaway type, Vicky is shamelessly flirting with Lynn's husband right in front of Lynn. Worse, she seems to be getting through to him with all that "Lex" and "handsome" stuff—he looks to Lynn like he's on the verge of an orgasm. Still, Lynn is forced to admit that Vicky does a good job of bolstering her husband's efforts—adding her own emphasis to the message Joe is trying to convey ("I just know how much Joe Miller thinks of your man, Lynn.")

This latter observation makes Lynn (to whom we now turn) acknowledge that she isn't that sort of wife to Alex. Not only doesn't she do the kind of stuff that might further his career, but Alex even chides her on occasion for some ill-considered remarks. She realizes she should be proud of him, but her feelings are ambivalent—note the adverse comparison she makes between what Alex does and the then current exploits of Anwar Sadat. Her husband is so intent on his work that there's little time left for her, and she sits home alone at night watching TV. Overlayering all this is a strong streak of cynicism, which we recognize right from the start with her "he forgot to add 'wife-neglecting'" thought in the second paragraph.

Lynn doesn't seem interested in her work. What she wants to do is have kids—a subject Alex keeps putting off, while her biological clock ticks away. It's a major—although largely unspoken—issue between them.

To be sure, we don't get to hear Alex's side of all this. But we learn enough to infer that, at least of late, Alex hasn't handled the marital relationship well. It's a predicament that's familiar enough (we saw a bit of it in "Father's Day") to deserve a cautionary comment.

Practicing law can be very demanding and, unless you're careful, all-consuming. You have to step back periodically and check how this may be affecting those closest to you—in particular, your spouse. Giving marital advice isn't my bag, and I won't presume to do so here. But (based on painful personal experience) I feel comfortable in recommending that lawyers devote at least the same degree of intensity to their marriages (and their kids) as they do to their clients.

At the time the stories in this collection take place, most of the lawyers were male, so the shortchanged spouse in question was typically a wife. In today's world, however, I would imagine that my recommendation has equal validity for a hard-charging woman lawyer with a less driven husband.

Getting back to Alex Gibson, he clearly hasn't been listening to my advice. He's rude to Lynn, makes her feel abandoned, and even refuses to discuss the subject that's nearest and dearest to her heart—children. And on this particular night, he goes one step further—virtually slobbering over Vicky in his wife's presence. Hey, Alex, that's not smart. . . .

This raises the explosive question for Lynn of how faithful Alex has been. On the one hand, she reasons, he has little time to fool around; on the other, he's been spending some of that time in the Miller home, without ever mentioning Joe's glamorous wife—is he trying to conceal something? Sex is all over the place in the late '70s, and this Vicky is plenty sexy. Sure, there's a lot of baggage involved, but could Alex withstand a "handsome Lex" come-on from her if he's had a little too much to drink? Lynn is forced to wonder whether her trust has been misplaced.

So that's the backdrop against which the main events of the story play out. The two couples are having an elaborate dinner in a fancy restaurant. Joe (who looks to Lynn like he's getting sloshed) is regaling the company with some recent exploits. One involves an instance that to Joe exemplifies the paradoxical maxim, "No good deed goes unpunished." Thereupon Alex, in the spirit of the evening, follows up with his tale illustrating what he christens the "corollary" to that axiom.

For any lawyer reading this, I want to issue a general note of caution. By all means, you ought to entertain (and be entertained by) clients and prospective clients. Social contacts of this sort can be helpful in cementing the personal aspects of the relationship. Just make sure not to lose control of yourself during those informal moments, especially if you've had a lot to drink. Offhand remarks that seem appropriate when uttered might not bear close perusal the next morning. And stay away from both extremes—avoid moments of arrogance as well as confessions of weakness. Also be careful in terms of the jokes you tell—you can never predict when your guileless stereotype might offend someone.

The particular tale that Alex relates is a good one that illustrates his point. The subject matter flows from Joe's story, so it doesn't just come out of nowhere. And Alex narrates it capably. But, let me ask you:

Do you think Alex is wise to recount this episode to Joe Miller?

On the plus side, I can personally vouch for the sentiment expressed. I've watched this play out for me enough times—related to events that occur both in the course of rendering professional services and also in a social setting—to be comfortable making it into an ironic generalization.

Further, I'm sure Alex never considered Joe Miller as the kind of client described in the tale. Joe has been emitting every indication that Alex Gibson will be his go-to guy for life. Alex is overlooking any distress signs that Joe may have been telegraphing. Most notably, Alex probably doesn't associate his corollary axiom with something occurring in nonprofessional surroundings like this—remember, his tale dealt with a client's infantile behavior during a late-night negotiation.

Still, Alex should realize by now that there's no such thing as a lifetime guarantee in lawyer-client relations. You may be the fair-haired boy (or girl) one day and out the door the next. Even if you've done nothing wrong, you can be replaced without any warning. Ten other lawyers are hustling that same client for business, and one of them may have recently steered something important the client's way, or another sits alongside the client on a prominent board, or a third just married the client's niece.

This is especially true where investment bankers are concerned. Many of them make no secret of the fact that they're influenced in giving out business by what a particular lawyer has done for them recently—such as getting an investment banker in the door to represent existing clients of the lawyer.

In view of all that, I don't think it's a good idea for you to tell one client a tale about another client—especially where, as here, the episode portrays your other client in a negative light. Even if you're trying to draw a contrast between the wonderful client in your presence and the imperfect client of the tale, it can still backfire. The client in the room may not be amused—envisioning you on some later occasion spinning negative yarns about him to other prospective clients.

Then, too, I'm uncomfortable with the implicit thrust of the tale—that because Alex performed well on one occasion, he was entitled to receive that client's subsequent business (and thus was wrongfully deprived of it when the client ceased using him). I can't think of anything with the potential to turn off a client more than a lawyer asserting a claim of entitlement to the client's business. I much prefer the deliberately modest tone and look of abject gratitude that Alex displayed earlier in the evening.

Turning now to the corollary axiom itself, you know my views on the subject, but let me ask you:

What do you think of this particular item of folk wisdom? Is it just something that's good for a chuckle, or is there a larger grain of truth lodged in there?

I suppose the answer to this query may depend on whether you've ever experienced something similar—which can happen, of course, in other relationships outside that of lawyer/client. But turning now from the general to the particular:

Do you think Alex will ever see any more business from Joe?

My response to this depends in part on what Alex does about the situation after the fact. Look, even if you take the corollary axiom to heart, it doesn't tell you how to react when the moment arises. "Don't see the client at his worst" may be good advice, but in many cases, the situation is unavoidable. Once Joe's distress at the table became obvious, Alex's response to walk him outside is the humane thing to do. In fact, not helping him at that moment might have damaged Alex's relations with Joe (and Vicky) even more.

So, if you were Alex, and assuming you wake up tomorrow and realize the inherent downside of what happened last night, I ask you:

What might you do to minimize the potential reverberations from the restaurant debacle?

Let me start with the obvious—whatever you do, don't exacerbate the situation. Recognize what a downer this is for the client. Say nothing that makes you appear judgmental, either at the time of the incident or later on. In fact, never refer to it at all—and certainly don't crow over having pulled the client's irons out of the fire.

If I were Alex, I'd call Joe Miller the very next day, thank him for the dinner, and—without a word about the bathroom scene—segue right into some professional talk. If I weren't working on something currently for Joe, I'd tell him about a new Delaware case that came down recently, or point out a wrinkle my partner is using in another deal that might be useful to Joe down the road. My intent is to show Joe that I've already forgotten about what happened last night and want to return to just being his go-to guy.

The real irony of the story is that even at the end of the evening, Alex is gloating about what a hero he'd been during Joe's horrible moment—utterly failing to see how this fits into the corollary axiom he was touting earlier at the table. Lynn sees the connection clearly— in fact, she's gleeful on the subject, because it ends her worries about Vicky—but I doubt she's going to mention the insight to her husband.

So, Alex may well go back to the firm, tell his partners all the nice things Joe Miller said about him, and predict a great influx of new business from that source. We don't know, of course, whether the corollary axiom will actually apply in this case, but I'll tell you one thing for sure—counting your chickens before they hatch is never good policy. If that new business Alex is crowing about doesn't materialize, his partners are likely to assume that Alex screwed up somewhere along the way. So—assuming Alex becomes aware of the evening's relevance to the axiom—he should hold off blowing his own horn to his partners until he's sure the barf scene won't affect his relationship with Joe Miller.

Finally, if I were Alex, and Lynn was eventually kind enough to open my eyes to the potential applicability of the corollary axiom, here's what I'd say to her: "Thank you, dear, for being so insightful. I've erred in underestimating how helpful you can be to me in my work. And, by the way, this weekend would be a good time for us to have that discussion about enlarging the family. . . ."

AWASH IN ASSOCIATES

A ssociates!" The word bellowed forth from Elliot Cheever's prim mouth, an emotional negative outburst uncharacteristic of the man and solely attributable to the frustrations of the moment. The ensuing thought, not uttered aloud, was more balanced—they can be helpful, sometimes downright indispensable, but they can also drive you crazy.

Cheever was sitting alone at the antique desk in his office. The outside light was fading, and the ceiling bulbs had not yet been turned on. The room was spacious, befitting a senior corporate partner of Jenkins & Price, with a decor and appearance that reflected Elliot's conception of himself—understated elegance. And, as he was always quick to note, there was none of that mess so common to the offices of his other partners.

Elliot sat in the dim light, brooding over the two associates of the firm he was currently dealing with. One of them—Gary Stone—he considered a royal pain in the behind, ruing the day Stone had been assigned to him for the latest Driggs acquisition. The other was Bob Gumley, who up until today Elliot had looked on as one of the good ones. Just my luck, he thought, that Gumley turns out to have a problem of considerable delicacy—a problem Elliot was finding quite difficult to deal with. What did I do, he implored the heavens, to deserve this?

The disquieting news had arrived at noon that day, a sparkling Thursday in May. Elliot had been invited to lunch at a fine midtown restaurant by one of his most important clients, Walter Sykes. As clients go, Sykes was a real gem—personable, not too demanding, never one to disturb Elliot on weekends or complain about his sizable bills.

The restaurant—which had been featured in a recent magazine article selecting 1979's Top Ten Eateries—had lived up to its billing. The food was excellent, the service flawless, the conversation spirited. And Walter had sweetened the repast by announcing that the Sykes organization was retaining Jenkins & Price to handle a major piece of new business.

Cheever was pleased by the news, but not surprised. Frankly, he expected no less, given the superior quality of the work product he and his colleagues turned out—at least most of them—and their consistent emphasis on serving the client's every need. Elliot considered the ability to generate significant new business to be one of his trademarks, as a respected and successful senior corporate partner of the firm.

Walter Sykes, a well-built man with an amiable countenance, took a final bite of the key lime pie, wiped his mouth with a napkin, and said, "Oh, by the way, Elliot, there's something a little awkward I feel the need to mention. It concerns Bob Gumley."

Cheever looked up in surprise. He considered Bob Gumley to be one of the most talented associates at the law firm. Elliot had brought Bob on to the Sykes team earlier in the year, and things had gone swimmingly ever since. Gumley's sure hand relieved Elliot of much of the day-to-day chore of dealing with Sykes and his lieutenants.

"Has Bob done something wrong?" Elliot asked.

"Oh, no, not at all—Bob's a terrific lawyer and we all have the highest opinion of him, except—except for one thing. . . ."

Cheever could see that Sykes was having trouble. If it didn't concern Gumley's lawyering, Elliot thought, what could the problem be? Had Bob made a pass at one of Walter's female executives? Might he have recorded some phony disbursements?

"It's just that . . ." Sykes paused, then seemed to gather up sufficient steam to put the issue on the table ". . . that Gumley exudes a very offensive body odor. Not just occasionally, but almost every time we meet with him. My people are all acutely aware of this. It fills the room—like the gamy aroma that radiates from the front seat of a New York City yellow cab in the middle of August. To be blunt, it's driving all of us crazy."

Cheever was, to say the least, taken aback by this unexpected revelation and the apparent fervor behind Sykes' words. Emanating as it did from an otherwise rational and valued client, Elliot realized this wasn't a bit of locker room joshing but rather unmistakably serious business—something that could, if not rectified, endanger their relationship.

From years of experience, Cheever knew that when a good client, for whatever reason, wants to change the associate who services his account, the law firm complies in order to mollify the client. So, although dreading the possible answer, Elliot asked, "Do you want us to replace Gumley with another associate?"

"No, we don't," Walter replied. "He's very smart, extremely personable, and everyone thinks highly of him—other than on the personal hygiene front. But frankly, Elliot, we don't think it's our place to confront Bob on this subject. That's why I've brought the matter up—so that you, as his employer, can do something about it. And, by the way, whatever you decide to do, just make sure not to identify us as the ones who raised the issue."

With that, Walter Sykes shifted to another topic, and nothing further was said about Bob Gumley.

On the way back to his office, Cheever reflected on what he'd been asked to do. An incident came to mind from years earlier, when he was a junior partner at the firm. Old man Jenkins, the managing partner, had called Elliot into his office one day. A client the two of them shared had voiced an objection to the beard grown by an associate who worked on the account. Jenkins was passing along to Elliot the responsibility for seeing that it got shaved off.

Even now, years later, Elliot still took pride in his response to Jenkins: "Tell the client to go to hell! If he wants a change of associates, we'll accommodate him. But I'm not going to tell this young lad he can't wear hair on his face, if that's what he chooses to do."

Although startled, Jenkins didn't protest. Presumably, he didn't repeat Cheever's tirade to the client. When nothing happened, the matter was simply allowed to drop, and the beard remained intact.

But now Cheever—ever aware of the lawyer's duty to assess the relevance of what might or might not be a controlling precedent—asked himself the sixty-four thousand dollar question: Are smelly armpits equivalent to facial hair? He then proceeded to conduct a brief internal debate, taking care to present fairly both sides of the question. Issues of social acceptability, voluntariness, personal hygiene, and group dynamics were raised and assessed. Elliot concluded that, on balance, a meaningful distinction did exist between the two situations, making it inappropriate for him to get up on his high horse to protect the dignity of this associate.

Besides, Cheever was forced to admit, Sykes had a point. Elliot liked Bob Gumley a lot, thought highly of him as an associate, and fully intended to propose him for partnership next year. But now that he reflected on it, Elliot realized he had been aware of the rank odor Bob frequently exuded, although heretofore shrugging it off as none of his business.

Cheever recalled a conversation with another partner a number of months back on this precise subject. The reason Gumley reeked, according to the other partner, was because several times a day Bob closed the door of his office in order to perform a vigorous workout, featuring a prodigious number of old-fashioned jumping jacks. There were no exercise facilities at Jenkins & Price, and nary a shower—ergo, Gumley's pungent scent.

Cheever tried to avoid thinking about the subject for the balance of the afternoon, but now, seated in his office as darkness fell, he could no longer shirk his painful duty. Yet the issue of how to handle this gave Elliot a lot of trouble.

Elliot had cut his teeth as a young lawyer in a day when associates wore three piece suits and a hat to the office. Juniors knew their place and would never have created problems like this for seniors to sort out. Moreover, Elliot had started out drafting trust indentures—meticulous work calling for old-fashioned methodical lawyering skills, of a sort unlikely to arouse dormant sweat glands.

Cheever knew what he ought to do, but was extremely reluctant to adopt a straightforward frontal approach to the problem. It might have been different if he could ascribe the indictment to someone else, but Elliot was under strict orders not to reveal that the complaint emanated from Walter Sykes—ergo, it would have to be transmitted as Elliot's own reproach.

He was not unaware of the touch of irony in the present situation. Many years ago, when he himself was a young associate at the firm, Elliot had been schooled by Dwight Bentley and other partners to apply "a smell test" for sniffing out disguised schemes of corporate chicanery. He had learned that lesson well, but now he found himself up against a very different kind of smell test. . . .

And so, strange as it may seem, this pillar of the legal community—who took on tough adversaries daily in often bruising confrontations—just couldn't bring himself to tell Bob Gumley about his body odor.

Still, Cheever realized he had to do something about the situation. With Walter Sykes—unlike the case of the beard-phobic client—it wouldn't just go away. And unless Elliot were able to quash the difficulty now, he would feel duty bound to reveal Walter's comment to his partners when Bob Gumley came up for partner next year.

At this point, Elliot's attention became distracted by some papers on his desk that related to the Driggs situation—forcibly reminding him of the other associate problem on his plate, the one featuring Gary Stone. . . .

Elliot Cheever had frequently been heard to say that, for a partner in a law firm who does business deals for a living, three things provide contentment. First was having a client he could reason with and who makes sensible decisions. Second was having an associate on his team who could be relied on to carry the ball, a veritable extension of Elliot himself. And third was having the negotiating leverage in the deal be on his client's side. When all three coalesced, he considered himself in clover.

But in the Driggs-Norton deal he was handling now, *none* of the three existed—which accounted for why Elliot was bemoaning his fate.

His client was Driggs Corp., a big private company owned by Jake Driggs, who ran it with an iron fist. Cheever well knew that Jake was one tough cookie, especially when he was buying something—like this smaller private company, Norton Inc., that he was now trying to acquire. Driggs Corp. had plenty of money, but Jake didn't like to overpay—even a little bit.

Elliot had seen that clearly three months ago in the first deal he worked on for Driggs. Jake was trying to acquire a company called Packet Ltd. After some hard bargaining, the two sides were very close to an agreement. All Jake needed to do was put a few more dollars on the table, and Packet was his—but Jake refused to do so. He wouldn't even let Elliot float a trial balloon with the other lawyer about the possibility of a splitting-the-difference compromise—that kind of thing, Jake said, would just show weakness on our part.

Unfortunately, as a result of his intransigence, Driggs lost the Packet deal to another buyer who surfaced out of nowhere and proved to be more flexible on price. When he heard the news, Jake's reaction was, "Good riddance!" Cheever surmised that Jake was one of those clients who never admit to any shortcomings in their performance—although Elliot sensed that losing the Packet deal came as a real blow to Driggs.

But was it a blow that Jake would learn from? Elliot doubted it. And the question wasn't moot, because precisely the same type of situation seemed to be developing in the Norton deal. After some spirited bargaining, in which Jake reluctantly increased his offer to $49 million, Norton reduced its asking price for the company to $50 million—accompanying its last move with an unequivocal message that it was unwilling to sell for a price under $50 million.

Cheever could see that most of the leverage in the deal was in the Norton corner. Since the acquisition would fill an obvious large gap in the Driggs product line—something no other transaction could do—the Norton people knew that Jake Driggs very much wanted to see the transaction happen. By contrast, Steve Norton, the dominant stockholder of Norton Inc., seemed to be under no necessity to sell if he couldn't get his price. What's more, there were a number of other potential buyers—anxious to get their hands on the Norton product line—who would be likely to step in and offer a full price if the negotiations with Driggs proved unsuccessful.

Given this state of affairs, Cheever was convinced that Norton would stand firm at $50 million, and he told Driggs so. But Jake replied, with some firmness of his own, that he was unwilling to go any higher than the $49 million of his last bid. Elliot was worried that if this stalemate continued, Steve Norton would either take his company off the market or solicit some other buyer who would be more amenable to walking the extra mile.

If Cheever wasn't happy with his client or his side's negative leverage in the deal, he was even less pleased about Gary Stone, the fourth year associate who had been assigned to him for the project. He had never worked with Gary before, but had received plenty of negative feedback about the associate from other partners—and from what Elliot could tell so far, several weeks into the deal, it was all justified.

Gary Stone simply wasn't at all like the typical buttoned-down, conservative J&P associate—especially those in the corporate department. Gary was, and apparently always had been, a nonconforming individualist. He started out as a peacenik in the mid-1960s, then moved on to a hippie lifestyle in Haight-Ashbury. He decided to go to law school in the early '70s, but even there marched to his own drummer. There were stories of him roaring up to the classroom building on his crimson motorcycle, helmetless, his long locks flowing.

Stone managed to do well enough academically to get a job offer from Jenkins & Price, but it soon became clear that he wasn't cut from the same mold as the other associates. Serious questions were raised about his work ethic, along with mutterings over his attitude. Elliot had also heard unflattering descriptions of Gary as a "sideways" thinker—invariably coming at problems from a different perspective than the rest of his colleagues.

His idiosyncrasies weren't limited to the office. For example, while other associates shared a house in the Hamptons or went skiing at Stratton, Gary Stone's idea of a vacation was to fly out to Las Vegas and spend ten hours straight at the craps table. No, thought Elliot, he wasn't your ordinary Wall Street corporate associate by a long shot.

Nothing Cheever had seen from Stone so far in this frustrating Driggs-Norton deal made the slightest dent in the unfavorable image Elliot harbored about the associate. And the fact that he was saddled with Gary for the duration—coupled with today's alarming heads-up about Bob Gumley from Walter Sykes—did much to account for Elliot's current negative state of mind. "Associates!"—he blurted out the word once again, and it echoed around his darkened office.

Elliot Cheever, master legal strategist, now proceeded to come up with a plan to handle the sticky circumstance of Bob Gumley. Although he wouldn't have conceded the label, others might have characterized it as a sideways approach. The challenge for him was to devise a course of action that wouldn't embarrass himself or devastate the associate but yet would resolve the problem. After all, thought Elliot as he contemplated his next move—his face wreathed in one of those "aren't I clever?" expressions—this is what I do for a living. I take on a problem, analyze it, and come up with an imaginative solution that no one else has thought of. If it works in corporate finance with all the attendant complexities, why shouldn't it handle a simple case of BO?

The next day, Cheever called Bob Gumley to his office to discuss some pending matters. By now, he was acutely conscious of the rank aroma wafting across his desk. After five minutes of legal analysis, Elliot put down his pen and shifted into phase one of his action plan.

"By the way, Bob, I happened to be walking by your office the other day. Although the door was closed, there was a distinctive sound coming from inside, which could be heard quite clearly in the corridor. I was puzzled for a minute, and then I recognized what the sound was—the occupant of the room was doing jumping jacks!" Elliot paused, a quizzical expression playing about the corner of his eyes. "Was I correct in my observation?"

Gumley managed a sheepish grin. "Yes, very likely. It's no secret that I do jumping jacks on a regular basis. My father was a big fan of the Royal Canadian Air Force exercise routine, and he drilled it into me at an early age. I find it helps me stay alert and energized."

"Well, Bob," said Elliot, adopting an avuncular tone, "I have nothing against jumping jacks, which are certainly an admirable form of exercise that I should probably do more of myself." He patted his paunch a few times by way of acknowledging the omission of the renowned RCAF exercises from his daily routine. "But I must say—and I feel others would concur with me here—that the resultant thudding one hears so clearly in the corridor is not in keeping with the dignity of a law office, especially for a first-rank firm like Jenkins & Price. So, as they say, a word to the wise . . . Now, about that latest draft of the agreement you sent me yesterday. . . ."

When Gumley entered Cheever's office the following day, the partner took a quick sniff and was distressed to realize that the associate's musty aroma still persisted. This was belied, however, by Bob's self-satisfied look. At the first opportunity, he broke the news to Elliot.

"I want you to know that I took what you said yesterday to heart."

"You did?" said Elliot, an unwitting trace of sarcasm creeping into his voice. "Does that mean you stopped exercising in your office?"

"No," replied Gumley, flashing a triumphant smile, "I went out and bought myself a stationary bike. A good buy, too—only $54.99. It's very quiet. I had one of the guys check the hall outside my office while I was pedaling, and you can't hear it at all—none of that thudding noise you noticed before."

Elliot managed a weak affirmative shake of his head to acknowledge the improvement in sound quality. He was beginning to realize, however, that his task might prove more difficult than anticipated.

His next foray into rectifying the problem took place at a partnership meeting a few days later. After routine matters had been covered and the floor was opened to new business, Cheever addressed his partners.

"I've been thinking that in this day and age of heightened health consciousness, it would be wise for us as a firm—in terms of recruiting new associates and keeping our existing staff fit and happy—to put in a small exercise facility on the premises. A stationary bike or two, some barbells, a few workout mats, a shower."

After a brief discussion, the Cheever proposal was shot down on the grounds of insufficient space available to construct such a facility. Still, Elliot wouldn't let go of the subject. "Well, then, how about the firm sponsoring memberships for associates at Good Health—that splendid new exercise club a few blocks from the office? It would be a desirable fringe benefit for the young lawyers, and we'd all benefit by the improvement in their physical condition . . ." But the consensus of his partners was that the associates were already making too much money, and what the firm really needed was to keep its expenses down.

"Hey, Elliot," asked Lenny Tatum, one of his partners, "how come you're so determined on this subject? I bet you saw that movie last year, *Pumping Iron*, with that beefcake guy, Arnold . . . what's his name? . . . Schwarzenegger or something like that. Are you thinking of getting in shape yourself?" Amid a chorus of chuckles, the pear-shaped Elliot Cheever replied, "Oh, no, nothing so radical—just an idea my wife had that I decided to pass along."

Later that day, Cheever was discussing the Driggs-Norton situation with Gary Stone in Elliot's office. Stone was sitting with his left leg up over the arm of the pull-up chair, his long hair flowing down past his shoulders. Since the day they started working together, Elliot had been bothered by this annoying habit of Gary's—lounging there, his gaze directed to the ceiling, conveying the impression that he could care less about what was happening in the deal and would much rather be somewhere else.

Cheever was doing most of the talking. Given the lack of feedback, he decided to use the time to instruct Stone on some of the finer points of negotiating.

"Now clearly, to a rational businessman, this situation might seem absurd. I mean, the $1 million difference between the parties' positions is roughly 2 percent of the total price. In the overall scheme of things, it's negligible—especially since this acquisition is a real prize and a matter of much importance to Driggs Corp. I've pointed that out to Jake Driggs, of course, but he's very stubborn—I have a hunch his manhood has somehow gotten mixed up in this."

Without lowering his eyes from the ceiling, Gary said in an offhand, seemingly bored manner, "But isn't this the ideal spot for a splitting-the-difference type of compromise resolution?"

"Of course it is," Elliot replied. "Now don't get me wrong, I'm not a disciple of splitting the difference when the positions of the parties aren't that close—say, if the spread were between $45 and $55 million. But at this narrow gap of only $1 million, it makes a lot more sense. Still, Jake doesn't want our side to propose the split. If only there were some neutral observer who could recommend it without causing either side to change position . . ."

"Why is that important?" asked Gary, showing a bit more interest while smoothing his long hair with the palm of his hand.

"Because the key tactical decision at this point often comes down to this—which side is going to be the one who suggests splitting it down the middle? If you wait for the other side to make the move, it may never happen. If you do it yourself, you run a certain risk."

Cheever paused to see if Gary was following his train of thought. The associate didn't give him the satisfaction of even a grunt, but Elliot decided to go on anyway. "To illustrate, let's say our side suggests a split at $49.5 million. If Norton doesn't accept it, then our implicit new position—regardless of what caveats we attach to the proposal—is $49.5 million, because Norton now knows that we're willing to go at least that far. Meanwhile, Norton is still at $50 million. So, if a compromise is ultimately struck, it's more likely to be in the neighborhood of $49.7 or $49.8 million than the halfway point we proposed."

Gary evidently had been listening. "How about if the suggestion comes from you to the Norton lawyer, as an aside?"

"I could do that and attach a disclaimer—such as, 'Hey, it just occurred to me that perhaps I could sell my client on a number somewhere in the middle, if you're willing to make a similar effort with yours.' But if they're any kind of negotiators, the Norton people are going to assume that my seemingly offhand proposal has been precleared with Jake Driggs. So, once the words are out of my mouth, the damage is done."

They sat there in silence for a few moments. Cheever was about to suggest that they move on to other matters when Gary actually tilted his head forward and looked in the partner's direction for the first time. "Hey, Elliot, I've got an idea here—courtesy of Las Vegas."

Cheever couldn't believe it. So *this*, he thought, is where Stone's mind has been! I'm consumed with the looming threat of another busted deal, and Gary's head is out in the Nevada desert . . .

"I know," Elliot replied, in a rare foray into what he took to be Las Vegas patois, "we offer to comp the entire Norton team at the Sands for a week if they'll drop their price into our range."

"No, I'm serious"—and as if to buttress his sincerity, Gary brought his elevated leg down to the floor and sat up straight. "Let's shoot craps to determine the compromise price."

Now Elliot was impatient. "Sure, and then we can play blackjack to decide who pays for the photographer at the closing."

Stone looked at him with an expression Cheever hadn't seen from the associate before—a glum recognition that Elliot was just another in a long line of uptight lawyers that Gary had been forced to deal with over the years. "Okay," said Gary, "just forget it." And his leg went back up over the arm of the chair as his gaze swept skyward.

Elliot realized he might have been a trifle heavy-handed. "Oh, don't be so sensitive—I'm just engaging in some playful banter. If you've got a constructive suggestion, I'd be happy to listen to it."

Gary looked over at Elliot warily, as if deciding whether or not to proceed. A few moments passed, and then he said, "Have you ever shot craps in a place like Vegas?"

"Actually, I have on one occasion, although I can't say I'm experienced."

"This doesn't require craps expertise—it's purely a matter of mathematics, the simple math of craps shooting."

"Go ahead—but it's safer for you to assume I don't know anything about it."

Gary took a deep breath, and then the words flowed from him in a gusher. "Look, each die is numbered from 1 to 6. So two dice can produce 36 possible numerical combinations. That translates into 11 different numerical totals, ranging from 2 to 12. Are you with me so far?"

Elliot gave him an affirmative nod.

Gary continued. "The number 7, the number most often rolled, can be made 6 different ways—6-1, 5-2, 4-3, 3-4, 2-5, and 1-6. So, with 36 possibilities, the odds against the dice coming up 7 on a single roll are 6 to 1. The next most common numbers, 6 and 8, can each be rolled 5 ways; the 5 and 9, 4 ways; the 4 and 10, 3 ways; the 3 and 11, 2 ways. Snake eyes—the number 2—and boxcars—12—can each be thrown only one way." Gary paused, as if checking to see that Elliot was following him.

"Go on," Elliot said in a noncommittal tone. He thought he saw where this was heading, but the whole thing violated every lawyerly instinct in his body.

Gary breathed deeply again. "My notion is to link the final purchase price to a roll of the dice. Since the dice can produce 11 possible totals, an increment of purchase price would be assigned to each number. For example, since 2 is the lowest dice total, that can serve as the low end of the bargaining range, $49 million. The highest dice total is 12; that can be the top of the range, $50 million. And it just so happens that each number in between can be assigned a $100,000 increment." He smiled at the elegance of the mathematics, and then added, almost as an aside, "Actually, whatever the bargaining gap is, dividing it by 10 creates the appropriate increments. So, for example, with a $500,000 gap, the increments would be $50,000 each."

Elliot knew he would have to react. It was clever, he had to admit, and a pleasant interlude in his otherwise troubled day. But now the time had come to get back to business.

Before Elliot could say anything, however, Gary appeared to get a sudden impulse and reached down to pick up the yellow pad that had been on the floor at his feet.

"Give me two minutes and I'll diagram this—give you a table to illustrate what I'm suggesting." Stone seemed so earnest and enthusiastic—so different from heretofore—that Elliot didn't have the heart to cut Gary's exposition short. The associate began to write furiously on the pad—words, numbers, columns—not stopping to alter a single stroke. When he finished—which didn't take much longer than the predicted two minutes—he handed Elliot the results. What he had written down looked something like this:

Dice Total	Purchase Price	Ways to Roll (out of 36 Possibilities)	Odds Against
2	$49 million	1	35-1
3	$49.1 million	2	17-1
4	$49.2 million	3	11-1
5	$49.3 million	4	8-1
6	$49.4 million	5	6.2-1
7	$49.5 million	6	5-1
8	$49.6 million	5	6.2-1
9	$49.7 million	4	8-1
10	$49.8 million	3	11-1
11	$49.9 million	2	17-1
12	$50.0 million	1	35-1

While Elliot was examining the table, Gary resumed speaking.

"As the table shows, the numbers 5 through 9, which relate to prices from $49.3 million through $49.7 million, account for 24 out of 36 possible combinations. In other words, the chances that a roll would fall somewhere in this midstream are 2 out of 3. You could further minimize the likelihood of a more extreme result by providing for several rolls and averaging the results."

And all of a sudden—although the idea of it went against everything he had held sacred for thirty years—Elliot saw how the dice idea might work to resolve a small-margin impasse at the end of a long price negotiation. And, not incidentally, how it might enhance Elliot's stature with his client. It was the tabular presentation that did the trick—for just a moment, Elliot flashed back to when he was a young associate himself, plowing methodically through the multiple sections of a long-winded trust indenture.

"Gary, I think you're on to something here."

Stone sat back in his chair, his face wearing a sort of loopy grin—a bit like the cat that swallowed the canary.

Elliot then began to grapple in earnest with the concept. "At least it could be feasible in a case such as this, where the parties are privately owned. If a *public* seller were involved, everyone would be gasping in horror: 'How dare you deal with the stockholders' money in this fashion?' I can just picture the paragraph in the proxy statement that solicits shareholders to approve the acquisition of the company: 'In arriving at the negotiated purchase price, the parties took into account the company's results of operations for the past five years, its net worth, present and historical market values . . . and then rolled dice for the last $1 million!'"

Gary chuckled. "Yeah, I'm not sure the SEC is ready for this quite yet."

"But the real question is whether Jake Driggs is ready for something like this—especially since he's likely to end up paying more than $49 million."

"He may not be," said Gary in a serious tone, "if he's really unwilling to go higher than $49 million for Norton under any circumstances. But if what's at stake here is more a matter of machismo or saving face or whatever, then the dice roll might give him an acceptable way of arriving at a deal."

"That's right—and with Jake being such a numbers man, he might be intrigued by the mathematical aspect. I think it's worth a shot—we certainly don't seem to be getting anywhere with our client in traditional bargaining terms."

In the silence that followed, Cheever reflected upon his task in going to Driggs with this proposition next week, when Jake would have returned from a business trip. Elliot tried to picture Jake's reaction. One thing he knew for sure was what Jake's big question was likely to be, and it was a tough one to answer. Well, thought Elliot, I'll deal with that when I have to. . . .

Cheever wasn't about to give up on his sports club idea. Thwarted at the firm level, he now took matters into his own hands—signing up for a personal membership at the nearby Good Health club. Utilizing his celebrated negotiating and drafting skills, he worked out a deal with the club which permitted a family member "or other designee" of Cheever's to use the facilities.

The next day, Cheever invited Bob Gumley to be his guest at Good Health. After apologizing for the lack of health facilities at the firm, Elliot told Bob he could have free use of the Good Health club—"it comes with my membership." Gumley, appreciative of Elliot's generosity, immediately began to make extensive use of the club's facilities. These included—as Elliot had been careful to note upon his initial inspection—a spanking new locker room with abundant shower stalls and a table full of assorted deodorants.

On the basis of several semifurtive expeditions past Gumley's office—the door to which now stood open—Elliot confirmed that Bob had removed the bicycle and abandoned on-the-job jumping jacks. Elliot congratulated himself on the apparent success of his plan.

Meanwhile, the new Sykes deal was moving ahead, and a preliminary meeting was scheduled with the client for the next day—a time when Cheever was required to be in Washington on other business. Bob Gumley attended the meeting on behalf of Jenkins & Price. The following day, unable to contain himself, Elliot called Walter Sykes on the phone.

"Well, Walter," said Elliot, "I assume you were satisfied with the results of yesterday's meeting."

"I was," Sykes replied.

"And everything was okay with Bob Gumley?"

"Everything," said Sykes, "except he still reeks."

Elliot was shaken to the core. Could it be that Gumley spurned postworkout showers, even in the glistening locker room facilities of Good Health? Or was something more sinister afoot?

Once more Cheever put on his problem-solving hat, so prized by admiring clients. Introducing the concept of a third party, he pondered whether someone who was closer to Gumley could be approached to act as an intermediary. Bob had no wife nor, to the best of Elliot's knowledge, any steady girlfriend. Elliot briefly contemplated using another associate or possibly Bob's secretary to relay the news, but rejected these options—fearing that his behind-the-scenes role would get back to Gumley with embarrassing consequences.

Cheever's ruminations then took on a more imaginative cast. He contemplated sending an anonymous letter in an untraceable literary style—perhaps something as nonlegalistic and direct as, "Hey, Bob, check your armpits!"—but this wasn't Elliot's preferred mode of communication. The idea of surreptitiously placing a large can of antiperspirant on Gumley's desk had the virtue of clarity, but lacked the subtle touch Elliot considered appropriate to the situation.

The question lingered in Elliot's mind as to whether or not Gumley even realized he was malodorous. Perhaps, he pondered, the man has no sense of smell. He thought about devising a means to test this—by sending him some roses, perhaps, or a large wheel of aged Liederkranz cheese. . . .

But none of these tactics filled the bill, and Elliot reluctantly came to the conclusion that he needed to handle this man-to-man with Gumley.

Cheever had an appointment later that day to see Jake Driggs. Before going over there, he knew he had a decision to make—should he bring Gary Stone and reveal that the dice toss was Stone's idea, or should he leave Gary home and present it as his own brainstorm?

On the one hand, he reasoned, Jake didn't really know Gary, so adopting the idea as his own would give it some added gravitas. He tried not to think about the obvious corollary—the advantage to him, if the client liked the idea, of Jake considering it the product of Elliot's brilliant imagination.

But Elliot couldn't help worrying about the obverse reaction—Jake thinking the proposal to be foolish and dismissing it out of hand. In that case, Elliot would certainly prefer it not to have emanated from him, but rather be dismissible as a humorous brainstorm of his slightly kooky associate—something Elliot was just passing along for Jake's amusement.

Elliot ultimately decided he was on such unfamiliar ground here that to claim personal credit for the idea presented too big a risk. He would bring Stone along and introduce it as Gary's notion. Then he'd wait to hear Jake's initial reaction before deciding whether to endorse it personally—assuming Jake seemed intrigued—or to laugh it off, if Jake treated the concept with scorn.

So, later that day, Cheever and Gary Stone went to see Jake Driggs. They met in Jake's office, which was a no-nonsense facsimile of the man himself—all business, almost no personal touches.

After some chitchat, Elliot put forward the proposal this way. "Listen to this novel idea that Gary came up with, to try to bridge the gap between Driggs and Norton. . . ."

The incredulous look on Jake's face when Elliot first mentioned the concept of using dice almost caused Elliot to disown the idea before going any further. But he decided to stick with it and noted a gradual change in Jake's expression as the client grasped the logic of the proposition. Sensing Jake's growing interest, Elliot was careful not to throw cold water on the concept. At one point, he actually found himself saying, "It's offbeat, to be sure, but I can see its value in this situation." He emphasized the prospect of it closing the final gap and ensuring the deal—albeit at a figure slightly in excess of the $49 million that Driggs had staked out as his top price. Elliot included plenty of caveats, though—making sure not to sell too hard—because he didn't want it to appear that he was talking Jake into this.

Driggs, who was now taking the proposition seriously, asked several questions, explored some of the ramifications, and then said, "But Elliot, here's the real negotiating problem created by this idea. If and when we raise it with Norton, won't they view it as a signal that we're willing to pay top dollar—$50 million—not just the $49 million I've been trying to get them to accept, and not even the $49.5 million they could infer if we just offered to split the difference in traditional fashion? And won't that knowledge tempt them to reject our proposal and hold firm at $50 million, in hopes that we'll ultimately come around?"

It was the question Cheever knew Driggs would ask, but somehow, in the rush of things, he hadn't prepared a decent answer. He decided to play for time, in hopes that something would occur to him. "That's a good point, Jake, and the risk is definitely there—especially since we've made such a big deal out of $49 million being our top figure. Now, uh, it seems to me . . ." But nothing persuasive was bubbling to the surface.

Just then, Gary spoke up, interrupting Elliot's makeshift response. "But Jake, we can reduce this risk substantially by the manner in which we suggest the proposition. After all, there's a big difference between a buyer who's willing to pay $50 million—and it's *willingness*, not *capacity*, that's usually at issue—and a buyer who's willing to take a 3 percent risk that he'll have to pay $50 million. A risk, I would add, with a correlative opportunity to make the purchase for $49 million. So your pitch should be something like, 'I don't want to pay $50 million—but I'm a gambler, and if you are too, here's a way we can resolve this impasse.' If Norton rejects the proposal, we're still at $49 million, no matter what reading they choose to make of the situation."

Cheever was impressed with Gary's acumen, and he could tell that Driggs was also. "He's got a point," Elliot said, and Jake nodded affirmatively.

After some further discussion, Jake authorized Elliot to give the dice resolution a try. Elliot was very pleased, and it made such good sense. Driggs Corp. obviously had the wherewithal to pay up to $50 million for this deal, and Jake was enough of a gambler to try it this way—without violating his macho approach to the power aspects of negotiation.

Jake Driggs emphasized, however, that in dealing with Norton, the idea couldn't seem to have originated with Jake. Elliot guessed he was still concerned over the risk he'd raised earlier, and probably also worried that the dice idea might be construed as undercutting the seriousness with which he was approaching the negotiations. "You handle it, Elliot," he said, "and don't attribute it to me." Cheever couldn't help recalling the similar words from Walter Sykes concerning the Bob Gumley problem.

The next day—D-Day, in Cheever's mind—following one of Bob Gumley's workouts at the Good Health club, Elliot invited him to lunch at a small Italian restaurant near the office. The overpowering aroma of garlic that pervaded the premises served to mask the better part of Gumley's personal scent.

Employing a carefully patterned line of conversation, Elliot took a circuitous path before arriving at his punch line.

". . . and, as I've always said, to be successful requires full use of *all* of one's senses—not just the obvious ones of sight and hearing."

Gumley, wolfing down a forkful of ravioli, nodded in acquiescence but showed no signs of grasping Cheever's desired linkage. So, making a subtle conversational segue, Elliot tried a different tack.

"As lawyers, we should always attempt to put ourselves in the shoes of others—not only our adversaries, but also our clients— to do our damnedest to figure out what's going on in their minds, with special attention paid to how they're reacting to us, even as to concerns they may have that we're not aware of. . . ."

"That's good advice," Bob murmured, taking a bite of his salad.

Elliot pursed his lips, then once again switched subjects adroitly, maneuvering himself within a few minutes to where he could say, " . . . and so, that's why my wife and I like living in the country—the clean fresh fragrance you breathe on an early morning stroll, as compared to some of the horrific odors one encounters in the big city."

But it was no use—none of Elliot's cunning tactics worked. He had to face the fact that Bob Gumley was completely unaware of having a problem. And so, much as it pained him, Elliot was at last forced to confront the matter directly. As he cleared his throat to begin, he was grateful that a powerful stench had overcome the garlic mist and worked its way across the dining table, in tacit justification of his mission.

"Ahem . . . Bob, there's a matter I'd like to bring to your attention. . . ."

"What's that?" asked Gumley, looking up but seemingly clueless as to what he was about to hear.

"Well, the fact is, Bob, that you regularly emit a rather strong and unpleasant bodily odor. . . ." There! Elliot rejoiced inwardly at having gotten it out.

"Oh, my God." said Gumley, clearly shocked at the news. "I can't believe it's still a problem."

"Still?" asked Elliot.

"I used to have a problem, but I honestly thought it was solved."

"I don't know what the problem used to be, but the present one is bad enough," said Elliot deadpan.

"Let me explain," said Gumley, the words now tumbling out in a rush. "Something chemical happens to me when I exercise. And it doesn't matter that I take a shower afterward—which I always do, when there's a shower available. The juices are still flowing, and the odor persists. Not that I can detect it—I have a very poor sense of smell, so nothing seems out of the ordinary. But I've been told about it periodically over the years. Of course, I tried using deodorants. The problem is, I have a terrible allergic reaction to deodorants—my skin breaks out in a rash that's worse than poison ivy. But recently somebody recommended one that doesn't cause a rash, which I've been using on a regular basis. And I thought it was working, because no one has given me any negative feedback in the past few months. Oh, my God, this is awful."

Elliot, impressed by the young lawyer's frank revelations, promptly switched over to his avuncular mode. "Now, now, Bob, this is not the worst thing in the world. It's easy enough to avoid the problem by simply refraining from exercising—"

Bob interrupted, "But I love to work out. It fires me up like nothing else—gets my adrenalin pumping. I'd have a lot of trouble giving it up."

"Well, then," said Elliot, "it's a matter of simple prudence. A case of timing. Do your workout at the end of the day, when you can go right from the club to your home—rather than in the morning or at noon, when you'll be heading over to the office or a meeting. I'm sure you'll be able to take control of this problem. Now, let's move on to a more edifying subject. . . ."

Elliot, pleased that the deed was done, applauded himself for his decisiveness in dealing with the problem. He was sure it would now be promptly resolved—and a good thing too, because they had a big meeting with Walter Sykes and his group the very next day.

Cheever was riding high now on both fronts. The pesky matter involving Bob Gumley was apparently a thing of the past, thanks to Elliot's prompt intercession. And the dice concept had cleared its first big hurdle—Jake Driggs, the client—thanks to Elliot's forceful presentation of the plan's merits.

As for the associates, Bob Gumley, who had suffered a serious olfactory slump from his prior elevated status, was now on the verge of a prodigal return to Elliot's good graces. And Gary Stone, whom Elliot had seriously underrated on the basis of unreliable office gossip, was proving to be a real diamond in the rough—abetted, of course, by Elliot's shrewd tutoring.

The time had now come to take the next step for Driggs Corp. It was one thing, Elliot knew, to have gotten his own client on board—it was quite another to win over the other side. The biggest obstacle would be the typical cynicism one encountered from an adversarial negotiator—the knee-jerk reaction that such a novel proposal must be designed to benefit the proposer at the expense of the recipient.

There were two hurdles here—the other lawyer, a man named Vance Jones, and his client, Norton, in the person of its owner and president, Steve Norton. The key, in Elliot's mind, was the lawyer. If the lawyer was opposed to it, there was little hope of reaching his client. But if Vance Jones could be persuaded that the idea had merit, then *he* could sell it to Steve Norton—with a much higher chance of success than if Cheever or Driggs were trying to convince Norton directly.

Elliot favored the approach of trying out the dice concept on Vance Jones lawyer-to-lawyer, with no clients around. The pitch he would make was that if both of them liked the idea, then they'd attempt to sell it to their respective clients. He considered such a plan preferable to surprising the opposing lawyer with a controversial concept like this in front of his client. The hazard of surprise was that, even if the other lawyer liked the concept, he might well balk initially—since he wouldn't know at that point how the idea had gone over with his client.

Cheever was sitting in his office with Gary Stone, preparing for their meeting with Vance Jones. By now, Elliot's view of Gary had completely changed. He was no longer a rude hippie. Rather, Elliot considered him a brilliant and constructive young associate whose opinion the partner valued highly—and whose presence at both strategy and negotiating sessions was requisite.

Elliot spoke first. "You know, there's a real tactical decision to make regarding how to bring up the proposition with Vance Jones. To keep it from being attributed to Jake, I should probably appear to have made up the idea on the spot—the proverbial light bulb flashing on above my head."

"Yeah, but the problem then is that you'd have to spend some time fussing with the numbers—it couldn't appear to flow too smoothly."

"That's right. And I can't help thinking that the proposal might stand a better chance of being accepted if I handle it so as to suggest this isn't something new—that gaming solutions occur all the time. You know, most people don't like to be out ahead of the pack."

Gary nodded. "You could buttress that by having a pad of printed score sheets available. In effect, you'd be saying, 'Another day, another roll of the dice.'"

Elliot laughed. "That's a good concept. But then, of course, the risk of it being attributed to the client is much greater."

After further discussion, Elliot decided to approach Jones on an in-between basis. He hadn't just thought this up—it had been percolating in his mind for a while, so he had the numbers down pat—but on the other hand, he didn't claim to have used it in other deals. And he would imply that he hadn't yet dared to run it by his own client.

So, a few hours later, Cheever and Gary Stone met with Vance Jones in the latter's office. Jones was a capable, experienced attorney with a strong practical bent.

"We've got a somewhat offbeat idea to break this logjam," Elliot began, and he could sense from the outset real interest in the lawyer's eyes. When Elliot first mentioned the dice, those eyes widened in surprise—but as Elliot proceeded with the analysis and handed over the table of values, it was clear that Jones was taking it seriously. Apparently, he considered it a constructive way to get the deal done—something that he knew his client wanted to see accomplished. And Jones must have sensed his client was enough of a gambler—and wary of Jake Driggs ever meeting his $50 million price—that the idea would fly.

"But, listen, guys," Jones said, "here's the legal question I have for you. If they decide to roll the dice, are the parties bound to do the deal at the dice price?"

Elliot hadn't really thought about that, but he took a stab. "I guess in order for them to be bound, we would have to draft and negotiate the entire agreement for the deal *before* throwing the dice—leaving only the purchase price blank, to be filled in and the agreement signed once the dice are thrown."

Now Gary spoke up. "But even there, the guy who doesn't like the result can just refuse to sign. To really button it up, you'd need to have a signed agreement before the roll, reciting the dice procedure to be followed in order to fix the price."

"That's right," said Jones. "But that document may become public some day, and I'm not sure you'd want to broadcast what we did to the world."

They discussed it some more, and in the end agreed they would rely on moral suasion—the two parties having agreed in principle in advance of the roll that they would move ahead on a deal at the price determined by the dice.

Sure enough, Jones got back to Elliot late that afternoon to say that Norton was willing to "roll dem bones." They worked out the particulars and set the ceremony for two days hence.

Lying in bed that night—pleased as punch with how things were going—Elliot indulged in some uncharacteristic fantasy thinking. He envisioned the process somehow getting disclosed, at which point a disgruntled one percent owner of Norton sues both sides for being irresponsible with the stockholders' money. He could almost hear the judge delivering his opinion orally from the bench, in these words:

> Admittedly, the gaming conclusion to the negotiations was rather bizarre, to say the least. But the defendants have advanced a simple justification for their actions—it clinched the deal. I find that to be the crucial factor, particularly since the evidence is unclear whether, without this device, either party would have budged from its prior position . . . Judgment for the defendants.

Hooray! Elliot's nocturnal mind then took off from there. Following the judicial seal of approval, the idea of shooting dice catches on as a handy solution for this kind of problem. In fact, when deals reach a certain point in the bargaining, it becomes common for someone to suggest, "Well, how about the Cheever resolution?"—and no one has to explain what it is, sort of like the Stayman convention in bridge. Elliot's name has become synonymous with the process. All over corporate America, men in pinstriped suits are carrying dice in their attaché cases, right next to their calculators, just in case the opportunity might arise.

A few more years go by in his fantasy. Now, the lawyer proposing the Cheever resolution doesn't even have to say anything. He just opens his case, takes out the dice, and rolls them in his palm—like Captain Queeg in *The Caine Mutiny*, with his little steel balls—until the other side takes the hint.

Time passes. Now every conference room across the land is equipped with a pair of dice, perched in the middle of the table near the pencils and yellow pads—like the doubling cube on a backgammon board. Whoever wants to suggest their use reaches out and pushes the dice toward his adversary, raising one eyebrow ever so slightly. The people on the other side exchange glances; their leader then nods in agreement. A green felt pad is spread across the table. A certified public accountant—resembling one of those vote tabulators at the Academy

Awards—is produced. He fills in the numbers on a printed scoring pad, then picks up the cubes. The seller yells "Boxcars!" The dice are thrown— It's a deal!

And on that blissful note, Elliot fell asleep.

Cheever and Bob Gumley got together in Elliot's office for a few minutes prior to the big meeting with Walter Sykes and his team. Although he didn't want to be obvious about it, Elliot couldn't help taking a few tentative air samplings from different angles. He was delighted to detect no odor at all emanating from Bob. As they left for the meeting, Elliot said, "Your, uh . . . *appearance* is splendid this morning, I must say." Bob, who appeared a trifle glum, acknowledged the meaning behind Elliot's words with a nod.

In the Sykes conference room before the meeting began, Cheever could have sworn that Walter Sykes was sniffing the air with a vengeance. It reminded Elliot of the grand ballroom scene in *My Fair Lady*, where the Hungarian linguist is furiously nosing around, determined to prove that Eliza is a fraud. When the conference room atmosphere proved to be sweet-scented, Walter's face lit up in a big smile. The rest of the Sykes team followed suit, all appearing extremely pleased. Elliot savored his moment of triumph.

About ten minutes into the meeting, one of the Sykes lieutenants made reference to a provision in a document Gumley had previously prepared, asking whether the point was still applicable.

"I'm not sure," said Bob. "Do you have the document? I can't remember exactly what it said. . . ."

A few minutes later, with the subject having changed to another issue, Gumley said, "Well, why don't we sell those shares *before* the other transaction is even announced?"

"We could do that," replied the Sykes tax man, "but then we'd have a whopping tax bill and no offsetting expense to match against it."

"Oh," said Gumley, "I see."

The meeting finally adjourned, to be continued the next day. As they were leaving, Elliot overheard the Sykes inside counsel say to Gumley, "You look tired, Bob—did you get enough sleep last night?"

Cheever and Gumley held a brief postmortem in Elliot's office after the meeting.

"You weren't very sharp today," said Elliot.

"I know," said Bob. "I was terrible."

"Why?"

"Because I didn't work out ahead of time. I need that to get my juices flowing. I've always made it a point to exercise right before a big meeting."

After Bob left the room, Elliot realized with alarm that he may have thrown out the baby with the bath water. He was forced to acknowledge how difficult it was to make someone into something he's not. Elliot's mind drifted to a recent example—the transsexual tennis player Renée Richards, née Richard Raskind, who entered the 1978 U.S. Women's Open with high hopes, but had been beaten 6-1, 6-4 in the first round.

Elliot assessed the choices that the Cheever-Gumley team appeared to be faced with. Exercise, be sharp, but stink up the meeting. Don't exercise, smell sweet, but come across as a dunce. He didn't like either alternative.

Later that day, Elliot was in his office with his new best friend, Gary Stone. Elliot must have looked temporarily dispirited, because Gary asked him, "Is everything okay?"

"Oh, it's nothing really. I'm just faced with an either-or choice in another deal, where neither alternative is appetizing—and it's been weighing on my mind."

Gary nodded in sympathy. "I know what you mean. I used to be bothered by the same thing until one day I had a flash of insight."

Elliot perked up. "What was that?"

"It happened years ago at a delicatessen counter. I ordered a ham and cheese sandwich, and the counterman asked, 'On rye or pumpernickel?' I could see each of the loaves and both looked delicious, making the choice difficult. And then I suddenly realized I didn't have to make the selection being forced on me. I told him, 'I'll take one slice of rye and one slice of pumpernickel, please.' I can still feel the moment of pleasure I experienced then—breaking out of that false either-or mentality. I hark back to it all the time."

When the adjourned meeting with the Sykes team began the next morning, Elliot was sitting at their conference table, looking a bit like the Cheshire Cat.

"Okay," said Walter Sykes, "we're all here from the company—Sykes, Cornwall, Akers, and Jackson. As for counsel, Elliot Cheever is here, and Bob Gumley . . . is plugged in by phone. Bob, are you there?"

"I am," came the disembodied but energetic voice from the speaker in the middle of the conference table. "And I've figured out a neat solution to the tax problem we were wrestling with at the end of the meeting yesterday."

Elliot Cheever, master strategist, beamed. A slice of rye, a slice of pumpernickel. What he would say about this to his partners next year, when Bob Gumley came up for partnership, was a matter for another day. . . .

They were all assembled for the dice roll that afternoon in a conference room at the Jones law office. Jake Driggs and Steve Norton shook hands to initiate the proceedings. The conference table was cleared of papers and coffee cups. The procedure was reiterated once more. Elliot proudly produced a pair of dice.

But at that moment, before things went any further, Steve Norton said, "I don't want to imply mistrust, but how do I know these dice aren't loaded to produce a low number?"

This caught everyone by surprise and, as might be expected, caused the Driggs team to do a lot of huffing and puffing about its inate honesty, about Norton's obvious implication of mistrust, and so on. Elliot wasn't sure where this was going, but he knew that with a novel proposition like rolling dice for a deal, everything was very fragile—the whole edifice could easily come crashing down.

Suddenly Gary Stone broke in and, speaking directly to Steve Norton, said, "If you're worried about that, we'd be prepared to reverse the whole thing and let the low dice numbers stand for the higher prices."

Norton smiled. "Smart boy—that's just what I wanted to hear. You've solved my problem. There's no need to switch the numbers. Let's proceed as planned."

They had agreed that there would be two rolls of the dice—each side would handle the cubes for one of them—and the final number was to be an average of the two results. Jones and Cheever were given the rolling honors. Vance promptly rolled a seven. Elliot picked up the dice, resisted the temptation to blow on them or cock them by his ear, and rolled a nine. The average of eight produced a $49.6 million purchase price. Driggs and Norton shook hands again—the deal was sealed.

Driggs and Cheever left the conference room at the same time and got into the elevator together. No one else was around. Elliot was feeling quite pleased with the procedure that had resulted in a deal. Evidently, Jake wasn't.

"You and your idiot ideas," he said. "Forget the fact that you rolled a nine—that's just physical incompetence. But not only do I end up paying $600,000 more than I wanted to for this deal, it's $100,000 more than if we had just split the difference at $49.5 million—which I now know Carroll would have been agreeable to, regardless of all your talk about his credibility in sticking at $50 million." He paused briefly and looked straight into Cheever's face. "You know what, Elliot? I'm going to deduct that $100,000 from your firm's fee."

Elliot waited for Jake to chuckle and say he was just kidding, but it didn't happen. As the elevator reached the lobby and Jake walked away without even a goodbye, Elliot realized that when he submitted the bill, he was going to have a real fight on his hands.

As for Gary Stone, Cheever mused in the taxi back to his office—well, if it weren't for Stone's cockamamie dice idea, he wouldn't be in this mess. How dare the associate put the partner in such a distressful situation? And once again, Elliot was reminded that all those unfavorable things he'd heard from his partners about Stone over the years were right on the money—Gary just wasn't J&P's kind of lawyer. . . .

Commentary on
Awash in Associates

The idea behind "Awash in Associates" is to show a senior-junior relationship from the senior's point of view. This is in contrast to "On-the-Job Training," which comes at it from the junior's vantage point.

The classic senior-junior relationship in a law firm is that of partner and associate. (This is explored more fully in chapters 5 and 10 of *Lawyering*.) The Jenkins & Price partner in the story is Elliot Cheever, whom we haven't encountered previously. Elliot is a senior partner who, as a young lawyer, cut his teeth drafting meticulous trust indentures, in a day when associates not only knew their place but wore three-piece suits and a hat. He fancies himself as a model of understated elegance. No bellowing tirades for Elliot—he's busy practicing a *profession.*

The story, which ranges over the course of about a week, is told by a third-person narrator, who takes us inside Elliot's head but no other—so we don't have any observations on Cheever from the perspective of the associates involved.

Elliot is working on two matters simultaneously (like Ralph Landry in "On-the-Job Training"), each with a different associate. Right at the outset, he candidly expresses his general attitude toward associates: They can be helpful, sometimes downright indispensable, but they can also drive you crazy. Although Elliot is feeling frustrated, his view isn't far away from what I've experienced personally (and heard echoed by many colleagues) over the decades.

The two foils for Cheever in the story are Bob Gumley, a senior associate one year away from being considered for partnership, who is working with Elliot on a deal for his good client, Walter Sykes, and Gary Stone, a fourth-year associate, who is on Elliot's team for the Driggs Corp. acquisition of Norton. The narrative in "Awash in Associates" bounces back and forth between these two assignments, but I'm going to take them up separately in this commentary, beginning with Bob Gumley on the Sykes deal.

In the first scene, Elliot is riding high. He has been invited to dine in a fine restaurant by a valued client (Walter Sykes), who sweetens the repast by announcing the retention of Jenkins & Price to handle a major piece of new business. This just feeds Elliot's rather large ego. In his view, we (for which read "I") deserve to generate significant new business, because we (I) turn out a superior work product and serve the client's every need.

A few moments later, however, this self-styled paragon of a business lawyer is taken aback by Walter's unsavory bulletin regarding the problem with Bob Gumley. Remember all that discussion in "The Smell Test" about the need to sniff out disguised schemes of corporate chicanery? Well, Elliot Cheever now finds himself smack up against a very different kind of smell test. . . .

Now, I freely admit to having chosen this particular associate shortcoming for some of the humorous possibilities it opened up, and I hope you'll chuckle along with me. Nonetheless, it does serve to illustrate the broader issues of client dissatisfaction with an associate and the need for constructive communication between partner and associate.

When Elliot gets the news about Gumley's gamy aroma, he reacts the way most client-conscious business lawyers would respond—asking Sykes whether he wants Bob replaced by another associate. The instances in which a client complains about an associate can take a number of different forms—ranging from perceived inferior work to a clash in chemistry—but in most cases, in order to mollify a good client, the firm will offer to change associates.

Here, however, that's not what the client is looking for. Sykes and his team value Bob's work highly and would like him to stay on the assignment—but without (pardon the vernacular) stinking up the joint. And since Elliot is Gumley's employer, Walter drops in his lap the task of getting Bob's glands under control—with the significant caution that Elliot can't attribute the complaint to the Sykes people.

Now I have a confession to make. The incident that comes to Elliot's mind as he later reflects on his mission actually happened to me. That's right—I was the young partner who (much to my own amazement at the time) took the principled stand against the client who wanted the associate's beard shaved off, for which I suffered no apparent repercussions.

But Elliot (and yours truly) never had to deal with smelly armpits. So he falls back on the exercise drilled into his brain from the first year in law school—assessing whether the armpits are distinguishable from the beard. He runs down the various considerations and concludes that the pits don't rise to the level of the face—ergo, he doesn't need to protect Gumley's dignity. And he can't really quarrel with Walter's complaint, since he recalls being himself aware of Bob's odor. Like so many of us who find ourselves in a similar position, he has previously shrugged it off as none of his business— but now it's very much Elliot's business. And, however reluctantly, Elliot realizes he has to deal with the situation.

Before getting into his response, though, let me ask you:

If you were Elliot, how would you deal with the Bob Gumley problem?

There's much to be said, of course, for the straightforward approach—"Bob, a word to the wise . . ." —but then I wouldn't have a story! And, by the way, over the years a number of friends (in non–law firm situations) have confessed to me that they shared Elliot's reticence in taking the direct path.

The next few segments are devoted to indirect approaches that Elliot tinkers with in trying to resolve the odor problem. He gets Gumley to cut out the jumping jacks on the fictitious basis of the thudding sound, but this just produces a silent stationary bike. Elliot tries (to no avail) to have the partnership install an exercise facility with showers. He joins the Good Health club with its palatial aroma-killing facilities, and arranges for Bob to have the use of it—but Bob still reeks. He ponders some creative alternatives: using a secretary or girlfriend as an intermediary, placing an aerosol can on Bob's desk, wheeling in a wheel of Liederkranz cheese. Even at the lunch when Elliot has decided he must confront Gumley head-on, he first tries out several circular paths—for example, the fresh fragrance of country air—without success.

Allow me to pull back briefly from this painful restaurant scene to make a more general lawyering observation. When you're attempting to convey information or a point of view to another party, there are times, to be sure, that it's advantageous to adopt a subtle approach—permitting the recipient to grasp the point without suffering any possible indignity attached to your having conveyed it directly. For instance, with a client who is taking an irrational position in a negotiation, you want to be able to move him off the position without telling him he's irrational—a chore that usually calls for some oblique persuasion strategy. But too often, when an important message needs to be conveyed—especially when it's not likely to be well received by the target—we beat around the bush, use euphemisms, and the like. As a result we fail to get across the full impact. When that happens, we're not giving our client the best service.

I see an analogy here to the other side of the coin—when you're trying to obtain (rather than transmit) information. This comes up often in negotiating, where you're seeking some disclosure from your adversary lawyer that will be helpful in devising your strategy. (This subject is addressed more fully in chapter 3 of *Smart Negotiating*.) The information you'd like to have (e.g., why the seller is selling the house and whether anyone else is bidding on it) frequently concerns one of the leverage factors that impact the deal—such as necessity, desire, competition, or time.

There are instances when it may be worthwhile to orchestrate an indirect means of garnering the knowledge you seek—going after it obliquely, hoping to put your counterpart less on his guard, so that he lets something slip from which you can draw a valuable inference. But my experience has been that in most cases, when you're after information that's clearly relevant to the subject matter of the negotiations and there's no downside risk to putting it on the table, you might as well phrase your questions directly ("Why is he selling the house?" or "Is anyone else bidding on it?"), so as to compel your counterpart to give you a straight answer. This can put the other side in a quandary, where a truthful response ("He's selling because he badly needs the money," or "We haven't had a single nibble") gives away too much too early, while an untruthful answer is an ethical no-no. So don't be afraid to pose tough questions to your counterpart. The worst that can happen is you'll be told it's none of your business—a response that itself may transmit valuable information your way.

Getting back to the story, Elliot finally has to resort to blurting out the real concern. Gumley, taken aghast, explains his chemical problem. Elliot—ever the problem-solver, now feeling pleased with himself for his "decisiveness in dealing with the problem"—advises Bob to work out at the end of the day, so he can then head right for home.

Unfortunately, though, we're living in a world where very little is that simple—everything seems to involve trade-offs. At the next meeting with the Sykes team, Gumley proves to be a dunce, which he blames on not having exercised (as he usually does) right before the big meeting. A bemused Elliot sees the situation in terms of two unappealing alternatives: Exercise, be sharp, but stink up the meeting. Don't exercise, smell sweet, but come across as a dullard.

Viewed in more general terms, this is the kind of thing we lawyers face on a daily basis. People are always posing for us matched pairs of alternatives to elect between—the pernicious either-or syndrome. It's neat and it's tidy, but in nine out of ten cases, it presents a false universe. Invariably, other options are available if you're able to avoid rigidity in your thinking. When an impasse arises in negotiating, for example, many experts stress the importance of inventing options—possible solutions, not readily apparent, that advance shared interests and reconcile differences in a creative fashion. Gary Stone's analogy to rye and pumpernickel was my own insight that brightened one well-remembered day many years ago. So now let me ask you:

If you were Elliot Cheever, how would you have dealt with this either-or problem?

Well, I like Elliot's approach, at least in the short run. A slice of rye, a slice of pumpernickel—Gumley on the speaker phone, his wisdom (but not his odor) permeating the airwaves. And so we leave Elliot, the self-proclaimed master strategist, sitting there beaming—but clearly with more work to do in orchestrating a permanent solution.

We turn now to the interaction between Elliot Cheever and Gary Stone. Elliot's opening riff on the three things that provide contentment for a business lawyer in a deal is right on the money. Give me a sensible client, a reliable associate, and some negotiating leverage, and I'll go to town every time. But poor Elliot—he doesn't appear to have any of the three.

Cheever's client, Jake Driggs, reminds me of a lot of clients we've all known—he doesn't like to overpay for anything, to the point where he's even willing to lose a deal rather then attempt to compromise by making a small move beyond what he deems appropriate. Oh lord, save me from these inflexible types . . . That kind of stance already cost Jake the Packet deal several months ago—losing out to another more flexible buyer who suddenly surfaced from nowhere.

You'd think Jake would have learned from that experience, but as we join the parties, it doesn't look to be the case. The same thing is happening in the current Norton deal. Norton has reduced its asking price to $50 million, but is unwilling to sell for less; Driggs has increased his offer to $49 million and has told the other side he's unwilling to go any higher. The resulting stalemate has Elliot worried that Norton could sell to another buyer or take the company off the market.

Worse still, the negotiating leverage appears to be with Norton. They're under no necessity to sell, if they can't get their price; other potential buyers are plentiful; and Jake has an obvious strong desire to make this deal, which fills a large gap in the Driggs product line that can't be achieved elsewhere. As a result, Cheever is convinced Norton will stand firm at $50 million.

So Elliot has a tough client and faces negative leverage, but to top it off, he also has to deal with a less than satisfying associate. Gary Stone, ex-hippie, is a nonconformist with a reputation around the firm for a questionable work ethic and idiosyncratic ways—such as enjoying the craps tables of Las Vegas. Elliot is peeved at having to put up with this guy on the Driggs-Norton deal.

So Elliot decides to pass the time instructing Gary on the finer points of negotiating. His analysis is perceptive. At this level of narrow difference between the parties, a splitting-the-difference compromise makes a lot of sense. But the party who suggests the split is at a disadvantage, because the other side now knows that the offering party is willing to do the deal at the split amount, while the recipient is still at his previous figure. The ultimate resolution is then more likely to end up somewhere between the split figure and the recipient's position. Although lawyers can be helpful in trying to broker the split, they are usually seen as just mouthpieces for their clients. And if Driggs waits for Norton to propose the split, it may never happen.

So that's the point at which Gary Stone comes up with his Vegas resolution. Before I comment, let me ask you:

What do you think of it? What do you see as the pros and cons?

Well, ladies and gentlemen, what can I tell you—this is my baby. I wrote an article on it over two decades ago, fully expecting to be inundated with favorable comments, a passel of "Isn't he clever?" remarks, and maybe even some legal business from budding disciples. What greeted me instead was a wave of silence. Maybe it was too far out, but I can't think of a better way to solve this negotiating problem, at least where no public stockholders or the SEC (both of whom can be sticky) are involved. Who knows, maybe this time. . . .

In addition to seeking your indulgence in treating this seriously (or at least mock-seriously) as a solution to the problem, I'd ask you to note how well it functions in raising several general issues that negotiators have to face.

After receiving Gary's briefing on the Vegas resolution, Elliot comes around to its possibilities and then envisions taking the concept to his client Driggs. In trying to anticipate Jake's reaction, Elliot knows what the client's big question will be, and it's a tough one to answer. When Elliot mused about this, were you able to guess what the question was that he knew Jake would ask?

When we next observe Elliot on the Driggs matter, he's ruminating on the upcoming meeting with his client—pondering whether to leave Gary home and present the dice idea to Jake as Elliot's own. I ask you:

If you were Elliot, how would you have come out on this one, and for what reason?

My strong hunch is that most of you wouldn't have done this, using the rationale that Elliot shouldn't try to steal Gary's thunder. Elliot comes out the same way, but on a more pragmatic basis—there's too big a risk that Jake will dismiss the idea, which might then reflect badly on Elliot as its proponent. If he labels it as Gary's idea, however, Elliot can then endorse it if Jake seems amenable ("Hey, look what a smart associate I have") or laugh the whole thing off should Jake turn thumbs down. It's not too attractive a line of reasoning on Elliot's part, but you frequently run across this kind of self-preservation analysis in the practice of law.

So Elliot and Gary present Gary's concept to Jake, who (after an initial quizzical reaction) seems interested—at which point Elliot starts to get behind it. Then Driggs pops the question Elliot knew would be coming (but hadn't prepared a reply to): Won't Norton view this as a signal we're willing to go all the way to their price of $50 million, which might tempt them to reject the dice proposal and hold even firmer at their bottom line?

Elliot fumbles around with this, but Gary steps right up and belts it out of the park. He points out the difference between willingness to pay and willingness to risk—there's only a three percent risk of paying $50 million, with a correlative opportunity to cement the deal at Jake's own $49 million figure. For those willing to gamble, that's a reasonable proposition. And it serves to underscore the message—which has more general applicability in negotiating—that if Norton rejects the dice toss, Driggs is still at $49 million.

Jake, impressed with this line of reasoning, authorizes Elliot to try to sell the idea to the other side—but cautions that it mustn't seem to come from Jake. You can't help noting the similarity to Walter Sykes not wanting his fingerprints on Bob Gumley's armpit problem earlier in the week, Bill Price not wanting his on Dwight's ultimate Breckenridge turndown in "The Smell Test," and Susan Collins not wanting hers on how to deal with Cathy Weaver in "On-the-Job Training."

With his client on board, Elliot must now decide how best to present this offbeat proposition to the other side.

If you were Elliot, how might you go about this?

I agree with Elliot's approach. Steve Norton's lawyer, Vance Jones, is the key here. Whenever you're presenting a controversial proposal to the other side, it makes a lot of sense to try to get their lawyer behind it—because if he opposes it, that's the kiss of death. If Jones likes the notion, he's in a better position to sell it to his client than if the thought were transmitted directly from the Driggs side. And it's usually preferable to try it out first on the other lawyer without his client being present. With his client in the room, the lawyer has to worry about the client's reaction and, perhaps for that reason, won't want to risk making an affirmative response even if he's favorably inclined.

I've been acting as a mediator of disputes in recent years, and I see an analogy between this last point and what goes on in a mediation. As a lawyer for a party dealing with a mediator, you have two key objectives: getting the mediator disposed toward your view of the dispute, and persuading the mediator to communicate that opinion to the other side under the mediator's imprimatur, which is what it takes for mediation to have a real impact. (For more on this, I refer you to my article "Calling All Deal Lawyers—Try Your Hand at Mediating Disputes," 62 *The Business Lawyer* 37 [Nov. 2006].)

By now, Elliot has begun to appreciate Gary's abilities and spends time strategizing with him. One issue they face in presenting the idea to Vance Jones is whether it should appear to be a sudden brainstorm or—at the other extreme—something that occurs all the time. This is an issue that negotiators often focus on (or at least should) in introducing a new concept, since the manner in which it's brought up can be decisive in determining its potential acceptability. Elliot's in-between approach seems to me just about right in this case.

Vance Jones responds well to the idea. Here's a smart lawyer who is properly focused on what's important for his client—namely, getting the deal accomplished—and isn't hung up by the novelty of the proposal. But Vance then poses an interesting legal question—will the parties be legally bound by the throw of the cubes? The lawyers end up deciding, for the reasons expressed (with which I agree), that there will merely be an agreement in principle to abide by the roll.

What do you think—should the dice be given more weight than just moral suasion—and if so, by what means?

When word comes back that Norton agrees to the throw of the dice, Elliot goes off on a fantasy that is pure Freund. I lulled myself to sleep with that one many a night—and it still remains a tasty bit of phantasmagoria.

So the scene is set, and the cubes are ready to be rolled. There's a final hiccup, but Gary solves it—taking the steam out of Norton's "loaded dice" implication by offering to change the relation between dice totals and purchase prices. Smart kid!

Then come the two climactic ironies. One is lawyer-client. Driggs gets his deal done, for which he should be delighted—but he's not. The dice roll results in his paying a little more than he wanted to (a risk of which he was clearly cognizant). Jake threatens to take the difference out of J&P's hide. Such ingratitude!—but clients have been known to turn on a dime like that. Let's just say it goes with the territory.

The final irony is partner-associate. Talk about Jake's ingratitude—the specter of Elliot turning on Gary (he's "not J&P's kind of lawyer"), after all the initiative and acumen Stone has shown, isn't pretty. I hope none of us has ever been guilty of something like that. Up until that point, my report card on Elliot was mixed, but this pushes him off the charts—over into Ralph Landry's nasty league.

For associates reading the story, please understand that Elliot Cheever is not representative of the vast majority of law firm partners. The typical partner is vitally interested in having you succeed. The better you perform, the happier the partner is—the more he can depend on you. Your success also supports the partner's self-image as a good person and role model. In my experience, few partners are so jealous of their clients or so insecure within the firm as not to root for your ultimate success.

SEX, LIES, AND PRIVATE EYES

I'm sitting here stunned. It's not the first time a client has terminated my services, but I've never been as shaken as when Cliff Cook sacked me two minutes ago.

And you know what the most upsetting part is—I don't disagree with his decision. If I were in his place, I'd have fired me!

No, no, I'll tell you what the worst thing is—that it never had to happen. I could have headed it off many times along the way, but I didn't.

Now, sure, everything's clear as crystal, but I just couldn't see it back then. Each time I thought I was doing something to strengthen the relationship, I was actually sowing the seeds of its destruction. And now it's too late to do anything about it.

I remember the day it all began, in that conference room adjacent to Cook's office. . . .

"Okay," said Cliff Cook, "let's get this meeting under way." He made a gesture with his hands to the several executives of Seacrest Corp. seated at the long table, who responded to their CEO with attentive expressions. "I think you all know our lawyer, Jack Lawrence, from the firm of Jenkins & Price. Jack has been handling our litigation for a number of years now, and very capably, I might add."

I acknowledged the compliment with a modest smile and a mock salute. It was true, though—I had done a lot of good work for the company. In the process, Seacrest had become my most significant client.

"Thanks for the plug, Cliff," I replied. "And this young man seated to my right is Kevin Dodge, one of our premier associates, who will be working with me on this case, his first for Seacrest."

I was, in fact, quite pleased that Kevin Dodge had been assigned to me for what promised to be an arduous assignment. We had worked together once before, representing a different client. I found him to be bright, articulate, and diligent. I was also aware, although I usually didn't notice such things, that Kevin was quite good-looking—a handsome face capped by a shock of jet black hair. I viewed him as a litigation star-in-the-making, almost certain to become a partner when his class came up for consideration in a few years.

I needed someone like Kevin to help me handle the supercharged Cliff Cook, who was a very demanding client. But I'll say this for Cook—unlike some clients, if you performed well for Cliff, there was no trouble with the fees. And so far, I was sitting pretty.

Speaking of sitting pretty, seated across the table from Kevin and me was Emma Searles, Seacrest's inside general counsel. She was a very attractive young woman—face, figure, brains, the works. Emma reminded me of a young woman I'd wooed in San Diego back in my Navy days—the one who broke my heart when she passed over this bushy-tailed ensign for a grizzled war hero lieutenant commander. . . .

I had long suspected there was more going on between Cliff Cook and Emma Searles than a purely professional relationship. It wasn't simply that Cliff made sure she was present at every meeting, even if the subject was out of her bailiwick. No, it was just something about their interaction. . . . But I didn't know for sure, and Cook had a wife and family. I've never been too observant of that kind of thing. Women—such as my wife—are a lot more perceptive and intuitive. And I certainly never felt it was my place to inquire further.

Fred Grant, Seacrest's chief financial officer, began to describe the new case. Seacrest was getting ready to sue a company named Congruent, which sold a subsidiary to Seacrest a year ago. It turned out that the subsidiary's financial statements had been inflated.

At one point, Kevin broke in to ask a question. "What measure of damages are we going to be able to prove here? Can we produce a good record of how we went about valuing the deal, in order to justify a hefty multiplier effect on the disappearing earnings?"

Before Fred Grant had a chance to reply, Emma spoke up, in a warm husky voice reminiscent of Lee Remick. "Good question, Kevin. In fact, it's the key to the entire case. Let me describe what we have on this, as well as what I wish we had but can't seem to lay our hands on. . . ."

Listening to the dialogue that ensued between Emma and Kevin, I focused entirely on the substance of what was said. In retrospect, some sparks may have been flying even then, but I was too oblivious to notice it.

I sit there in shock as Cliff Cook turns and walks out of my general counsel's office. This isn't the way I thought things would end up—not only being tossed out of his bed but needing to dust off and circulate my résumé! I thought I could have it all—the prestige job, the power relationship, the American Express card Cliff covered every month. Talk about hubris. . . .

I remember the day that, in retrospect, it started to unwind—the day Jack Lawrence brought Kevin Dodge over to that first meeting on the Congruent case. Sure, I was attracted to Kevin—good-looking, smart, and obviously on the make. He reminded me a little of John Travolta in last year's hit movie 'Saturday Night Fever'. But I might not have been so receptive if things had been going better with Cliff. In fact, just the previous night, he and I had done battle in his office. . . .

"Now, Emma, about this Congruent case. . . ."

"Goddamit, Cliff, forget the goddamn case. I want to talk about us. I'd like to know whether you've told your wife that you're leaving her."

"Oh come on, don't be so unreasonable. . . ."

"Me unreasonable? I tell you what's unreasonable. Spending Thanksgiving by myself last week, munching on a turkey TV-dinner, watching the Detroit Lions game—while you, Madame Cynthia, and those adorable kids of yours warmed each other around the family hearth, sipping hot apple cider."

"I'm sorry about that—"

"I don't need your sympathy—I want you! And out in the open, too. This is no life for me. Whenever we're together, we're always in hiding. I'm sick of skulking around."

He patted my hand—like you'd soothe a little kid—and said, "Look, Emma, I understand your frustration. I love you very much, but it's very difficult to leave a wife of twenty years and abandon a couple of teenagers. Rest assured, though, I'm working on it—trying to get over the hump."

"Hah!—the hump that's about to be over for you is the one that's been taking place in my bed! Your reluctance to commit is driving me crazy."

And I proceeded to stomp out of his office, slamming the door behind me. I was mad as hell—not just putting on an act—although I guess it was a little over the top. But that's what's necessary in dealing with Cliff Cook, who has to be pushed hard to accomplish anything. Whatever I'd been doing up to that point hadn't worked. So when I met Kevin, I must have realized subconsciously that it was time to move to the next level.

The subconscious became conscious the evening after our first meeting. Kevin and I were alone in my office, sitting next to each other at a small round table, working on the Congruent case. I've fixed up my office with a lot of personal touches—I wouldn't call it a boudoir, but it's not your everyday stylized executive quarters. Kevin said, "Here's the way I see the carve-out from the indemnification provision—" but I interrupted him.

"Let's take a little break from the case, Kevin. Tell me about yourself. Are you a native New Yorker? Where did you go to college? Is there a Mrs. Dodge?"

Kevin leaned back and replied to my three questions—yes, Dartmouth, and no. Then, after offering a brief autobiographical sketch, he asked me about myself. I replied in kind. It turned out we had both graduated from different law schools at the same time six years ago—in '72, the year Nixon was elected to a second term, just before Watergate moved into high gear.

"If I may be so bold to ask," said Kevin in a playful voice, "how did someone so youthful get to be general counsel of a big company like Seacrest?"

I fluttered my eyelashes and replied, "I take it that what you mean by that incredibly rude question is—who did I have to screw to get to this place?"

Kevin leaned back, put his palms on the table, and said, "I'm going to let that one pass."

I reached out and placed my hand on top of his. "As we get to know each other better, Kevin, I'll reveal all. . . ."

For just a moment, Kevin put his other hand on top of mine. With my free hand, I blew him a kiss. . . .

Our next meeting on the Congruent case took place three days later in the Seacrest conference room. Cliff Cook wasn't there, so Fred Grant and Emma Searles were leading the discussion. As the meeting progressed, I began to get an uncomfortable feeling that something not purely professional was going on between Emma and Kevin.

For instance, I noticed that when either of them talked, the words were directed right at the other—accompanied by certain penetrating looks—which had the effect of virtually ignoring the rest of us at the table. And their discourse was sprinkled with shared references and double entendres—the kind of thing you weren't used to hearing in a conference room.

At one point, for example, in trying to underline the distinction between whether Congruent's misstatements had been intentionally fraudulent or just negligent, Kevin quipped, "It's like the difference between rape and everyday intercourse." Emma replied, without missing a beat, "Sometimes, it's not so easy to tell the difference"—to which Kevin winked and said, "Touché."

I, of course, promptly retreated into my traditional turtle mode—trying to ignore the byplay, or at least to explain it away. Assuming I was correct in my suspicion that Emma and Cliff Cook were romantically linked, it would be disastrous for Jenkins & Price if the client were to catch a J&P associate trying to cut in on the CEO's girl—to say nothing of the ethical implications. So, notwithstanding the visible evidence, I went into denial.

That is, until a few days later. I had an early morning flight to catch and I wanted to speak to Kevin before I got on the plane. So at 6:30 A.M. I put in a call to his home number. It was answered on the third ring by a sleepy female voice with a familiar sound. "Yes?"

"May I please speak to Kevin?"

I then heard the same voice, but now turned away from the mouthpiece, say, "Oh shit, Kevin, wake up. I thought I was home and picked up your line by mistake. Someone wants you—I think it may be Jack. I'm putting the phone on the pillow."

This time, there was no mistaking the husky tones of Emma Searles. . . .

Well, after my stupid mistake that morning with Kevin's phone, I real-ized Jack Lawrence probably knew what was up, which raised the ques-tion—was he likely to run to Cliff with the salacious news? I seriously doubted it. Jack didn't seem like that kind of guy—and the risk was mini-mized because the other offending party was one of his own associates.

But then I remember thinking, hey, do I really care whether Cliff finds out about me and Kevin? Or to take matters a step further, do I affirma-tively want Cliff to know? I'm so mad at him. He just takes me for granted. Nothing I've said or done so far has shaken him up enough to leave his wife—maybe it'll take a little dose of paramour cuckolding to do the trick.

It's not that I didn't realize this was risky business. But I guess I was cocky—everything in my life up to that point had been a piece of cake. And besides, this guy Kevin really turned me on, in a way that Cliff never had—although he lacked Cliff's stature and bankbook. Maybe Kevin wasn't my long-term cup of tea, but now that I'd started in with him, I wasn't prepared to readily give him up—he really suited my purposes just then. So, I decided to play it out and see where things would go. . . .

When I returned the next day from that business trip, I sum-moned Kevin Dodge into my office. "Look, Kevin," I said, "I don't like to interfere in the personal lives of my associates, but I can't continue to turn a blind eye here. I'm too worried about what it might mean to the firm. I'm going to ask you a few questions, and I want you to be absolutely straight with me."

Kevin, seated in a chair across the desk from me, had a look of concern—but hardly panic—on his face.

I decided to start out in a formal mode, akin to the tone of a judicial opinion. "Based on the following facts—my hearing, at 6:30 A.M., a voice on your home phone that I recognized as belonging to Emma Searles; that voice calling out your name; and her remark about leaving the phone on the pillow—I've come to the conclusion that you're having an intimate relationship with Emma. Am I right?"

"You're right," replied Kevin evenly.

"Am I also correct in my long-held suspicion that Emma is Cliff Cook's mistress?"

"Well, the term you're using is a little old-fashioned, but if you're asking whether they've been engaged in a long-term affair, then—at least according to what Emma has told me—you're correct."

"And I take it that Cook doesn't yet know about you and Emma?"

"As far as I know, he doesn't."

I stood up to give my next words added emphasis. "Well then, you've simply got to break this off with Emma, before you endanger the firm's relations with Seacrest. If Cook were to find out about it, he'd be mad as hell at us—and rightly so. In fact, he'd likely show us the door. And I've worked too hard to get to where we are with Seacrest—I'm not about to let that happen."

Kevin paused before replying. He had obviously anticipated this confrontation and prepared himself for it—as I'd expect a good lawyer to do.

"Jack, I hear what you're saying; I understand your concern; and I consider it entirely appropriate for you to bring up this subject. Here's the thing, though. As far as I'm concerned, I'd be willing to end this relationship with Emma. She's a tantalizing woman, that's for sure, but I'm not taking it too seriously—and, without being immodest, in my present circumstances there are plenty of other fish in the sea. Hey, when I saw *Annie Hall* last year, I decided I wanted to meet Diane Keaton . . . Still, there's a downside to my breaking this off, which you ought to be aware of."

"What's that?" I snapped, immediately suspicious of Kevin's motives.

"Emma is more into our fling than I am. I'd like to think that's because she considers me a great lover, but I'm pretty sure there's another reason. She's really mad at Cliff Cook, who has refused to leave his wife for her. I suspect she's using me to get back at him. But either way, it comes down to the same thing. If I break off with her abruptly, and for no discernible reason, she might speculate that our firm is pulling the strings. She could then get mad as hell at Jenkins & Price. And this woman wields a lot of power at Seacrest. She could get us fired just like that"—and here he snapped his fingers—"without ever telling Cook what the real reason is."

I had to admit that Kevin had a point, although by no means a conclusive one. "So what are you saying?"

"That we've got a better chance of staying on as Seacrest's counsel if I keep the affair with Emma lukewarm for now and then gradually extricate myself—which I'm willing to do."

"Yeah, right, it's tough work, but someone has to do it. . . . But I'm still worried that Cook will find out."

"Don't worry. I'll be discreet."

But it wasn't Kevin's discretion I was worried about—it was Emma's. Especially if she were trying to get back at Cook . . .

I was still not convinced this was the right course to take, but I knew I wasn't too good at this kind of stuff. So I gave Kevin the benefit of the doubt, while emphasizing to him the need for discretion.

Watching Kevin at an all-hands meeting at Seacrest a few days later, I really couldn't fault him on that score. But as for Emma—she was something else entirely. Even though Cliff Cook was right there in the room, Emma managed to do something provocative whenever he was distracted for a moment. At one point, for instance, she slid a sheet of paper across to Kevin which I could see contained doodles of hearts. When they passed by each other at the coffee machine, she patted Kevin on the rear end.

I don't think Cook noticed any of this. But I realized that as the case moved forward and with Emma being so daring—almost as if she wanted to get caught in the act—it would only be a matter of time before Cliff woke up to what was going on.

The situation now called for more drastic steps. I had an idea, and later that day called Kevin into my office.

"I know, I know—" said Kevin before I could even open my mouth.

"Look, Kevin, after that scene this morning—which I concede was not your fault—I've decided to replace you on the Congruent case with Jill Marsh. If you feel the need to keep your affair with Emma lukewarm during the phase-out period, then do so—but strictly on an outside-the-office basis. Cliff Cook is much less likely to catch on if the two of you aren't playing grab-ass in his conference room."

Kevin pondered this for a moment. "Well, I'll admit it was getting uncomfortable for me in there, so I'm okay with your idea—provided it doesn't look like I'm getting fired from the job."

I had anticipated this reaction on his part and was prepared to deal with it. "That's fair enough. I'll say to Cliff and Emma that a client of the firm you've been servicing for several years just got sued on a deal you know a lot about. In view of your past knowledge, the client specifically requested your services. You're not yet so deep into the Congruent case—although, I'll try to resist adding, apparently quite deep into something else. . . . So, we're replacing you on the Congruent team. To make it more palatable to them, we won't charge Seacrest for the time you've put in on the case up to now, nor for the time necessary to bring Jill up to speed."

Kevin nodded his head in approval. "That's pretty ingenious. But I'd like to try it out on Emma first before you announce it publicly."

"Negative on your last," I replied, lapsing back into some old Navy jargon. "I don't want her to say 'no,' at which point we'd be proceeding over her objection. It's better to present them with a fait accompli."

I didn't realize it then, but the real genesis of my Seacrest problem was cooking up that false story about some other client requiring Kevin's services. It seemed innocent enough at the time—just a little professional lubricant to make things go down smoother. But I couldn't tell that same story to Jill Marsh, or to anyone else at the firm for that matter, because they would know there was no such other client. So later that day in my office, when I told Jill she was going to be working on the Congruent case, I had to come up with a different bogus explanation.

"Look, Jill, let me be perfectly candid." (I didn't warn her that when somebody begins that way, watch out!) "I sense a certain chemistry problem between Kevin and the Seacrest people, which will only get worse as time goes by. Although they haven't met you, I'm sure you'll be a much better fit. But I can't really say that to Seacrest—and I don't want to embarrass Kevin by making it seem he's being ousted. So I'm going to tell them a little white lie about Kevin's services being required for one of his long-term clients. Are you okay with that?"

"No problem," said Jill, who seemed pleased at getting involved in a major case and uninterested in the cover story.

So that's the way I played it the next day at Seacrest's office. Cliff and Emma registered some surprise. But with Jill sitting right there, basking in my enthusiastic description of her skills—and in light of the "no charge" fee adjustment I proffered with some flair—there wasn't much they could say on the spot.

The news that Jenkins & Price had taken Kevin off the Congruent case really caught me by surprise. So, I didn't react to Jack during the meeting, but my mind went to work on the situation later that same morning.

Once the initial shock wore off, I was mad as hell at Kevin for not warning me about what was happening. Given our intimacy, you'd think he would have—but then, as I pondered it further, I realized that Jack may have put him under wraps. And I began to wonder whether that "other client" story was true or just an excuse Jack used to get Kevin off the case. The timing was simply too convenient—and I did see the disapproving look on Jack's face when I was flirting with Kevin in the conference room. . . .

I realized I was going to miss having Kevin around the office. The heart doodles, the pat on his ass—I knew what I was doing. And I did want Cliff to notice that something was up—just enough to make him jealous and uneasy, but without him knowing that anything serious was taking place.

There was another thing that gnawed at me. The Congruent case gave Kevin and me a great excuse to be together—not only in public, but privately too, and late at night in my office. If Cliff had stumbled upon the two of us, I had a built-in excuse for Kevin's presence.

And then my mind went into high gear, along these lines. We don't have to stand for this; we're a major Jenkins & Price client; we had Kevin first—let's fight to get him back. Since Jack knew I had a "special interest" in the matter, it would be stronger if the "we want Kevin back" plea came from Cliff. I figured I could arrange that without him becoming unduly suspicious. . . .

A few days later, Cliff Cook called to say he was coming over to my office—an occurrence that was unusual enough to cause some trepidation on my part.

When Cliff arrived, he skipped any small talk. "Let me get right to the point, Jack. Emma and I are unhappy that you took Kevin Dodge off the Congruent case. Jill Marsh is affable enough and I'm sure she's a competent lawyer, but we both feel that Kevin is a lot more capable than she is. He's a very special guy, we had him first, and we want him back."

This presented me with a real problem. Still, I had to smile inwardly at the irony of Cliff Cook pleading for the return to duty of the young man who was banging his girlfriend! The good news was that, at least to that point, Cliff had no idea something was up between Emma and Kevin.

"I'll see what I can do, Cliff, although I think I'm powerless in this instance—it was a Jenkins & Price decision. But listen, Jill Marsh is a very good associate—just be patient for a week or so while she gets up to speed. And I promise you I'll spend more of my own time on the case than ever before."

Cliff seemed somewhat assuaged by this. But then, just as he appeared ready to leave, he said, "Jack, there's something else I want to talk to you about—a personal problem unrelated to the Congruent case."

When I heard that—even though Cliff made it seem like a casual afterthought—I realized that what I was about to hear was the real reason for his visit to my office.

"Jack, I know we've never talked about this subject, but by now you've probably figured out that Emma and I have been engaged in a long-term intimate relationship."

My guard immediately went up. This was the last subject I wanted to be discussing with Cook. I murmured something unintelligible in reply, which neither confirmed nor denied my knowledge.

He went on. "Even though I'm happily married and at heart a family man, my relationship with Emma has assumed a very important role in my life—one that I find immensely satisfying. But lately, Emma has been different. In the past, she was always available to me, but now she sometimes claims she's busy. I'll spare you the gory details, but the sex—which was incomparable—just isn't the same. She's become testy and irritable, mainly on the issue of me leaving my wife—even though Emma has been well aware I'd never do that while my kids were still in their early teens. In short, I have a hunch she's seeing someone else on the side."

Oh my God, I thought—and then wondered, why is he telling me this? I made a real effort to keep my facial expression as neutral as possible—I didn't want an inadvertent glimmer to betray my state of knowledge.

"Jack, I need to find out what's going on. You're my most trusted advisor. I want you to hire a private detective to observe Emma's every move over the next two weeks. I'm determined to get to the bottom of this. But, needless to say, Emma can't have any idea what's happening. And should she suspect something is up, I don't want my fingerprints to appear. Got it? Okay, go to work."

With that—and before I could respond—Cliff rose from his chair and strode out of my office.

After he left, I sat there in shock—musing about what to do next. I knew I had to hire the private eye—that was a direct order from the client. But how about *before* that? What I really wanted to do was tell Kevin about the detective, have him tell Emma, and then have them cool it while Sam Spade went about his thing. But Cliff had been insistent that Emma *not* know about this—I couldn't violate that direct dictate of confidentiality.

Still, I reasoned—or perhaps, in retrospect, "rationalized" is a more appropriate term—that this didn't mean I couldn't tell Kevin about it, as long as I extracted a promise from him that he wouldn't pass the word along to Emma. My justification was that Cliff hadn't said anything specific about *that*—a justification which conveniently overlooked the fact that Cook had no idea I knew the identity of Emma's playmate. I did wonder, though, whether I could rely on Kevin not to tell Emma, since he wasn't the one Cook put that burden on—I was.

But even assuming Kevin would preserve the secret—for which I planned to extract his solemn vow—I questioned whether he would be able to induce Emma to cool it for the duration of the detective's investigation. She was obviously a very determined woman. Then I hit upon a scheme—a pretty clever one, it seemed at the time, although I can see now how it caused me to plunge deeper into the morass.

I broached my plan to Kevin later that afternoon in my office. "I had a visit from Cliff Cook today. The bad news is that he knows something is up with Emma, because he asked me to hire a private detective to tail her for the next few weeks. So, obviously, you two have to cool it during that time. The good news is that he obviously doesn't suspect you're the problem, because he asked me to bring you back onto the Congruent case. I'm going to tell him that's impossible, but we've still got the detective problem. And you can't say anything about that to Emma, because Cliff was very insistent that this not get back to her. I want you to promise me that you won't tell her."

Kevin thought for a moment before replying. "I promise—but if I can't tell her, what will I say is the reason we have to cool it?"

"I've thought about that, and here's my idea. I'm going to send you to England for a fortnight, as they say. Get you the hell out of here. That way, there'll be nothing for the detective to discover."

"But what do I say to Emma?"

"Well, she thinks you left the Congruent case to work for another Jenkins & Price client. So just tell her you have to go to London to depose or interview some key witnesses in that other case."

"I guess that'll work. But what are you going to do about Cliff wanting me to come back on Congruent?"

"I'll just tell him I tried my damnedest but can't extricate you from that other case. But I'm not going to say anything to him about your going to London—there's no need for him to know that."

"What will I do over there?"

"I've considered that. You might as well be productive. For a while now, Jenkins & Price has been secretly considering opening a London office to service some of our multinational clients. I'm one of the partners in charge of the project. We haven't made a final decision yet—especially in view of the weakness of the dollar against the pound—but while you're over there, you could scout out possible locations. Since we're still undecided, though, we don't want our associates to know we're even thinking about a London office. So you can't tell anyone what you're doing over there. Just leave town—don't talk about it. Let them think you're on vacation."

"What if someone—like, for instance, another client—asks my secretary about my whereabouts?"

"Just tell her to say, 'He's out of town'—with no elaboration. Maybe they'll think you went to Turnberry." I don't know if Kevin got the reference—it was the place where Tom Watson beat Jack Nicklaus by one stroke in last year's British Open.

Kevin didn't look pleased with the deception. No doubt I should have been more bothered by it myself, but—I hate to admit this—I was so wound up in the scheme that I almost felt a sense of exhilaration. I was really on a roll, with three or four fabrications working at different levels. And I wasn't through yet.

"Now Kevin, you have to tell Emma not to phone you over there—and you can't call her, either at her home or her office, since the detective will probably be tapping those lines."

"What will I tell her is the reason we can't talk on the phone?"

"You have to figure that out, but remember, you can't mention the private eye. Try blaming it on yourself—maybe something to do with the other case you're working on, a fear that your adversary may be investigating *you*. . . ."

I never really resolved all the loose ends here. After Kevin left my office, I recall sitting there very much alone. The temporary sense of exhilaration had passed, and all I could see was how much deeper and deeper I was sinking into this quagmire. *What a tangled web we weave, when first we practice to deceive.* Worse still, I couldn't avoid some nagging ethical questions, such as whether I was violating an obligation to my client by impeding the detective's investigation.

I was reminded of the situation I faced last year representing Alan Carter in that stock fraud case, when all of a sudden I awoke to the realization that Will Wilson's crucial testimony on Carter's behalf had probably been purchased by the client. I dithered around back then, but ultimately did nothing about it. That was bad enough. But there's a big difference between that kind of passive nonfeasance—after all, I didn't knowingly sponsor Wilson's false testimony— and the active malfeasance I had gotten myself involved in here. Or is one just an inevitable step up the ladder from the other . . . ?

My ruminations were broken by a call I needed to take on another matter. What the hell, I thought as I picked up the phone, the next move is to hire the detective. He certainly should be competent, but he needn't be, shall we say, world-class.

Life became really boring for me with Kevin over in London, and not even communicating by phone. I missed him—and I also missed the opportunity to put some more pressure on Cliff. Since I'm an activist by nature, I realized I had to do something about the situation. . . .

The next few days were relatively quiet. The private detective I'd hired was on the job, but with Kevin in London and staying out of touch with Emma, there was nothing for him to discover. It began to look like I'd dodged the bullet.

That temporary state of euphoria was shattered the next afternoon, at a meeting with the Seacrest people. Cliff was there, but not Emma. "Will Emma be joining us?" I asked him.

"Oh, Emma left town last evening. She had to make a trip to London to put out a fire at our subsidiary over there."

It was, in retrospect, sort of delicious. The flight over was okay, although I wish I could have traveled on the Concorde that made its first trans-Atlantic crossing not too long ago. When I got to London the next morning, Kevin had gone out to have breakfast. I told the desk clerk at Kevin's hotel that I was his wife, slipping into town to surprise him on his birthday, and got the clerk to let me in to Kevin's room.

At the airport, I had bought a large towel decorated with the British flag. I took off my clothes, wrapped myself in the towel, and lay down on the bed. When Kevin opened the door, I began to sing, "There'll always be an England," as I slowly unfurled the flag. . . .

I'm sure he was glad to see me. He did seem concerned, though, that if and when Jack found out I'd crossed the pond, the partner might think his associate cooked up the whole rendezvous. I let him stew over that for a few minutes and then steered him in the direction of more important things. . . .

When I got back to the office, I called Kevin in London to tell him Emma was on her way. "I'm aware of that," he said, "In fact, she showed up to surprise me this morning. But I want you to know, Jack, I had nothing to do with this—it was strictly Emma's idea."

I didn't know whether to believe him or not. Maybe that was because I'd been lying so much myself—it tends to have a disabling effect on your own credibility detector. At any rate, there wasn't much I could do about it at this point, and the two of them were unlikely to be discovered.

But later that day, I got a call from the detective. "So far," he said, "I've come up with nothing. But Miss Searles has just taken a trip to London that struck me as a little sudden. That kind of thing always makes me suspicious. Am I authorized to go over to England to follow up my instincts?"

What a spot this put me in! I didn't want to tell him to go, since he would undoubtedly catch the two of them canoodling. I didn't want to tell him *not* to go, since that smacked of impeding his investigation. I realized I couldn't decide this question—I had to get Cliff Cook involved. I told the detective I'd call him back.

I picked up the phone, called Cook, and repeated to him what the detective said. "What do you think, Cliff? Obviously, there'll be some added expense if we authorize him to go."

Cliff thought for a moment before replying. "Hmm . . . I suppose it's possible she's fooling around over there. That trouble at our subsidiary did seem to come out of nowhere . . . But she doesn't have any friends in London that I'm aware of . . . I don't know, Jack. You're my trusted advisor—what do *you* think?"

It was a tough moment for me, but I handled it the only way that seemed feasible at the time. "Well, Cliff, I'm your advisor on litigation matters—not matters of the heart. I think you'll have to make the call on this one."

"Okay," said Cliff. "Since she'll only be gone a few days, tell the detective not to bother. But I'll find out what plane she's coming back on, and you get word to him to check the airport to see if she's flying alone. Then he can resume his coverage back here."

I breathed a sigh of relief. Still, I felt a funny feeling in the pit of my stomach. Had I done the right thing by my client?

Around noon the next day, I got a call from Cliff Cook. His voice had a sharper tone than usual. "Jack," he said, "I need to talk to Kevin Dodge about a matter that came up in the early days of the Congruent case, when he was still on our team. It involves something the other side said that I can't quite remember, but it's important—and Kevin, who was there, would probably recall the details. How do I get in touch with him? I called his secretary who said he's out of town—but then she clammed up."

I promptly lied and said I wasn't sure where Kevin was, but I'd find him and have him get in touch with Cliff. But Cook's request, coming out of the blue, made me uneasy—although not nearly as uneasy as I felt when, just before hanging up, Cliff said, "Oh, by the way, Jack, I've rethought the subject. Have the detective make a quick trip to London. Emma is staying at the Dorchester. So long."

Kaboom! I sat there trying to figure out just how much Cliff knew or surmised, and what to do about it. A few minutes later, the answer appeared at my office door in the person of Jill Marsh.

"Jack, I just wanted to fill you in on something that happened this morning in my meeting with Cliff Cook. Everything about the case itself was fine, but something else struck me as possibly troublesome. At one point, Kevin's name came up.

I happened to mention that he was over in London. Cliff seemed extremely interested in the news and ended the meeting a short time later—a little prematurely, it seemed. . . . I hope I didn't do anything wrong."

I thanked Jill for her report and provided the necessary reassurance. She left my office. It was now clear—especially with the reversal of his decision on the detective—that Cliff had a strong hunch what was going on. And not only in terms of Emma and Kevin—by now he was undoubtedly suspicious of my role in this as well. It would only be natural for Cliff to assume that when he told me Emma was on her way to London, I must have known Kevin was over there. The time had come for me to reevaluate the situation.

I saw then, for the first time and with harsh clarity, that in order to hang on to this prized client, I had gotten deeper and deeper into a tangled web of deception. And I realized that this is what happens with lies—they breed other lies, and then you begin to tell one thing to one person and something else to another. It becomes tough to keep track of just where you're at.

Not only that, but if you're in a position of relative power—like I was as a partner—you often recruit other people to lie for you in order to perpetuate the deception. I had done that with my associates. Kevin was forced to tell Emma he'd been preempted by a nonexistent client, who had sent him to take imaginary depositions in London, where he couldn't phone Emma because of nefarious fictional adversaries trying to pin something on him. Even the innocent Jill Marsh had been put in the position of having to support the tale of Kevin's invented long-term client.

Now, that much is true for anyone who lies. For a lawyer, though, it's much worse. I'd found myself rooting for the detective to give an "all clear"—to be able to transmit to Cook a report that no boyfriend existed—when I knew damn well there *was* a boyfriend. And the boyfriend was my own associate! Is that good client service? Is that a satisfactory measure of loyalty? The questions seemed almost rhetorical. I could just imagine how our ethics guru, Dwight Bentley—whom I understand is not in very good shape nowadays—would respond to them.

So I decided I had to put an end to this travesty. I could no longer impede the way things played out. But what I quickly learned
was that it's not so easy to extricate yourself from a situation like
this without having it appear you've been dissembling from the
outset—especially when you have been! To keep that from happening, it often takes a few more lies to unravel the knot.

Here's the way my mind was working that day. I realized I
was under no compulsion to protect Kevin and Emma from the
consequences of their actions. The only guy I had to look out for
was myself—and, by extrapolation, my firm, Jenkins & Price.
In short, I was now willing for Cliff to find out that Kevin and
Emma were having a fling, as long as this information didn't
jeopardize the firm's relationship with Seacrest.

So then I thought about what I'd say to Cliff if I were really
to come clean. The mea culpa would have to go something like
this:

> I knew very early on that Kevin and Emma were lovers. When
> you told me you suspected Emma was having an affair, I with-
> held my knowledge that she was.
> The detective I hired for you wasn't the best available.
> When I took Kevin off the Congruent case, I lied to you about
> another client requiring his services.
> I dispatched Kevin to England to cool things down, so the detec-
> tive wouldn't discover their affair.
> I didn't advise you to send the detective to London, even though
> I knew that Emma was over there with Kevin.
> When you asked me where Kevin was, I lied and said I didn't
> know.

What the hell, I just couldn't do it! I'd look terrible—disloyal to
the core. So, the question then became, what *can* I do? I had to
follow Cliff's order and send the detective to London. But I didn't
have to warn Kevin the detective was on the way—in which
case, presumably, he and Emma would be caught in the act.
Most important, I had to let Cook know what was going on.

Cliff himself happened to be out of town that day. Knowing
this—and not wanting to get into a telephone discussion with

him on the subject—I sent a note over to his office by messenger, in an envelope marked "personal." The note read: "Cliff, to update you, I phoned the detective and told him to get on the next plane to London, to check out Emma at the Dorchester. Then, when I inquired at the firm, I found out that Kevin is also in London. I'm pretty dumb about these things, but the thought has occurred to me that maybe Kevin and Emma are there together. So I reached the detective before he left and told him to also check out Kevin at the Savoy, and to focus on whether the two of them were spending time with each other. If it turns out my suspicions are true, I'll be mortified. In that event, I apologize fervently to you, both on a personal basis and on behalf of the firm. The problem is, we can't always control our associates all the time. . . ."

Well, to make a long story short, the detective crossed the pond and caught Kevin and Emma together in clearly compromising circumstances. He reported his finding back to me by phone. I waited until I knew Cliff was again out of the office and then passed the news along to him via another personal note-cum-apology.

You know, I had a funny feeling Kevin and I were being watched in London. Sure enough, the morning after I got back in town, Cliff came into my office. He barely greeted me, and when he spoke, his voice was very cold.

"I'll come right to the point, Emma. In recent days, I've suspected you of fooling around with someone else, but I didn't know who. I had Jack Lawrence hire a private detective, who tracked you to London. He saw you in an unambiguous embrace with Kevin Dodge."

I tried to be flip about it. "Gotcha!" I said.

"Is that all you have to say?"

"No, it's not, I would also like to state for the record that I can't believe I ever gave my heart to a sick bastard who had the nerve to put a detective on my tail."

Well, it just went downhill from there. I not only admitted the affair with Kevin—I actually went into some detail about the whole thing and how it evolved. I explained how frustrated I'd been by Cliff's reluctance to leave his wife and that this kind of thing can happen when a woman is resentful. But then my tone changed, and I told him I was prepared to end things with Kevin. I sang a few bars of the Billy Joel song, "Just the Way You Are," to show Cliff I wasn't trying to change him. I even fluttered my eyelashes as an invitation to set things right.

That sort of thing has almost always worked for me in the past, so I really wasn't prepared for Cliff's response. But I realize now that affairs of the heart—or, for that matter, of the lower organs—are in some ways like telling lies. You get yourself in deeper and deeper, things get out of hand, and you can never predict where it will all end up. Cliff's final words came as he turned to leave my office.

"I understand your frustration, Emma, although I believe I've been forthright with you from the start—I'm not leaving my wife while my kids are still teenagers. You might give up Kevin, but this kind of affair could be repeated, and I can't handle any more Kevins. So, as of right now, our personal relationship is at an end. And by the way, Emma, you're fired. Arthur Greene, a partner from the Sampson firm, has agreed to come aboard as general counsel, effective immediately. You've got thirty minutes to clear out your things."

Cliff Cook came to my office today. We hadn't spoken since I'd sent my two notes to him. He didn't bother to sit down or even take off his overcoat.

"Just so you know, Jack, I've spoken to Emma and told her I had her tailed by a private detective, who spotted her in London going at it with Kevin Dodge. She admitted their affair. In retrospect, I think she almost wanted me to find out about it—to make me jealous enough to leave my wife."

I started to say something, but Cliff waved me off. "She also told me that you knew about their relationship early on—that this was why you took Kevin off the Congruent case and later sent him to London."

Dammit, I thought, Kevin must have said something to Emma. You just can't control other people. . . .

"So, Jack, what it comes down to is that you've been lying to me all along. Listen, if you'd told me the truth at an early stage, I wouldn't have blamed you or your firm, because Emma was the person primarily at fault here. Kevin was just a convenient tool for her to use for her own purposes. Hell, even at the end I might have forgiven you as a stand-up guy, if you'd come clean and told me the whole sordid tale.

"But lying to me, and then not telling the whole truth when you switched gears—that's no basis for a lawyer-client relationship. How can I trust the guy who's been deceiving me? As of now, Seacrest's professional relationship with Jenkins & Price is finished. I've already switched the Congruent case over to the Sampson firm—send them the files." And he turned on his heel and departed my office.

So that's where things stand—although it's not quite the end of the tale. An hour has passed since Cliff left, and I'm still sitting in my office ruminating. What has me worried now is the story I'm going to tell my partners about why the firm got bounced off the Congruent case—especially since I made such a big deal about it when we got hired.

I hate the idea of lying to my colleagues, but Cliff's diatribe about my personal conduct being the basis for him firing the firm would not go over well in the councils of the partnership. I can just visualize it being used against me when the subject of partner compensation comes up later this year. So, if I'm reluctant to tell my partners the truth, what else can I say to them?

One possibility is to blame our dismissal directly on Kevin Dodge for porking the client's girlfriend. When Cook found out, I could say, he was so furious that he took it out on Jenkins & Price.

Of course, that will be tough on Kevin. In fact, he's likely to be fired. Even if he stays on, his chances of making partner—with this black mark against him—are nil.

Under this scenario, I guess I'd have to compound things by lying that I didn't know anything was going on between Emma and Kevin—that I only found out about it too late to save the client relationship. Otherwise, the question will inevitably be asked—if I did know, why didn't I do something about it?

But do I want to get involved in another round of lies, especially to my partners? And by the way, I'd be at some risk of being caught in the act. For instance, Cook might relate the real story to one of my young litigation partners—he knows a few of them pretty well.

Kevin is more of a danger, especially if he becomes angry over being fired. He might never find out exactly why Seacrest terminated the firm—although if he stays intimate with Emma, she could easily tell him. But even without that, Kevin knows I've been aware of his affair with Emma all along, so he could refute my protestations of innocence.

That's why I'm sitting here now in a real dilemma, uncertain of the best path for me to take . . .

My secretary buzzes to say that Emma Searles is in the reception area and would like to see me. I'm obviously intrigued and invite her in.

Emma settles herself in an armchair, crosses her legs to reveal a bit of shapely thigh, and states her business.

"Jack, my sources at the company tell me you've been scolded by Cook and your firm has been bounced as Seacrest's counsel. You may not be aware of this, but I too have been scolded by Cliff—and then not only bounced out of his bed but also out of my job. So, it seems we have something in common."

I nod but don't interrupt her.

"Although we haven't conversed much directly, I feel I know you pretty well through our mutual acquaintances, Cliff and Kevin. And it occurs to me that we're really not very different people. I cheated, you lied—it's all pretty much the same thing."

Actually, I'm thinking, what I did was a lot more reprehensible than what she did—so I take her correlation as a back-handed compliment.

Emma continues. "I'm a damn good lawyer, as I think you're aware, but I've come to the conclusion that I wasn't cut out for corporate life. So I've decided to relocate to one of the good law firms in town. Jenkins & Price is the firm I know best, think the most of, and could do more good for than any other. And so, Jack, I've decided to ask you for a job. I could come in as a senior associate, and if I proved myself capable, be eligible for partnership in a year or two."

Not having expected this, I don't answer right away. A lot of thoughts flash through my mind in the next few moments. I have no questions about Emma's competence, but based on recent experience, her judgment is certainly suspect. More to the point, though, and assuming she and Kevin are still an item, I'm concerned what impact her arrival on the scene will have on whatever spin I decide to put on the reason for our dismissal as Seacrest's counsel.

Emma smiles. "I think I can guess some of the things going through your mind, Jack. Such as, can she be relied upon—this babe who pats guys on the ass and fabricates a tale to justify going over to London on the company dollar. Look, I can't justify the past and won't try to—but I have learned my lesson, my former hubris is virtually defunct, and I'm ready to give my all in this new job at J&P."

I nod in acknowledgement, but I think she can see there's something else on my mind—this woman is *very* smart—which she now proceeds to address.

"And Jack, there is one respect in which I can be extremely helpful to you. I'm sure you must be wrestling with the question of what to tell your partners about the reason why Jenkins & Price was so unceremoniously dumped as counsel in the Congruent case. Well, I can be your star witness."

I guess I must look a bit alarmed, because she quickly says, "Don't worry, I won't rake over the gory sexual details. No, here's what I have in mind. I've been replaced as general counsel of Seacrest by Arthur Greene from the Sampson firm—the same firm that has taken over from Jenkins & Price as litigation counsel on the Congruent case. I'll just tell your partners that, for personal reasons having nothing to do with my competence, Cliff Cook decided to replace me with Greene as general counsel. And the first thing that Greene did on taking over was to substitute his old firm for Jenkins & Price on the case. This way, it takes the onus off you completely. And there's even a grain of truth in it."

This woman is a genius. . . .

I clear my throat and make a stab at sounding official. "Well, of course you'll have to go through the hiring committee, but I'm sure we'll be able to find a place for you." Then, reverting to my normal voice, I add, "One condition, though—you have to give up Kevin. Otherwise, people who know he was on the case originally might put two and two together. . . ."

Emma nods in acquiescence to my condition, smiles, stands up, reaches across the desk to shake my hand, and says, "As Humphrey Bogart said to Claude Rains at the end of *Casablanca*, 'I think this is the beginning of a beautiful friendship.'"

Commentary on
Sex, Lies, and
Private Eyes

I n this story, we get to spend some more time with
one of J&P's litigation partners, Jack Lawrence.
You'll remember him from his courtroom wake-up
call in "You Gotta Get Me Off!" We also meet Cliff
Cook, the CEO of the firm's client Seacrest Corp.; the
Seacrest general counsel, an attractive young woman
named Emma Searles; and a J&P fifth-year associate, Kevin Dodge, whom Jack has called "a litigation
star-in-the-making."

In the previous story, "Awash in Associates," one associate (Bob Gumley) had an odor problem and another
(Gary Stone) liked to shoot craps. In this tale, the associate (Kevin Dodge) turns out to be a budding Don
Juan. And the object of his lust isn't just anyone, but the
general counsel (Emma Searles) of J&P's good client,
Seacrest. And Emma isn't just any general counsel, but
the mistress of the client's CEO (Cliff Cook). So, come
in, Houston, we've got a problem. . . .

I'm not aware of any such real-life triangle, but it
certainly could have happened. At any rate, I've tried

to avoid being salacious about the sexual high-jinks—a forbearance you may find disappointing—and focus on the effect this predicament has on Jack Lawrence.

The effect, in a nutshell, is to cause Jack to lose his ethical bearings. (There's an analogy to the "Partner-gate" cover-up that Paul Garson contrived in attempting to cloak a misstep of his favored partnership candidate, Ted Ashburn.) The libidinal problem here might not have had such a dire effect on another lawyer, but, as we saw in "You Gotta Get Me Off!"—where Jack became paralyzed into inaction when he suspected his star witness was lying on the stand—Jack Lawrence is not the staunchest guy in town.

A word about the format of this story. It begins in the present tense for the opening scene, then flashes back into the recent past for the bulk of the events, and ends up again in the present for the final encounter. The narration is in the first person, mostly by Jack Lawrence. One limitation of this is that the reader can only know what Jack knows. So to cover other ground and add some spice, I've included several segments recounted by Emma Searles. Just remember, as you read the tale, that both Jack and Emma are central characters, so neither can be considered a disinterested observer.

Now to the story. Emma is frustrated in her relationship with Cliff, which is going nowhere. Kevin is a young man on the make. They meet in connection with Seacrest's case against Congruent, and sparks fly. Although the two of them leave clues aplenty, Jack—who is deep in denial—sees very little. But since he suspects that Emma is Cliff's mistress, the contemplation that a J&P associate may be going at it with the client's lady is just too much to bear. And then one day—having heard Emma's distinctive voice over the telephone from Kevin's bedroom at 6:30 A.M.—Jack can no longer turn a blind eye to what's occurring.

In today's world, what Kevin is doing here constitutes a specific violation of the rules of professional conduct.

Moreover, a lawyer who has knowledge of it (like Jack) arguably has a duty to inform the appropriate professional authority. Back when the story takes place, states dealt with lawyer-client sexual relations under more general rules dealing with misconduct or conflicts of interest, with the principal concern being whether the lawyer was taking advantage of his position or abusing the client's trust—factors not apparently applicable to the savvy Ms. Emma Searles.

For her part, Emma is so mad at Cliff—mainly for not leaving his wife—that she's willing to take the risk of a fling with Kevin. She may even want Cliff to suspect that something's up—hoping his jealousy will induce him to come around. Although she realizes Jack knows the score, she appears unworried that he'll do something about it.

The first question I want to pose to you is this:

What are your views on the actions of Emma and Kevin up to this point? Should either or both of them have exercised more restraint before getting involved? Were they misguided in ignoring the possible effects on their careers? Does this kind of thing actually happen today?

At the risk of sounding hopelessly antiquated, I must confess to an irresistible urge to put Kevin over my knee and give him a good spanking. As Kevin himself tells Jack when confronted, "there are plenty of other fish in the sea"—so why then is he trolling in these protected territorial waters? I'll tell you something else—in my day, Kevin's bad judgment in this regard would, if known to the assemblage, have seriously hurt his chances when the partners got around to evaluating his fitness for partnership.

As for Emma, I'm a little more reluctant to offer her any counsel in this particular sphere. And I have to admit that the flirting in the conference room, the late-night strategy sessions, the double entendres—they do hold a certain fascination. I guess if Emma came to me for advice, I'd focus on the concept of hubris, a trait she displays in such reckless abundance. I'd tell her what I've observed over the years—that a serious case of hubris generally contains its own self-destruct button. Come on, Emma, there must be better, less risky ways to put a little amatory pressure on the boss.

Unlike Elliot Cheever in "Awash in Associates"—who has trouble bringing himself to confront Bob Gumley's aroma—Jack Lawrence now springs into action. He challenges Kevin Dodge, obtains his carnal admission, and tells him to break off the affair—citing the dire effects it would have on J&P's relations with Seacrest if Cliff were to find out. I'm comfortable with this approach, but let me ask you:

If you were Jack, is that what you would have done? If not, what steps would you have taken?

Kevin then talks Jack out of insisting that he break off with Emma. To do so, he says, will result in her blaming J&P for the lothario boycott, and her anger will cost the firm the Seacrest business. Since losing the client is Jack's main concern, he reluctantly accedes to Kevin's plan to keep the affair "lukewarm."

If you were Jack, would you have agreed to Kevin's plan? If not, how would you have reacted to it?

I think I would have said, "Nice try, Kevin," and turned it down. I'd have told him to muster all his credibility, pretend that he has good judgment and a conscience (sorry for the sarcasm, Kevin), and tell Emma that he—not Jack or J&P—has decided it's improper for him to engage in this affair while serving as Seacrest's counsel in the Congruent case. I'd also warn him to be careful not to say anything that implies he's passing judgment on her actions. Emma may not be happy at this turn of events, but hopefully she would have some respect for his scruples. Given the unusual circumstances, and the good work J&P has been doing for Seacrest up to this point, I think it's unlikely she would use this as the basis for firing J&P as Seacrest's counsel.

Well, they try it Kevin's way, but things don't work out. Even though the associate attempts to be discreet, Emma doesn't—causing Jack to fear that Cliff will eventually notice what's going on. Jack now realizes that more drastic steps are required, but instead of reiterating his demand that Kevin break off relations with Emma pronto (which he should have done), he decides to change associates on the Congruent case. This will allow Kevin to keep his affair with Emma lukewarm outside the office, where Cliff is less likely to observe them in action.

Whatever the dubious merits of such a plan, it's what Jack does to accomplish the associate switch that causes problems. When Kevin says he doesn't want it to look like he's been fired, Jack is ready to go with his first falsehood. He'll tell Seacrest that a firm client Kevin has been servicing just got sued on a matter Kevin knows a lot about, and the client has requested Kevin's services. In Jack's view, it's just a white lie—"a little professional lubricant to make things go down smoothly." And Jack, ever the pragmatist, will make it more palatable to the client by not charging for Kevin's time or for the hours it takes his replacement, Jill Marsh, to get up to speed on the case.

What do you think of Jack's rationale to the client as to why he's replacing Kevin on the case? Is this how you would have handled it? If not, what would you have done?

Now, I'm not going to pretend that I never used a little professional lubricant myself with a client, or didn't throw in a white lie or two. Albert Schweitzer, I'm not. And this happens to be a situation where the whole truth is not an appetizing alternative. But that's the point of the story—to illustrate what a dangerous course a prevaricator sets out on when he concocts his first lie, with all the sub-falsehoods and diversions he has to employ to buttress the basic untruth.

I think Jack should just have told the client that he needed to replace Kevin on the case "for reasons that I can't go into"—refusing to be drawn into a discussion of the circumstances—while proffering an equal caliber associate and credits on the fee. What can Seacrest do? This may not be ideal, but at least it's not a lie that requires a lot of distasteful shoring up.

At any rate, Jack does it his way, and the first problem he encounters is that he can't use the same story with Jill Marsh and others at Jenkins & Price, since they would know there's no such other client. So Jack levels with Jill that he's telling Seacrest a white lie about Kevin and gets her to go along. By the way, he's not even totally truthful with her—pretending that the reason for the personnel switch is a "chemistry" issue between Kevin and the Seacrest people. (Hmm. . . maybe the definition of that word can be stretched to fit the actual facts.) Anyway, let me ask you:

What are your views on how Jack handled Jill in this instance? Can you think of a better way for him to have proceeded with her?

Here's what I would have said to her: "For reasons I won't go into, Jill, I've decided that I want you to replace Kevin on the Seacrest-Congruent team. If they ask you why the switch occurred, just say that you don't know and refer them to me."

The street-smart Emma privately questions the stated reason for the switch. She enlists Cliff to plead with Jack to get Kevin back on the case. Pretty good irony, huh?

When the request is made, Jack focuses on the good news—that Cliff obviously doesn't know about Kevin and Emma. Jack urges Cliff to give Jill Marsh a little more time and promises to devote more personal hours to the case.

If you were Jack at this point—where Cliff has made a special plea for Kevin to return, and you know he's available—would you bring him back on the Seacrest-Congruent team?

I think I would have done so. If a client goes to pains to ask that the firm accommodate him, my inclination would be to do so. Of course, I would couple this with instructions to Kevin to break off the affair with Emma immediately.

Then Cliff drops his bombshell about Emma—acknowledging their intimate relationship and voicing his suspicion that she's "seeing someone else on the side." Cliff asks Jack, as his "most trusted advisor," to hire a private detective to spy on Emma—but she's not to know, and (does this sound familiar?) Cliff's fingerprints can't appear anywhere. So, let me ask you:

As Jack, how would you respond when Cliff reposes his confidence in you and engages your assistance to hire the detective?

Right now is probably the last point at which Jack can turn this thing around without incurring lasting damage. The following lines wouldn't have been easy for Jack to utter, but let's try them out: "Hearing your suspicions, Cliff, and putting two and two together, I very much fear that if you're right, the 'other man' is my associate Kevin Dodge. I'd certainly like to be able to help with your personal problem, but I think I'm conflicted; so I suggest you use another intermediary to hire the detective. If your suspicions and my fears turn out to be accurate, I apologize profusely in advance for Kevin's misconduct." What do you think?

Instead of this, Jack rationalizes, concocts falsehoods, ponders various schemes, and comes up with a self-styled brainstorm. What makes things even worse is that he confesses to feeling a sense of exhilaration, "with three or four fabrications working at different levels." Ouch!

Jack knows that Emma can't learn of the private detective, but he decides it's all right to tell Kevin, while extracting the associate's promise not to pass it on to Emma—after all, Cliff hadn't specifically banned him from doing that. Come on, Jack—don't you think that if Cliff suspected Kevin of being Emma's playmate, he would have had a few choice words to say on the subject?

Jack starts out with a lie to Cliff that he can't get Kevin back on the case. Then—realizing that if Emma doesn't know about the detective, she won't abstain from dallying with Kevin during the investigation —Jack devises the notion of shipping Kevin off to London for a fortnight. Out of sight. . . etc. But that requires a false story to Emma as to why Kevin is heading overseas. It also calls for a phony assignment (looking for office space), the involvement of Kevin's secretary to say he left town without elaboration, and a fake reason why Emma and Kevin can't speak on her tapped phone. Jack tops it off by deciding that the private eye he'll hire won't be world-class. I won't even ask your opinion of this whole rigmarole. It's painful, isn't it, to observe Jack slowly sinking into the quagmire.

Along the way, Jack ruminates on how this situation relates to the one in "You Gotta Get Me Off!" There's a big difference, he starts out thinking, between that kind of passive nonfeasance and the active nonfeasance he's gotten into here. But on further reflection, he asks himself (presciently, I think), "is one just an inevitable step up the ladder from the other?"

What do you think?

Emma now gets bored and creates a fictitious excuse to visit Kevin in London. When Jack finds out and calls Kevin, the associate says he had nothing to do with the visit—it was strictly Emma's idea. Jack doesn't know whether to believe him or not—cognizant that the difficulty in judging Kevin's veracity is due to Jack lying so much himself, which "tends to have a disabling effect on your own credibility detector." Amen!

The detective now seeks authorization to follow Emma to London. Jack calls Cliff—after all, it's the CEO's decision—but Cliff puts the issue right back to Jack: "You're my trusted advisor—what do *you* think?"

Jack punts and leaves it up to Cliff, who decides not to send the detective. Jack heaves a sigh of relief, but wonders—has he done the right thing by his client?

What do you think—has he? Would you instead have recommended that the detective go to London? Not go? Something else?

Here's another point at which Jack can undergo one of those "oh, my God" moments, reveal that Kevin is in London, and say this confirms his fears that Kevin is the other man ("for which, my abject apologies in advance"). At the very least, if Jack decides not to go all the way—but can sense what's in the wind—he's better off having recommended to Cliff that the detective be sent across the pond.

Things then start to unravel. Cliff calls Jack to say he wants to get in touch with Kevin about some earlier matter. (This is Cliff's own lie, but after all, what should we expect—he's the guy who's been cheating on his wife for years.) Jack dissembles right back, saying he's not sure where Kevin is. Then Cliff announces he has changed his mind and wants Jack to send the detective to London. A few minutes later, when Jill reports her inadvertent remark to Cliff that placed Kevin in London, Jack realizes what has happened. He's now reasonably certain that Cliff knows what's going on—including Jack's own role in the proceedings—and starts to rethink things.

Jack has some useful thoughts here for all of us—about lies breeding lies, the practical difficulty of keeping track of what's been said to each person (since the stories told tend to differ), and the need to recruit others to do one's dirty work. It's a bad state of affairs generally, and even worse for a lawyer. As to whether Jack's rooting for the detective to strike out is evidence of client loyalty, I won't even ask.

Do you know what I found the most interesting aspect in concocting this mess? It was the discovery that when Jack finally decided to end the deception—but didn't want to appear as having been lying from the outset—there was no easy way to extricate himself. Just reread the part of the story in which Jack realizes what he'd have to say if he were really to come clean. He's appalled—it makes him sound like a monster—and he decides he can't do it.

If you were Jack at this juncture, could you see yourself telling Cliff the whole truth?

The reason that a total confession sounds so terrible to Jack is because it presupposes an ignoble motive on his part—trying desperately to hang on to the client. That does happen to be Jack's actual motive. But the narrative might not seem quite so terrible if it had been undertaken for a different motive.

Let me try out an analogy to the world of negotiating. Everyone agrees that misrepresentations of facts that relate directly to what's being bought and sold are clearly off limits. On the other hand, many phony rationales are used to justify positions taken (for instance, the reason stated by one party as to *why* he can't give a certain protection requested by the other). I don't encourage this sort of thing, but the reality is that it's generally condoned, on the theory that one side isn't entitled to see the inner workings of the other side's mind. (That's why I warn negotiators to take nothing at face value and examine closely all ostensible rationales.)

I'm not recommending this to Jack Lawrence, but if he'd really like to come clean on the facts (but can't face the ignominy of his actual motive)—and if he can get over the distinction between what might not be considered inappropriate in a negotiation and what's called for lawyer-client-wise (which I can't)—then he could consider something along the following lines: "In my misguided way, Cliff, I was trying to protect you from finding out that your mistress was misbehaving, and I was subconsciously hoping their fling would evaporate, with an ocean between them. It was bad judgment on my part. Now that you've become aware of the secret, I can only say mea culpa."

Jack takes the other route, generating some additional lies to unravel the knot. He sends Cliff a note, implying he just woke up to the notion that Kevin and Emma might be an item, and further suggesting that he's helping the detective to uncover the truth about them. The thought of this mortifies him—it's something for which he fervently apologizes—but what can you do about these associates nowadays. . . .

The denouement is brief but painful. The detective catches Emma and Kevin canoodling. Cliff fires Emma from both bed and office. Cliff then confronts Jack, giving his weak excuse short shrift—since Emma has told Cliff that Jack knew about the affair from the start, and that this is why he took Kevin off the case and sent the associate to London.

As I note later on in my commentary to "The Reluctant Eulogist," I've found over the years that when I take a position with a client based on an ethical principle, it goes down much easier with the client if coupled with a practical consideration that points in the same direction. And most of the time I'm pleased to discover that just such a consideration does in fact exist. I see an analogy between this and the situation with lying. Not only is lying an ethical no-no, but on a practical basis, it's a terrible idea. And one of the main reasons for this is that the liar simply can't count on what other people involved in the deception will say or refrain from saying—as a result of which, the truth usually comes out, to the liar's dismay. That's just what happens here.

Cliff then says that if Jack had come clean at the outset, Cliff wouldn't have ousted J&P, since he understood it was primarily Emma's fault. Even if Jack had 'fessed up at the end, Cliff would have given him some points for being a stand-up guy. But the consistent falsehoods have eroded the lawyer-client relationship irreparably, and so Cliff fires the firm.

Does anybody disagree with what Cliff does here?

I don't. Even Jack (at the beginning of the tale) says, "I'd have done the same thing."

I'll close with a word about the coda to the story. People like Jack and Emma are, in a word, survivors—like Ralph Landry in ("On-the-Job Training") and the apprentice survivor Ted Ashburn (in that story and "Partnergate"). And survival is what the coda is about.

The issue facing Jack is how to spin this debacle to his partners. The truth is troublesome for him, none of the other possibilities are good, and he's in a dilemma. All of a sudden—deus ex machina—Emma comes barging through the door with a solution to the problem. The cynical bond between them is forged—reminiscent of Humphrey Bogart and Claude Rains marching off arm-in-arm to the Free French garrison in the final scene of *Casablanca*. I hope you realize I'm not endorsing this kind of thing—just indicating that it does happen.

Now let me turn to what's really critical. When I get around to writing my sequel to this tale, set at a time two years later, what do you think:

Will Emma have made partner at J&P?
Is Kevin still around, and are the lovebirds more than friends?
How about Jack—do he and Emma have their own affair?
Most important, does J&P get Seacrest back as a client?

Stay tuned. . . .

NEGOTIATING 101

I t's just negotiating Andy—don't let it get you down." Mack took a sip of his scotch on the rocks. "This Chapman knows his stuff. And he hates the idea of paying top dollar for anything. So don't take it personally."

Andy fingered his glass of beer. They were in the cocktail lounge of the small hotel on lower Park Avenue where Andy was staying. At 4:30 in the afternoon, most of the tables were empty. Andy had offered to come to the lawyer's office, but Mack suggested the lounge as a more comfortable locale. This struck Andy as odd, but he reckoned it was just one of those urban idiosyncrasies he'd be encountering in the days ahead.

Five foot ten and physically fit, Andy looked younger than his thirty-six years. His pleasant features fell just short of handsome. He wore a short-sleeved shirt, a knitted tie, and a skimpy seersucker jacket that exposed part of his tanned forearms.

Andy eyed the man across the table. Michael McKinley—apparently known to all as "Mack"—looked to be in his late sixties, rumpled, overweight, and balding, with prominent circles under his eyes and reddish veins in the fleshy area of his nose. Mack exuded experience and self-confidence—qualities that Andy, at least in his big city incarnation, knew he lacked.

His own experience was in the English Department of Cromwell College, nestled amid the foothills of New Hampshire's scenic White Mountains. He thrived in the academic setting, even on the paltry salary of an associate professor. Along with wife Carol, and son, Billy, he kept his distance from what he viewed as the pollutants—both environmental and human—of urban life.

Now, however, he was seated in a Manhattan cocktail lounge—horns honking in the street, the sultry August heat poised to smother him the minute he stepped outside the cool interior. He recalled hearing all about the 1977 blackout that paralyzed the city and the capture of serial killer "Son of Sam" a month later. Enmeshed in an involuntary situation that seemed beyond his capacity, Andy Potter longed for the cool hills and white frame houses of North Cromwell.

He reflected on the irony of the circumstances. Here he was, knowing next to nothing about business, about finance, about negotiating—occupations he had shunned all his life. Then, out of the blue, he'd been charged with the major responsibility of selling his late father's business. Was it any wonder he was floundering?

He could almost recite by heart the words of his father's handwritten note to him:

> You're probably wondering why I'm entrusting you with the sale of my business. God knows, it's not because of your training or experience—I'd be surprised if you've ever looked at a balance sheet—though I do think you've got the stuff to handle it.
>
> But the real reason is that I don't trust anyone but my own blood to do this job. All the rest of those bastards—bankers, lawyers, accountants—are just looking out for themselves, not their clients. And I certainly wouldn't rely on any of the guys who work for me to sell the business—they'd rather buy it themselves, on the cheap. As for Jeannie, well, she's been a hell of a wife, but business and numbers aren't her thing.
>
> So, it's all yours, Andy, except that it won't happen, and you'll never get to read this, because I'm going to outlive all of you.

But his father's heart hadn't bought into that prognosis of longevity. A few weeks ago, Phil Potter was alive and well, sitting behind the president's desk at Potter's Paints, barking out orders. The next day, he was supine in an ambulance, DOA at the emergency entrance to New York Hospital.

Andy took it hard, although it wasn't as painful as twenty years ago when his mother died in a tragic automobile accident while he was in high school. He'd been very close to his mother, but the same wasn't true with his father. Phil Potter could never understand why Andy chose to teach Keats and Shelley to future MBAs, when he should have been learning how to manage a twenty-unit chain of hardware and housewares stores in four boroughs of the nation's largest city. Phil's longstanding disappointment with his son's career path had undermined their relations. Still, Andy never expected his father to be gone so suddenly, or to leave him feeling so alone.

"Now, if I'm going to help you, we need to review the situation to make sure I've got all the key facts." Mack's crisp words brought Andy back to the reality of the cocktail lounge. As Andy began the narrative, Mack signaled the waiter to refresh his drink.

"All right. My father, Phil Potter, died two weeks ago. He left a will naming me—his only child—and his wife Jeannie, who's not my mother, as coexecutors. It provides that the business he owned, Potter's Paints, should be sold upon his death."

"How do the proceeds of the sale go?"

"Fifty-fifty between Jeannie and me."

"Is there a lot in his estate other than the business?"

"No, not too much. A co-op apartment, a few small investments—but the company is really the major asset."

The waiter arrived with Mack's scotch on the rocks. He took a sizable swallow from the glass.

"My father left a letter with his secretary that he'd signed in front of a notary. It gave me total responsibility for handling the sale, deciding on the buyer, agreeing to the price, and so on—all at my 'sole discretion,' it said. He also left me a personal note, explaining why he'd done this, which we don't need to get into."

"Okay. So, what's happened since then?"

"Well, after a short mourning period, I met with my father's personal lawyer, Jonas Hearn, who drew the will and is handling the estate. Jonas told me that three days after the death notice

appeared in the *Times*, he was approached by a man named Thomas Chapman. Evidently Chapman knows Hearn's son-in-law, a guy named Robert Browning."

Hey, Andy thought to himself, isn't that odd—the same name as the poet we study in one of my English lit courses. . . .

"Anyway, Chapman is the president of a successful conglomerate called DX Corp.—their stock is traded on the New York Stock Exchange."

"I've heard of them."

"Hearn said that DX has made several acquisitions of retail chains in related businesses. Chapman told him they've been interested in Potter's Paints for some time. So, when he learned of Dad's death, he contacted Hearn to inquire whether the business might be for sale." Andy paused to take a small pretzel from the bowl on the table.

"And how did Hearn reply?"

"Hearn told him that the will called for the company to be sold—"

"Ouch!"

"—and that Phil Potter's son would be happy to meet with him." Andy paused. "Why the 'ouch'?"

"Look" said Mack, in a tone Andy identified with that of an adult addressing a small child, "when a prospective buyer knows that a company needs to be sold, that solves one of his two big problems."

"What's his other problem?"

"We'll get to that." Mack took a generous swallow of his scotch. "Keep going."

"So anyway, I met with Chapman. At first, he was very pleasant, very complimentary about my father, very understanding of the difficult spot I've been put in."

"Was anyone with you when you met him?"

"No, just the two of us—he took me to lunch at that famous seafood place in midtown."

"Did you tell him that you teach English and profess to know nothing about business?" There was a playful edge to Mack's question that Andy failed to detect.

"Sure."

"Did you notice any saliva coming out of the corners of his mouth?"

"What?—I don't understand. . . ."

"Nothing, nothing. So, what did Chapman say?"

"He said he was interested in acquiring Potter's Paints—that it would make a good fit with some other holdings of DX. He wanted to know if I had a price in mind."

Mack leaned forward across the table, his eyes engaging Andy's. "Did you?"

Andy took a sip of beer. "Well, soon after the funeral, I met with Harry Bell, my father's accountant, to go over the company's financial statements. Harry told me that Dad thought the business was worth $10 million. Harry was skeptical about the amount and never mentioned it to anyone—not even to Jonas Hearn. And, of course, Dad never discussed the subject with me . . . I must say, for someone like me who gets by on a salary of $25,000 a year, that's a staggering number—"

Mack interrupted Andy's musings. "So how did you reply to Chapman? Did you mention the $10 million?" From the urgency in Mack's voice, Andy could tell he considered the point significant.

"No, I didn't. I wasn't sure whether this was something I ought to tell Chapman or not. I thought maybe I should throw out an even higher number, but I didn't want to risk him losing interest. So I just punted—told him I didn't have a specific price in mind."

Mack stirred the ice in his drink. For the first time, Andy was aware of the elevator music being piped into the lounge. The lights had been turned up as the glow of the late afternoon sun waned.

"Did I do the right thing?" asked Andy.

"I'd rather not be judgmental at this point. Let me hear the rest of the story."

Andy paused, recalling how flustered he'd felt when Chapman popped the big question, right out of the blue. He hadn't expected things to move along so quickly at a first meeting. At the time, he sensed that his answer might shape the tenor of the deal, but he just didn't know how best to respond. He wondered whether Mack considered him an idiot.

"Please continue," said Mack, glancing at his watch.

"Well, that ended the first meeting. Chapman asked for some numbers and information on the business, which I had Harry Bell send over to him. Then, less then a week later—the day before yesterday—Chapman and I had a second meeting in his office, but the mood was completely different."

Mack gave a knowing nod. "The condolence period was over, and this was business as usual."

"I guess so. Chapman proceeded to dump all over Potter's Paints—it was strictly a mom-and-pop operation, there was no management in place below my father, the stores were poorly located, the inventory was full of obsolescent stuff. He made a big deal out of the company's exposure to a problem it had in Queens back in 1975—'massive overhanging liabilities,' in his words. Then he talked about the current sluggish economy and the 7 percent unemployment rate."

"I can tell where this is going."

Andy grimaced. "Chapman ended by saying the business wasn't even worth $5 million. However, 'out of the goodness of his heart,' he was willing to pay $6 million—not a penny more—but only on the condition that I accept his offer within a week."

"Some heart!" Mack emitted a wry chuckle, as if never ceasing to be amazed at the hypocrisy of negotiators. "Did he give any reason for the haste?"

"Yes, something about a DX finance committee meeting coming up, and he needed to know my answer before then, because they were considering an alternate use of the funds."

"And what did you say?"

"Not much of anything. By that time, I was in shock. I told him I'd be in touch. I came back to the Potter's Paints office, proceeded to get very mad—"

"I told you, it's just negotiating."

"—and then I telephoned Harry Bell, Dad's accountant, to tell him what happened."

"How come you didn't call Jesse Hearn, your father's lawyer—the one who introduced you to Chapman?"

"I didn't feel he'd be helpful. By the way, his first name is Jonas."

"Sorry."

"Frankly, I have the impression Hearn doesn't know much about selling a business. And it bothers me that every time I talk to him, he seems so intent on my striking a quick deal with Chapman. So I turned to Bell, and that's when Harry suggested that what I needed was a lawyer who had lots of experience negotiating acquisitions. Harry said he'd worked recently with someone who filled the bill—a sole practitioner who used to be a partner of the Jenkins & Price firm, and who knew his way around. And that turned out to be you."

"Right. I got a call from Harry yesterday, which brings us up to the present."

"Yes." Andy's mind began to drift. He realized now that his father's $10 million figure was going to be a problem, especially after his dinner last week with Phil's widow, Jeannie. . . .

A week had passed since Phil Potter's funeral. Andy's wife, Carol, had taken their son Billy back up to New Hampshire. Andy and Jeannie were dining at a neighborhood Italian restaurant on the upper West Side, near the Potter apartment.

Andy looked across the table at Jeannie whose long brunette hair framed her oval face. She was only five years his senior—still a hell of a good-looking woman, he thought, not much different from when his father introduced her to the family fifteen years ago. He was conscious of the fact that, in the eyes of other diners, his stepmother Jeannie could pass for his date.

The conversation was muted and listless, ranging over some unkempt details left behind in Phil Potter's wake. Then, without giving it any prior thought, Andy repeated his father's remark to Harry Bell about the business being worth $10 million. Jeannie's eyes widened. Although she made no direct comment, Andy could tell that she hadn't heard the number before and that it was much higher than she'd anticipated. He knew immediately that he should have kept his mouth shut.

Later, over cups of espresso, Jeannie looked at him searchingly for a moment. He felt she was groping for the right words to express a thought that was troubling her. When she spoke, the words were barely audible.

"Do you think you can handle this sale, Andy?"

From the expression on her face and intonation, he could tell she had considerable doubt. "I'm going to give it my best shot."

She paused and then said, almost as an aside, "I hope that's good enough."

"All right. I've only got a few minutes, so I'll get right down to basics." Mack's voice, terse and direct, recaptured Andy's attention.

"If I had been in this from the beginning, I would have handled matters differently. Still, we're not in such bad shape, provided we do a few things soon."

"What did I do wrong?" asked Andy, his voice displaying equal doses of curiosity and trepidation.

Mack polished off the rest of his drink and put the glass down on the table. "Look, what counts in negotiating is leverage—both the reality of power and also the perception of strength. It can take various forms. For instance, Chapman now knows that you're required to sell the business. He, on the other hand, doesn't have to buy it. That puts him one-up—as I said before, it solves one of his two main problems."

A few rays of late afternoon sun slanted through the lounge window. Several more tables were now occupied.

"You asked me what a buyer's other problem is—the answer is competition. You may be forced to sell, but as long as there are several possible buyers, then Chapman has to worry. Right now, he thinks he's the only game in town, which is causing him to come on strong. We have to whittle down that apparent strength."

Andy, listening intently, nodded in agreement.

"It's too late now to suggest the possibility that the business might not be sold. But we can certainly make Chapman aware that he's in a contest with other bidders. That'll tip the leverage back toward the center."

Andy's face took on a quizzical expression. "Do you mean I should pretend to be talking with someone else at the same time I'm negotiating with Chapman?"

Mack frowned. "No, no. I don't like the ethics of inventing a fictitious buyer. Besides, it's tough to make fiction plausible. No, what I had in mind was for you to actually initiate talks with other parties. And then we'll let Chapman find it out for himself—that'll increase the credibility of our having an alternative."

Andy pondered this for a moment. "Yes, I can see that—but won't Chapman be miffed that I'm not negotiating just with him?"

"He might have some cause to be sore if he'd been led to believe he was operating under an exclusive arrangement, but that hasn't been the case, has it?" Andy shook his head. "Good. So let's make sure Chapman realizes he doesn't have a lock on things."

Andy's curiosity now outweighed his trepidation. "How else did I screw up?" he asked.

Mack didn't mince words. "You should have been prepared when Chapman asked what price you had in mind. It was one of those rare instances where the truth, the whole truth and nothing but the truth was the perfect answer. If I were you, I would have said"—and here, much to Andy's surprise, Mack gently parodied the New England twang Andy had acquired during his years in academe: "Well, Mr. Chapman, I'm just a schoolteacher and I don't know much about these kinds of things. But my late father told us, just a few weeks before he died, that Potter's Paints was worth every bit of $10 million. I don't think he'd be happy if I ended up with something less than that. . . ."

Mack now returned to his natural speaking voice—a fast-paced, Manhattan-accented, no-nonsense delivery. "Sorry to be maudlin, but you can see the force of that, can't you? In effect, Chapman would have had to negotiate against a dead hand." Mack rotated his head slightly, as if ruminating over the lost opportunity. "But it's too late for that speech now—it would seem contrived. Like so many things in negotiating, you either do it on the spot or it's gone forever."

Andy was feeling acutely uncomfortable. He didn't like the idea of having blown it. He worried what would happen if Jeannie were to find out. And his big concern was how Mack's last dictate—*Do it on the spot or it's gone forever*—would play out in future negotiations.

"But don't fret, there are other ways to attach credibility to a number. We'll just have to work a little harder at it."

"I *am* fretting. Look, I've never had to negotiate anything significant. You might even say I've been anti-negotiating all my life—maybe a knee-jerk reaction against my father, who loved to bargain. All I know about the subject is what I've been told by a faculty buddy of mine at Cromwell—a guy who spent some time at that new negotiation program they have at Harvard."

"Yeah, I've heard of that."

"According to my friend, the Harvard instructors take a cooperative approach to bargaining. They want both sides to put their cards on the table and engage in what they call a mutual search for common ground."

"Yeah, right."

"And their goal is to use objective criteria to reach an agreement that's fair to both sides."

Mack scowled. "Listen, you won't hear anything about fairness from old Mack—that's an elusive concept I can't get my arms around. *Satisfaction* is the gospel I preach. You need to have a strenuous process—plenty of give and take, back and forth. Then , if both sides are satisfied with the result, they're likely to feel it's *not unfair*, which is close enough for me."

"I never thought of it that way."

"Hey, I'm sure many aspects of that cooperative approach are laudable, but it misses the mark in today's deal-making business world. Want to know why? Because the very thing those birds want to eliminate—what they call the 'positional dance'—is the key to getting both parties satisfied, which is what's needed for them to reach agreement."

Andy nodded. "I think I understand. Look, Mack, I'd really like you by my side for all future meetings with Chapman. But he made a big point of his preference to work these things out one-on-one—'between the two principals,' he put it, and without all that . . . uh, I think his words were, 'excess baggage' of lawyers and financial advisors and so forth."

"He would adopt that posture with you, wouldn't he? Listen, if you want me to be there, you can simply insist on it. And even though Chapman may kick and scream, he'll have to go along."

Mack motioned to the waiter to bring the check. "But I don't think that's our best strategy. Once Chapman sees me, then everything we do or say will seem to him invented for the purpose. Right now, he probably thinks. . . ." He paused, as if searching for an apt phrase.

". . . that he has a real hayseed on his hands!" Andy smiled as he completed Mack's sentence. "Thanks a lot—but I guess I deserve it."

"No offense, but yes, that's sort of what I had in mind. On the other hand, that naive image will provide a lot more credibility for whatever you do."

Andy nodded slowly in assent. "I get the picture. But your warning about blowing it if things aren't done right the first time out of the box—aren't I likely to make some irretrievable errors? It's not like teaching, where I can correct my mistakes in the next class session and no harm done."

"That's a risk we'll have to take. But you're obviously smart and, I'd guess, a quick study. Assuming we talk through the possibilities in advance—and for that purpose, we should plan to meet again tomorrow afternoon—I can provide enough guidance to keep a disaster from happening. And then, at the right point, I'll emerge out of the shadows and shepherd it from there."

The check arrived at the table. Andy realized that he, as the client, should take care of it, and reached into his wallet for a credit card. "Okay," he said, "let's see if we can get this back on track."

"Daddy, Daddy, it's you!"

"Hi, Billy, how's my boy doing?"

"I miss you, Daddy. When are you coming home?"

Andy cradled the telephone in the crook of his neck and shoulder. His kid sure had a way of getting to him—so direct, right to the point, emotions out on the table.

"Soon, Billy, very soon, I hope."

"Mr. Chapman, I certainly appreciate the interest you've shown in Potter's Paints and the courtesies you've extended to me in these difficult days since my father's death."

Andy was in Chapman's spacious, elegant office in a midtown skyscraper, a day after his second briefing with Mack. Framed photos of Chapman in the company of various celebrities adorned an entire wall. Chapman—a portly, well-groomed man in his mid-fifties—was seated behind his oversized desk, leaning back in the chair, hands clasped behind his head. Andy sensed from the supercilious smile playing around the corners of Chapman's mouth that his host was relishing this meeting—probably on the assumption that Andy had come to capitulate.

Andy wet his lips and continued. "You placed a firm deadline on your offer, and that's why I'm getting back to you promptly. I'm afraid I must reject your $6 million bid for Potter's Paints. You see—"

Chapman, any relish gone from his face, interrupted. "If it's a matter of taking a little more time, I'm sure that can be arranged. I know how difficult it must have been for you to pick up the reins—"

"No," said Andy, shaking his head slowly from side to side, "that wouldn't help. Look, Mr. Chapman, I listened to your speech about what bad shape the company is in. Fortunately for me, your outside view of the situation at Potter's Paints doesn't match the reality I've seen on the inside. But I sense such conviction on your part that it seems fruitless to try to persuade you otherwise—and I just don't have the time to devote to it. So, thanks very much again, and I wish you well."

Andy stood up to leave, offering a handshake. Chapman, ignoring Andy's outstretched hand, took a deep breath and spoke rapidly in a loud, intimidating voice.

"You're making a big mistake, a big mistake. Don't overestimate the value of your father's business. Those of us who spend our lives buying and selling companies know about these things. You haven't been exposed to what it's like in the real world."

Mack had prepared Andy for this reaction. "You're right. I'm no expert here. That's why I've consulted other professionals who know about value, to confirm my hypothesis."

Chapman's tone shifted from intimidation to an attempt at conveying total sincerity. "I'm your best buyer, Andy."

"I had hoped so, and I was prepared to conclude a deal with you on realistic terms, without the need to look elsewhere. But selling a good business for an inadequate price is not the accomplishment I want to be known for. The least I owe my father is to do this the right way."

"And what, may I ask, is the right way?"

It was precisely the question Mack had hoped Chapman would ask. "To see just what alternatives there are. As a matter of fact, I'm on my way now to the offices of Flynn & James, who I understand are quite reputable business brokers. And I must say, on the basis of my conversations with them so far, there seems to be a lot of potential interest in Potter's Paints."

"You should have seen the look on Chapman's face when I walked out the door!" Andy had telephoned Mack's office to relate what happened during the meeting that took place earlier in the day.

"I'm impressed, Andy—you handled yourself very well."

Andy, though pleased at the compliment, was uneasy about the outcome. "Still, the fact is he let me walk out."

"Chapman is a good negotiator. He had to do that. He's testing whether you're serious or not."

There was a pause in the conversation. Andy heard a tinkle that sounded like liquid being poured over crackling ice cubes.

"So, what's next?" asked Andy.

"Well, you have an appointment tomorrow with one of those potential buyers that Flynn & James found for you."

"Right."

"We need a way to get the news back to Chapman that you're actually in discussions with other purchasers. Here's my thought. I've done some checking around and learned that one of the division heads at DX, a guy named Sam Jones, used to buy supplies from your dad. Just tell the new buyer that if he wants a customer reference on Potter's Paints, he should call Sam Jones. That will get the word back to Chapman plenty fast."

"But what if Chapman doesn't . . . uh, how did you put it earlier . . . come back to the table?"

"He will, Andy, he will. . . ."

Jeannie and Andy were seated in the living room of the Potter apartment on West End Avenue. The unpretentious decor of the rooms mirrored Phil's plainspoken personality, though an occasional decorative touch reflected Jeannie's hand. The sticky August heat defied the efforts of a window air conditioner.

"I've always thought this is a nice apartment," Andy said. "Will you hang onto it?"

"If we get $10 million from the sale of the business," Jeannie replied tersely.

The tone of their meeting had not been pleasant. Jeannie appeared very much on edge, her face unsmiling, her words hurling a challenge.

"I don't know, Jeannie. That might be hard to accomplish, based on what I've seen so far."

"Do you really believe you're the best judge as to the value of the business? Don't you think your father knew a little more about this subject—after all, he'd devoted his whole life to Potter's Paints."

Andy couldn't miss the sarcasm in her voice, but he held his ground. "Sure, he knew more about the business than I'll ever learn. But he never tried to *sell* it. And from what Mack tells me, you don't know what price you can get till you put the property on the block."

"Mack this, Mack that—that's all I've heard from you tonight. It really bothers me that you're not taking your advice from Jonas Hearn, your father's lawyer."

"That's because selling companies isn't Hearn's area of expertise."

"And, by the way, Jonas has told me plenty about your man Mack, which doesn't exactly fill me with confidence."

"Such as what?"

"Such as why he's no longer with a law firm—he used to be a partner of Jenkins & Price, you know—and why he doesn't handle major deals any more."

"Why?"

There was a corked bottle of sherry on the table next to her. Jeannie grasped it by the neck, tilting it up at a rakish angle above her open mouth. "Glub, glub. . . ."

"Oh, come on," said Andy. But her gesture left him uneasy.

Her voice took on a note of urgency. "I can't believe you've broken off negotiations with Chapman. Jonas thinks that was a major mistake—he tells me DX is our absolute best bet. What do you know about negotiating with the big boys? Aren't you in way over your head?"

He was preparing to respond when Jeannie resumed speaking—but now in a tone of quiet desperation that struck Andy as genuine. "I hate to admit it, but I'm just plain scared. Phil was always full of confidence and had me believing he'd take care of me for life. I gave up my own career a long time back to cater to Phil's needs. Now, without any warning, he's gone—and I'm going to have to take care of myself. To do that, I really need every dollar I can get from the sale of the business."

Later that evening, Andy sat alone in his small, sparsely furnished hotel room, reflecting on his troubled meeting with Jeannie.

It was the first time the two of them had been at odds, and it didn't feel good. What made things worse was that the issue at the core of Jeannie's concern—a lack of confidence in his ability to manage the sale of the business—was a worry he also shared. In a way, he couldn't blame her, especially in light of Jeannie's legitimate anxiety over her own financial prospects.

Her negative attitude toward Mack was also disquieting, to say the least. It reminded him that he'd placed his total faith in this singular man he didn't know at all, who—at least according to Hearn's gossip—was no longer a Jenkins & Price partner due to a drinking problem.

Andy wanted to disbelieve this, but couldn't help recalling his initial meeting with the lawyer—in a cocktail lounge, for God's sake!—when Mack downed several tumblers of scotch. And during their recent afternoon phone call, the unmistakable sound of a drink being poured came through the receiver. If the rumors were true, did that mean the hard-nosed negotiating advice he'd been getting and following was ill conceived? Andy shuddered at the thought, trying without success to put it out of his mind.

"Honey, we hardly remember what you look like. Come home before Billy thinks the electrician is his father."

Carol's tone on the telephone was joshing, but there was a bite to it that made Andy uneasy.

"Sweetheart, we're at a very sensitive stage in the sale of Dad's business. There's a terrific pot for us at the end of the rainbow, but I've just got to stick with it for the time being. . . ."

Andy was seated at the desk in his father's office. It was not where he wanted to be. But if the business didn't get sold, he could see himself in this chair indefinitely.

The intercom buzzed. "Mr. Chapman is on the line."

Whew!—just the words Andy longed to hear. Chapman had waited a whole week before calling. As each day passed, Andy's concern over the wisdom of Mack's approach had increased.

He picked up the phone. "Good morning, Mr. Chapman."

"Good morning, Andy. Please call me Thomas. How are things going?" Chapman's voice sounded to Andy like a jug of North Cromwell maple syrup.

"Just fine, Thomas, just fine."

"Look, I wasn't happy with the way our last meeting ended, and I'd like to get together with you again. I've got some new thoughts that might prove useful."

Bingo! Chapman's purchasing guy must have gotten a call from the other potential buyer. "All right."

"How about tomorrow at ten in the morning?"

"I'm sorry, but I have a meeting scheduled for then," said Andy, trying to keep the specter of other interest alive. "The afternoon would be better."

"All right," said Chapman, without hesitation. "Two o'clock at my place."

Andy, flushed with a heady sense of being on a roll, decided to double down. "I'd prefer meeting over here at Potter's Paints.

There's an important call I may have to take, and I wouldn't want to miss it. . . ."

It was true. Andy was expecting a call from his son.

Chapman, apparently in no mood to be confrontational, replied, "All right, I'll see you there at two."

"Now, Andy, let's get down to the central issue." They were in Mack's small office later that afternoon. The walls were bare of ornaments; the desk, tabletops, and windowsills were strewn with manila folders, reference books, and piles of papers. As he talked, the lawyer paced slowly around his desk.

"The key to this upcoming meeting with Chapman is for you to get across the $10 million number. We've talked about how to do that, but what concerns me is the obvious question he's likely to ask: 'If this is so important to you, Andy, why didn't you mention it back when I first asked whether you had a price in mind?'"

They had been strategizing for almost an hour now. Andy was getting tired and a little irritable. "It's all a game, a goddamn game."

"That's right," said Mack, his voice rising, "but hell, give the bugger its due. It's not just 'a game'; it's the great American business game—the acquisition mating dance! And you're playing it in New York—the veritable temple—where the inhabitants prize 'doing a deal' over everything else."

"Mating dance?"

Mack reached into one of the drawers of his file cabinet, producing a bottle of scotch and two glasses. "By my reckoning, the sun's just about over the yardarm in Newfoundland. How about a little drink?"

Andy, frowning, demurred with a shake of his head—pondering whether this was the time to take a stand for temperance in the workplace. Mack, ignoring the frown, poured a generous shot into one of the glasses, took a swallow, and turned back toward Andy.

"Let's face it," said Mack. "Building a company from within is hard work—long, drudging hours, not much positive feedback. But an acquisition—ah, that's something else entirely. That's what gets the adrenalin flowing for top executives and others involved. And the biggest kick lies in the negotiating—the matching of wits with an adversary. And what's the best part of the negotiating? It's the initial mating dance, where the parties try to pin down the deal at a price each of them can live with." He paused, took another sip from the glass, and then blurted out—with the first hint of passion Andy had seen in him—"I love it!"

Andy didn't love it, but he was beginning to see what it was about deal-making that fascinated grown men.

"And for me," continued Mack, "even though most of the deals you read about in the paper are acquisitions of large public companies, the smaller deals like this are the most fascinating. In those public acquisitions, there are dozens of people involved—the actions and reactions are too diffuse. But here, it's just one-on-one—you're much closer to the maneuvering."

"Daddy!" His son's voice had a sense of urgency that the telephone couldn't mask. "Guess what? Adam Hickock's father bought him one of those new hand-controlled robots that you can make do anything—it's unbelievable."

"That must be fun to play with," said Andy.

"Oh yeah, it's terrific," said Billy. "Adam's father said he'd gotten a great deal on the robot at a store in Manchester."

Andy, realizing he was being set up by his own kid, moved to contain the damage.

"Billy, I know it would be exciting to own your own robot, but we just can't afford that kind of thing right now."

"Oh, no, Dad, I didn't ask you to *buy* me one. I was just telling you about Adam's robot. . . ."

Chapman eased his bulk into the armchair in Phil Potter's office. Andy, still uncomfortable about sitting behind his father's desk when anyone else was around, pulled up a small chair nearby.

Chapman started right in without any small talk. "Let me come right to the point. I made what I considered a decent opening offer for Potter's Paints. The next thing I knew, you broke off the negotiations. What's up? Why can't we do business?"

Andy was ready for him. "I'm glad you're direct, Thomas, because that's my style, too. So here's the way it is. My father was very proud of Potter's Paints. Before he died, he let those around him know that, in his mind, the business was worth at least $10 million. Dad felt this was a realistic number. Then you came in here and dumped all over the business. That really rubbed me the wrong way, given that the company was my father's 'other baby'—my stepbrother, so to speak. The lowball valuation, the haste to sign me up—it looked like you were trying to steal the company while the Potter family was still in a state of shock."

"But, Andy," Chapman replied evenly, ignoring the accusation, "I inquired at the time if you had an asking price. Why didn't you tell me about the $10 million then?"

There it was—the question Mack had known would be coming. They had discussed at some length how to handle it. Andy himself came up with the response they decided to use.

"It was my own inexperience. I had heard that, in negotiations, the minute you tell the other side a number, they start whittling it down. On the other hand, I was reluctant to suggest a higher number that I didn't feel any conviction about."

Well, Andy thought, it came out a little rough. but that's the way Mack wanted it to sound—honest, unrehearsed, with all the naïveté left in.

Chapman's voice was cold, his irritation barely controlled. "So what are you telling me—that $10 million is your price?"

"That's right. That's what my father's widow is expecting, and that's what my advisors tell me I should be able to get. . . ."

"Well, don't keep me in suspense—what the hell finally happened?"

It was the evening after Andy's meeting with Chapman. Alone in his hotel room, Andy had called Mack's home to brief him on the day's events. There was a huskiness in the lawyer's voice that Andy hadn't previously noticed.

"Well," Andy replied, "after a good deal of fencing, Chapman finally blinked. He said that since I'd made such a big point about how far off his valuation was, it might be . . . uh . . . I think 'productive' was the term he used—productive for his numbers man to meet with Harry Bell. Perhaps then they would learn something that would enable DX to increase its bid—although, he was at pains to point out, obviously not up to the $10 million level."

"Ah—pay dirt! And how did you handle that?"

"Well, I wasn't sure what to do, but I didn't see how it could hurt, so I said all right. Was that correct? Or have I blown it again?"

Mack took some time before replying. Andy found himself wondering what Mack was doing—refilling his goddamn glass?

"Yes. . . yes, I think you did the right thing. Chapman took that tack so as to give himself a basis for decreasing his bid without losing face—"

"You mean *increasing* his bid," Andy interjected.

"—Yes, of course, *increasing* his bid; that's what I meant to say. And you were right to let him do it—although it might have been a good idea to mutter that you didn't see much purpose in it, because the two of you were so far apart."

"I thought about that, but I was worried Chapman would then feel boxed in and might cancel the numbers meeting." Andy was surprised to hear himself questioning his lawyer's judgment.

There was a perceptible pause before Mack responded. "You know, I think you may be right on this one. It's probably just as well you didn't say that. . . . Hey, Geoff Chaucer, you're getting pretty good at this stuff."

The next morning, a few minutes after Andy's arrival at Potter's paints, a call came in from Jonas Hearn.

"The reason I'm calling, Andy, is to make clear to you how seriously concerned Jeannie Potter is with the unsettled state of affairs regarding the sale of the company."

"Don't think I'm not anxious about this, too," Andy replied.

"I'm sure you are, and that's exactly my point." Hearn's voice had an unctuous quality that always bothered Andy. "I'm aware of your father's desire that you undertake this task. Still, when your coexecutor—and, more importantly, your cobeneficiary— loses confidence in your ability to carry it off, then, as the attorney for the estate, I have to consider my fiduciary responsibilities."

"I'm not sure what all that means, but I don't think I like the sound of it."

"I'll tell you what it means. DX Corp. is not only the best buyer of Potter's Paints—it may be the *only* real buyer at any decent price. You're playing a game of chicken—orchestrated by a character of questionable repute and dubious sobriety—with what might be the estate's only hope to achieve fair value for its primary asset. I can't stand idly by and let that happen."

Later that morning, Andy went to Mack's office and briefed him on the call from Jonas Hearn—omitting, however, the unflattering reference to Mack.

The lawyer dismissed the subject impatiently. "Don't get distracted by that bird. He's just pissed off that he's not getting a fee for selling the business. Let's get right to the matter at hand—your next meeting with Chapman. Do you have any questions for me?"

"Yes. How about other issues, like job security for the employees—when do I bring those up?"

"I don't want us to raise any other issues until Chapman shows some willingness to play in our ballpark in terms of price. It would send the wrong signal—that we're not as determined to stick near the $10 million figure as we say we are."

"How about these two other guys I'm talking to about acquiring Potter's Paints? They seem somewhat interested, but so far neither has made an offer."

"Just keep talking to them, so you can truthfully tell Chapman he's got real competition."

"Should I go further? What about hinting to Chapman that one of them is already at $9 million and—in your phrase—heading north?" He was surprised to hear the thought come out of his mouth.

"No, no, let's not make up any stories. This may be a game, but I believe in playing by the rules—and one of the chief rules is, no lies. A little puffing may be okay—the other side expects that—but no factual misrepresentations."

Andy's eyes were drawn to Mack's left hand which appeared to be noticeably shaking. To another observer, it might have signified the onset of Parkinson's; to Andy's newly suspicious mind, it suggested a case of the DTs.

Andy twisted in his seat. "One thing is bothering me. I have to get back to New Hampshire soon for the fall semester."

Mack looked up from the doodles on his pad. "That's a problem I've been concerned about. Chapman may be moving slowly here for precisely that reason—betting that when the leaves begin to turn, you'll experience Keats and Browning withdrawal, go into a panic, and make a quick sale to DX. It's the old story—the person under time pressure in a negotiation is often at a real disadvantage. Has the Cromwell subject come up with Chapman?"

"No."

"Then, I think *you* ought to raise it—but only to assure him that you have—" and here, Mack's voice took on a stately, measured cadence "—all . . . the . . . time . . . in . . . the . . . world . . . to hold out for a full and fair price. Make a few calls up to Cromwell—then you can tell Chapman you've worked it out for some of your colleagues to cover any classes you have to miss."

"I get it. Anything else?"

"Yeah, one key item. It's time to find out what price you'll ultimately be willing to accept for Potter's Paints. Otherwise, it's difficult to know how to negotiate when Chapman bumps his bid—and don't worry, he will. Let's sit down with Harry Bell and the Flynn & James firm, and figure out once and for all whether your father's $10 million number was just a pipe dream or the real thing."

"I've made some real progress as a negotiator, but frankly, Carol, I'm still nervous that I'll make a bad goof when something unexpected comes up. And if that happens, there may be hell to pay with Jeannie."

There was no warmth in his wife's voice at the other end of the phone line. "Jeannie, Jeannie, that's all I hear whenever we talk. The next thing I know, the two of you will have twenty-five dollar seats on the aisle for *Annie.* Just how much time are you spending with her?"

Chapman stood up from his office desk and walked over to the window before speaking.

"Andy, my people have spent a good deal of time on the figures, and we're prepared to raise our bid. Obviously, we could go up in small increments, negotiating all the way, but that's not my style. I'm going to put my best price on the table, to see if we can make a deal."

Andy recalled Mack's words to him prior to the meeting: *I guarantee that Chapman's number—which he'll tell you is his ultimate stretch—will be under $8 million.*

"The figure, Andy, is $7.5 million. It's a hell of a price—DX will be taking some substantial risks, especially with those liabilities from the Queens fiasco—but so be it."

Andy had worked out with Mack how to handle this moment. "Well, that's certainly a constructive move in the right direction, Thomas, and I appreciate your willingness to rethink your valuation. However, it just doesn't get up into the range I need to close off the selling process we're going through now."

Chapman, frowning, returned to his seat. His voice was stern. "Don't make too hasty a judgment here. We're able to go this high because of the potential synergies between the companies. We can earn back the excess element of the purchase price through the cost savings we anticipate. No one else will be able to pay this much. If you turn us down without having a better offer in your pocket, you're making a big mistake."

Andy tensed his body to avoid squirming in the chair. He realized that Chapman was trying to get to him, banking on the fact that Andy had nothing else in hand. And what made it difficult for Andy was that Chapman was right. Still, Andy knew he had to stand firm at this moment.

"Don't think I'm acting hastily. I've given this a great deal of thought, I've received expert advice, and I know what I'm doing."

Chapman rose to his feet before Andy could initiate his own exit. "I hope you do," said Chapman, extending his hand toward Andy. "And, as you must appreciate, we can't simply leave this offer open-ended. In all candor, I have to tell you that we're in serious talks to acquire another company with a product line that's similar to yours. They're anxious to know where we stand, and I need to be able to tell them. So I'd like to have your response no later than the end of this week."

Andy's response was immediate. "Don't pressure me, Thomas. You tried that once before and saw how I reacted. I won't discuss this with a gun to my head."

"And that was it. We managed a cold handshake, and I went home."

"But how was it left?" asked Mack. It was late afternoon and they were once again in the lawyer's office.

"Well, I said, 'I'll get back to you.'"

"NO!" Mack exploded, shaking his head vigorously from side to side. "Don't you see, that makes it seem like you're going to give the $7.5 million serious consideration."

Andy winced, wondering whether he'd ever get this stuff right.

Mack quieted down. "All right, no big deal. Anyway, at this point, it's your turn to move. Chapman is certainly not going to bid against himself. And by the way, his remark about being in talks to acquire another company like ours—apparently, that's not a bluff. One of Harry Bell's contacts passed along some information to him that confirmed what Chapman said, so we have to treat it as credible."

"This keeps getting more complicated."

"Let's step back a minute and review the rest of the picture. First of all, based on our pricing meeting with Harry Bell and the Flynn & James guys yesterday, I think it's clear that something in the $8 to $8.5 million area would be a reasonable price for the company. Phil didn't really appreciate those potential liabilities arising from the Queens fiasco in '75, and he closed his eyes to the large amount of slow-moving inventory. His $10 million estimate overstated what the business was worth by maybe 15 or 20 percent. Do you agree?"

"I do."

"Not only that, but the chances of getting Chapman up into the $10 million area of Jeannie's dreams appear very remote."

"Slim to none."

Mack shook his head from side to side. "Jeannie reminds me of so many clients I've had over the years. You know the line—" and now his voice took on a mimicking tone—"Don't break off the negotiations, Andy, even if Chapman is firm at $7.5 million. Just make sure not to come back with a penny less than $10 million."

Andy managed a tight smile. He understood an anomaly when he heard one.

"Now, from what you've told me, things don't look too bright on the alternative purchaser front."

"That's right," Andy replied. "One of them just doesn't seem that interested—he's moving at a snail's pace, even though he knows others are actively looking. As for the other guy, well, he asked me what price I had in mind, and when I told him the story about my father and dropped in the $10 million number, his eyes almost bugged out of his head."

"Hmm . . . that's not good."

Andy looked glum. "It's worse than that. The Flynn & James people—who, after all, have a real incentive to find me a buyer other than DX—are beginning to sound very negative about the prospects. And just yesterday, one of my father's top managers told me he was resigning to take another job. I'm afraid of what may happen with our key people during this period of uncertainty."

Mack pondered matters for a moment. "We've got to move fast here, while you've still got the leverage of several 'interested' buyers. Keep the other negotiations going—tell those guys you have a lot of flexibility. I'm sure Chapman's spies know they're talking to you, so let's not change the dynamics."

Mack got up and walked over to the file cabinet from which he'd produced the bottle of scotch a few days earlier. As Mack reached into the drawer, Andy's anxiety bubbled over, and he found himself saying, in an agitated voice, "Mack, I'd really appreciate it if you would hold the drinks for later on."

Mack's eyebrows knitted together as he turned to look directly at Andy. After a moment, Mack slowly replaced the bottle in the drawer, closed the cabinet, and returned to his desk chair.

"It's getting late, Andy. Why don't we break now and resume talking tomorrow afternoon?"

Andy arrived back at his hotel, still a little shaken from the file cabinet incident in Mack's office. He knew he'd have to figure out how to deal with this.

A letter had arrived from the dean of the faculty at Cromwell. Although its tone was sympathetic, the message was clear—we need to know *now* whether you'll be teaching in the fall. The clear implication was that if Andy chose to stay on in New York, he could and would be replaced. So much, he thought, for the old school spirit.

He was about to shower when the phone rang.

"Hi, Daddy, it's your son—your son, Billy. Remember me?"

"Billy? Billy? I don't think I know anyone named Billy. . . ." But the absence of reaction at the other end of the line—not even a chuckle—made Andy realize that his feeble attempt at humor was misplaced.

"Hey, just kidding, son. As a matter of fact, I'm sitting here now looking at a picture on my nightstand—the one we took just below the chairlift at Stowe last February. . . ."

"Right"—it was Carol's voice, chiming in from another phone extension in the house—"and we're looking at a picture of you, too, but it's fraying and turning brown around the edges—much like our uncut front lawn. . . ."

Carol told Billy to go watch television, and she and Andy proceeded to have a serious talk about the situation. Carol's pitch was straightforward. Of course she realized Andy wasn't away on a lark—that he was conducting important business. But should *he* be the one doing it? Surely competent people could be retained to handle the sale. Andy ought to leave that big city den of iniquity and come back where he belonged—to home, family, college, and the cool hills of New England.

It was ironic, Andy thought, that the two women in his life both wanted the same thing from him—that he leave New York and return to New Hampshire. Sure, Carol had different reasons from Jeannie—she wasn't used to him being away, she wanted him around, perhaps she felt threatened by his attractive stepmother—but at bottom, both of them shared a lack of confidence in his ability to do the job.

"At least come home for a week," Carol said, "even if you have to go back."

"I'd love to, but things are happening fast now, and I'm afraid I would miss something important." What he didn't say was that he feared Jeannie and Jonas would seize the opportunity to replace him. "Why don't you and Billy come down here?" he asked—to which she replied with a dozen weak negatives. Andy realized that Carol's real reluctance stemmed from her sense that a conjugal visit to Manhattan would just encourage him to remain longer at his post.

The conversation was frustrating, with no satisfying resolution. It didn't help things when, in response to Carol's query as to what he was doing that evening, Andy gave a truthful answer—dinner for two at a French restaurant with Jeannie.

"And so, that's where things stand at the moment." Andy completed his update on the situation and took a sip of espresso. The restaurant was crowded, noisy, and reeked of garlic.

Jeannie leaned forward across the table, her expression quite serious, and began to speak in measured tones. "I'm not happy about this. Not only has Phil's $10 million disappeared, but now you're playing chicken with our best and maybe only hope for a deal."

Andy noted that she used the same expressions—"playing chicken" and "only hope"—that Jonas Hearn had used with him earlier. He could see that Jonas was angling to get himself back into the action, stirring up Jeannie to achieve his goal. "I'm not playing chicken, Jeannie. I'm trying, with the help of a professional, to negotiate for the best deal possible."

But Jeannie wasn't in the mood to listen. "I've been talking to some professionals, too. Jonas and the others tell me that since your authority to handle the sale of this business comes from a letter—not from the will itself—it's not worth the paper it's typed on."

"What's your point?"

"I want you to resign and your buddy Mack to be fired. I want the sale of Potter's Paints to be handled by a real professional."

"Who do you have in mind?"

"Elliot Cheever, one of the senior lawyers at Jenkins & Price. He's evidently a master deal-maker and negotiator who comes highly recommended. I've met with him, and I'm very impressed."

"Jenkins & Price is Mack's old law firm."

"I know that—and after talking to Cheever, I know more than I want to know about this man whose advice you've been blindly accepting for weeks now."

When Andy didn't reply, Jeannie resumed speaking, her voice and manner now having shifted to a softer tone. "Andy, you're a good man. I've always enjoyed having you as my stepson. And I'm sure you're a fine English professor." Her voice then resumed its prior edge. "But this is a different world. The combination of risky advice from an inebriated lawyer and your amateur performance has put us in a deep hole—a hole we need to dig out of right away before we're engulfed."

Andy was stunned by her vehemence. "And what if I don't resign?"

"Then Jonas intends to go into court to get your authority under the letter overturned. I won't enjoy that, but there's too much at stake here for me to put my fortune in your inexperienced hands, however well-meaning you may be."

Later that night, lying on the bed in his hotel room, Andy ruminated on the situation.

There were a number of good arguments for his bowing out. He never saw himself in this role or sought it out. He very much wanted to go back north to his family and his job. The second-guessing that would be inevitable if he screwed up was bleak to contemplate. He disliked the idea of jousting with Jeannie in court—whatever way that came out, it was a no-win situation, especially since the two of them had to continue to work together as coexecutors of his father's estate.

If Andy were on a psychiatrist's couch, he knew a prime topic would be his fear of failure. Over the years, it had caused him to duck some major undertakings—to quit the high school basketball team before the coach decided on the starting five, to pass up the option of medical school. The most painful episode was the book he was going to write three years ago—the book that would have taken his academic career to a new level. It went by the boards in a welter of rationalizing factors—family considerations, time commitments, confrontation with other scholars, and most notably, *Am I up to it?*

Andy was pained at the lack of support from New Hampshire. Billy was worried that his father didn't remember him; Carol envisioned him shacked up with his stepmother—and both of them were pleading for him to come home. And to add to the pressure, Cromwell College had stepped forward to place his cherished job in jeopardy.

The issue of Mack was intertwined with his own situation. He could see one possible compromise to get Jeannie and Jonas off his back—where he stayed on as point man, but replaced Mack with Jenkins & Price. It wouldn't mean stepping down in quality—he'd heard that Jenkins & Price was one of the best firms, and he assumed its senior partner, Elliot Cheever, was a skilled strategist and negotiator. Andy considered Mack's advice so far as constructive, although not without risk. But he worried that Mack's drinking problem—for he'd come to think of it in those terms—might cause difficulties ahead. And Mack's role certainly seemed to inflame Jeannie and Jonas. He didn't like the idea of firing someone—it was a task he'd rarely been forced to confront—but he hadn't known Mack long enough to feel bound by ties of loyalty.

Andy moved from the bed to the desk and took out a blank pad. Suppose he did decide to resign—how might he communicate the news that he was stepping down? Would he attach conditions—such as the need to keep him informed of progress, to give him an opportunity for continued input, and to make any proposed deal subject to his final approval? How about a time limit? Should he retain the right to resume his present role?

Then he scribbled some formulations under which he stayed in place but replaced Mack with Jenkins & Price. If so, he'd require Jeannie and Jonas to agree not to contest his authority. If Jenkins & Price proved unworthy, he needed the right to replace them. How about with Mack? Or would he be limited to some new advisor?

The more Andy thought about it, the more he realized that the only reason he was sticking it out was the personal letter from his father entrusting him with the task. But he had qualms about how Phil Potter would feel now, if he were around to reevaluate the situation. Based on where things stood, he might wish he'd designated a pro for the job. After all, as Phil said, he never expected the letter to come into play. . . .

And then an idea came to Andy—to engage in an imaginary dialogue with his father. After all, he knew how Phil Potter's mind worked, and he needed to determine how his father would come out on the question. Andy went back to the bed, lay down on his back, looked up at the ceiling, and began speaking out loud.

"So anyway, Dad, here's what has happened so far. . . ." Andy gave a synopsis of the events occurring since the funeral, replied to a few questions he thought his father might raise, and then asked, "Well, Dad, what do you think?"

Phil Potter's reply came from on high without a moment's delay. The words reverberated in Andy's head, as loud as if Phil were standing in the room next to him.

"Hey, Andy, screw 'em all. Poor Jeannie has been brainwashed. Jonas sounds like he's not showing all his cards. I knew you'd have some problems negotiating, but you're the guy I trust. And after all, along with Jeannie, you've got the biggest stake in a good outcome. So I'm satisfied your heart's in the right place—and if you keep at it, I bet your head and brains will get there too! No son of Phil Potter quits on his father. . . ."

The fog had cleared. Andy knew he had to stay on. Mack's future, which his father didn't address, was another matter—Andy realized he'd have to confront that shortly.

He got up from the bed, went back to the desk, and emptied the contents of his briefcase. He began poring over a number of documents he'd assembled in preparation for the resumption of negotiations with Chapman.

As he was thumbing through the DX annual report, a name caught his eye—Robert Browning. No, it wasn't the poet. This Robert Browning owned a company that was involved in a big joint venture with DX. He pondered where he'd heard that name recently? And then it came to him—Robert Browning was Jonas

Hearn's son-in-law, the man who had introduced Chapman to Hearn. . . .

Late the next morning, Andy and Mack were meeting in the lawyer's office. Andy had just finished briefing Mack on the previous night's dinner with Jeannie, relaying her demand that Andy and Mack be replaced by Jenkins & Price in the person of Elliot Cheever. He hadn't yet gotten around to recounting his own hotel room epiphany.

"Look," said Mack, "you should stay right where you are, running the show. You're doing fine—they have nothing to complain about." He put down his pen.

"As for me," he continued, "I think I've given you good advice so far, and could continue to provide more of the same. But if getting rid of me will lift them off your back, then I'll step aside. I'm no fan of Jenkins & Price, but I know Cheever well, and although this guy is very full of himself, he's a good business lawyer—you'll be in capable hands."

Andy decided not to comment directly on Mack's overture but instead said, "I've never asked, but now I'm curious—how did you happen to part company with Jenkins & Price?"

"Oh, it's a long story that I won't bore you with, but here's the short version. When a partner of J&P turns sixty-five, as I did several years ago, a committee of the firm votes on whether or not to extend the partner's tenure for another five years. They voted not to extend me. After thirty years at the firm, I was out of there on my ass."

"Did they give a reason for not extending you?"

"No, they didn't. It's like when a Manhattan co-op board turns you down—they don't have to say why. I happen to know the real reason, although they dropped a lot of innuendo about something else."

"I don't mean to pry—and if you mind my continuing this conversation, I'll end it—but what was the 'real reason'?"

"Hey, under the circumstances you're entitled to know. I'm sure Elliot has already filled Jeannie's ears with J&P's version. The real reason is that my most recent billings were down appreciably. This was due to the fact that my two biggest corporate clients had both been acquired a few years back—acquired by larger companies that substituted their own lawyers for J&P. The firm didn't think I'd be able to get back up to that level of business."

"What was the innuendo you referred to?"

"That I had a drinking problem. Hey, I enjoyed a drink and still do, but I didn't have a problem then and I don't now. I never gave bum advice under the influence; I never embarrassed the firm. But they didn't want to admit they were dumping me on just a cold financial basis."

Andy said nothing, so Mack went on. "I knew you were troubled by my drinking after your slap on the wrist yesterday."

"My reaction yesterday wasn't called for. I was full of anxiety and it just came out. I apologize."

"No need. You're entitled to sober advice—I was off-base reaching for the bottle."

Andy had made up his mind. "Mack, we're a good team. I wouldn't think of breaking it up."

"I appreciate that."

"Now let me tell you what else went on last night." And he proceeded to report his "conversation" with his father.

When he finished, Mack smiled and said, "I'm glad you decided to stay on the job. Phil Potter would be proud of you."

"Thanks for the vote of confidence."

"And thanks for your confidence in me."

Andy then told Mack about the Robert Browning reference he'd found in the DX annual report, relating his suspicions about the tie-in between Chapman and Hearn.

Mack snorted. "That Jonas Hearn is a real rat, but now it's time to squash him—and I think I know just how. Let's keep going with Chapman. By the time Hearn gets around to going to court—if he ever does—this deal will either be made or it'll be history."

"My sentiments exactly. So what's the next step with DX?"

Mack reflected for a moment. "Listen, Andy, did you ever get to make that speech to Chapman about having all the time in the world to devote to this, with other teachers covering for you, and so on?"

"No, I never had the opportunity. And by the way, now that you mention it, Cromwell is starting to get on my tail."

"Good! Let's change signals here. I think you should tell Chapman that you *need* to get back to New Hampshire. As a result, if you can get a quick commitment from him, you may be willing to take less for the company than your $10 million asking price—but not under, say, $9 million. That will serve to narrow the gap somewhat. It'll also show him you're flexible—at least to a point—which should lead to further moves, all designed to produce a final price north of $8 million."

"But what about your speech the other day on the importance of time, and how it can be used against you?"

A little smile played around Mack's eyes. He shook his head slowly, savoring the moment. "Andy, Andy, don't you recall what Emerson—one of *your* guys!—had to say about a foolish consistency being the hobgoblin of little minds? Now that we know $8 to $8.5 million is the right range, you need a graceful way to descend from the $10 million level."

"Well, Jeannie, after a lot of thought, I've decided—for various reasons, which I'll go into if you're interested—*not* to resign as the man in charge of selling Potter's Paints. Nor will I accept Jenkins & Price as a substitute for Mack. So, if you want to oust me and Mack, you'll just have to go to court."

It was later the same night at her apartment. Andy hoped she wouldn't ask him to expound on his reasoning—but if she did, he'd decided not to mention his "conversation" with Phil, which might come across as both morbid and self-serving.

"I'm sorry to hear that. You're leaving me little choice."

"Just two further thoughts. The first is that Mack and I have worked out a strategy to rekindle the negotiations with Chapman, at a price level lower than $10 million. As I've told you before, the Flynn & James people think the right price for the company is in the $8 to $8.5 million area, and that's what I'm hoping to achieve. So you might want to wait to see how that works out before you start the court challenge."

"I have a notion myself about valuation, but before I get into that, what's your second thought?"

"Well, didn't you ever consider it strange that Jonas Hearn was so anxious to see Potter's Paints sold to DX? Remember, he was pointing us in that direction even when Chapman was offering only $6 million for the company! Sure, he might have been unaware of Dad's $10 million figure, but on the other hand, Jonas wasn't saying, 'Well, let's see if we can get a better offer somewhere else'—he was just pushing us into Chapman's arms. At the time, I tried to pass it off as Jonas being worried about closing out the estate—needing the business to be sold in order to get funds to pay the estate tax. Still, I wondered—why the emphasis on Chapman?"

Andy paused briefly to look at Jeannie's face. Although she said nothing, her expression confirmed that she had pondered the same question.

"Well, last night, going through some documents, I got my answer. If you recall, the guy who introduced Chapman to Potter's Paints was Jonas Hearn's son-in-law, a guy named Robert Browning. It turns out that Browning has an important joint venture with DX. What better way for Jonas to promote Browning's interests with DX than for him to deliver Potter's Paints to Chapman at a cheap price? Now, I can't prove that—there's probably no smoking gun—but if I were you, I'd be very cautious taking advice on the sale of the business from Jonas Hearn."

Although she said nothing, the slight bulge in Jeannie's eyes and tightening around the mouth telegraphed to Andy that this revelation stunned her. As Mack had said, it was much better to handle it this way than to confront Jonas directly. Any clout Jonas might possess had to come from Jeannie, and Andy was now satisfied it wouldn't be forthcoming.

After a few moments Jeannie regained her footing and said, "That may be the case, although I find it hard to believe. But Jonas isn't the only person I've been getting advice from. As a matter of fact, I've been talking to that lawyer, Elliot Cheever— a smart man. And he has a low opinion of the firm you hired to help evaluate and sell the business—what's their name . . . uh, Flynn & James. So he introduced me to another company, called the Sherman Group. I met yesterday with Bart Sherman, the head man there. And he thinks we should be able to get at least $9 million for the business."

"Would that it were so," Andy murmured. He had become skeptical about everyone's motives of late, and this prediction sounded like someone inflating expectations in order to "get the business."

"So, Andy, I'll agree to hold Jonas off from going to court if you'll replace Flynn & James with the Sherman Group. That way, I'll feel my interests are being well served."

Andy reflected for a few moments before replying. The events of recent days had made him acutely aware that negotiating wasn't just something you did when selling a business. It was going on all over the place—people jousting, positioning themselves, attempting to use leverage. Jeannie was giving him the works right now. But when Carol joked about Billy calling the electrician "Daddy," or made insinuations about Jeannie, wasn't she doing the same thing? And even Billy, with that robot? He had the distinct feeling that everyone was hustling him, everyone except Mack—and, Andy figured, that would probably change at some point, too.

"I can't promise you I'll hire them, but I'm certainly willing to meet with Sherman." As he spoke, a plan began to form in his mind. "And I'd like you to be there when I do."

"I wish you could have been in the room, Mack—it was my finest hour!"

Mack and Andy were having dinner in an Indian restaurant near the theatre district. "Tell me about it," said Mack, spearing a chunk of kebab with his fork.

"Well, this Bart Sherman—a kind of self-important guy, who obviously had Jeannie snowed—is going through his patter and I'm sitting there listening. Now I decide to set him up for the kill. So I say, 'Listen, Bart, I'm impressed with this $9 million figure you've been using, since I've been told $8 million is more likely.' And he bites. 'Don't worry, Andy, we can get you the $9 million.' And then I spring the trap."

"Go on—I'm enjoying this."

"I say to Sherman, 'Okay, then I assume you'll be willing to take a lower-than-usual fixed fee for your services, with a proviso that if you achieve $9 million, you'll earn a higher-than-usual total fee.'"

"Oh," Mack cooed, "very nice, very nice indeed."

"Well, you should have seen Bart Sherman sputter around for the next ten minutes. But basically—as I had guessed—he wasn't about to accept that type of arrangement. While this unfolded, I looked over at Jeannie and could see by her expression that she realized these guys were phonies."

"The key was having her there in the room when you sprang the trap."

"Yes. And I could also tell—just from the way she squeezed my hand when we parted—that she *now* realized I was up to this job."

The complex pungent aromas of Indian cooking filled the room. Mack put down his fork. "I've known that for a long time."

"Thanks. Okay, now with that sideshow out of the way, let's talk about the meeting I had with Chapman."

"Shoot."

"In brief, I went down to $9 million with my Cromwell speech. But Chapman didn't waver—he just kept reiterating what a stretch the $7.5 million was. The meeting ended inconclusively. So what do I do now?"

"Well," Mack replied, taking a sip of his Indian beer, "we're at a delicate stage. If we just leave the price gap sitting there, we face the risk of DX disappearing—and because we have so little else to work with, that would be a disaster. On the other hand, even though Chapman is trying to sound intractable, you really don't want to bid against yourself."

Andy broke in. "Here's what I've been thinking, Mack. With him at $7.5 million and me at $9 million, the midpoint between us is $8.25 million. That's a price at which we'd be willing to do the deal. Why don't I just suggest to him that we split the difference?"

"No, no," answered Mack, "that would be the wrong thing to do. Splitting the difference only makes sense when the positions are much closer than they are now. Besides, here's what happens. Once you make the offer to split, then he knows you're at $8.25 million—that's your new position, in effect—while he's still holding firm at $7.5 million. If you're lucky, you'll end up with a deal at around $7.8 or $7.9 million."

"So then, what can we do?"

"Well, maybe we have to get out of this one-dimensional bargaining." Mack punctured the poori bread with his fork. "We need to shake up the equation a little."

"Do you have something in mind?"

"Yes, as a matter of fact, I do." Mack spoke slowly, as if testing his idea as it emerged. "Look, the potential claims against the business from that Queens fiasco in '75, worst case, are roughly $1 million. Chances are they could be settled for a lot less than that, although it's doubtful the company will get off scot-free. And Chapman has been using those claims as one of his main justifications for keeping the price down."

"He sure has—I'm sick of hearing about them."

"But precisely because of that, this is one of those bargaining opportunities where we can turn his own words against him— hoist Chapman by his own petard, so to speak."

"Very Shakespearean, I must say."

"Chapman doesn't want to pay you $9 million and still be stuck with a potential $1 million of liabilities. So here's a deal we could make, which gives us a graceful way to come off the fixed $9 million figure."

"I'm all ears."

"Chapman pays $9 million, but $1 million of it is put into escrow to cover those claims. That way, since the claims are covered and DX isn't otherwise responsible for them, Chapman gets a much more valuable business for his $9 million. And he can't very well argue about what a big benefit this is to him, since he's made such a point of the claims."

"No, he can't."

"Now, if the claims have to be paid in full, you end up with $8 million—but that's probably all the business is worth under those circumstances. On the other hand, since it's your money at stake, you would control how the claims are handled. If we can work out a more favorable settlement with the claimants, say for $500,000, then we get to keep the balance of the escrow and end up with $8.5 million."

"I think I understand what you're saying, but please go over it again."

"I will, in a minute." Mack gazed up at the fan turning lazily below the ornate ceiling, as if he were alone and thinking out loud. "The only problem is, if we introduce it that way, we'll probably end up with around $7.5 million as the fixed amount. So let's propose it at the $9.5 million level—$8.5 million fixed with a $1 million contingency—which we can rightly characterize as a reduction from our $9 million noncontingent position. And then"—now he turned to face Andy—"let me suggest how you handle things when Chapman goes for the concept, but tries to substitute $7.5 for $8.5 million as the fixed amount."

It was two days later. Andy was back in Mack's office, relating what had happened.

"So anyway, Chapman liked the idea right off the bat—but just as you predicted, he wanted to start with $7.5 million as the fixed number. We sparred for a while, but he was adamant, and the tension was building."

"Well, did you do what I suggested?"

"No, I didn't. The whole idea of getting exasperated and stalking out of the room just did not appeal to me. And after what you said the other day, I didn't want to be the one to offer to split the difference. So, I decided to improvise."

"Calling your own signals, huh? An audible at the line of scrimmage . . . pretty dangerous stuff." Mack's tone was half playful, half concerned.

"I know, and believe me, I had some trepidation."

"So, tell me—what did you do?"

Andy paused—it was his turn to savor the moment. Here's what I said to him. 'Up at Cromwell, Thomas, I teach a course on George Bernard Shaw.' Chapman grunted back at me, 'What's that got to do with this?' And I replied, Well, what's happening here reminds me of a story—possibly apocryphal—that they tell about the great man.

" 'It seems that Sam Goldwyn, the American movie mogul, was trying to buy the film rights to Shaw's plays and driving a very hard bargain. The two of them struggled at great length over the price.

It finally ended up with Shaw declining to sell. And Thomas—do you know how Shaw summed up the situation? He said, "The trouble is, Mr. Goldwyn, that you are interested only in art, and I am interested only in money!" ' "

"Oh," chortled Mack, "I like that one!"

"Well, it worked. Chapman laughed and the tension was broken. All of a sudden, he looked at me and said, 'You're really serious about getting top dollar for this business, aren't you?' And I said, 'I sure am.' And then he said, 'Okay, but not one penny over $8 million fixed with the $1 million contingent.' And I said, 'Thomas, you've got yourself a deal.' We shook hands on it."

Mack got up from his chair, walked around the desk to where Andy was seated, and placed a hand on his shoulder. "Congratulations."

Mack's secretary buzzed the intercom. "Mrs. Potter is returning Andy's call. It's on the second line."

"Thanks," said Andy, picking up the phone. "Hello, Jeannie. I've got good news for you. We have a deal with DX at a price of at least $8 million, and we could end up with maybe half a million more."

"That's wonderful." Jeannie sounded genuinely pleased.

"So, I guess there's no need to have me replaced as the man in charge."

"Oh, I never really considered doing that."

"You didn't? Well, what was all that tough talk the other evening at dinner?"

"Oh, come on, Andy." Her voice was warm and she seemed amused. "I thought you were a negotiator. Don't you recognize a little stepmotherly leverage when you see it?"

Andy's face broke out in a broad smile. "Hell, Jeannie, of course I knew what you were up to all along—what do you take me for, some kind of hayseed?"

After Andy hung up, Mack asked him: "Tell me, Andy, how will you ever manage to go back to Cromwell, now that you've had a taste of making a deal in the Big Apple?"

Andy visualized Carol against a landscape of red and gold leaves; he pictured Billy waking up Christmas morning to find a robot under the tree. "I'll survive."

Then Andy stood up and walked over to Mack's special file cabinet. He opened the drawer and took out the bottle of scotch. "By my reckoning," Andy said, "the sun's just gone down over the Reykjavik yardarm. I think we both need a little drink." He poured them each a shot.

Mack smiled as he raised his glass. "You did real good."

"Thanks, but I couldn't have managed it without your help."

"I appreciate that." They clinked glasses. "In fact," said Mack, without missing a beat, "this might be a good time to talk about my fee. . . ."

Commentary on
NEGOTIATING 101

This story differs from the others in that it views the lawyer-client relationship from the client's vantage point. The central character here is Andy Potter, an academic who's having a lot of trouble handling a business transaction; and while there's a third-person narrator, we spend a lot of time inside Andy's head.

Then, too, all nine other stories feature active partners in the law firm of Jenkins & Price. The lawyer here is Michael McKinley—known to all as "Mack"—and you may recall a reference to him by Helen Bentley (Dwight's wife) in "The Smell Test." Mack, a former partner of Jenkins & Price, was cast out by the firm when he turned sixty-five. (We'll come back to the particulars of that presently.)

Anyway, Mack is on his own, operating out of a tiny rumpled office—one gets the sense he's not faring too well financially. But he's still a lawyer to be reckoned with in negotiating a deal, which—at least on the surface—is what this story is all about. There's also a lot going on in terms of human factors—most notably, for our purposes, lawyer-client relations.

Andy's father, Phil Potter, has died quite suddenly, leaving behind instructions that have placed Andy in charge of selling Phil's business, Potter's Paints, a chain of hardware and housewares stores in New York City. Andy, an associate professor of English at Cromwell College in New Hampshire, knows nothing about business, finance or negotiating. He's an odd choice for the assignment perhaps, but Phil trusted no one else. This selection, however, makes Phil's widow, Jeannie (Andy's stepmother), quite nervous, as she's relying on her half of the sales proceeds for her future support. Moreover, the attorney for the estate, Jonas Hearn, is miffed because Andy isn't using him on the sale; Andy is under pressure from his wife (Carol) and son (Billy) to leave the Big Apple and come back to New Hampshire; and he's up against a savvy adversary (Thomas Chapman). All of this puts Andy—racked with self-doubt about his ability to handle the job—in a tough position.

This is where Mack steps in. Introduced to Andy by Phil's accountant (Harry Bell), Mack takes on the chore of guiding Andy in his assignment. Their relationship, and Mack's crash course for Andy on how to negotiate, lie at the core of the story.

The first lesson takes place (appropriately enough, as we shall see) in a hotel cocktail lounge. Andy is relating to Mack the tale of how, right after his father's death, the estate attorney (Jonas Hearn) was approached by the president of the DX Corp. conglomerate (Thomas Chapman), who knew Hearn's son-in-law (Robert Browning). DX had made several acquisitions of retail chains in related businesses, and Chapman was inquiring whether Potter's Paints might be for sale. Hearn responded by telling him that Phil Potter's will instructed the estate to sell the company.

Mack's reaction upon hearing this—"Ouch!"— introduces his first negotiating pointer for Andy in the session. It goes to the issue of leverage, also discussed in the commentary to "On-the-Job Training." (For a more detailed treatment, see chapter 2 of *Smart Negotiating*.)

Most bargaining situations contain a variety of factors that either favor or disadvantage a party. Only rarely is there a level playing field. As a negotiator, you have to constantly deal with this state of affairs—taking advantage of leverage that runs your way and attempting to offset leverage that adversely impacts you.

One of the negative leverage factors is necessity, as exemplified by the seller who is forced to sell. The ability to walk away from the table if acceptable terms can't be worked out puts backbone into one's bargaining posture. By contrast, having to sit there glued to the seat—afraid to do anything that might cut short the negotiations, forced to endure whatever indignities the other side chooses to inflict—can be excruciating, and may well pressure a seller into accepting less than he would otherwise hold out for. There's no reason for Chapman to know up front that the estate must make this sale, but now he does know (thus the "ouch"), and the Andy/Mack team will just have to deal with the reality of that knowledge.

The next issue concerns the asking price for Potter's Paints. Andy has no idea of the actual value of the company. But his father's accountant, Harry Bell, told him that Phil thought it was worth $10 million—a figure Harry was skeptical about and didn't discuss with anyone other than Andy. Knowing this, let me ask you:

If you were Andy, how would you have replied when Chapman asked at their first meeting whether he "had a price in mind"?

This question raises several issues that call for comment. (They are also discussed in "On-the-Job Training" and its commentary; for more detail, see chapters 7 and 8 of *Smart Negotiating*.) First, I don't like to put an initial asking or offering price on the table until after having attempted to determine my client's realistic price expectation—the number at which he'd be well satisfied to do the deal and can reasonably anticipate the other side's acquiescence. Since this hasn't been determined at the time of Chapman's question, Andy's response that he didn't have a specific price in mind is justifiable.

A related issue here is who puts the first price on the table. In brief, although the conventional wisdom is to let the other side go first, I often counsel clients (at least those who know where they want to end up) as to the desirability of getting their own number out there first. The reason is to try to take control of the price issue—to let their counterpart know that if she wants to play ball, here's the ballpark where the action will occur.

Another applicable issue is how much room to give your side when starting out. You'll need some bargaining space to be able to conduct the negotiations so as to arrive at your client's realistic expectation. Your opening proposal should be sufficiently reasonable to be viewed constructively by the other side (and thus to evoke a positive response), but it should give you enough room to move deliberately to your expectation without being forced to stretch beyond it. And it should be a number to which you're able to attach plausible rationale, because without that, your proposal lacks backbone.

That's the general framework. In this case, Mack tells Andy that it's one of those rare instances where a truthful answer by Andy—"My father told us right before he died that he thought the company was worth $10 million"—would have been a good response. The rationale here isn't objective (such as a price/earnings multiple or discounted cash flow analysis), but rather an attempt to make Chapman negotiate against a dead hand. Of course, the unspoken premise of Mack's advice is that Potter's Paints is worth less than $10 million. It wouldn't be such good advice if they were later to discover that Phil underestimated the company's value.

Mack then points out that to make the speech now would seem contrived, adding the thought, "Like so many things in negotiating, you either do it on the spot or it's gone forever." This may be overly dramatic, but timing is indeed important. That's why I so often caucus with clients in advance of a meeting at which we anticipate the other side will bring up something important, in order to rehearse how they should react on the spot to various possible formulations. A spontaneous reaction by the client has more credibility than a lawyer's response, and I want to make sure we're sending the right message (usually negative, to be sure, but also nuanced) to the other side.

You've probably guessed this by now, but I'll say it anyway: The nonjudgmental aspect of the "getting to yes" school of negotiating has never appealed to me. In the commercial world we inhabit, it sends the wrong signal to the other side. (Envision a lawyer reporting to his client on a recent meeting with a nonjudgmental adversary: "Hey, I dropped that lowball offer on them, but they didn't flinch, they wrote it down and discussed the terms—nobody called me a jerk or bottom-fisher— so maybe they don't value their property that highly.") Mack's views on this (as stated in the story)—including his emphasis on satisfaction rather than fairness— happen to mirror my own.

At any rate, Andy declined to put a number on the table when invited to by Chapman. Later, when he and Chapman had a second meeting, the DX president dumped all over the business of Potter's Paints, emphasized its overhanging liabilities, claimed it wasn't worth even $5 million, but offered to pay $6 million if the offer was accepted within a week. The reason Chapman gave for the haste was an upcoming DX finance committee meeting at which alternative uses of funds would be discussed. This, by the way, is the kind of "creative motivation" I referred to in the commentary to "Sex, Lies, and Private Eyes." Be warned, all you negotiators: take nothing at face value and examine closely every ostensible rationale.

Mack advises Andy to try to neutralize the "necessity" leverage working in Chapman's favor by fostering competition among possible purchasers. Competition puts pressure on a buyer to pay top dollar, while stiffening the seller's resolve to hold out for it. Even a seller operating under necessity is then able to say, hey, don't get too hard-nosed with me, because I've got an alternative. But inventing fictitious competition is an ethical no-no, so Andy needs to actually initiate talks with other parties. When Chapman finds out about this, he'll realize he doesn't have a lock on things.

Chapman has asked for future meetings to be between the principals, without lawyers or financial advisors present. In their first session, Andy told the DX president that he knows nothing about business, which presumably caused Chapman to salivate at the prospect of further one-on-one negotiations. Mack assures Andy that if this makes him uneasy and he wants Mack in the room, Chapman will have to go along. But Mack suggests a different strategy—letting Chapman think he's dealing with a "real hayseed" (Andy's words), which will attach more credibility to whatever Andy says than would be the case if the words were spoken by a lawyer or financial advisor. To be sure, Andy might blow some things, but Mack is willing to take that risk—sensing that he can provide enough guidance to make the risk manageable.

What do you think of Mack's judgment on this issue—is it wise, or should he insist on being present for future Chapman-Andy sessions?

I think it's risky, and I don't know whether I'd have done the same thing in Mack's place. But in that case, we wouldn't have had much of a story!

During this initial lawyer-client dialogue, we learn several other important details:

that Jonas Hearn, the estate lawyer, not only doesn't know much about selling a business but, in Andy's phrase, "seems so intent on my striking a quick deal with Chapman";

that Andy has mentioned the $10 million number to Phil's widow, Jeannie, thereby setting up an expectation that will be difficult to fulfill; and

that Mack likes to drink scotch in the late afternoon, even while conducting business.

That's about it for Andy's first meeting with Mack. This is followed by a brief interlude in which Andy's son, Billy, provides some "come home, Daddy" pressure. The scene then shifts to Andy's next meeting with Chapman (for which he has been prepped by Mack), at which Andy will respond to the DX $6 million/one week proposal. Before I discuss this session, let me ask you:

How do you think Andy handled this meeting with Chapman? Would you have done anything differently, and if so, what?

Let's go over what Andy accomplishes at the meeting. He rejects the $6 million bid, characterizing it as not being in accord with the reality he's seen "on the inside" of the company. He declines to put his own number on the table, nor does he invite an increase in Chapman's bid, because "I sense such conviction on your part that it seems fruitless to try to persuade you otherwise." He gets across the fact that he's not doing this on his own but has consulted professionals, dropping the Flynn & James name and noting that there's a lot of potential interest in the business on the part of other unspecified buyers. Finally, he ignores Chapman's efforts to rekindle the discussions and walks out the door.

Pretty good work, wouldn't you say? (Hey, I wrote it. . . .)

By the way, please note that the meeting took place in Chapman's office. I assume Andy had some choice in this matter, and here I think he chose wisely. If you're going to end the meeting by making a dramatic exit, make sure it's at the other guy's office—it's much more difficult to get up and walk out of your own!

Andy then telephones Mack to report on the encounter and receives a compliment on his performance. Mack works out a way to have the word get back to Chapman that Andy is meeting with other potential buyers. And he soothes Andy's concern that Chapman might not return to the table ("He will, Andy, he will."). The only disconcerting note occurs when Andy hears "a tinkle that sounded like liquid being poured over crackling ice cubes."

A troubling session between Andy and Jeannie follows, at which she criticizes his tactic of breaking off negotiations with Chapman, citing Jonas Hearn's view that this was a "major mistake" because "DX is our absolute best bet." Jeannie is confrontational and sarcastic, telling her stepson that he's in way over his head. She also manages to strike a note of quiet desperation—alone in the world, with no career (foregone, while she catered to Phil's needs), and hungry for "every dollar I can get from the sale of the business." Along the way, she takes a few swipes at Mack—aimed at his drinking problem, which (she says) is why he's no longer a J&P partner and doesn't handle major deals.

The Mack stuff hits home with Andy. Alone in his hotel room later that evening—unhappy over the rift that seems to be developing between himself and Jeannie—he reflects on having reposed total faith in this man reputed to have been severed from J&P over his alcohol intake. Andy recalls the tumblers of scotch at their first meeting and the sound of a drink being poured during their recent telephone call. He wonders whether the hard-nosed negotiating advice he's been getting from Mack—and dutifully following—may be ill advised. This fuels a lack of self-confidence in his ability to manage the sale of the business, which Jeannie certainly did nothing to dispel.

A week passes with some more Carol/Billy pressure and Andy's growing anxiety over the wisdom of Mack's approach. And then—voila!—Chapman gets back to Andy. Mack is vindicated, at least so far. I like the way Andy plays a little hard to get for his next meeting with Chapman—not because the place where the meeting takes place is important (which I've never believed to be the case), but because Andy uses it to promote the concept that he's being actively pursued by other buyers.

Prior to meeting with Chapman, Andy caucuses with Mack in the latter's office. They focus on the key question of how best for Andy to get the $10 million number across to Chapman. (I'm assuming that by this time, although they may not have received specific advice as to the company's value, they realize that $10 million is something of a stretch and thus would be an acceptable asking price.)

In the course of the meeting, Mack gives a little speech about the "acquisition mating dance"—the great American business game. His thoughts mirror the way I used to think about M&A during the '70s and '80s—I even used the phrase as the title for one of my books. Later on, my enthusiasm faded somewhat (that's a story for another time and place), but I'm still comfortable with the sentiments Mack expresses—including the point he makes about the fascination of one-on-one negotiations.

But Mack also does something very stupid at this meeting. In the middle of the strategizing, he reaches into his file cabinet for a bottle of scotch, pours himself a drink (after Andy demurs), and swallows it neat.

I'm not competent to determine whether Mack is an alcoholic, and I'm unsure whether his drinking influences his negotiating judgment, but I do know one thing—it has adversely affected his lawyer/client-relations judgment. I'm sure that in Mack's mind a few drinks don't undermine the wisdom of his advice. But Mack must realize there is some public suspicion (perhaps fanned by Jenkins & Price) that his drinking had something to do with him no longer being a J&P partner. He can also be reasonably sure (given Jonas

Hearn's evident unhappiness at Mack's ousting him from the deal) that Andy has been made aware of the history. Notwithstanding this, Mack proceeds to do the very thing that constitutes a damaging confirmation of this nasty rumor.

So, pardon my preaching, but let me say this to any lawyer who drinks a lot more than just on occasion: If you're not willing to give it up, then at least do it on your own time—not when you're in the middle of providing advice, especially to a client who may already be suspicious of your proclivities.

Moving ahead now, and after Andy's son, Billy, gets in another dig, Andy comes face-to-face with Chapman again. Chapman starts out by accusing Andy of breaking off the negotiations after Chapman had made "a decent opening offer," and then he inquires, "Why can't we do business?" Let me ask you:

What do you think of Andy's response and his method of getting the $10 million number on the table? Would you have handled it differently, and if so, how?

Andy, who is acting here on the basis of Mack's advice, works in Phil's $10 million valuation, with a plausible explanation of why he hadn't mentioned it at their prior meeting. He buttresses the valuation by noting that this is what his professional advisors are telling him he should be able to get. He goes on to assert that Chapman's bad-mouthing of his father's business, coupled with the lowball $6 million offer, and "the haste to sign me up," created the inference that Chapman was trying to steal the company while the Potter family was still in shock. Very well done, Andy, if I do say so myself.

Assume, for these purposes, that Andy's professional advisors have *not* been telling him he should be able to get $10 million. The question then arises:

Does Andy's characterization that they are doing so—when they're not—violate ethical principles of negotiation?

Not that I encourage it, but I think this kind of puffery about the value of what one is selling—which doesn't misstate a transactional fact—is probably acceptable. The players understand the ground rules and treat this as part of the game. My answer would be different if Andy were to pretend he had received a specific offer from a bona fide purchaser at that level, or even if he were to say he'd received a formal opinion letter from an investment banker confirming that value (when he hadn't).

I recall a helpful test one commentator suggested as to where to draw the line here. It depends on whether the deception causes some unfairness in the bargaining situation. The issue isn't whether there's intent to deceive or mislead, but rather whether the nature of the statement makes it likely that the negotiator will succeed in doing so. Here the element of justifiable reliance becomes critical. The more specific the statement, the more likely it will be treated as a factual representation; the less specific, the greater likelihood of it being considered more opinion or puffing.

At any rate, Chapman blinked at the meeting and delegated his numbers man to meet with the Potter's Paints accountant, Harry Bell. Perhaps through that process, he said, they might learn something enabling DX to raise its bid, although certainly not to the $10 million level (Chapman, after all, is a savvy negotiator). Andy acquiesced to the meeting without further comment.

Do you agree with what Andy did here?

Mack suggests that Andy might have coupled his acquiescence with a disclaimer that he didn't see much purpose in the meeting, since we're "so far apart." But Andy replies that he was worried Chapman might use this as an excuse to cancel the numbers session, and Mack, after reflection, confirms Andy's view. I do, too, and my view is delivered cold sober—apparently unlike Mack's, whose husky voice and verbal slip in substituting "decreasing" for "increasing" suggest otherwise.

Tipsy or not, Mack did the right thing here. When you're advising a client on negotiating strategy but haven't attended a particular session, and your client (who did attend) makes a determination at the meeting based on the existing circumstances, you ought to give that determination substantial latitude. It's tough to make negotiating decisions when you're not in on the action. And these are, after all, matters of judgment—it's scarcely an exact science. Moreover, when the client's judgment trumps your own view, you should validate that judgment (as Mack did), especially when advising an insecure client like Andy.

Next comes the threatening call to Andy from Jonas Hearn, referring to Andy's "game of chicken—orchestrated by a character of questionable repute and dubious sobriety"—hey, that's our boy, Mack. Again, though, there's Hearn's puzzling reference to DX being "the best buyer"—the only real buyer "at any decent price"—implying that Chapman's $6 million offer is praiseworthy. What is this Jonas up to?

The ensuing strategy session between Andy and Mack touches on some important points. They finally decide to sit down with the estate's investment advisor and accountant to ascertain the company's real value, which will determine their response to Chapman's likely increased bid. Mack advises Andy to keep talking to the other semi-interested buyers, so that he can truthfully tell Chapman that DX has competition—Andy shouldn't even think about making up any fictitious bids.

Andy expresses concern about having to get back to New Hampshire for the fall semester. Mack speculates that this may be why Chapman is moving slowly—hoping for professorial panic to set in and result in a quick sale to DX. Time pressure is a leverage factor that's often present in deals and must be dealt with. Here, Mack wisely suggests they alter Chapman's perspective by affirmatively raising the issue and assuring him that Andy has all the time in the world to hold out for a full and fair price.

Andy asks Mack when he should bring up other issues, such as job security for employees. Mack gives him sound advice on this score. When you're trying to deliver a message of firmness on price (here, at the $10 million level), it sends the wrong signal to be fussing with lesser issues—making it seem as if Andy recognizes that he'll eventually have to come down in order to make the deal. It's more prudent to defer raising these other issues until Chapman shows he's prepared to be realistic about price.

It's a useful caucus, with the only sour note being Andy's awareness of Mack's shaky left hand—suggesting to Andy a case of the DTs.

Carol now gets on Andy's case about Jeannie. It sounds like a little jealousy has entered the picture. Poor Andy—not only is the jealousy unwarranted, but Jeannie is actually making his life miserable.

Then Andy has his next meeting with Chapman, who announces he's prepared to raise his bid. At their preceding strategy session, Mack had virtually guaranteed to Andy that Chapman's number would be under $8 million and that he would tell Andy it's his "ultimate stretch." That's just what Chapman does—making a $7.5 million offer which he characterizes as his "best price."

My advice to you lawyers is that, as your self-confidence and judgment increase, you should not be afraid to make predictions to a client under appropriate circumstances. It can prove useful to the client in anticipating trouble and taking preventive measures. Here, it serves a dual purpose—lowering Andy's expectations, so he's not disappointed that Chapman's increase isn't closer to $10 million, and giving Mack a useful reputation for prescience. By the way, don't worry too much if your prediction doesn't turn out quite the way you said it would—such shortfalls are rarely remembered or held against you, since you're only dealing in suppositions.

Here again, Mack has gone the extra step and advised Andy how to react to the offer he anticipated would come—that's so much better than leaving it up to chance. Their approach is to label it as "constructive"— a useful all-purpose word that acknowledges the effort without signing on to the substance—and then have Andy go on to say that it "doesn't get up into the range I need to close off the selling process we're going through now."

What do you think—did Andy handle this well? What might you have done differently?

I like the way Andy handled it, even though Chapman then proceeds to give him some grief. And when Chapman tries to put time pressure on him to accept the offer, Andy wisely responds by denouncing the "gun to my head." The meeting closes with Andy saying to Chapman, "I'll get back to you."

When Andy reports this last remark to Mack, the lawyer explodes. To him, it sends a signal that Andy is giving the $7.5 million serious consideration. Mack may be right about this, but the explosion is wrong— and Mack, sensing this, quickly calms down and moves on to what they should do next. He confirms (through information received by Harry Bell) one aspect of what Chapman said—that DX is in talks to acquire another company similar to Potter's Paints. This is the flip side of the leverage created by the competition factor, and it's often used by a buyer to put some reciprocal pressure on too cocky a seller.

Conversations with Flynn & James and Harry Bell have established that something in the $8 to $8.5 million range would be a reasonable price for the company, especially in view of the potential liabilities from the so-called Queens fiasco. Furthermore, there seems little chance of getting Chapman "up into the $10 million area of Jeannie's' dreams," the alternative purchasers aren't panning out, and key employees are starting to resign. So it's necessary to move fast, while the other buyers are still in the picture.

At this point, Mack heads over to the file cabinet (bad move), Andy tells him to "hold the drinks" (justifiable), and Mack breaks off the meeting (a very questionable decision).

The pressure on Andy keeps increasing. His college writes to notify him that if he stays in New York, he can and will be replaced; Carol and Billy convey another dose of family guilt; and Jeannie is going all out to get him, even threatening a court action to overturn his authority. Jeannie wants Andy and Mack to resign, at which point the estate would bring in—guess who?—Elliot Cheever of Jenkins & Price (remember Elliot from "Awash in Associates"?).

Next is Andy's big soliloquy scene ("to negotiate or not to negotiate")—lying alone in his hotel room, weighing all the factors. (It's something like Dwight Bentley's musings in his little room that night in "The Smell Test.")

There are good reasons to bow out, which Andy explores. The issue of Mack's drinking is very much on his mind. He tries out some resignation formulations. He wonders how his father would feel at this juncture—would Phil be sorry he didn't designate a pro for the job . . . ?

Then there's Andy's dreamlike epiphany—a conversation with his dad, and Phil's response: "Screw' em all . . . No son of Phil Potter quits on his father." Andy now knows what he has to do. And minutes thereafter he makes a discovery about the cozy relationship to DX of Jonas Hearn's son-in-law, Robert Browning—the man who introduced Chapman to Hearn.

The next scene is a caucus between Andy and Mack, at which Andy briefs Mack on Jeannie's demands. Mack insists that Andy stay on, but offers to resign himself if it will lift the pressure from Andy—Elliot Cheever is, after all, a competent lawyer.

At one point, they segue into a discussion of how Mack and J&P parted company. He says it was because his billings were down, due to his two biggest corporate clients having recently been acquired. But the firm encouraged the innuendo that Mack had a drinking problem, which he denies had anything to do with J&P's decision. He apologizes for "reaching for the bottle" with Andy at yesterday's session. Andy is mollified and tells Mack he won't break up the team.

Andy relates his discovery about the Hearn-Browning-Chapman connection. Mack licks his lips and comes up with a plan of how to handle it.

At an earlier time, Mack had advised Andy to let Chapman know that he had all the time in the world to negotiate this deal. Andy never got around to mentioning this to Chapman. Now Mack changes that advice, counseling Andy to tell Chapman that he needs to get back to New Hampshire. Let me ask you:

What do you think of Mack's new advice here? Does it bother you that it's inconsistent with his prior counsel?

Mack justifies his change of gears here by labeling it a graceful way for Andy to descend from the $10 million level of his father's assessment to the level ($8 to $8.5 million) where a deal can actually be done. I agree.

I can't count how many times that Emerson quote about consistency being the hobgoblin of little minds was proffered to me by one of my senior partners, as he deftly moved on to new ground that I questioned. Let me provide the full quote, which I find very instructive—particularly with all this political talk nowadays about flip-flopping. "A foolish consistency is the hobgoblin of little minds, adored by little statesmen and philosophers and divines. With consistency a great soul has simply nothing to do. . . . Speak what you think now in hard words, and tomorrow speak what tomorrow thinks in hard words again, though it contradicts everything you said today."

Andy then confronts Jeannie and tells her that he and Mack aren't resigning. He tries to get across to her the $8 to $8.5 million valuation figure they've arrived at. And he opens her eyes to the Chapman-Browning-Hearn connection, which is a much better way than confronting Hearn directly, since any clout Jonas has must emanate from Jeannie (and now won't be forthcoming). He does agree to meet with the valuation firm that Elliot Cheever has recommended, whose principal she quotes as having said "we should be able to get at least $9 million for the business."

I echo Andy's reflections here that negotiating isn't just something you do when selling a business. It's going on all over the place—domestically and otherwise. Everyone is trying to get to him except Mack, and he muses (prophetically) that even this will probably change some day.

In the next scene, Andy relates to Mack how he handled Bart Sherman. It involves the same technique as Mack's petard-hoist price compromise that I'll discuss in a moment. The key was having Jeannie in attendance when he performed the maneuver—it wouldn't have had the same impact otherwise. Jeannie now realizes that Andy is up to the job.

This still leaves the question of how to make a deal, with Andy having come down to $9 million and Chapman seemingly sticking at $7.5 million. What next, Coach?

Here's where Mack comes up with some creative thinking. When there's a substantial unknown factor affecting valuation—a factor whose ultimate dimension will become knowable at some point in the not-too-distant future—it may be possible to structure a deal that lets a portion of the price turn on the outcome of the unknown factor. That's what Mack did here, making the deal price partially conditional on the outcome of the claims from the Queens fiasco.

The key to the compromise is that Chapman has been playing up the enormity of the Queens claims as a justification for keeping the price down. Here's one of those opportunities that a negotiator cannot afford to pass up—the chance to foil an adversary right out of his own big mouth, hoisting him on his own petard, so to speak. Chapman can't very well shift gears and claim, all of a sudden, that those liabilities are minuscule. And if they turn out to be as large as he says, then under the Mack/Andy formulation, Chapman has cut a fine deal. (Similarly, Bart Sherman's "we can get you $9 million" sets up Andy's offer to pay a higher-than-usual fee conditioned on that price being achieved.)

If this had been a novel rather than a short story, I would have served up the final negotiating session between Andy and Chapman in its entirety, placing the narrator right there in the room with the two combatants. Reaching agreement on a deal—especially after undergoing hard-fought negotiations—is one of those dramatic moments that should be viewed up close and personal. But in the short story, we have to make do with Andy recounting the major details to Mack.

There are five points I want to make about this climax to the negotiations. The first is Mack's realization that although he had devised an acceptable method of compromising the parties' differences, Chapman wouldn't go for it right away—even if the DX president liked the concept. So Mack worked out in advance how to give Andy some bargaining room to reach the ultimate compromise. He had Andy propose an $8.5 million fixed price, with a $1 million contingency based on the outcome of the Queens claims. Even with the extra $500,000 padding, Andy can justly characterize this proposal as a reduction from his prior $9 million fixed price position. Mack then predicted (rightly, it turns out) that Chapman would try to substitute $7.5 million for the $8.5 million fixed portion of the price, and he advised Andy how to negotiate to arrive at their $8 million realistic expectation.

Stated in more general terms, the point I'm making is this. Too often, when we manage to devise a creative compromise, we're so pleased with our accomplishment that we jump right in with it. That may be the favored modus operandi in a "getting to yes" world, but it's not recommended in the commercial sphere we business lawyers inhabit. Rather, we have to figure that the other side will want to take a whack at whatever we come up with, and accordingly we need to give ourselves some operating room to absorb the hit.

The second point to note is that Andy didn't follow the advice that Mack seems to have given him—namely, to stalk out of the room if and when things went badly. Andy, sensing there was a deal to be made that day, stuck with the process. I give Mack low marks here on the advice, and I applaud Andy for having the courage of his convictions.

The third point is that Andy (having received prudent advice on the subject from Mack) didn't want to be the one who offered to split the difference between the $8.5 and $7.5 million fixed price components of the two sides. (This subject is discussed in "Awash in Associates.") Mack and Andy rightly feared that if they were to propose the $8 million split while Chapman was still at $7.5 million, the deal would probably end up being made somewhere around $7.7 or $7.8 million.

Fourth is Andy's decision to break the tension with his Shaw-Goldwyn anecdote. It was not only well timed but also pertinent to the situation—if George Bernard Shaw (the admired subject of Andy's teaching efforts) was interested in getting top dollar, so was Andy. It had the effect of forcing Chapman to recognize that he wouldn't be able to snare Potter's Paints at a bargain price.

Here's the final point. Some observers might argue that when Chapman went to $8 million, Andy ought to have used that as a baseline for continued negotiating—striving for a price in excess of that number. I don't agree with them. Notwithstanding the emphasis I place on the process of bargaining, the virtues of perseverance, the search for advantages, and such, I'm convinced that a smart negotiator has to know when to stop the music and grab a chair. The opportunity to make a deal today may well be gone tomorrow. People can change their minds, or new factors (such as competition) can intervene. I don't know how many times over the years—usually late at night in a formerly smoke-filled room—I've maneuvered my client into a corner and whispered in his ear, "Don't let this guy out of the room until you've shaken hands on a deal." The resulting agreement may not be all you could hope to achieve by prolonging the process; but when the risk of losing the deal altogether doesn't justify the possible incremental advantage, that's the time to come to terms.

This is how I feel about the acquisition from Andy's standpoint. The $8 million fixed component achieves his realistic expectation. Chapman undoubtedly considers his $8 million proposal to have been a major move on his part, designed to close off the bidding. There's no telling how Chapman might react if Andy keeps pushing him. So instead, Andy "grabs a chair," and I commend him for it.

Jeannie finally gets around to complimenting Andy, while Mack does, too. And now (as Andy breaks out the tumblers), about Mack's fee. . . .

I'll close this commentary with some general thoughts on the subject of negotiating. For roughly three decades, I relished negotiating as a business lawyer—it was my favorite professional activity. I also taught it in law school, lectured extensively, and wrote books and articles on the subject. Although toward the end I got more involved in resolving disputes, the great bulk of my negotiating was of the deal-making variety.

What I've always appreciated about negotiating transactions is that, unlike a lawsuit where there's a winner and loser, in a deal the ultimate goal is for both sides to reach a mutually satisfactory agreement. This goal of mutual satisfaction is what makes negotiation unique. It's not solely getting your own way—you need to bring the other party along in order for the deal to take place. I like to say, it's winning him over that counts—not winning over him.

But, of course, you also have to take care of your own side's interests. My guideline for this is to look for the favorable middle ground—where my client is pleased with the resolution and the other party is satisfied enough to do the deal.

Here's what I said about this in *Lawyering* almost thirty years ago (and I still feel the same way today):

> Most of what takes place in the course of negotiations can be characterized as either attempting to get a leg up on your adversary or striking a compromise between your respective positions. I firmly believe that the key to effective negotiating lies in achieving a functional balance between these two seemingly inconsistent aspects. If all your efforts are directed toward gaining advantages over your adversary, you will undoubtedly come on too strong, and where the parties possess relatively equal bargaining power, with freedom to consummate the transaction or not, you may cause your client irreparable harm—such as losing the deal. On the other hand, if you don't push a little—if you never strive for advantages in drafting or stake out positions that invite rebuttal—then your client is unlikely to achieve his share of obtainable rights and protections.

Now, all that is true of negotiating generally. What always gave the process a special flavor for me as a lawyer was that I wasn't negotiating for myself but for a client. This adds a whole other dimension to the picture. On the one hand, you can be a better negotiator for others than for yourself. When your own property or interests aren't at stake, you can be more objective, more relaxed, more creative. Conversely, if you're too anxious about the outcome, you may not trade wisely.

On the other hand, it's not an unmixed blessing. The need to find out what a client really wants, the task of shepherding him through the bargaining process, the necessity of explaining to him the significance of what's going on, the ability to handle those difficult moments when the two of you find yourselves in disagreement—all these and more add a real burden. And lots of tough questions abound, such as how deeply the lawyer ought to get involved in the client's decision-making. When should the lawyer make a specific recommendation, and conversely, when should he hold back from doing so, either because it's not in his area of expertise or because he has a client who thinks lawyers ought to know their place? So it's fascinating, but can often be frustrating.

Unfortunately, my experience has been that a lot of lawyers—even good ones—don't treat negotiating as something worthy of serious consideration. They just let it happen, trusting to their instincts; and as you might expect, those with good instincts usually turn out to be competent at the bargaining table.

But the sad fact is that a large number of otherwise skilled lawyers are mediocre negotiators at best. They become so immersed in difficult substantive questions that they rarely stop to analyze how best to achieve their goals. They neglect to size up their adversary, to peer inside his mind and discover what's really troubling him. They seem to lack adeptness at devising effective compromises. Their inventiveness is reserved for matters of substance— new ways to structure a deal for tax purposes and the like—while the equally creative and necessary task of circumventing a difficult sticking point with the other side remains ignored.

Yet lawyers are the logical persons to handle negotiations in business transactions. A legal mind is invaluable for clarifying situations—for example, to identify the cause of a seeming disagreement as a simple failure to distinguish between separable issues. Lawyers possess the training and experience to ask the hard questions so crucial to the bargaining process. And it's usually the attorney who realizes that the parties' minds haven't actually met on an issue which is seemingly resolved.

For most of my years in active practice, I was in the trenches, conducting negotiations on a daily basis. And then, as I passed age sixty, the wear and tear got to me, and I found myself no longer so eager for the fray.

When I wrote *Smart Negotiating* in the early 1990s, I had a recurring fantasy—that clients would read the book and come to me for negotiating advice (which I still enjoyed dispensing), at which point other individuals (younger colleagues, agents, the clients themselves) would carry out my instructions, leaving me free to move on to the next counseling session without having to sully my hands. That was around the time I wrote "Negotiating 101," the earliest of my stories, and it seems (in a manner I wasn't aware of at the time) to have reflected that fantasy. I didn't have his drinking problem, but I must have subconsciously seen myself as Mack—counseling, strategizing, predicting, and then sending Andy off to do battle with Chapman.

Well, I soon learned to my dismay that this wasn't to be my lot in the real world. Clients who were willing to pay the kind of fees I was charging insisted on my active participation in the process. And you know what—they were entitled to it. And so, when I found getting down and dirty to be more of a burden than a thrill, that's the time I retired.

In that sense, this story isn't typical of what we lawyers do for a living. But don't worry—now that Andy and Chapman have shaken hands on a deal, Mack is going to have to emerge from the shadows and take a plunge into the nitty-gritty with the DX lawyer, or that purchase agreement will never see the light of day.

Gordon was alive, Dave functioned as a supersalesman, traveling a lot. Gordon handled all the home office matters that required a lawyer. But with Gordon's passing, Dave came in from the road to take over the reins of the family business.

I paid my respects to Dave shortly after Gordon's funeral. Dave said he was preoccupied with estate details—our firm isn't handling that end of things—but would be calling me soon about some matters that needed attention.

At the time of Gordon's death, there was one major deal in the offing—the acquisition by Keating Enterprises of Fiberpack Corp. Gordon and I had discussed it in depth just the week before his passing. When I spoke to Dave, I asked him if the deal was still on. He said it definitely was—that he'd asked the Fiberpack people for some time because of his dad's death, and they'd complied.

A few days ago, Dave called me to say he'd be coming over to my office today for two purposes. One, as I anticipated, was to discuss the Fiberpack deal.

The other was to talk about the terms of a new employment contract with Al Pruitt. I know Pruitt well from my prior dealings with the company. He's a longtime key employee of Keating Enterprises—probably the most important single executive next to the boss. His present five-year contract will be expiring in a few months. So, it makes sense to focus on this as soon as possible, and I'm glad that Dave and I will have a chance to do that today.

Dave Keating enters my office. He's in his early thirties and prematurely balding. There are beads of perspiration on his brow. He holds an unlit cigar between his pudgy fingers.

After a brief greeting. Dave sits down and starts right in. "Glad we could get together. We'll talk about Fiberpack after we're finished with Pruitt."

Seeing Dave in action, I can't help recalling how his father would start out a meeting. Gordon always liked to schmooze a little—commenting on current events, asking about my kids and such—before getting down to business. It's a marked contrast— the first difference I notice between the two of them.

Looking closely at Dave's face, I can see a family resemblance to Gordon—a youthful, still unlined version of his father.

I wonder whether I'll have a problem working for someone who's more than a decade younger than myself. But let's face it, youth is taking over everywhere. How about that thirty-two-year-old guy who was elected governor of Arkansas last year—his name is, uh, Bill . . . Bill something . . . Oh, that's it, Bill Clinton.

Dave's voice is loud, his delivery rapid. "Pruitt's contract is up in about two months, so he's been after me to work out his deal going forward. I didn't feel I could put it off any longer, so that's why we're meeting with him today."

"Meeting with *him*? He's coming here today?"

"Right—in about ten minutes."

I'm taken aback. Dave never mentioned that we would be negotiating with Pruitt today—I thought just the two of us were meeting to discuss the terms we'd later propose to Al. I can assure you, Gordon never would have sprung something like this on me—that's the second father-and-son difference I observe. And whenever Gordon and I were planning to negotiate with the other side, we always gave ourselves a lot more than ten minutes to prepare for the bargaining—I guess that's the third difference.

"Well," I say, trying hard to keep the surprise out of my voice, "in that case, I better line up a conference room for us to meet with Pruitt and his lawyer."

Dave gives a dismissive wave of his hand. "Not necessary, your office is fine. And by the way, Al won't be bringing a lawyer."

My eyes widen. "He won't? Hey, wait a minute, that makes me uncomfortable—negotiating with him without his lawyer present."

"Don't worry. Al has great respect for you and doesn't feel the need to hire a lawyer."

I'm not happy about this turn of events—the extra level of responsibility imposed, the potential for a claim of unfairness. If I'd known about this earlier, I might have headed it off. But it's too late now. . . .

Well, to protect myself, I'll get the lawyer issue on the table with Al right at the outset. As far as his contract goes, I wasn't involved when it was signed five years ago, but I've had a chance to read it over. The terms are pretty cut-and-dried. Assuming what Dave has in mind for the renewal is in line with the existing provisions, and as long as I don't press Al too hard on anything, I guess I can get through the meeting.

"Dave, I'm uneasy about doing this, but I can see why it's important for you to lock Pruitt in on a long-term basis. After all, he knows so much about the business, he has all the contacts—your father's right-hand man and a real salt-of-the-earth guy."

Dave leans forward in his chair, waggling the unlit cigar. "Actually, it's *not* so important to me. I'm gonna let you in on a secret, George—I *don't* intend to renew Al Pruitt's contract."

I'm jolted by the news. "Why not?"

"Because I found another guy who's better and cheaper than Pruitt to take his place."

So much for institutional loyalty—a fourth difference with his old man. . . . Well, what the hell, it's Dave's company now—he can do what he pleases. I'm still bothered, though.

"This comes as a real surprise, but I'm sure you know what you're doing. Here's what I don't understand, though—if you've got someone else on tap for Pruitt's job, why are we sitting down to negotiate with Al today?"

Dave rocks back in his chair. "Because the new guy hasn't given me a final 'yes' yet. All signs are positive, but I can't afford to dump Pruitt until it's in the bag. I'll know for sure in a week or so. But Pruitt was itchy, so I agreed to this meeting."

I don't like the sound of this at all. "So the negotiation today is essentially a charade?"

"In one sense, yes. But it's more than that."

"How so?"

"Pruitt has a lot of friends at the company. If I just out and out show him the door, they're gonna be upset—and that's not good for my business. I want to be able to say to the troops that when we talked about renewing his contract, Pruitt asked for too much—he got greedy—and that's why I had to replace him when his term was up."

I shake my head vigorously. "But Dave, I've gotten to know Al pretty well over the years, and he's not greedy at all. I've found him to be quite reasonable. His current contract reflects that, and he isn't likely to ask for the moon on this go-round—especially now, right after the death of your father, who was his close friend."

Dave flicked an imaginary ash on the carpet. "I know that. But we can't afford to come to an agreement on terms with him. So—"

"So?"

"So, you'll have to take some tough positions on the big issues—positions that Pruitt can't agree to."

I'm sputtering now. "You—you want me to take deliberately unreasonable positions with him?"

"Yeah—but not obvious ones. I want to be able to tell everyone that it was Pruitt who acted unreasonably."

Now the beads of perspiration begin to appear on *my* forehead. Nothing like this could possibly have happened when Gordon was alive—there's the fifth difference.

"Let me get this straight. You want me to propose some terms that will be onerous and unacceptable to Pruitt but won't appear so bad to others?"

Dave stands up. "You got it. Take a few minutes to think up some good ones—I'm gonna go outside and make a phone call." He points his cigar at me. "And remember, I want these provisions to come from you, so that as far as Pruitt is concerned— and anyone he talks to later—*I'm* not the bad guy, *you* are."

Dave leaves my office in search of a phone. I'm in a state of shock. This is very upsetting—a sham negotiation, taking deliberately tough positions to ensure there won't be an agreement, and with *me* as the villain. That last aspect is the sixth difference between Dave and his father—Gordon was out front and forthright in all his negotiations.

I can't believe it—and Dave has given me just ten minutes to come up with the goods. What a bummer! And what makes it even worse is I really need to read over the Northvale contract that's being signed tomorrow, and I still have to write the eulogy for Dwight Bentley. . . .

From what I can see, I don't know if I'll ever feel comfortable lawyering for Dave. This precise situation may not arise again, but what assurance do I have that he won't ask me to do other things I consider unethical or unreasonable?

I take a few deep breaths to calm down. I remind myself to keep my eye on the ball. Keating Enterprises is a major long-term client of mine. And Keating has a big deal with Fiber-pack in the offing. Why, the billings from that one acquisition could mean the difference between a great year and a merely good one for me at the firm. And in that kind of deal—when we're up against a sophisticated adversary—Dave will know better than to ask me to try anything as bush league as what he wants me to do with Pruitt.

God knows, I dislike the chore he's given me here—but, I ask myself, is it really unethical? Look, in two months Dave Keating will be free to enter into a new employment contract with Pruitt or not—and he's chosen not to. Now, the way that Dave wants to appear he's arrived at that junction isn't to my liking, and I guess I'm abetting the deception Dave wants to pull on his other employees. But the *legal* effect is no different than if Dave simply said to Al, "I've decided not to renew your contract."

How about the fact that Pruitt won't have a lawyer with him? Dave says Al hasn't even bothered to hire one. I don't like the set-up, but it's not as if Dave is asking me to interfere with Pruitt's *existing* contract rights. So, in that sense, Al not being represented by counsel is less significant. It would be different, of course, if Dave wanted me to coerce a lawyerless Pruitt into signing a new contract on unconscionable terms—but that's not what Dave is asking me to do. . . .

I wonder, though—am I rationalizing my decision to go ahead and do something so distasteful just because I'm hot to keep Keating Enterprises as a major client?

What finally persuades me is something I'm always mindful of—that as a lawyer, I'm an agent. If I want to serve my client, I have to do what he wants me to do—including play the role of the bad guy—even if I don't like it, as long as it's not illegal or unethical.

So, after a few moments of indecision, I find myself jotting down on a notepad some positions I can take with Pruitt that fit Dave's instructions. It's not pleasant work, but I manage to do it. When Dave returns to my office five minutes later, I run my suggested items by him. He appears satisfied.

Al Pruitt arrives, and Glenda shows him in. Al is a man in his early fifties, well dressed, with an earnest look and manner.

After greeting Dave, Al gives me a firm handshake and a warm hello. We exchange a few sympathetic words on Gordon's passing. He sits down in one of the pull-up chairs by the desk. Dave is seated over on the couch, out of the line of fire.

"Al," I say, "we've gotten together today to discuss the terms for renewal of your employment contract. You understand that you're entitled to have a lawyer represent you."

Al smiles. "I do understand, and it's very gentlemanly of you to remind me of that. But I've known you for many years, George, and while I realize you're not representing me here or giving me legal advice, I have complete faith in your good judgment. Besides, I'm assuming the terms will parallel those in the present contract, even though you weren't involved back then. So I don't feel the need for a lawyer."

Al's little speech hasn't made what I'm about to do any easier, but I proceed. "I appreciate your confidence in me, Al. But I must dispel your notion about the terms being the same as at present. Almost five years have passed since the last contract was signed, and the world—to say nothing of Keating Enterprises—has changed quite a lot in the interim."

Pruitt looks puzzled. "I'll grant you that, but what needs to be changed in my contract?"

"Well, let's start with the financial terms. Right now, you receive a $100,000 salary and a $50,000 guaranteed bonus. We can continue your salary at the same level, but there's no longer going to be any concept of a guaranteed bonus. Your bonus will be discretionary with the company's board of directors, as it is for executives in most other companies."

Al frowns at me. As he speaks, he glances periodically over at Dave for support. "Look, in all candor, I'm disappointed that my salary isn't being increased, as I certainly expected it would be after five good years. But what troubles me a lot more is the idea of making my bonus discretionary. Gordon and I always considered my compensation to be $150,000. The way it was divided up in the contract between salary and guaranteed bonus was for other corporate reasons—which didn't bother me, as long as I could count on receiving the full amount."

Pruitt pauses, as if awaiting some confirmation from Dave. Hearing none, he goes on. "I have fixed expenses—a big mortgage, two kids at college, my parents in a retirement home—that require every penny of the $150,000. Making the bonus discretionary changes the equation entirely."

He's right, of course, and it's difficult to argue with his logic. But I have to try. "I can't speculate on what might have been in Gordon's mind five years ago. But these are tough economic times we're in now. And while Keating Enterprises has performed well to date, it can't commit itself to levels of compensation that would be inappropriate if matters were to take a real turn for the worse. That's especially true in the uncertain period that follows the death of the company's founder and chief executive."

"I hear you," says Pruitt, his lips tightly pursed, "but I don't agree. Let's pass that for the moment, though. What else do you have in mind?"

"Well, I was frankly surprised when I read the early termination provisions in your present contract. In order for the company to fire you 'for cause,' you'd just about have to commit murder or, at the very least, arson. This has to be brought into line with the more usual formulation—to include such matters as disobeying a direct order, or failure to achieve anticipated company-wide profit levels."

Al grips the arms of his chair. "But I don't have total profit responsibility—so that would mean I can be fired if other people fail to accomplish their goals."

I decide it's better not to argue this point with him—since he's clearly right—and just press ahead. "And under the present contract, if you're terminated without cause, you receive $100,000 per year for the full term—without any mitigation, even if you take a job elsewhere. So you'd be collecting your full salary without working a day for Keating Enterprises—or worse, while you're employed by one of its competitors."

Pruitt, visibly agitated, interrupts me. "But that's the whole idea of having a contract—the company is not supposed to fire me without cause. That's why we included some stiff severance provisions."

I sneak a glance over at Dave, whose clenched jaw and piercing eyes warn me not to dare flinch from my duty. So I move on. "And as for the noncompete provisions, should you decide to leave voluntarily, these have to be tightened up quite a bit."

"Leave?" Al's tone is incredulous. "Me leave—voluntarily? Why would I do that? Keating Enterprises is my home."

"Well, you asked what the changes would be, and I'm just telling you."

Pruitt shifts in his chair to face Keating and implores him. "Dave, your father never would have done this to me."

Dave shrugs his shoulders. "What can I do, Al—I have to take my lawyer's advice."

I cringe inwardly, but realize I cannot contradict my client.

Al says, "I can't accept these terms."

Dave's voice now becomes soothing, the supersalesman at work. "I'll tell you what, Al. Don't make any rash judgments now. You're probably still upset over Gordon's passing. Why don't you take a few weeks and think about it. We'll sleep on it too, and then let's see if we can reach a meeting of the minds."

Al grunts in acquiescence. He stands up, shakes hands with Dave, and leaves the office—without even glancing my way.

I look over at Dave and grimace. "That was painful."

"You handled it well, George."

"Okay," I say, determined to put this unpleasantness behind me, "Let's turn our attention to the Fiberpack deal."

"Yes," says Dave, waggling his unlit cigar, "I wanted to talk to you about that. It's back on track." Dave suddenly stands up, looking for all the world as if he's about to leave my office.

I have a sinking feeling. My God, I think, am I about to discover the seventh difference?

"But here's the thing. I've decided to hire Mike Lucas of Cliff & Lucas to represent Keating Enterprises on the Fiberpack deal. He's got a lot more experience in mergers and acquisitions than you have. . . . Anyway, thanks for your help on Pruitt."

And with that, Dave walks out the door.

I'm stunned. Here I'd just finished taking care of Dave's dirty business with Pruitt—ever the loyal servant—and this is how I'm repaid. . . . Why, that son of a bitch!

And now I proceed to get mad as hell, uttering a string of expletives and banging my fist on the desk with such force that the papers fly all over the room.

There's a goddamn lesson here somewhere, I'm sure, but I'm too irate to think clearly. All I know is I want to strangle someone—preferably Dave Keating, but if that's not possible, then the next guy to cross my path. Grrrr. . . .

And so it is that when, after a few minutes of fuming, I turn my attention to the Bentley eulogy, I'm in one helluva lousy frame of mind.

As I think back on my time working for Dwight, I remember those years as the worst of my professional life. His practice was so far out of the firm's mainstream that I felt like a recluse. It wasn't just that, though—it was the man himself. Bentley was a nice enough guy, but just impossible to work for.

It all comes back to me now. How, for instance, everything moved at a snail's pace—so tedious and repetitive. "Now, George," he would say, "I think you should go back to the library and check those cites one more time." And Dwight's approach was so narrow, so by-the-book. "We can't give a legal opinion on that issue, George—it's a mixed question of law and business judgment." And he didn't change with the times—just ask Alex Gibson about Bentley's prissiness when Alex tried to take on that Breckenridge deal a few years back.

Worst of all, the man had absolutely no sense of how to attract new business, how to grow the practice. He just sat there, waiting for the phone to ring. He didn't even have a business card—thought it smacked too much of solicitation. I always had the feeling that he looked on the rest of us—out hustling deals—as no better than ambulance chasers.

So what do you think—should I put all that in the eulogy?

I glance at the headline in the newspaper on my desk: "Iranian Student Mob Storms U.S. Embassy in Tehran—Takes 90 Hostages." This is terrible news. Crazy things are happening in this world of 1979, and I'm sitting here writing a eulogy for a man whom life passed right by. And—lest I forget for a moment—also having to deal with a scumbag like Dave Keating. . . .

I push aside the file of Dwight's personal papers that his secretary sent up to me at Bill Price's request. What the hell, I'm getting nowhere with this eulogy, so I may as well do something productive.

I pull out the file for the Northvale deal that's set to be signed tomorrow. All day I've been trying to do a final read-through of the principal agreement—a demanding job that requires my full attention. This is another reason I'm so irritated at having to spend time on Dwight's eulogy—to say nothing of having to play the villain in that Pruitt charade.

For the next forty minutes, I manage to concentrate on the Northvale contract—checking the text of this long and complicated document that I negotiated, on behalf of my buyer client, with Rob Phelps, the lawyer for the seller. Everything seems in order. As I'm nearing the end of the document, though, something catches my eye—buried in a complex provision concerning indemnification for uncollected accounts receivable.

I reread a certain long-winded sentence, and then it hits me. The sentence contains a double negative, the effect of which is to give the buyer—my client—a valid claim against the seller under certain circumstances. But what I clearly remember— because I personally negotiated the provision, although one of my associates drafted the language—is that my client was *not* supposed to have any recourse against the seller in that situation. So, the legal effect of the garbled language is just the opposite of what was intended—and it runs in our favor!

As Mel Allen would say, "How about that!?" This thing has gone through a number of drafts, and no one ever caught the double negative. . . .

Well, screw it, that's *their* problem. Hey, I'm not their lawyer—Rob Phelps is. This glitch is for him to catch—that's what they're paying him for. My lips are sealed.

What's my risk here? I play it out in my mind. Let's say Rob does notice it on his final read-through of the contract before signing, and brings it up. I'll just say I missed it—hell, so did he the first few times around. On the other hand, if Rob discovers it *after* we sign but before the closing, I can still give it up—but then maybe I can swap it for something *I* need. . . .

What if Rob only finds out about it after the closing, six months down the road, when the provision actually comes into play? Well, I can say that I just don't recall what the original intention was—and we'll probably end up with some compromise resolution.

It just goes to show how carefully you have to read these lengthy contracts—which is why I shouldn't be distracted by something like writing a eulogy. Still, a glance at my watch shows that it's getting late, and Bill Price wants something on his desk by the end of the day. So I've got to put aside the Northvale deal for the moment, and get back to Dwight Bentley.

What can I say *good* about the old man? Listen, I'm smart enough to realize a eulogy has to focus on the good stuff and ignore the bad, but it's not in my nature to say something is good that's definitely not. I don't mind exaggerating or putting a spin on things, but only where there's a positive basis for it. But where's the positive here?

I leaf through the file that Dwight's secretary sent me. There's a letter of some kind he was working on recently—and look, in the small print at the bottom, it says "draft no. 8." I don't doubt it for a minute—the man was a real fuddy-duddy. You had to go over each word and phrase with him a hundred times before he was satisfied—such overkill. But I guess I could put something in the eulogy about "how dedicated Dwight was to the pursuit of excellence."

Another sheet of paper catches my eye. It's a schedule that one of the firm administrators must have prepared for Dwight personally some years ago—I've never seen anything like this circulate around. It lists the firm's then partners and associates, with each one's hometown, college, law school, spouse's name, and children. It brings to mind all the hours Bentley used to waste with me and other associates, asking us questions about our early years, our schooling, our wives—hours which could have been spent making money for the firm. Well, I suppose I can say that "he had an inquisitive mind and was a good listener."

But the Bentley I knew back then wasn't just about listening. The man loved to talk—especially about the way things used to be. All those reminiscences, repeated ad nauseam—about the

early days of the firm, when there were only seven lawyers. . . .
Even then, the man was living in the past. But I could spin
that to read, "Dwight had a good memory and a vivid recall of
events."

Going from seven lawyers to the seventy-five we have now—
hey, that didn't happen because of Dwight. In fact, it happened
in spite of those Old Guard guys like Bentley. If things were left
to them, we'd all be sitting around the library, dreaming up hypothetical problems to research. We've only gotten to where we
are because other guys—guys like me—went out into the world
and hustled new business. While Dwight was busy reminiscing
about the past, we knew how to "ask for the order"—which is
what it takes, if you're going to prosper in the legal profession.

I rummage around in the file a little more and find some papers that relate to Bentley's wartime service. I remember how
Dwight relished talking about those days—landing in Norman-
dy on D-Day plus two, the breakout from St. Lo. And, of course,
the story he never tired of repeating—about how, during the
Battle of the Bulge, the Germans were just about to overrun his
unit when their panzers ran out of gasoline. By the way, I hope
that sonuvabitch Dave Keating runs out of gas, right in the middle of the goddamn Long Island Expressway, with no shoulder
to pull off on. . . .

Well, I can certainly throw in something about Dwight's "admirable military service," although I have to admit I'm growing
tired of all that World War II stuff. The only thing those old
guys are good for is when you run into one of them blowing on
the dice at a Vegas crap table. I call them "troopies" and can
visualize them huddled in a circle on the lower deck of a troop
ship, the evening before the landing on Iwo Jima, rolling the
dice against a bulkhead. Those are the guys I like to bet along
with—hell, if they could make a couple of passes with the entire
Japanese army poised to blow them sky-high, I figure they can
hold the dice for a big roll at the Flamingo.

I come upon a carbon copy of a January 1970 letter from
Dwight to a guy whose name I recognize as one of his wartime
buddies—Willy Weeks. I'm not getting anywhere with this anyway, so I decide to read it.

In the letter, Dwight recounts a trip that he and Stan Gault, another of his military pals, had recently taken on the twenty-fifth anniversary of the Battle of the Bulge. Dwight and Stan went back to the Ardennes—only this time, in a rented Mercedes.

On the first page, Dwight describes how they traced the troop movements of the Wehrmacht's last-gasp winter offensive in December 1944. The two of them drove the same road as Patton's tanks, roaring up from Neufchatel to lift the siege of Bastogne. They visited the mammoth concrete memorial just outside town, with its museum of vehicles, ordnance, and wax figures dressed in wartime uniforms. It was, in Bentley's quaint term, a "rousing pilgrimage." I turn to page 2 and continue reading Dwight's words.

The next day, Stan and I left to return to Brussels, traveling through the Ardennes along a series of scenic back roads. As we paused at one remote intersection, I noticed a small sign, "Cemetière Britannique, 1940–1945," with an arrow pointing in a direction away from our route. Our travel literature hadn't mentioned anything about a British cemetery in this area. But you know how it is, Willy—something told us to make this detour.

The road—not much wider than a single lane—led outside the little town, winding up a hill. Cows stood in the open fields. It was very quiet.

The cemetery was just off the road, on a mesa cut out of the hill. It covered about an acre—perhaps a thousand graves, in neat rows, marked by small uniformly shaped tombstones. In the middle was a careful grouping of cherry trees.

At first glance, it looked more like a meticulously pruned English garden—like the one you and I visited near Oxford in the fall of '43, Willy—than a repository for victims of violence. The mood was serene, yet seemingly passionless.

 Hey, I didn't know Dwight could write this kind of stuff . . . I move on to page 3.

The dates of death told the story. When the German offensive was mounted in late December 1944, these British troops had occupied one of the sectors attacked. Most of them had fallen by the early days of 1945, repelling the assault and driving Hitler's armies back into Germany.

As Stan and I looked across the rows of granite markers reaching to the borders of the cemetery, it struck me that here was a burial place whose unvarying dimensions had been forged at the moment of its creation. The arrangement was complete—no more beardless Scot Greys or Welsh lads were meeting their maker on Belgian soil.

You know, I never really saw this side of Dwight. . . .

It was very peaceful in the cemetery. One man, probably a caretaker, tended some flowers. Even the cows across the road appeared to be asleep.

In fact, Willy, the only sounds came from the gravestones. Not just the names, ranks, and regimental insignia, though these we heard; not so much the dates of death or youthful ages of the deceased—the vital statistics of tragedy. No, what spoke so loudly were the messages engraved at the bottom of each tablet.

These epitaphs came from next of kin. Some of the inscriptions were quite formal, suffused with patriotism and religiosity—phrases like "He gave his all for King and Country," or "For the greater glory of God," or "Greater love hath no man." For these, Willy, I had a mental picture of working-class Brits, dressed in their Sunday best, standing awkwardly at regimental headquarters to check off their choice from a large selection of memorials appropriate to the occasion—"Yes, that sounds nice, luv."

But it was the personal messages that got to Stan and me.

A light has gone, a face we loved so dear,
A place is vacant which never can be filled.

Or

A corner in our hearts is set aside for you,
Not just today but always,
Ma and Dad

And

At the going down of the sun
and in the morning
We will remember him.
Sleep, Daddy

I find myself reading more slowly as I turn to page 4 of Dwight's letter.

And gradually, stone by stone—after days of reliving the adventure, the glory of battle—Stan and I once more came to understand what the Bulge was all about. These men lying in the ground had been real. They were very young, most in their late teens or early twenties—just like we were, Willy. They died here, away from home and those who loved them, fighting a relentless enemy.

And that fate, my friend, could well have been ours—if the Germans hadn't run out of gasoline. We might be lying in the Ardennes today—like our buddies, Irv and Hick, buried over near St. Lo.

Stan and I walked down the line of graves, weeping openly. We were far from the Panzers and the monuments, but—for what we then realized was the first time—we seemed very close to what happened in the Ardennes twenty-five years ago.

As we drove away, Stan and I both had the same mixed feelings—how lucky we were not to be under the earth in a European grave, and how guilty we felt that, unlike those poor lads, we were able to live such full and constructive lives.

I finish the letter and close my eyes. A calm has come over me— the tension I've been feeling is gone. And then—how can I explain this?—it's as if a long-closed door in my mind has just opened. For the first time today—in fact, for the first time in years—I can see the true Dwight Bentley in his prime.

And *now*—as the thoughts flood into my brain—I know exactly the words to put down in the eulogy.

How Dwight's door was always open. He made himself available to everyone, from senior partner to newest associate. There was no cult of personality with Bentley—none of that aura of self-importance that everyone seems to emit today.

How thoughtful and courteous he was, such a gentleman. And truly interested in his colleagues—that's why he had that list of home towns, colleges, and spouses prepared. I recall seeing a copy of a letter he wrote just last month to a young partner, Stephanie Carroll, congratulating her on an article she'd written, full of encouragement. There's not much of that generosity of spirit around nowadays.

How loyal he was to the firm. His rehashing of the early days at Jenkins & Price wasn't just a fond reminiscence. It had a real purpose—to inculcate in us a sense of our history, to foster continuity, in an age of declining institutional loyalty.

How he treated his partners. Dwight was always a team player, who frowned at internal rivalries—like the one between Paul Garson and me. He was truly pleased when one of his partners did something of note, which he felt benefited us all.

How he handled associates, drilling us on how to do things the right way. A real craftsman, Dwight preached the gospel of seeking excellence in our work. He conferred with us on legal matters and gave weight to our views. He provided us with feedback on our performance—praise when we were deserving and constructive criticism where warranted. And he was sensitive to our needs—to the times, for instance, when we were overworked and needed a night or weekend off.

How he dealt with lawyers from other firms—showing them respect, striving to create a civil atmosphere. Dwight didn't attempt to take advantage or let himself be taken advantage of. The friendly adversarial relationship that good deal lawyers have to know how to cultivate—he had it down pat. And he always preached the virtue of balancing what you do to improve your client's position with what you have to do to make the deal happen.

How he serviced his clients. Dwight relished the lawyer's counseling function, the giving of advice. But he didn't want his advice accepted just because of his expertise—he refused to dazzle a client into submission. Instead, he was anxious to persuade the client that his advice was right, as he went about explaining everything very carefully. And if the client, after fully grasping the pluses and minuses, decided not to take the advice, then Dwight didn't pout but moved on to the next issue.

How impeccable were his ethics. He was, as a southern friend of my father used to say, "straight as six o'clock." Dwight had wonderful judgment, and a number of the firm's high-powered partners used to run things by him for a reaction. Come to think of it, he probably saved us from a lot of embarrassment—or worse—if we had taken on that Breckenridge business of Alex Gibson's. I now realize that when I'm faced with questionable situations down the road, I'll be asking myself, "What would Dwight have thought about this?"

And by ethics, I'm talking about something that goes beyond just the canons. Dwight had a sense of what was right, what was appropriate, how people should deal with each other. Let's face it, he wouldn't have done what I just did to Pruitt—not for all the tea in China. He would have told Dave Keating where he could shove that rotten plot.

I feel a sudden impulse to pick up the phone and call Pruitt's office. I'm not sure what I'm going to say, but I know I need to talk to him. I dial the number. His secretary says he hasn't returned yet, so I leave word for Pruitt to call me. I'm confident that by the time he does, I'll know what to say. I think I'll just run the situation past Dwight. . . .

I locate the Northvale file, and place a call to Rob Phelps, the seller's lawyer. His answering machine picks up, so I leave a message. "Rob, this is George Troy. If you look at Section 3.14(a)(ii), you'll discover a double negative that changes the meaning of the clause in my client's favor. I realize this wasn't the original intention, so you might want to come up with a new wording to have it come out your way."

I'm about to hang up, but then I pause for a moment. I know I should leave it like that . . . but what the hell, the devil makes me do it—

"Oh, and Rob, old boy—just remember, you owe me one."

Commentary on
The Reluctant
Eulogist

This story is narrated in the present tense by George Troy, a J&P midlevel corporate partner. We met him briefly in "Partnergate."

He was Paul Garson's rival there, championing the partnership candidacy of Curt Bell. That ended badly when Curt—having been passed over—attempted to blackmail Garson, was uncovered, and got booted out of the firm. Troy's service as Bell's sponsor didn't exactly enhance his own standing in Jenkins & Price. But life goes on, and George Troy—like Ralph Landry in "On-the-Job Training" and Jack Lawrence in "Sex, Lies, and Private Eyes"—is a survivor. On the day we join him in this tale, he's attempting to juggle three assignments at once.

This is the last story in the book and, in a way, serves as a bookend to the first. Dwight Bentley, the aging protagonist of "The Smell Test," has just passed away. We haven't met up with him in the intervening several years, although there were references along the way to his declining health. Bill Price, the firm's managing partner, is going to be delivering a eulogy at Dwight's upcoming funeral service. Bill has asked George Troy to prepare a first draft, which Bill needs on his desk today.

Presumably, Price selected Troy for the task because, as a young associate, George had worked steadily for Bentley, and Dwight held him in high esteem. But this chore—one that might have been construed as an honor by someone else—is seen by George as a pro bono burden, interfering with his other billable activities, and he's not shy about letting us know how he feels on the subject.

At first, Troy is just dismissive of the old man—not a factor in the firm, no clients, no real work for him to do. Perhaps if George weren't feeling the pressure of the other stuff on his plate, he might be in a more eulogistic mood. But that's not the case today, as he tells us right off the bat—"I'm on goddamn overload." What happens then with Dave Keating really sets him off, and he takes out his anger and frustration on poor deceased Dwight.

We'll come back to that presently, but let's turn now to the Keating matter. Here again, death has intervened—in this case, it's the passing of Gordon Keating, the head of Keating Enterprises and a longtime friend and appreciative client of George Troy and Jenkins & Price. Now Gordon's son, Dave, whom Troy barely knows, has taken over the business. As the story opens, the son is on his way to the J&P office to meet with George.

Viewed more broadly, this kind of situation can be a difficult one for an outside lawyer like George Troy. Especially with small and midsize business clients, the passing of the guard at the company is a common cause of lawyerly concern, unless the lawyer has developed a close relationship with the successor honcho. When there's new blood in the corner office, things can change quickly, and one of these things is the selection of the outside lawyer.

The discouraging aspect of this for you as the outside lawyer is that being replaced may have nothing to do with how good a job you've been doing or are likely to do—the new chief exec just has a close lawyer friend and feels more comfortable having her on board as his advisor than you (whom he doesn't know that well). Or the issue could turn on dollars—you've been charging the company fair but high fees and the new boss thinks he can obtain a comparable level of service from another firm at cheaper rates.

By the way, you're not immune from this problem when the client in question is a large corporation. I recall several instances where a change of general counsel occurred at large corporate clients of mine, and not long thereafter I found myself right out the door—replaced by the GC's good friend or former colleague.

I don't have any magic formula to offer on how to deal with this situation. I do advise, however, that you get over any hubris you may harbor about your indispensability to the client and recognize the need to take steps to cement your relationship with that fresh face. Trying to satisfy the new boss—that's what George Troy ends up doing against his will here, and the question raised is how far a lawyer should go in bowing to his client's wishes.

Dave Keating is coming to J&P to discuss two matters. One is relatively small—the terms of a new employment contract with Al Pruitt, a longtime key employee of the company. The other is what Troy considers the big enchilada—an upcoming major acquisition by Keating Enterprises of Fiberpack Corp. A week before he passed away, Gordon Keating discussed this deal with George, and Dave has indicated that it's still on track. For a business lawyer like George, that kind of transaction is a hearty meal to feast on, and he's excited by the prospect.

Once Dave arrives, Troy quickly discovers that the son is unlike his father in various respects. The first shock for George is Dave's announcement that Al Pruitt, who wants to talk about the renewal of his about-to-expire contract, is coming over to meet with them in ten minutes. George would liked to have known about this in advance and to have more time with Dave to prepare for the meeting. He's correct, of course—this isn't the right way for Dave to treat his lawyer. But what can I say—it happens to all of us; and if that's the only problem, Troy just has to suck it up and make the best of things.

But, as we soon learn, this isn't the only difficulty. Dave tells George that Al Pruitt will not be bringing a lawyer along. The prospect of negotiating with Pruitt without his lawyer present makes George uncomfortable, but Dave assures him that Al "has great respect for you and doesn't feel the need to hire a lawyer."

What do you think?

If you were George at this point in the proceedings, would you agree to hold the meeting with Pruitt?

The ethics of this situation are governed today by rules 4.2 and 4.3 of the Model Rules of Professional Conduct, which were enacted after the scene in the story took place—although the disciplinary rules then in effect were substantially the same. If you know that the other person is represented by counsel, you can't meet or communicate with him on the matter without the other lawyer present, unless the other lawyer has consented to it. And this is true even if the other person initiates or consents to the meeting. If (as in the story) the other person isn't represented by counsel and is willing to meet or communicate with you, then your main obligations are not to state or imply that you're disinterested and not to offer him any legal advice (other than that he should get counsel).

Let's assume your conduct complies with the Model Rules. The question remains whether it's a good idea to hold a negotiating session where the other side isn't represented by counsel but is willing to meet nonetheless. For me, it depends on who the other party is, what's likely to be discussed, and whether anything irreparable is going to take place.

For example, in the M&A takeover world I inhabited for so many years, the roles of the players were often all mixed up, and I frequently found myself negotiating with the principal on the other side, or his investment banker, without any of their lawyers in the room or on the phone. I would check with the other lawyers ahead of time to see if they had any objection; I'd ask the business people at the outset if they wanted their counsel present or on the line; and when no one seemed to care—and the subject matter under discussion, usually price or some other business or financial deal term, wasn't "legal" in the narrow sense—we were off to the races, without any real qualms on my part.

At the other extreme, if the purpose of a particular meeting is to discuss contractual terms having a substantial legal component, and the guy on the other side is inexperienced in such matters, and the session is expected to culminate in the signing of an agreement—well, I wouldn't go near that one with a ten-foot pole, unless a lawyer representing the other side is present and accounted for.

Obviously, other situations fall somewhere in between. At this point in the story (things do get more complex in a minute), if I were George, I'd probably have gone ahead and met with an unrepresented Al Pruitt. Of course, I'd confirm with Pruitt at the outset that he has no lawyer, doesn't feel the need of representation, and realizes I'm not neutral but strictly Keating's lawyer. At this juncture, I'm still expecting that the renewal terms will be close to what's in the present contract; I know Pruitt to be a knowledgeable guy; and the renewal agreement won't be signed in this session— at most, it might result in an agreement in principle that Pruitt can back away from if he decides to consult counsel later on. In such a meeting, if the parties were to reach agreement in principle on a term with a legal component (such as noncompetition), I'd probably advise Pruitt to seek counsel at least on that point after the meeting—thus implying that if his lawyer has a problem with what was agreed to in principle, we wouldn't consider it to be reneging on Pruitt's part should he reopen discussions on the point.

Then Dave drops the bombshell—that he has no intention of renewing Pruitt's contract. Keating is going to replace him, but since the new man hasn't yet agreed to terms, and Pruitt is itchy to start talks, Dave has agreed to hold this meeting. The session will be, in George's word, a "charade." But it's worse than that. Dave wants to be able to tell Pruitt's friends at the company that the reason Al's contract isn't being renewed is because he got greedy and asked for too much. Since that's unlikely to happen on its own, Dave tells George to take some deliberately (but not obviously) unreasonable positions on certain issues. And to top it off, these positions have to appear to emanate from George the lawyer, not Dave the client (or, in Dave's phrase, *"I'm* not the bad guy, *you* are"). Dave then exits, giving George ten minutes to come up with some good stuff.

Well, what do you think:

Should George take on the unpleasant assignment that Dave has given him?

As we soon learn, George does agree to do this, after briefly agonizing over it ("a few moments of indecision," as he later terms it). The thought pattern by which he arrives at this decision is instructive, so let's examine how he gets there.

His initial reaction is one of outrage at being asked to conduct a sham negotiation, with himself as the villain. Who is this guy Dave, anyway—I don't think I'll ever feel comfortable representing him.

Then George calms down. And what's the first thought that then intrudes? It's that Keating Enterprises is a major long-term client, with the big Fiberpack deal on tap—the billings from which "could mean the difference between a great year and a merely good one for me at the firm." That's really the basis for everything that follows in George's mind, to wit:

The Fiberpack people are sophisticated—Dave wouldn't ask me to do any of this funny business with them.

I dislike the chore, but it's not really unethical.

In two months, Dave Keating can choose to decline to enter into a new employment contract with Pruitt anyway, so what's the harm?

I'm not interfering with Pruitt's existing contract rights, so it doesn't matter that he isn't represented by counsel.

And then comes the thought that George says finally persuades him to go ahead. He realizes he's just an agent, who has to do what his principal wants him to do—including playing the role of a bad guy—even if he doesn't like it, as long as it's not illegal or unethical.

What do you think—do these arguments sway you?

There's something to be said for each one—they're not off the wall. But for me, the whole thing amounts to a series of rationalizations that George goes through to convince himself to do something distasteful because—and only because—he wants to keep Keating Enterprises as a client and do the Fiberpack deal. Look, George Troy isn't a guy who completely lacks scruples. Do you think he'd agree to go through this charade if it weren't based on that juicy prospect?

Let me discuss briefly some of George's rationalizations. The first is that Dave won't pull a stunt like this with the more sophisticated Fiberpack folks. Listen, I belong to the school that says people, like leopards, don't change their spots. The absence of scruples Dave displays in dealing with Al Pruitt—who, after all, was his deceased father's closest colleague—is something that will undoubtedly be repeated in different forms on various future occasions, to the great discomfort of his lawyer. If George signs on with this guy, that's what he has to look forward to.

As for whether or not the task Troy has been called upon to undertake is unethical, I think it does cross the line into unwholesome territory. Even if it could somehow be justified vis-à-vis Pruitt, it's intended (as George himself recognizes) to deceive the other employees—a deception in which he would clearly be aiding and abetting.

To be sure, Dave is free not to renew Pruitt's contract when it expires in two months. But the harm here lies in the way Dave and George are proceeding to get to that place—by covering up the real reason and making this look like something it isn't.

Just because George isn't interfering with Pruitt's existing contractual rights doesn't serve to validate Al's being unrepresented by counsel at this meeting. If Pruitt had a lawyer there, he or she would be able to expose George's demands as unreasonable, thereby undercutting the charade that Dave has designed to fool the other employees.

George's point about just being an agent who needs to follow his principal's lead is more difficult to deal with, because it possesses a certain validity in the abstract. As a lawyer, you do have to serve your client's interests. So, for instance, you need to find out what the client really wants, which may be different from what you think she wants or ought to want. You should be sensitive to any differences in risk-taking profiles between you and your client—it's hers that counts, not yours. You need to adapt to the client's idiosyncrasies. And sometimes you have to grit your teeth and follow the leader, even if you disagree with the way she's proceeding.

Of course, if you strongly disagree with something the client wants to do, you should tell her so, and try to talk her out of it. She's entitled to hear your views, even if they don't match her own. Still, at the end of the day, if what she's proposing isn't illegal or unethical, you probably have to go along—after all, it's her nickel.

But where an ethical issue is involved (and for this purpose, I define ethical broadly), not only should your voice be heard loud and clear recommending against taking the proposed action, but if the client persists, you've simply got to bow out. (I'll leave to others the detailing of the more rigorous present-day requirements where public companies are involved.)

When I found myself in disagreement with a client over a proposed course of action that I considered unethical, I tried not to moralize too much—I didn't want to make the client feel like a sinner. It was generally an easier pill for the client to swallow if I included a practical argument that pointed in the same direction, such as, "Not only is it wrong, but you'll probably arouse the commissioner's otherwise latent wrath." And, if possible, I'd attempt to come up with a constructive suggestion regarding a better way to handle the matter, so that it didn't cross over the line.

Well, I think you can guess how I come out on the charade in the story. George should refuse go to through with Dave's planned deception—to take it on is a real mistake on his part. Just how he should present that decision to Dave depends on whether he'd like to keep doing future business with Keating Enterprises—itself a real question, now that George knows the kind of guy he'll be working for.

If George doesn't care about Keating's future business, he can just tell Dave to shove it and kick him out of the office. But let's assume that although George is unwilling to participate in this charade, he considers Dave sufficiently redeemable to be given another chance— and, after all, George would like to continue to represent the company. So, let me ask you:

As George, how would you handle the rejection of Dave's charade so as not to sever all ties with Keating Enterprises?

There's no one best way to proceed, but here's how I might handle such a presentation to Dave:

Dave, let me be candid with you. I'm sure neither of us is comfortable with treating Al Pruitt this way, nor would your father be. But in addition to the discomfort we feel, there's also a strong practical reason why it's not advisable.

The purpose of the charade is to deceive the other employees (Al's friends) as to why his contract isn't being renewed. I'm not willing to assist in that deception, but even if I were, it wouldn't work. After they receive an earful from Al about what went on in this office—buttressed by the views of the lawyer Al is sure to hire after the meeting—those employees (who aren't dumb) would understand exactly what we were up to. And even if the provisions appeared to emanate from me, they'd assume you were calling the shots—at which point, as the new head of the company, you'd be off to a terrible start in terms of employee relations.

How much better it would be for you to just stall with Pruitt until you have your other guy signed up, and then level with Al as to your reasons for making a change; give him a nice severance package and a gold watch; and then talk with several key employees to explain the situation as belt-tightening or whatever.

I don't know whether this would work with Dave or not, and if it didn't, George would just have to stand his ground—but it's certainly worth a try.

Anyway, in the story George buys in to the charade, and some painful moments ensue. I'm not even going to discuss the specifics of the points George raises. I'm sure, though, that the two worst times for him are, first, when Al Pruitt tells him, "I have complete faith in your good judgment" (that's another juncture at which George should have said, "I can't go through with this"), and second, when Dave says, "What can I do, Al—I have to take my lawyer's advice" (which is what George signed on for, so there's not much he can do about it at this point).

George completes the unsavory task with Pruitt, receives a compliment on his performance from Dave, and then—irony of ironies—is told that Dave has dumped J&P from the Fiberpack deal and hired another law firm. All I can say to you, George, is that it serves you right. . . .

George is now mad as hell and in a terrible frame of mind as he turns his attention to the Bentley eulogy. And it shows. He reflects back on the years working for Dwight as "the worst of my professional life"; he scorns Dwight's practice as out of the mainstream; he remembers everything he worked on as being tedious and repetitive; he decries Dwight's narrow by-the-book approach. Then he muses about Dwight having no idea how to attract new business—why, the man actually "looked on the rest of us—out hustling deals—as no better than ambulance chasers." And George asks himself, with a heavy dose of sarcasm, whether he should put all this in the eulogy.

At this point, George takes a break from the eulogy, turning his attention to the agreement for the Northvale deal, which needs to be gone through page by page before the signing scheduled for the next day. The necessity to perform this tiresome but vital chore serves as a further irritant to George's attitude toward writing Dwight's eulogy—a nonbillable assignment that he views as undermining the full attention the contract requires.

In regard to what's needed for the Northvale deal, I have to agree fully with George. No matter how many times you've been over particular clauses of an important agreement as they're negotiated and resolved, it's always wise to make one final trek through the entire document, to see whether it all hangs together and if anything was missed. And this is something that partners can't assign to a junior lawyer—they have to do it themselves.

Sure enough, George comes up with something that hasn't been caught on previous perusals. It's a double negative in a complex sentence, the effect of which is to reverse the effect intended by the provision. George knows what the original intent of the parties was because he negotiated the provision (although he didn't draft the language). And guess what—the impact of the error runs in favor of George's buyer client, providing the buyer with recourse against the seller in a situation where the buyer wasn't supposed to have any recourse. This raises the issue of what George should do about his discovery.

If you were George, what would you do about it?

George's immediate response is to do nothing. I'm not their lawyer, he says; Rob Phelps is—let him find it himself.

It's a hard-nosed response, which George must realize. That's why he goes over in his mind how things would play out if Rob does catch the glitch before the signing, after the signing but before the closing, or after the closing. And George plots how he'd plead innocence on the first of these and try to turn the other two to his client's advantage. Note that Troy has already cooked up the lie he'll tell Phelps if the error is discovered down the road— that he doesn't recall what the original intention was. I have a view on this, but I'm going to hold it until later.

Now Troy turns back to the Bentley eulogy. Perhaps it was the sheer joy of discovering a mistake that worked to his client's advantage in the Northvale contract, but at least now George is looking to find something good he can say about Dwight. Still, he says, there has to be a positive basis for it. So he lists some of the man's traits, reflecting on how he might spin those characteristics he found so tedious into something affirmative:

Dwight's fussiness with documents could become "the pursuit of excellence."

The hours he wasted in small talk with associates reveal "an inquisitive mind."

His long-winded reminisces constitute "a vivid recall of events."

But the honeymoon doesn't last, and pretty soon Troy slips back into low gear. According to George, the reason for the firm's growth and success has been entirely due to "guys like me" who hustled new business, while Dwight was sitting there "reminiscing about the past." It's a refrain that's reminiscent of Alex Gibson's thinking in "The Smell Test"—another instance of Old Guard versus Young Turks.

With George Troy, nothing seems to be sacred. Even Dwight's military service (which George is willing to call "admirable") only leads him into an irreverent vision of war veterans rolling the dice at a Vegas crap table.

And then George comes across Dwight's letter to a wartime buddy about the Battle of the Bulge cemetery he accidentally encountered. (I have a confession to make here. That cemetery was my discovery on a similar trip I made through the Ardennes in 1984—the fortieth anniversary of the battle. The sentiments Dwight expresses— other than those relating to his own army service—are close to what my own feelings were at the time.)

At any rate, George reads the letter and has his epiphany—seeing, for the first time, the true Dwight Bentley in his prime. And he proceeds to delineate those professional traits that made Dwight special.

I don't know that there's anything I need to add here to George's resulting compilation. It represents my idea of a number of qualities that an esteemed member of the bar would possess, and I found it personally very satisfying that George finally awoke to reality. How about doing me (and yourself) a favor by going back and re-reading that part of the story—and then try to measure up to what came so naturally to Dwight Bentley.

George now knows how to write his eulogy, but he has also discovered a few other things in addition. He realizes that Bentley would never have countenanced what he just pulled with Al Pruitt—Dwight would have told Dave Keating off in no uncertain terms. On an impulse, George puts in a call to Pruitt's office. He doesn't reach him, but he will eventually; and although he's not sure what to say, when the time comes he'll "run the situation past Dwight."

And then George calls Rob Phelps, the lawyer representing the seller on the Northvale deal. He leaves a message, telling Rob what he found and that he's willing for the provision to be changed to its original meaning. George knows that this is just what Dwight would have done. I also count myself as a disciple of Dwight on this one. Not only is it the right thing to do, but you'll get credit from your counterpart and others for your integrity—and most important, you'll feel good about yourself.

So, after a lot of Sturm und Drang, my book of short stories ends on a relatively high note—with reverential memories of the admirable traits that a departed senior partner exemplified. Dwight's passing seems to have generated at least a temporary epiphany in one of the young business hustlers.

Oh yes, about those last few lines in the story—where George concludes his message to Phelps with, "Oh, and Rob, old boy—just remember, you owe me one." Well, that's just my way of saying that even in fiction, you can't expect miracles. Guys don't really change that much—remember Ted Ashburn under siege by Bill Price at the end of "Partnergate" or Jack Lawrence waltzing off with Emma Searles in the concluding scene of "Sex, Lies, and Private Eyes." George may have had his epiphany, but he just has to show that there's plenty of the old George Troy still left.